HISTORY OF MYSTICISM

The Unchanging Testament

Third (Revised) Edition

By S. Abhayananda

ATMA BOOKS
OLYMPIA, WASH.

Library of Congress Cataloging-in Publication Data

Abhayananda, Swami, 1938-
    History of mysticism : the unchanging testament /
by S. Abhayananda. -- 3rd rev. ed.
        p.   cm.
    Includes bibliographical references and index.
    ISBN 0-914557-09-2 (pbk.)
    1. Mysticism--History.   I. Title.
BL625.A297 1996
291.4'22'09--dc20   95-35127
                                                                CIP

ACKNOWLEDGEMENTS

I wish to acknowledge my indebtedness, and offer my sincere gratitude, to the following publishers and authors for the use of brief quotations from their works:

Beacon Press, for quotations from *The Gnostic Religion* by Hans Jonas.

Bobbs-Merril Co., for quotations from *Recollections Of Socrates by Xenophon*, by Anna Benjamin.

Chicago University Press, for quotations from *Giordano Bruno And The Hermetic Tradition*, by Frances A. Yates.

Doubleday Anchor Books, for quotations from *The Spiritual Heritage Of India*, by Swami Prabhavananda; *The World Of The Buddha*, and *Zen Poems, Prayers, Sermons, Anecdotes, Interviews*, edited by Lucien Stryck.

Frederick Ungar Publishing Co., for quotations from *The Vision Of God*, translated by Emma G. Salter.

George Allen & Unwin, for quotations from *The Philosophy Of Ibn 'Arabi*, by Rom Landau; and *Selections From the Sacred Writings Of The Sikhs*, by Trilochan Singh, et al.

Grove Press, for quotations from *Essays In Zen Buddhism (First Series)*, by D.T. Suzuki; and *Manual Of Zen Buddhism*, by D.T. Suzuki.

Harper Torchbooks, for quotations from *Meister Eckhart, A Modern Translation*, by Raymond B. Blackney.

Harvard University Press, for quotations from *Ancilla To The Pre-Socratic Philosophers*, by Kathleen Freeman.

ICS Publications, for quotations from *The Collected Works Of John Of The Cross*, translated by K. Kavanaugh & O. Rodriguez.

Jewish Publication Society, for quotations from *Selected Religious Poems Of Solomon Ibn Gabirol*, translated by Israel Zangwill.

Martinus Nijhoff, for quotations from *Hierarchy And The Definition Of Order In The Letters Of Pseudo-Dionysius*, by Ronald Hathaway.

Oxford University Press, for quotations from *The Early Church Fathers*, by Henry Bettenson, *The Essence Of Plotinus*, by Grace Turnbull, and *Tibet's Great Yogi Milarepa*, by W.Y. Evans-Wentz.

Pantheon Books, for quotations from *Teachings Of Ch'an Buddhism,* by Chang Chung-yuan.

Paulist Press(Missionary Society of St. Paul the Apostle in the State of New York), for quotations from *Philo Of Alexandria*, translated by David Winston, *Ibn Arabi: The Bezels Of Wisdom*, by W.W.J. Austin, *Meister Eckhart: Essential Sermons*, by Edmund Colledge, O.S.A. & Bernard McGinn, and *Fakhruddin Iraqi: Divine Flashes*, by W.C. Chittock & Peter Wilson.

Penguin Books, for quotations from *The Upanishads,* translated by Juan Mascaro, and *The Bhagavad Gita,* translated by Juan Mascaro.

Princeton University Press, for quotations from *Plato: The Collected Dialogues*, by Edith Hamilton & H. Cairns.

Ramakrishna-Vivekananda Center, for quotations from *The Gospel Of Sri Ramakrishna*, translated by Swami Nikhilananda.

Samuel Weiser, for quotations from *Essays In Zen Buddhism (2nd Series)*, by D.T. Suzuki.

Shrine Of Wisdom, for quotations from *Mystical Theology And The Celestial Hierarchy*, by the Editors of the Shrine Of Wisdom.

Society For Promoting Christian Knowledge, for quotations from *The Areopagite on The Divine Names And The Mystical Theology*, translated by C.E. Rolt.

University of Notre Dame Press, for quotations from *Unity And Reform: Selected Writings Of Nicholas Of Cusa*, by John P. Dolan.

Vedanta Press, for quotations from *Narada's Way Of Divine Love*, by Swami Prabhavananda, *How To Know God: The Yoga Aphorisms Of Patanjali*, by Swami Prabhavananda, and *Shankara's The Crest-Jewel Of Discrimination,* by Swami Prabhavananda.

CONTENTS

CONTENTS
- Cont'd. -

IV. Mystics Of The Late Middle Ages

V. Mystics Of The Modern Era

PREFACE

I am one of those who have been privileged, by the grace of God, to experience the ultimate Truth of existence. This "mystical experience" occurred, for me, on the night of November 18, 1966. Since that time, I have easily recognized, by their various descriptions of it, those who have also directly experienced that absolute Truth. And it has become abundantly clear to me that, over the course of man's long history, many individuals of differing cultures, languages, and religious traditions have known that same unitive experience. Contained in this book are the accounts of the lives and teachings of some of the best known of those individuals, for whom I feel great empathy and comradery, as my own experience coincides with and confirms their own. In fact, their experience is my experience; for all who have realized the Truth have known that same eternal Self.

The material contained herein presents no speculative philosophy; it offers no metaphysical hypothesis. Rather, it is the collected legacy of those who have experienced, first-hand, the unitive Truth underlying all existence. It is a record of the voices of the illumined souls of the past, all of whom gave their hearts, their very lives, to sharing their transcendent knowledge with unborn humanity. And so, to the prospective reader, I say: mark well what you read here. This is no ordinary history of people, places and events; it is the secret history of man's perennial journey on the ultimate Quest, where all the travellers, arriving from widely diverse paths, arrive at the self-same unitive Truth. It is really the greatest, the most thrillingly wonderful, story ever told. May it awaken you and inspire you to join the great Quest.

S. Abhayananda

"Ask of those who have attained God; all speak the same word. ...
All the enlightened have left one message; ... it is only those in the
midst of their journey who hold diverse opinions."

-- Dadu

INTRODUCTION

Mysticism is that point of view which claims as its basis an intimate knowledge of the one source and substratum of all existence, a knowledge which is obtained through a revelatory experience during a rare moment of clarity in contemplation. Those who claim to have actually experienced this direct revelation constitute an elite tradition which transcends the boundary lines of individual religions, cultures and languages, and which has existed, uninterrupted, since the beginning of time. It is, as Aldous Huxley points out, the "perennial philosophy" that resurfaces again and again throughout history in the teachings of the great prophets and founders of all religions.

When we study the many speculative philosophies and religious creeds which men have espoused, we must wonder at the amazing diversity of opinions expressed regarding the nature of reality; but when we examine the testimonies of the mystics of past and present, we are struck by the unanymity of agreement between them all. Their methods may vary, but their ultimate realizations are identical in content. They tell us of a supramental experience, obtained through contemplation, which directly reveals the Truth, the ultimate, the final, Truth of all existence. It is this experience which is the hallmark of the mystic; it goes by different names, but the experience is the same for all.

By many of the Christian tradition, this experience is referred to as "the vision of God"; yet it must be stated that such a vision is not really a "vision" at all in the sense in which we use the word to mean the perception of some 'thing' extraneous to ourselves. Nothing at all is perceived in "the vision of God"; rather, it is a sudden expansion, or delimitation, of one's own awareness which experiences itself as the ultimate Ground, the primal Source and Godhead of all being. In that "vision," all existence is experienced as Identity.

We first hear of this extraordinary revelation from the authors of the Upanishads, who lived over three thousand years ago: "I have known that spirit," said Svetasvatara, "who is infinite and in all, who is ever-one, beyond time." [1] "He can be seen indivisible in the silence of contemplation," said the author of the Mundaka Upanishad. [2] "There a man possesses everything; for he is one with the ONE." [3]

About five hundred years later, another, a young prince named Siddhartha, who was to become known as the Buddha, the enlightened one, sat communing inwardly in the forest, when suddenly, as though a veil had been lifted, his mind became infinite and all-encompassing: "I have seen the Truth!" he exclaimed; "I am the Father of the world, sprung from myself!"[4] And again, after the passage of another five hundred years, another young man, a Jew, named Jesus, of Nazareth, sat in a solitary place among the desert cliffs of Galilee, communing inwardly, when suddenly he realized that the Father in heaven to whom he had been praying was his very own Self; that he was, himself, the sole Spirit pervading the universe; "I and the Father are one!" he declared. [5]

Throughout history, this extraordinary experience of unity has repeatedly occurred; in India, in Rome, in Persia, in Amsterdam, in China, devout young men, reflecting on the truth of their own existence, experienced this amazing transcendence of the mind, and announced to everyone who would listen that they had realized the truth of man and the universe, that they had known their own Self, and known it to be the All, the Eternal. And throughout succeeding ages, these announcements were echoed by others who had experienced the same realization: "I am the Truth!" exclaimed the Muslim, al-Hallaj; "My Me is God, nor do I recognize any other Me except my God Himself," said the Christian saint, Catherine of Genoa. And Rumi, Jnaneshvar, Milarepa, Kabir and Basho from the East, and Eckhart, Boehme and Emerson from the West, said the same.

These assertions by the great mystics of the world were not made as mere philosophical speculations; they were based on experience -- an experience so convincing, so real, that all those to whom it has occurred testify unanimously that it is the unmistakable realization of the ultimate Truth of existence. In this experience, called *samadhi* by the Hindus, *nirvana* by the Buddhists, *fana* by the Muslims, and "the mystic union" by Christians, the consciousness of the individual suddenly becomes the consciousness of the entire vast universe. All previous sense of duality is swallowed up in an awareness of indivisible unity. The man who previously regarded himself as an individualized soul, encumbered with sins and inhabiting a body, now realizes that he is, truly, the one Consciousness; that it is he, himself, who is manifesting as all souls and all bodies, while yet remaining completely unaffected by the unfolding drama of the multiform universe.

Even if, before, as a soul, he sought union with his God, now, there is no longer a soul/God relationship. He, himself, he now realizes, is the one Existence in whom there is neither a soul nor a God, but only the one Self, within whom this "imaginary" relationship of soul and God manifested. For him, there is no more relationship, but only the eternal and all-inclusive I AM. Not surprisingly, this illuminating knowledge of an underlying 'I' that is the Soul of the entire universe has a profoundly transformative effect upon the mind of those who have experienced it. The sense of being bound and limited to an individual body and mind, set in time and rimmed by birth and death, is entirely displaced by the keenly experienced awareness of unlimited Being; of an infinitely larger, unqualified Self beyond birth and death. It is an experience which uniquely and utterly transforms one's sense of identity, and initiates a permanently acquired freedom from all doubt, from all fear, from all insecurity forevermore. Little wonder that all who experience such liberating knowledge wish to share it, to announce in exuberant song to everyone who will hear that, through the inner revelation of wisdom, "You shall know the truth, and the Truth will make you free!"

If we can believe these men, it is this experience of unity which is the ultimate goal of all knowledge, of all worldly endeavor; the summit of human attainment which all men, knowingly or unknowingly, pursue. It would seem, then, a valuable task to study and review the lives and teachings of those who have acquired this knowledge. In this book, I have sought to present just such a study and anthology; it is presented in an historical perspective in order to better view the long-enduring tradition of mystical thought, and to reveal more clearly the unity underlying the diversity of its manifold expressions. Naturally, it has not been possible to include every single instance of mystical experience, or to touch upon all the myriad extensions of mystical knowledge, but I have attempted to tell the story of the lives and teachings of those who most intelligibly represent the mystical tradition as it has manifested throughout the ages. It is a story that begins long, long ago, in a past so remote that it is but vague and faint, beyond the reach of our straining vision, obscure in the hazy mists of time.

I. Mystics Of The Ancient Past

PRE-HISTORY OF MYSTICISM

Where, we must wonder, did mysticism begin? Who was the first to experience the transcendent vision? To these questions, there are no answers; but it is reasonable to assume that the experience of unity is as old as man himself, and occurred to a few searching souls even in the most primitive of times. The mystical experience of unity is entirely independent of advancements in learning or civilization. Indeed, it would seem, if anything, to be more likely to occur in a simpler, less "civilized" environment, since such an experience requires a totally interiorized state of mind, undistracted by external stimulii. One can easily imagine how spending one's nights beside a fire under the canopy of the stars might enhance one's contemplation of eternity. It is perfectly reasonable, therefore, to suppose that seers of the Infinite existed even in the very remotest unrecorded period of man's history. Unfortunately, however, these ancient mystics are lost to us forever in the dark abyss of time.

Yet, while we do not possess the written testimonies of the mystic sages of the dim past, there is some evidence for the antiquity of mysticism to be found in the popular religious symbols which have come down to us as the artifacts and mythologies of primitive cultures. When we examine the mythologies of these earliest civilizations, especially those myths which describe the origin of the cosmos, we find a curious similarity in the religious symbols used by widely separated cultures. In almost every instance, we may discover the legend of an original Father-God, whose first Thought or Word, symbolized in the form of a Mother-Goddess, is said to have given birth to all creation.

In nearly every part of the globe these two have appeared, albeit with many names. He, the Father-God, has been called An, Apsu, Huan, Prajapati, Purusha, Yahweh, El, Tem, Atmu, Ptah, Ra, Shiva, Brahman, Dyaus, Zeus, Vishnu, Ahura Mazda, Ch'ien, and Tao, among countless other names. He is the absolute Stillness, the pure Consciousness, the unclouded Mind, the unmanifest Ground, who exists as the substratum upon which all this universe is projected. Likewise, in nearly every recorded mythology, we find the Mother-Goddess; She has been called Inanna, Isis, Shakti, Kali, Devi, Chokmah, Durga, Maya, Teh, Cybele, Athena, Astarte, Mylitta, Tara, Juno, Prthivi, Freia, Sophia, Prakrti, Semele, Ishtar, and many, many other names as well. She is the creative effusion of the Father; She is

Mother Nature, the creative, manifestory Power of the Father-God, manifest as the entire cosmos.

In order to understand the vision of the earliest seers and mythologizers, we must look beyond the various names given to this primordial Pair, and try to grasp the meaning behind the words and myths. The reason for the similarity of view among the various primitive cultures is that the Reality, which their pictorial symbols are contrived to represent, is the common and universal Reality *experienced* in the mystical vision, a Reality that is the same for all who "see" It. Scholars who know nothing of the experience of unity postulate some cultural interchange to account for such similarities between the various primitive cosmologies, or postulate an "archetypal memory" from which these many identical images supposedly arose, it never dawning on them that the direct knowledge of the one Absolute and Its projection of the universe is an actual *experience* common to all seers of all times.

In this "vision" or "union," the mind is somehow privileged to experience itself as the eternal Consciousness from which the entire universe is projected. It knows itself as the unchanging Ground, or Absolute, and the world as Its own projected Thought or Ideation. The individual who contacts, through prayer or deep meditation, that universal Consciousness, experiences It as his (or her) own identity. He (or she) realizes, in those few moments, that he (or she) is indeed nothing else but that one Being manifest in a singular individual form; and that all this universe is the manifestation of that one Being, flowing forth from It as a wave of love streams out from a loving heart.

One who has known It sees clearly that this mystically experienced Reality has two distinct aspects; It is the pure, eternal One, beyond motion or change; and It is also the world-Thought which emanates from It, like the rays of a Sun, or the thoughts of a Mind. In this clear realization of Reality, the mind, while knowing itself as the undifferentiated Absolute, experiences concurrently the projection and reabsorption of the universe in a continuous cycle of outflowing and returning. The universal manifestation appears and disappears in a cyclic rhythm extending over eons of our temporal reckoning, but the eternal Awareness, along with Its manifestory-Power, never changes. It is ever immersed in Its own bliss.

So difficult is this two-in-One to speak of -- since It cannot be spoken of without differentiating the two aspects, and making It appear to be two when It is always One -- that the ancient seers tended to characterize the two aspects as male and female complements. In their attempts to explain this ineluctable duality-in-Unity, the seers of early cultures relied upon pictorial symbols -- such as the yin-yang symbol of the Chinese, or depicted the projection of the world of matter upon the Absolute in anthropomorphic or animistic images. In nearly every such instance, the unmanifested Absolute was depicted as Male, and Its projected image-Power, co-existent with It, was regarded as Female. He is the Father-God, the one Mind, the ultimate Source and Controller; but She, His projected "Thought" is the Creatrix, the Mother-Power from whom all creation flows.

That these two aspects of Reality should be so commonly symbolized as male and female should not surprise us; for what better pair of symbols can be imagined to represent the duality-in-Unity experienced by the mystic than the two sexes who, while retaining their individual characteristics, are joined as husband and wife, form-ing an indivisible unit? The human male seems an apt symbol for the immovable Absolute, the unchanging Consciousness, who witnesses, as the subjective Self, the drama of universal manifestation. He represents the Absolute in mythology as the wise and just Father and King, aloof and impersonal, the pillar of strength, governance, and protection. The human female seems equally well-suited to symbolize the creative Force which emanates from the witnessing Self. She is the Womb of Nature from whom all life is born; She is the Source and Nourisher, and She is also the object of desire. She represents the manifestory-Power in mythology as the ever-young maiden, the warm and tender Mother, the Giver of mercy, and the Fountain of all beauty and grace. Perhaps, in some mysterious way, these two -- male and female -- really *are* representative images, or manifestations, of the two comple-mentary aspects of the one Divine Reality.

Evidence exists to show that, by the 3rd millennium B.C.E., and no doubt long before that, worship of a transcendent Father-God and Mother (Nature) Goddess was widespread. The genuine mystics, the seers of Unity, were no doubt few then, as they are today, but there is repeated evidence in the Creation-myths of Egypt, Assyria, and Babylon that such seers did exist. In the cosmologies of many of these early civilizations we find the common conception of the One Reality as consisting of two aspects: the eternally transcendent Mind, and the dynamically creative Thought which is responsible for the formation and substance of the relative world. Representing this creative Energy in the 3rd millennium B.C.E., the Sumerian Goddess, Inanna, is made to say: "Begetting Mother am I. Within An (the Father-God) I abide, and no one sees me." [1]

Since She, the Mother, is actually the manifestory-Power of the Father, and therefore indistinguishable from Him, they are frequently pictured together, locked in an inseparable embrace; two, yet inextricably One. As we shall see, this mythic image of the Father-God and His ubiquitous Consort is one which recurs again and again in the metaphysical formulations of all cultures. It is this recurring conception which hints to us of mystical experience as the common origin.

When we delve even further backward, into the upper Paleo-lithic era (ca. 35,000-9,000 B.C.E.), we find it difficult to imagine how one might have communicated mystical experience in that time, long ago, even to one's peers, considering the limited language skills of the peoples of that time. But the challenge of communicating it to future generations without the benefit of a written language was even more immense. The transcendent Absolute is beyond even the most eloquent speech; how then was one to represent It in myth or legend?

Here is one possible answer: Let us suppose that many thousands of years ago some nameless mystic told his comrades of his experience of the great Unity. And, for century after century, that tale was passed down orally as an authentic description of the origin and beginning of all things; until, around 700 B.C.E., it finally appeared in written form as an allegorical tale, or myth, of creation. Here is that tale as it appears in the *Brihadaranyaka* Upanishad:

> In the beginning, there was only the Self. ... He
> reflected, and saw that there was nothing but Himself,
> whereupon he exclaimed, "I am" (*Aham*). Ever since, He has
> been known within as "I." Even now, when announcing
> oneself, one says, "I am ...," and then gives the other name
> that one bears.
> He was afraid. Even today, one who is alone is
> afraid. But then he realized, "Since there is nothing else but
> myself, what is there to fear?" It is only from [the presence
> of] a second [entity] that fear need ever arise. However, he was
> still unhappy. Even today, one is unhappy when alone. He
> desired a mate. And so he took on the form of a being the size
> of a man and woman joined in a close embrace; and then He

separated into two individuals: a man and a wife. Therefore, as
the sage Yajnavalkya has declared, this body, by itself, is like
half of a split pea. [In order to become whole again,] this
empty space must be filled by a woman. The male [half] then
embraced the female [half], and from that the human race arose.

But the female wondered: "How can he unite with me,
whom he has produced from himself? Well then, let me hide!"
She became a cow; he became a bull and united with her, and
from that cattle arose. She became a mare; he became a
stallion. She an ass, he a donkey and united with her; and
from that solid-hoofed animals arose. She became a goat, he a
buck; she a sheep, he a ram and united with her; and from that
goats and sheep arose. In this way, he poured forth all pairing
creatures, down to the ants. Then he realized: "All this
creation is actually myself; for I have poured forth all this."
One who knows this truth realizes that he, himself, is truly
the creator [living] within his own creation. [2]

A distorted version of this tale shows up a few centuries later
in Plato's *Symposium*, [3] where Aristophanes recounts the legend of
the original "androgynous" creature who was both male and female
rolled in one, and who was then divided into two by Zeus as a means
of checking its power. But Plato's version is without the profound
allegorical meaning of the original myth as retold in the *Brihadaranyaka* Upanishad. Let me attempt to explain:

In the One, there is no form, no experience at all. There is no
vision, and no knowledge. For, in order for there to be experience,
there has to be two: the experiencer and the experienced. For vision,
there has to be a seer and a seen; for knowledge, there must be a
knower and a known, a subject and an object. For any of these things
to be, the One must pretend to be two, must create within Itself the
semblance of duality. If there is only a seer and no seen, there can be
no vision. And if there is only a seen and no seer, again, vision
cannot be.

Figuratively speaking, the One is lonely being alone; so It
creates (images forth) a second, in order to experience (enjoy) Itself.
This is the primal division, the primary creation: it is an *apparent* bifurcation of the one Consciousness into subject and object, seer and
seen. In all existence, there are only these two -- and they are really
both the One. This Self-division of the One into subject and object is

the primal dichotomy alluded to in this allegory. The subject is, in actuality, the One; the object is, in actuality, the One. That One is, naturally, beyond gender; but, in Its (pretended) roles as subject and object, It becomes the male principle and the female principle.

The male principle, the subject, cannot be seen, touched or sensed in any way; only the object, the female principle, is sensed. The male principle is the unchanging witness, or seer; it is the pure, unmanifested, awareness that knows "I am." When there is the impulse of desire, a thought-object is produced to satisfy it; and as soon as that thought-form is manifested, that is the object of experience; that is the seen. This creation of duality occurs at the macrocosmic level, and it occurs at the microcosmic level. Mankind, the image of God, operates in the same manner as God, the universal Self.

Keep in mind that neither the seer nor the seen can exist without the other. They are complements. They depend upon each other for their own existence. The seer without a seen or the seen without a seer -- neither exists. When they are together, then we have experience. We have the enjoyment of life. We have the expression of the One as many. This is the meaning of the two "halves" seeking each other for the purpose of delight. Unless It becomes two, the One has no experience, no universe of forms, no delight.

This same bifurcation is continued throughout creation; the subject and object, as male and female, become the multitude of living forms, and through delighting in each other, continue to recreate themselves. This is the allegory of the cow and the bull, the mare and the stallion, the she-ass and the jack-ass. "Then he realizes, 'all this is myself!'" This is the wondrous knowledge that comes to man when he knows and understands his own true nature and the nature of all 'objective' reality. He is, indeed, the one Self of all, who lives within his own creation, experiencing the play of duality, while remaining the forever-undivided One.

This is the tale told by all who have been graced with the knowledge of the One who is their source and origin. It is, no doubt, the tale that was told by some mystic of the Paleolithic era, a tale which had the power of truth, and spread, becoming the archetypal myth or tale of the mystery of Being that was told 'round the nightfires and in the holy caverns across the continent of Old Europe, across the steppes of Central Asia, and eventually written down somewhere in the upper Gangetic plain.

The primitive artifacts brought to light by archaeology seem also to bear out our suspicion of a mystical influence going back thousands of years. For, today, archaeologists, having unearthed thousands of objects of representative art -- some of which date to over 20,000 years ago -- have greatly expanded our vision of man's pre-history from that of a century ago. Some of the most striking examples of this early figurative art come, not from the so-called "cradle of civilization," but from Europe -- an "Old Europe" -- which spawned a rich independent culture whose primary religious symbols turn out to be the same Father-God and Mother-Goddess who appear in a thousand guises in the East and, in fact, in every significant culture that appeared on earth. [4]

When we gaze in awe at the magnificent painted beasts stampeding 'cross the walls of the great Magdalenian caves of Altamira in Spain, of Lascaux and Les Trois Freres in France, dating from 17,000 to 12,000 B.C.E., we see a great preponderance of cows and bulls, mares and stallions, goats and rams, marked with symbols as to gender. In a chamber of the Tuc d'Audoubert cavern, stand a pair of coupling bison made of clay, from ca. 14,000 B.C.E. Can we help but wonder if it is not this very same allegory of the origin of life that is illustrated in the art of these many ancient sites? How frequently in both Paleolithic and Neolithic sites do we find representations of the bull, and sometimes just its horns, to be the premier symbol of the Divine! Is it only coincidence that it also figures as the premier creature in our ancient tale of creation?

There are other artifacts which seem to illustrate the familiarity of early man with that mystical tale of the One who became two. The most interesting was found near one of the oldest (ca. 20,000 B.C.E), and most familiar examples of Paleolithic art yet discovered: "The Woman With A Horn" (*Figure 1*), a 17" high relief carved into a sheltering overhang of limestone just above a 100 meter-long ledge, or terrace, at Laussel, in the Dordogne region of France, only a few miles from the spectacular caverns of Lascaux. Sometimes referred to as "the Venus of Laussel," she is a corpulent naked female, who is holding in one upraised hand a bull or bison's horn. The other hand is over her protruding belly. That she is intended to represent the great Mother (Nature) Goddess seems clear. In fact, it is evident that the site where this Goddess-figure appears was a Paleolithic shrine, or sanctuary, to the great Mother-Power; other emblems, symbolic of the female generative organ, are etched into the stone overhang adjoining the Goddess, along with several other female and one male form as well.

But most significant of all, and the artifact to which I wish to call your attention, is an adjoining carved relief which stands out from the rest: it is of a male and female united in a single emblem, or symbol (*Figure 2*). It has been suggested that the two figures are in a position of intercourse, with the female sitting atop a prone male. If so, it is reminiscent of certain modern representations from India of Shakti sitting atop the prone corpse of Shiva, symbolizing the dynamic activity of the creative Energy whose foundation and support is the unmoving Absolute. And if this is the case, the two works of art, though 20,000 years apart, may be fundamentally related. However, when one examines the ancient rock-carving closely, the two figures, female and male, seem not to be joined in intercourse, but seem rather to be designed to represent the two Principles joined into a single unit. It is not a realistic joining; in fact, certain elements of the arrangement are difficult to explain: if one looks at it reversed, with the (bearded) male at the top, his legs seem to extend along her left side, merging into and becoming her arm and breast, his feet becoming her head. Thus, each figure merges into the other, with a unifying border clearly designed to encompass them both.

Set as it is into this sanctuary of worship, this integrated male-female symbol would appear to be the earliest known example of the representation of the divine two-in-One upon which later mystics would so amply elaborate. Is this conjoined pair intended as an illustration of our primal myth of the original androgyne, prior to its separation into male and female principles? Some would protest that this is a concept too abstract, too sophisticated for a Cro-Magnon *homo sapiens* with a flint-chisel. But, as stated earlier, mystical experience is not dependent upon intellectual sophistication, and, without a written language, how else would some early mystic tell of his revelation to future generations except through myth and symbol?

But what are we to make of the bison's horn in the upraised hand of the Goddess? It is evidently intended as a prominent and recognizable symbol. But for us, 20,000 years removed, the tale told in that gesture must forever remain a mystery. Is it, as some scholars believe, a symbol for the moon? Or is it related to the fact that the bull, and sometimes just its two horns, was regarded in Paleolithic as well as Neolithic times as symbolic of the transcendent God? Could it be that the single horn in the uplifted hand of the Great Mother of Laussel serves to announce that She, herself, is one of the two

complementary aspects of Divinity? We shall never know for certain.
We may feel relatively certain, however, that She is intended to repre-
sent the female principle, the universal Mother, the great Womb of
Nature, who produces all this (objective) universe from Herself.

Another artifact depicting the great Mother (Nature) as a
pregnant naked female was found in the same region: it is a fragment
of reindeer bone from 12,000 B.C.E. on which is engraved a scene
showing the Father-God, symbolized by a bull, standing over the
Mother-Goddess. The Mother, symbolized by the pregnant female, is
below, supplicant, and receptive of the fecundation of the Father
(*Figure 3*). An inconceivable 8,000 years had passed since the nearby
'Woman With a Horn' was created; but the bull was still the primary
symbol for the Male principle, the transcendent Father-God, as it
would remain for at least another 10,000 years.

In the mystical experience of unity, there is seen, of course,
neither male nor female. The One, which contains in Itself all pairs of
opposites, is Itself beyond gender. However, It *is* apprehended under
two different aspects: It is the transcendent, quiescent Consciousness,
beyond the manifestation of time and space; *and* It is the Creative
Force which cyclically manifests and demanifests the entire universe.
And it is evident that, in almost every early culture, these two aspects
have been commonly represented in word and picture by those who
have apprehended them both, as the Father-God and the Mother-
Goddess (*Figures 4-6*). These two symbols of the primary duality-in-
Unity appear in abundance in the earliest myths and cultural artifacts
of pre-literate civilization, and they hint to us of the existence of
mystical experience transmitted orally and pictographically in the
early days of man's history. The transmission of actual personal
testimonies of mystical experience had to await the written record of
man's thought; and this occurred in various parts of the world during
the third millennium B.C.E., when hieroglyphs, ideograms, and
cuneiform writing first began to appear.

Where, then, do we find the earliest records of mystical
experience? We know that some of the most advanced early civilizations existed concurrently in the Nile, Mesopotamian, and Indus
valleys; and, while we may only conjecture about the development of
a mystical philosophy in ancient Egypt, Sumeria, and other Middle
Eastern regions, it is in India that we find the earliest explicit
testimonies of the mystics and the earliest development of an
advanced mystical philosophy, and so it is there we shall begin.

Figure 1. Limestone bas-relief of the great Goddess, known as "The Woman With A Horn," from Laussel (Dordogne region), France (ca. 20,000 B.C.E.). She is the great Mother Nature, from whom all creation flows, the Energy of the transcendent Self which manifests as the object-ive universe.

Figure 2. Opposing male and female figures from limestone shelter at Laussel (Dordogne region), France (ca. 20,000 B.C.E.), possibly intended to be symbolic of the one Reality experienced in the mystical vision which is both transcendent and immanent..

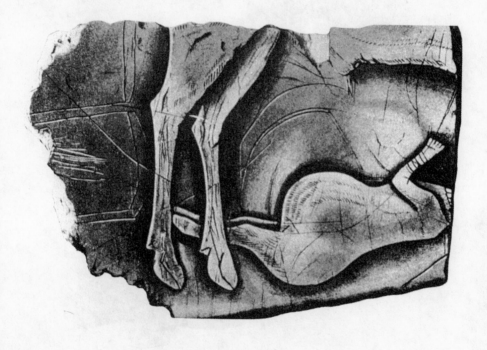

Figure 3. Engraving on reindeer bone (ca. 12,000 B.C.E.), from Laugerie Bass (Dordogne), France. The story illustrated is unknown, but the symbols are familiar: the Father-God is symbolized here by the bull; the creative aspect, or great Mother, symbolized by the pregnant female, is below, suppliant, and receptive of the Father's fecundation.

Figure 4. God-sculpture (4.5" high) from a grave-site in Cernavoda, at Hemangia on the edge of the Black Sea, present-day Romania (5000 B.C.E.). Often referred to as "The Thinker," He is clearly laboring in thought as the pure Mind from whom the world-thought emanates.

Figure 5. Goddess-sculpture found alongside the God-sculpture at the grave-site in Cernavoda (5000 B.C.E.). Appearing to be a modern abstract work, this ancient figurine represents the Great fecund Mother Nature, the creative thought-Power of the Father, the source and nourisher of all manifest creation.

Figure 6. Wooden carving of Zeus and Hera from Samos (ca. 625-600B.C.E.). Zeus (the Father-God) is holding forth the breast of Hera (Mother-Nature), signifying that, while it is She who nourishes the world, it is by *His* hand, since She is, indeed, *His* manifestory-Power. In an Orphic hymn, Zeus is referred to as "the foundation of the earth and of the starry sky, ... male and immortal female, ... the beginner of all things, the God with the dazzling light. For He has hidden all things within himself, and brought them forth again, into the joyful light, from His sacred heart, working marvels.'

Figure 7. The "prototype Shiva," an ithyphallic figure on a seal from the Indus Valley city of Mohenjo-daro (ca. 2500-1800 B.C.E.), is represented as a yogi, transcending the world of creation, while yet sustaining all creatures as *Pashupati*, "Lord of all creatures." Note the three faces and the carry-over of the bull's horns.

Figure 8. A sealing found in the excavated Indus Valley city of Harappa (ca. 2000 B.C.E.) On one side (top), two man-bull figures, and to the right the upside-down figure of the great Mother (Nature) from whose womb a tree, representative of all creation, grows. On the reverse (bottom), a female obeisant to a male figure. The lettered inscription is the same on both sides and has not been deciphered.

THE VEDIC HYMNISTS

When we attempt to discover the origins of mysticism, previous to the existence of written testimonies of mystical experience, we enter a dim, dark realm. For it is extremely difficult to ascertain whether or not a mystical philosophy was possessed by men living in India in a pre-literate period. Without the evidence of written documents, one must rely only on the slim evidence provided by the scattered artifacts taken from the ruins of ancient cities. In the case of India, the surprisingly large and elaborate cities unearthed at Harappa and Mohenjo-daro prove the existence of the remarkably developed civilizations of the Dravidian people who lived in the Indus Valley perhaps as far back as 2500 B.C.E.

Among the artifacts found in these cities was a seal containing a male figure which may be the prototype of the Father-God, Shiva (*Figure 7*), whose epithets are *Pashupati*,"Lord of all creatures," and *Yogeshvar*,"Lord of yoga." He is shown in his three-faced aspect, with a large crown of horns, sitting cross-legged in contemplation, with an erect penis; and he is surrounded by Shiva's traditional symbol, the bull, and other animals. In addition, there were found a number of phallus-shaped stones, known as *lingams*, which are also traditionally representative of Shiva, the world-transcending Absolute.

Along with these representations of the Father-God, however, were found a number of figurines and emblems of the Mother-Goddess, identifiable as Shakti, the fertile Mother of all creation. She is shown in one figure in a dancing pose, and in a sealing from Harappa she is shown standing on her head, her legs apart, with a plant or tree growing from her womb (*Figure 8*). There were also found a number of ring-shaped stones, called *yonis*, which are traditionally associated with Shakti, the Female principle of generation. And even a few figurines were found which appear to be androgynous, having breasts as well as what appear to be male genitals.

From the scant evidence found in these excavations we may assume that a mystical religious view which recognized the dual principles of the Absolute and Its creative manifestory-Power as complementaray aspects of the one Reality existed and flourished even in so remote a time. We are led to believe, therefore, that the religious view of these ancient peoples was inspired by one or more

seers of the ineffable duality-in-Unity which has been described in
more explicit and intelligible terms by mystics of a later era. Yet,
however convincing ths evidence may be, it cannot be considered
conclusive, but must remain forever a matter of conjecture.

Nevertheless, if we do accept this evidence, from the pre-
Aryan (Dravidian) civilization, of a full-blown Shiva-Shakti mythology, we may trace the manifestation of the Shaivite tradition to these
pre-Aryan peoples, and account for the appearance of two separately
developing traditions among the early Indian peoples: one, the long-
established tradition of the aboriginal races, and the other, the
imported Vedic pantheon of the invading Aryans. For the Dravidian
population, the Absolute Being came eventually to be known as *Shiva*,
and His world-manifesting Power was called *Shakti*; while the Aryan
tradition eventually adopted the name, *Brahman* for the Absolute
principle, and *Maya* for Its world-manifesting Energy. And, while
these two traditions eventually intermingled and became recognized
by the wise as representative of a common and identical world-view,
for many centuries each retained a semblance of independence while
co-existing alongside one another.

The earliest written records from India to convey the mystical
view of Unity are found in the collection of songs of devotion and
ceremonial liturgy known as the *Vedas* ("Wisdom"). The Vedas were
originally part of an orally transmitted legacy of the Aryans, dating
from 2000-1500 B.C.E., which was only transmitted to writing
centuries later. The *Aryans* ("Kinsmen") entered India from the
northwest via Persia and Afghanistan, originating from somewhere in
Central Asia. They were a light-skinned race who conquered and
absorbed the earlier Indus Valley civilization of the dark-skinned
Dravidian peoples, the builders of the vast complex cities at Harappa
and Mohenjo-daro. What later came to be called the civilization of
the "Hindus" (a corruption of *Sindhu*, the name of the river which
once served as the nation's northernmost perimeter), is an amalgam of
these two cultures, a sifting and blending of two independent traditions whose individual traces can still be found in the divergent racial
and religious traditions of present-day India.

For the early Aryan interlopers, the one God of all was called
by a great variety of names, according to the qualities intended to be
praised. Here, for example, in the following Vedic verses, He is
addressed as *Visvakarma* ("the all-Creator"):

O Visvakarma, Thou art our Father, our Creator, Maker;
Thou knowest every place and every creature.
To Thee, by whom the names of the gods were given,
All creatures turn in prayer. [1]

The Female Divinity was called *Prthivi* ("Nature"); and in a
prayer to Her, the seer cries:

May Earth pour out her milk for us, as a mother unto me her
son.
O Prthivi, beautiful are Thy forests, and beautiful are Thy hills
and snow-clad mountains. [2]

In yet another song from the Rig Veda, in which the Father-
God is spoken of as *Prajapati* ("Lord of all creatures"), His Female
Power of manifestation is called, not *Prthivi*, but *Vac* ("Speech" or
"Word"):

In truth Prajapati is the Father of the world;
With Him was Vac, the other aspect of Himself.
With Her, He begat life.
She conceived; and going forth from Him, She formed all
creatures.
And then, once again, She is re-absorbed into Prajapati. [3]

This is a depiction of Creation almost identical to the Egyptian and Judaic ones appearing around the same time (ca. 1500
B.C.E.), and is amazingly similar to the opening paragraph of the
Fourth Gospel by the Christian evangelist, John. Here, once again, we
have a symbolic representation of the perennial vision of the mystic
who perceives the Absolute and Its manifestory Power as an ineffable
duality-in-Unity, and characterizes It as the universal Father-Mother.

We find in the Vedas many different names for the Father-
God, each representative of a special power or quality of the one
Being. Sometimes He was called *Dyaus*, "the Almighty", or *Varuna*,
the power of the wind; sometimes He was *Indra*, whose thunderbolts
brought the rain. But as time went on, these various epithets came to
be recognized as but various aspects of the same one Lord:

They call Him Indra, Mitra, Varuna, or Agni, or Garutmat, the
heavenly bird.
Reality (*Sat*) is one; learned men call It by various names,
such as Agni, Yama, or Matarisvan. [4]

Too often, men take the names of God which accumulate over the centuries to represent separate and distinct entities, and then pit them one against the other. This was true of the early poets and mythologizers of the Vedas as well. As soon as one tribe or civilization absorbed another, it established its own name for God as the superior, and relegated the subjugated people's name for God to an inferior position. In this way, a polytheistic mythology accumulated in no time, peopled with all manner of anthropomorphized gods. This, however, is the work of the priests and mythologizers, not of the seers. As one Vedic mystic put it:

> With words, priests and poets make into many the hidden
> Reality which is but One. [5]

The Vedas are an amalgamated collection of many songs written by priests, sages, legalists, rulers and poets of the early Aryans, and they run the gamut from lyrical devotion to ceremonial doctrine; from primitive superstition to high philosophy. They represent not only a broad extent of time -- perhaps a thousand years of development -- but also a wide divergence of intellects. It was the poets and priests contributing to the Vedas who fashioned the liturgical and legal traditions of subsequent generations, but it was some unnamed mystic or mystics who gave expression to the exalted vision of Unity which is the cornerstone of the Vedas and the foundation upon which rests the great monistic tradition of Vedanta.

Others may attempt to speak of such things, but it is only the mystic whose words are capable of conveying the certainty and authority which is born of true experience. Here, in the *Creation Hymn* (X:129) from the Rig Veda, we have a description of the primal Reality prior to the manifestation of the world by a sage who had seen It for himself. In one of the oldest extant declarations of a true mystic, that one Beginning-place of all things is described:

1.   Then, neither the non-Real (*asat*) nor the Real (*sat*) existed.
       There was no sky then, nor the heavens beyond it.
       What was contained by what, and where, and who sheltered it?
       What unfathomed depths, what cosmic ocean, existed then?

2.   Then, neither death nor deathlessness existed;
       Between day and night there was as yet no distinction.

That ONE (*tad ekam*), by Its own power (*svadha*) breathlessly
breathed. [6]

First, let us understand that "the Real" (*sat*) refers to the
Absolute, the pure Mind, the one Origin and Father of all; and "the
unreal" (*asat*) refers to this illusory universe of form and apparent
substance that is, at bottom, truly only Energy (*svadha*). Elsewhere
we shall meet up with this same pair referred to as "Brahman and
Maya," "Purusha and Prakrti," or "Shiva and Shakti." Such terms
conceptually separate out the two aspects of the one Reality perceived
in the "mystical experience" of which our seer speaks. It is a conceptual division only, and does not represent a *real* division in the
ultimate Reality.

Then the Hymnist goes on in an attempt to explain how,
within the non-dual Existence, the creative impulse arises, bringing
about the manifestation of the universe:

3.   In the beginning, darkness lay wrapped in darkness;
        All was one undifferentiated (*apraketa*) sea (*salila*).
        Then, within that one undifferentiated Existence,
        [Something] arose by the heat of concentrated energy (*tapas*).

4.   What arose in That in the beginning was Desire (*kama*),
        [Which is] the primal seed of mind (*manas*).
        The wise, having searched deep within their own hearts,
        Have perceived the bond (*bandha*) between the Real (*sat*) and
        the unreal (*asat*).

Mystics of succeeding generations, who have seen THAT in
the depths of contemplation for themselves, have recognized the
author of the above Hymn as one who had also known "the mystical
vision." He was, himself, one of those sages he describes, who,
searching deep within themselves, perceived "the bond between the
Real and the unreal." He had seen THAT from which all Creation
emanates; for in that mystical experience of unity, one goes back --
not temporally, but causally -- to the Beginning of things, to that
eternal, unmoving Consciousness from which the world-manifestation
springs forth. There, in that perfect Stillness, night and day, life and
death, do not exist; they are indistinguishable in that state prior to the
coming into being of all such opposites. All these opposites, these
complements, rely for their existence on an initial differentiation
within the One, creating a perceiver and a perceived.

The subtle source of that differentiation, says our mystic, is "Desire;" i.e., the impulse within the One to create within Itself an object, an "other," for the purpose of experiencing enjoyment. Is it not the same with us? Does not the same subtle process occur in all our own mental constructions? First, arises a desire, followed by the formation of a thought or fantasy to gratify the desire, and then delectation. It is this subtle movement of desire which comes into expression as mind (*manas*) or mentation; and, by the production of mental imagery, we have created within our integral consciousness an artificial duality: a *seer* (the witnessing subject) and a *seen* (the object of inner vision). And so, within ourselves, we experience a microcosmic reproduction of the process which occurs as universal Creation within the one Mind [universal Destruction is likewise mirrored in the dissolution of a thought within the mind, as we return to self-awareness].

5.   They (the wise) have stretched the cord (*rashmi*) of their
      vision [to encompass the Truth],
      And they have perceived what is higher and lower:
      The mighty powers [of Nature] are made fertile
      By that ONE who is their Source.
      Below [i.e., secondary] is the creative Energy (*svadha*),
      And above [i.e., primary] is the Divine Will (*prayati*).

It is, we are reminded, the one Divine Consciousness which is the primary Reality (*sat*); the thought-creation is but illusion (*asat*). The Divine Will (*prayati*) is superior, or above; and the creative energy (*svadha*) of thought-imagery is subordinate, or below. This has been seen in contemplation by all the mystics of every time.

6.   [But, after all,] who knows, and who can say whence it all
      came, or how this creation came about?
      The gods, themselves, came later than this world's creation,
      so who truly knows whence it has arisen?

7.   Whence all creation had its origin, only He, whether He
      fashioned it or not --
      He, who surveys it all from highest heaven -- He knows.
      Or perhaps even He does not! [7]

Why on earth, we must all wonder at some time or another, would God have given birth to this dream-like realm, where individualized souls struggle for wisdom and contentment while continually buffeted by passions, blinded by ignorance, assailed by pain, and threatened with death? What could be His motive? As there were no witnesses to the initial Creation, there is no one to tell. But what of the mystic? Surely, while he is lost in the depths of the Eternal, he is in a unique position to explain the 'why' of Creation! Unfortunately, even the mystic perceives no 'why'. For, in that unitive vision, He alone is. The joyful expression which is the universal drama radiates from Himself, the one Mind. He alone is the one Cause. There is nowhere else to look for causation, for whatever appears from Him and before Him is His own most natural and unquestionable radiation of Bliss.

Another way of expressing this truth is to say that the appearance of the world-manifestation in and on the one Consciousness is simply the nature of That. All questions regarding the how and why of it are therefore alogical. It is like asking, "Why does light shine?" or "Why does a mind think?" Who knows why a desire arises? Who knows how a thought is formed? We are aware that our thinking processes are distinguishable from our background consciousness, which is merely a witness to the mind's activity. We are aware that the thought-producing aspect of our mind is superimposed on our consciousness, but we don't know how or why. It simply occurs. We say that it is merely the nature of consciousness to manifest as thought. Similarly, the nature of That, the one Consciousness, is to manifest as the phenomenal world. "Perhaps," says our Vedic author, "even He doesn't know the how or why of it."

Here is another passage from the Rig Veda (X:90:1-5) that points up the difficulty of explaining the relationship between the two complementary aspects of Reality:

> All this is He -- what has been and what shall be. He is the
> Lord of immortality. Though He has become all this, in real-
> ity He is not all this. For truly, He is beyond the world. The
> whole series of universes -- past, present, and future -- express
> His glory and power; but *He transcends His own glory.* All
> beings of the universe form, as it were, only a portion of His
> being; the greater part is invisible and unchangeable. He who
> is beyond all predicates *appears* as the relative universe; He
> *appears* as all sentient and insentient beings. [8]

In the above Hymn, we are taught the perennial paradox of duality-in-Unity: "Though He has become all of this, in reality He is not all of this." He is the transcendent, the Unchangeable, the Eternal; yet conjunctive with the absolute, unqualified voidness of that one Consciousness, is the shining forth of His "glory." This shining-forth as the universe of forms is not He, yet it is He. His "glory" stands in relation to the Absolute as the Sun's radiating light stands to the Sun. They are different, yet they are one. The rays of the Sun have no independent existence, and exist only because of the Sun; the glory of God which appears as the phenomenal universe also has no independent reality, but exists only as a radiation or emanation from that pure Sun of Consciousness. "He transcends His own glory," says the seer; remaining forever One, unchanging and pure, He appears as the multiform universe.

Such an understanding comes not from the mind of a speculative philosopher, but from the vision of the mystic. Only one who has plumbed the depths of his own mind, and passed beyond the mind to the Source of all mind and all manifestation, can know the truth of this unity-in-duality, this duality-in-unity. It is the knowledge of the Vedic seer which, as we shall see, has been throughout the ages the common knowledge of all who have passed beyond the "glory" of God, and have seen in the depths of inner contemplation the one Beginning and Ending of all things.

EARLY EGYPTIANS

So far, we have looked only at the early evidence of mystic-ism in a small portion of the sub-continent of Asia -- from the Indus Valley to the Gangetic plain. Now, let's turn to equally ancient Egypt, Mesopotamia, and the emerging nation of Israel.

When we examine any ancient civilization, we see before us a broad cultural tapestry of multiple mythic images. And yet, if we search carefully, we shall undoubtedly find in one small corner of that tapestry the evidence that a genuine seer existed, and spoke, and left his imprint on future generations. The popular polytheistic culture of ancient Egypt, with which we are familiar from the findings of archae-ology, was the product of its artists, poets, priests, and intellectuals. They invented a panoply of gods and goddesses, creatures of the religious imagination; yet, despite this apparent polytheism, the cornerstone of the religious consciousness of ancient Egypt was the recognition of an absolute Unity, which was called *Neter*, in which all gods (*neteru*), men, and creatures were included.

For the Egyptians of the early dynasties, the various gods, such as Ra, Horus, and Osiris, for example, were symbolic representatives of various aspects or attributes of the one universal Spirit, much as Indra, Varuna, and Agni personified various attributes of the universal Brahman in the Vedic tradition. The Unity, called *Neter*, was regarded as the one eternal Being, omnipotent, omniscient and inscrutable, in whom and from whom all the phenomenal and noumenal universe exists. Men, gods, creatures, and all objects were seen to be mental creations of the transcendent God, who, in Himself, remained eternally pure and unchanging. Here is a synopsis of their view of Creation, as presented by noted Egyptologist, Sir Wallis Budge:

> According to the writings of the Egyptians, there was a time when neither heaven nor earth existed, and when nothing had being except the boundless primeval water, which was, however, shrouded with thick darkness. In this condition, the primeval water remained for a considerable time, notwithstanding that it contained within it the germs of the things which afterwards came into existence in this world and the world itself. At length, the Spirit of the primeval water felt the desire for creative activity, and having uttered the word, the world sprang straightway into being in the form which had already been depicted in the mind of the Spirit before he spake the word which resulted in its creation. [1]

This view, it should be noted, is strikingly similar to the view, already cited, of the Vedic seers of ancient India. It should be noted also that, for the ancient Egyptians, it is the "Thought" or "Word" of the one Spirit which constitutes the world of creation -- a Thought or Word born of, yet distinct from the originating Mind. We find this view consistently held as far back as the 24th century B.C.E. at Memphis, in Egypt, where an independent religious tradition worshipped the One as *Ptah*. The rock-carvings on the walls of the pyramids, known as "the Pyramid Texts" (ca. 2350-2175 B.C.E.) declare:

> Mighty and great is Ptah, who gives power to all the gods; ... He is in every body and every mouth of all gods, all men, all beasts, all crawling things, and whatever lives, since He thinks forth and calls into being everything according to

His will.

  When the eyes see, the ears hear, and the nose breathes, these sensations are referred to the mind. And it is the mind that brings forth every word, for the tongue only repeats the thought of the mind. Likewise, everything has come into existence through the thought of Ptah and His word. [Through the mind of Ptah] all the gods were fashioned, ... and all the gods are at one with Him, content and united with the Lord of heaven and earth. [2]

This is undoubtedly the work of an ancient mystic, of one who has seen the origin of the universe in the clarity of mystical vision. But even more compelling evidence for the existence and influence of an ancient mystic may be found in a portion of *The Egyptian Book Of The Dead,* called "The Papyrus of Ani," which contains material dating back to the 30th century B.C.E., and may even have predated the dynastic eras in a purely oral tradition. Here, we find a number of recurring epithets for the one originating Principle, which clearly bespeak such a mystical influence:

  God is One and alone, and none other exists with Him; God is the One, the One who has made all things.

  He is eternal and infinite; ... He has endured for countless ages, and He shall endure to all eternity.

  God is a spirit, a hidden spirit, the Spirit of spirits, the Divine Spirit.

  He is a mystery to His creatures, and no man knows how to know Him. His names are innumerable; they are manifold, and no one knows their number.

  God has made the universe, and He has created all that is in it; ... He has stretched out the heavens and founded the earth. What His heart conceived came to pass straightway, and when He had spoken His word came to pass, and it shall endure forever.

  God, Himself, is existence; He lives in all things, and lives upon all things. He endures without increase or diminution; He multiplies Himself millions of times, and He possesses multitudes of forms and multitudes of members. God is life, and through Him only man lives. He gives life to man, and He breathes the breath of life into his nostrils.

  God is merciful unto those who reverence Him, and He hears those who call upon Him. He protects the weak against the strong, and He hears the cry of him that is bound in fetters. ... God knows those who know Him; He rewards those who serve Him, and He protects those who follow

Him. [3]

Scholars today view these epithets as merely an exceptionally early expression of monotheistic theory, predating that of the Judaic scriptures; but the mystic recognizes the author of these words, not as a theoretician, but as a person who has realized the ultimate Reality through direct experience, who has "seen" the Unity in the clarity of mystical vision. It is because his knowledge came of a God-given revelation that he was able to speak with such authority and conviction, and for that reason also his words endured to so deeply effect the religious sentiment of ancient Egypt and very likely that of the early Jews of Israel as well.

THE JEWS

Around the beginning of the 2nd millenium B.C.E. a small group of people left the city of Ur of the Chaldeans in Babylonia (near present-day Kuwait), led by a man named Terah and his son, Abraham, and travelled northward across the Euphrates river. These were the first people to later become known as *Ivriim*, or *Hebrews*, "the people who crossed over the river." Later, Abraham, at the age of seventy-five, told his few tribesmen that he had heard the voice of God speaking to him from on High, and the voice told him that they would become God's "chosen people" if they would follow the commandments God had given to Abraham. God would lead His people south into the land of Canaan (the land which now comprises Israel, Jordan, Syria and Lebanon) if they would agree to the circumcision of all their male descendents. Abraham's followers agreed to this covenant, and the Judaic religion was born.

For several centuries thereafter, Abraham's descendants wandered as nomads in the land of Canaan, worshipping their God, whom they called *JHVH* ("Yahweh"), perhaps as a variant of *Jahu*, originally the name of a tribal god of rain. Then, in the 16th century B.C.E., Joseph, a descendant of Abraham, led some of the Hebrew tribe into Egypt, and eventual slavery, while some others remained in the "promised land" of Canaan. Those Hebrews who had endured slavery in Egypt returned to Canaan in the 12th century B.C.E., led by a new leader named Moses, who, with his code of social conduct, helped to establish a lawful and integrated society. However, in the four-hundred years of their absense, the Canaanites (those who had remained behind) had evolved their own religious culture, borrowing much from their ancient Babylonian roots and other indigenous influences.

They had embraced the mystical concept of the two Divine aspects of the one Truth: They called the one aspect, which was transcendent and Male, *El* ("the First") or *Ba'al* ("the Lord"); and the other aspect, which was the creative Energy manifest as the world, they depicted as immanent and Female, and called Her *Elat* (the feminine form of *El*), or *Ba'ala* (the femine form of *Ba'al*). She was also known as *Anath*, *Athirat*, or *Asherah* -- all variants of the Syrian *Astarte* or the Babylonian *Ishtar*. This cult of *Ashera*, the Mother-Goddess, was anathema to the newly arrived Hebrews however. The Hebrew Bible contains more than 40 references to Her in which the newly-united peoples of Israel were warned against Her worship.

Nonetheless, it is clear that some segments of the Hebrews adopted the concept of the Goddess; for, in 1975 of the Current Era, at a site in the Sinai desert called Kuntillet Ajrud, archaeologists found fragments of a storage jar dating from the 8th century B.C.E., which contained three figures, one a female playing a lyre, with an inscription referring to "Yahweh of Samaria and His Asherah."[1]   The Asherah, or goddess, is also represented on these fragments by Her icons: the sacred tree, symbol of Nature's bounty; and the lion, Her frequent mount in representations from ancient Sumeria to India.

Between the 10th and 6th centuries B.C.E., the Canaanite cult of *Ashera* continued to resurface, as evidenced by the recurring injunctions against Her worship in many of the Old Testament books written during that time. And, eventually, the conflict between the Canaanite worshippers of the One in Its dual aspects which they called Baal and Asherah, and the Hebrew worshippers of the One in Its dual aspects which they called Yahweh and Chokmah resulted in the systematic slaughter of the Canaanites by the Hebrews. Ba'al was replaced by Yahweh, and Asherah was replaced by Chokmah. *Chokmah* (pronounced *Hoke-mah*), which means "Wisdom," was the Hebrew version of the creative Power of Yahweh, synonymous with *Prthivi* of the Vedas. Later, in the Jewish rabbinical tradition, She would become *Shekinah*; and the Greek seers of a later time -- notably the Stoics, and the Gnostics as well, would call Her *Sophia*,

their own word for "Wisdom."   By both Jews and Greeks alike She
was regarded, not only as the creative aspect of God, but also as the
principle of Intelligence inherent in mankind who is Her embodiment.

In the book of *Proverbs*, in the Old Testament of the Bible,
She is made to say:

> God made me [Wisdom] in the beginning of His
> works, as the first of His acts.
> ... Before God made the earth and the fields or the
> first dust of the world,when He set up the heavens, I was
> there;
> ... When He laid the foundations of the earth, I
> existed as His instrument. I was His delight every day,
> playing always before Him, playing on His inhabited earth,
> and my delights are with human beings. [2]

She was regarded as co-eternal with the unmanifested God,
being His Power of manifestation by which the universe came into
existence:

> *Chokmah* [Wisdom] is from the Lord; She is with
> Him eternally. ... It is He who created Her, ... and infused
> Her into all His works. [3]

She is the vibratory Energy from which all matter is produced,
a vibratory Energy which emanates from God, as the sound of a word
emanates from a person's mouth:

> Hear the praise of *Chokmah* from Her own mouth: 'I
> am the Word which was spoken by the Most High'. [4]

Yet, while the early seers of Judaism recognized the dual-
facetedness of the One, they were also keenly aware of the danger of
the hypostacization of the creative Principle as a second and separate
Divinity, and the consequent error of philosophical Dualism. For this
reason, they continually hearkened back to the declaration of the
singularity and unity of God:

> I am the one Lord; there is no other beside Me. I
> form the light and create the darkness; I make peace and
> create evil. I, the one Lord, do all these things. [5]

This great declaration of non-Dualism is perhaps the most

significant statement in all of the Hebrew Bible. It acknowledges the singleness of God, and stands as a bulwark against those who would divide the responsibility for the nature of things between a good Principle and an evil Principle, as has been done so often throughout history. Dualism -- the doctrine which asserts that there are two *independent* and contrary Principles at work in the universe is a belief which perennially resurfaces among the unlearned segments of the populace as a means of explaining the apparent injustice and suffering in the world. God is good and just, they reason; and so these things could not have originated with Him, but had to have been produced by some other.

Such a creed of Dualism existed during Biblical times as well, and required frequent reminders from the Hebrew prophets and seers that all that is comes from the one Lord. The creative Power, usually symbolized as a female Goddess, never was a separate and independent Divinity, but is merely a symbol of the creative Power of the One; they were never two. It is that one Lord who is the source of the creative Power from whom comes both good and evil; all such opposites: the light and the darkness, pleasure and pain, life and death, composition and decomposition, are complementary aspects of the one Life-force, while He, the transcendent God, is beyond all dualities, and is unaffected by the appearance of duality.

As those who have seen the Truth in the "mystical vision" tell us, He is always pure, always unaffected by the play of opposites which we experience as the world. Just as our own personal consciousness remains clear and unstained by the millions of thoughts and images which have paraded across it, or just as the sky remains clear and unmarred even though millions of thunder-clouds have passed across its face, so He is ever pure, ever-unchanged and unaffected by the manifestation of the countless thought-forms which constitute this universe.

To be sure, He is solely responsible for the existence of this universe; He is its sole Source and animating power. And yet, as is evident from the analogy with the human consciousness, He, in his own being, remains uninvolved, unaffected by the immensely complex activities and evolutions taking place within the cosmic drama. This is not to say, of course, that He is not as close as our own breath; we, and the objects of our world, are nothing else but His existence, and He is the Source and inner Self of everyone. He is the voice of reason, He is the fire of song within the heart; He is the compassion that stirs the soul, He is the light of wisdom shining, full of joy, within us all. It is He who, in the very creation of this world of opposites, has placed the dust of blindness before our inner eye, and concealed Himself in the fog of our ignorance.   And it is He, also, who increases His own light in the soul, causing it to yearn for total illumination, and then reveals Himself within as the Light of all lights, the Self of all selves.

Of all the various prophets and authors of the Hebrew Bible who yearned for a clear vision of God, the nameless author of the book of *Psalms* seems best qualified to be regarded as a true mystic. These noble and poetically beautiful songs of God-longing and praise have been attributed to David, king of Palestine (ca. 1000 B.C.E.), but it is very unlikely that they really were penned by that famous warrior-king. Whoever their author was, it is clear that he had experienced the yearning for God, and had received the grace of mystical "vision." His *Psalms,* apparently recorded around the same time as some of the songs of the *Rig Veda*, bear some similarity to those Vedic Hymns. His world, like that of the Vedic authors, was a harsh one of mysterious, unexplained forces, and violent, warlike men. He calls on his God to defeat them and to favor him and his own. In his plaintive songs to God, he oftentimes cries out in anguish at God's slowness in vanquishing the wicked, and granting victory to the righteous.

Like the Vedas, the Psalms run the gamut of human emotions, from humility to rage, from prayer for righteousness to prayer for conquest. They are songs from an obviously difficult time of savage and brutal struggle, and yet, it seems that, during the time of the Psalmist, there was a strong movement toward the path of devotion, and many who sought, through solitary contemplation, to know God. It was the Psalmist who gave voice to this movement, saying: "This is the generation of them that seek after Him, that seek Thy Face, O God. [6]   His one desire was to see God face to face; "As for me," he says in the 17th Psalm, "let me behold Thy Face through righteousness." Like Jesus, who was to come long after him, he declared that it is the pure in heart who shall see God: "The Lord loves righteousness; it is the righteous who shall behold His Face. [7]

Wherever we find a literature of loving devotion to God, we may expect also to find a seer of God. The Psalmist was just such a lover and seer. In his Songs of longing for the embrace of God, we find the forerunners of the songs of devotion written much later by

the saints of the *Bhakti* movement in India. In the period of his most
intense longing, he sings: "As a deer pants for the cool stream, so my
soul longs for Thee, O God." [8]   And in his anguish, he cries out,
"How long, O Lord? Wilt Thou forget me forever? How long wilt
Thou hide thy Face from me?" [9]   And then, when at last he attains
the vision he sought, and realizes the oneness and all-pervasiveness of
God, he sings:

> O Lord, Thou art behind me and before me, and Thy
> hand is ever upon me. This is a knowledge too wonderful for
> me to grasp! Whither shall I go from Thy Spirit? Or whither
> shall I flee from Thy presence? If I take the wings of the
> morning, or dwell in the uttermost parts of the sea, even there
> shall Thy hand lead me, and Thy right hand shall uphold me. [10]

In such utterances, we are able to hear the perennial song of
unity sung by the later mystic seers. The Psalmist clearly recognizes,
at least briefly, the all-pervasiveness of God, the all-inclusiveness of
God, and knows in that moment that even his own life is but an
expression of God's manifold being. But it is too wonderful, too
subtle, for him to grasp. And besides, the Psalmist is little concerned
with establishing a consistent philosophical world-view; his songs are
prayers to God, songs of rejoicing, praise, or wails of distress. Like
the Vedas, they originate from the primitive heart, which seeks in all
simplicity to know and follow the ways of the mysterious God who
holds in His hands the fate of all men. To their author, the
formulation of a 'philosophy of Unity' was unthinkable; he was a
lover, and he knew only that his beloved God had shown him His
grace.

Whether it was king David or some other who wrote the
Psalms, their author was a man who had undoubtedly received a
profound experience of God within himself, and who, because of that
grace, was able to provide inspiration and strength to men of many
later generations through his songs in praise of God. To be sure,
those ancient songs are mixed with the stain of bigotry, violence, and
other human weaknesses; but we must remember the time and
circumstances under which they were written. Their author stood
alone in a time of barbarism and stupidity, and fearlessly sang of his
God, and upheld the banner of truth and righteousness for his people
to follow. Today, so many centuries removed from his times and
trials, we may still catch a glimpse of the greatness of the Psalmist, and

hear the echo of his mighty voice across the mountainous years, resounding in praise of the ancient and everlasting God.

THE UPANISHADIC SEERS

In India, sometime during the first mellennium B.C.E., the Vedas were finally collected and put into an organized written form; and an additional, much later, collection of philosophical writings by the *rishis,* or seers, who had known God, were appended to those earlier hymns and religious precepts, and thereafter regarded as an integral part of the *Vedas.* These philosophical appendages, addressed to a more learned and intellectually sophisticated audience, were called the *Upanishads.* The Sanskrit word, *upanishad,* means "sitting beneath," and connotes those teachings which are received at the feet of a spiritual Master, or *Guru.* The Upanishads are also "sitting beneath" the Vedas as the final portion of the collection, and are therefore known as the *Vedanta*: the end (*anta*) of the Vedas.

Of the one-hundred and eight Upanishads said to exist, twelve are regarded as of primary importance and merit. In philosophical purity and persuasiveness, these few represent what, for most of us, are the Upanishads. Their names are the *Isha, Kena, Katha, Prasna, Mundaka, Mandukya, Chandogya, Brihadaranyaka, Aitareya, Taitiriya, Svetasvatara* and *Maitri Upanishads.* The authors and exact date of authorship of these separate spiritual treatises are unknown; we know only that they were written, by various anonymous sages who had realized that Truth of which they speak, sometime between ca. 1200 and 400 B.C.E. While they vary in length and in style, their one common theme is the inner realization of the identity of the *Atman* (Self) and *Brahman* (the one universal Consciousness). We may strive to know God, or we may strive to know our Self; but, say the Upanishads, when you find the one, you shall also find the other; and it is this discovery which constitutes Enlightenment.

It has long been recognized as a fact of religious psychology that, as a man grows in understanding of God, he grows correspondingly in understanding of himself. As his conception of God becomes more refined, his conception of Self undergoes a corresponding alteration, and *vice versa.* This intriguing fact is expressed most succinctly in a passage from the ancient Indian epic, the *Ram-*

ayana; in it, Rama, who represents the Godhead incarnate, asks his servant, Hanuman, "How do you regard me?"   And Hanuman replies:

> *dehabhavena daso'smi*
> *jivabhavena twadamshakah*
> *atmabhave twamevaham*

> (When I identify with the body, I am Thy servant;
> When I identify with the soul, I am a part of Thee;
> But when I identify with the Self, I am truly Thee.) [1]

These three attitudes represent not only progressively subtle stages in the conception of God, but progressively subtle stages of self-identification as well. While each of these three relational attitudes finds expression as the prevailing attitude within various individual religious traditions, they are actually representative of the viewpoint from these different stages of self-awareness.

We have seen, in the Vedas, how religious thought progressed from a primitive sort of nature-worship to monotheism, and finally to a monistic conception of reality. This progression of understanding is a duplication of the progression of understanding that takes place in the mind of every individual as well. We all begin as materialists, taking for granted that the phenomenal world before us is the sole reality. The idea of a transcendent God, or a unifying Principle inherent in the world, seems but a remote and hazy notion. Then, as our religious sense awakens, perhaps through some shocking reminder of our mortality, or a dawning clarity of mind while viewing the starry heavens or some quiet stretch of seacoast, we begin to reflect. And some inner logic seems to demand a Creator for so vast and mysterious a universe. We begin to sense an Intelligence beyond our own, an Intelligence with whom we can communicate, and of whom we are increasingly aware in all our thoughts and actions.

The second stage of our religious development comes when, after some deliberation and inner probing, we come to the conclusion that there is something within ourselves, a moral spirit, a guiding light, which is, itself, Divine, and partakes of God Himself. We call it our "soul," and we sense the longing of that soul to rejoin the Divine beauty and goodness from which, like a spark from a blazing fire, it emanated.

Finally, we experience the third stage in our journey when, in a moment of longing, contemplating our Divine Source, we know "the peace that passes all understanding," and suddenly, in a moment of unprecedented clarity of Intelligence, we know that one Divinity face to face. In that clear knowing, we realize that the seeker and the Goal, the knower and That which it sought to know, are one. Like the king of a vast kingdom, awakening from a dream in which he is poor and lost, we awake to the realization that we were never separate from the One, but only imagined a separateness where none existed. Then we know who we have always been: the one all-pervading Being, who, while transcending this world of light and shadow, is Itself the substratum and essence of all.

It is in the Upanishads that we first hear from those fully illumined seers who have reached the final stage of knowledge regarding God and the Self, declaring to us that the Self and God are one:

> Even by the mind this truth is to be learned:
> There are not many, but only ONE. [2]

We are easily able to understand the idea of an underlying Unity intellectually, but that remains an imperfect and ultimately unsatisfactory knowledge so long as we do not directly experience that Unity as *I*. Our very knowledge stands in the way of experiencing the Truth, because we retain the limited awareness of "I know". That very intellect which knows establishes a separation between the knower and what is known. Hear what the seers of the Upanishads say on this point:

> He is known by those who know Him beyond thought,
> not to those who imagine He can be attained by thought. ... If
> you think, "I know Him well," you do not know the Truth.
> You only perceive that appearance of Brahman produced by the
> inner senses. Continue to meditate. [3]

> What cannot be thought with the mind, but That where-
> by the mind thinks: know That alone to be Brahman.
> ... It is not what is thought that we should wish to
> know; we should know the thinker. "He is my Self!" This one
> should know. "He is my Self!" This one should know. [4]

And *that* knowledge, of the Self, or *Atman*, is obtained only through the direct experience that occurs when the knowing mind is transcended, and the knower and the known are realized to be one.

No amount of reasoning, no amount of philosophical understanding, can approach this directly-apprehended knowledge:

> He cannot be seen by the eye, and words cannot reveal
> Him. He cannot be realized by the senses, or by austerity or
> the performance of rituals. By the grace of wisdom and purity
> of mind, He can be seen in the silence of contemplation. [5]

> When a sage sees this great Unity, and realizes that
> his Self has become all beings, what delusion and what sorrow
> could ever approach him? [6]

> When awake to the vision of one's own Self, when a
> man in truth can say: "I am He," what desires could lead him
> to grieve in fever for the body?
> ... When a man sees the *Atman*, his own Self, the
> one God, the Lord of what was and of what shall be, then he
> fears no more. [7]

This "vision" of the Self is described in the Upanishads as Liberation (*moksha*). It is a freedom, a release, from doubt, from uncertainty, from the fears attending ignorance, forever. All questions are answered; all desires and causes for sorrow are put to rest; for thereafter, a man knows the secret of all existence. All previous notions of limitation and mortality, all darkness of ignorance, is swept away in the all-illuminating light of Truth:

> When the wise man knows that it is through the great
> and omnipresent Spirit in us that we are conscious in waking
> or in dreaming, then he goes beyond all sorrow. When he
> knows the Self, the inner Life, who enjoys like a bee the
> sweetness of the flowers of the senses, the Lord of what was
> and what will be, then he goes beyond all fear. [8]

> When a man has seen the truth of the Spirit, he is
> one with Him; the aim of his life is fulfilled, and he is ever
> beyond sorrow.
> ... When a man knows God, he is free; his sorrows
> have an end, and birth and death are no more. When in inner
> union he is beyond the world of the body, then the third world,
> the world of the Spirit, is found, where man possesses all --
> for he is one with the ONE. [9]

It is these truths, that "Brahman is the Atman," [10] "Atman is Brahman,"[11] and that man's realization of Atman-Brahman is man's ultimate "Liberation," which constitute the great message of the

Upanishads. But a further question remains: "How is this realization
to be attained?" In answer to that question, the various authors of the
Upanishads offer various answers, which to a perplexed student may
appear contradictory and mutually exclusive. But, with a little explanation, it can be easily understood that their directives are not contradictory at all, but complementary. For example, in the *Katha
Upanishad*, we are given three different explanations of the way to
know God. The first is "by the grace of God":

> The man who surrenders his human will leaves
> sorrows behind, and beholds the glory of the Self by the
> grace of God.
> ... Not through much learning is the Atman reached,
> nor through the intellect and the sacred teachings. It is reached
> by those whom He chooses; to His chosen the Self reveals His
> glory. [12]

The second is "by purity of heart":

> He is seen by a pure heart and by a mind whose
> thoughts are pure.
> ... When all desires that cling to the heart are sur-
> rendered, then a mortal becomes immortal, and even in this
> world he is one with Brahman. [13]

The third is by "one-pointed contemplation":

> Not even through deep knowledge can the Self be
> reached, unless evil ways are abandoned, and there is rest in
> the senses, concentration in the mind, and peace in one's
> heart.
> ... When the wise man rests his mind in contem-
> plation on our God beyond time, who invisibly dwells in the
> mystery of things and in the heart of man, then he rises above
> both pleasures and sorrows. [14]

These three, apparently diverse, methods or means to attain the
realization of God appear in one form or another throughout all the
Upanishads. And, in order to understand the integral relationship of
these three apparently different "paths," we must examine them in
the light of the experience of those who have reached the goal of Self-
realization. First, let us understand what is meant by "the grace of
God."

Those who have known that absolute Self realize that whatever
exists, and whatever occurs in this universe, is His doing. There is

nothing whatsoever that is apart from Him. This the sages have
clearly seen. Where, then, is that which is outside of His doing? Can
we suppose that the awakening of our understanding about God is
something apart from His doing? Or that our efforts, our devotion to
Truth, our desire for knowledge, is something other than His own
activity within ourselves? It is God's grace which inspires within us
the effort, the desire. The vision of God is not attained without effort,
but the effort itself is a manifestation of His grace. And the revelation
of Himself -- could that be accomplished without His doing it? We
are within God, and everything -- even our doubting, our rejection,
our foolishness -- is He. Can that inward journey to Self-realization
be inspired by someone other than He?

Regardless of what steps we take toward the realization of God,
it is God Himself who is playing out the drama. The light that fills a
room is nothing but light; how could we find a portion of that light
that is acting independently? Likewise, all this universe is the glory of
God, and nothing but Him. What, then, is not Himself? What is not a
manifestation of His grace? The authors of the Upanishads, like all
true seers of God who have come after them, have acknowledged the
fact that, ultimately, their turning to God, their thirst for Him, and their
eventual Self-realization, are all inspired and accomplished by His
grace. "He is indeed the Lord supreme whose grace moves the hearts
of men. He leads us unto His own joy and to the glory of His
light."[15]

Now, in the light of this understanding, let us examine the
qualification of "purity of heart." Though it is a vague and broadly
generalized phrase, it is one used repeatedly by the sages of the past
and present, including Jesus of Nazareth, to describe the state of mind
prerequisite to the "vision" of God. Pure-heartedness suggests guile-
lessness, simplicity and childlike humility. "He is unknown by the
learned, and known by the simple." [16] It implies tenderness, compassion, sincerity, and all those qualities we associate with "goodness." It is the state of the heart of one who knows that God is
universally present, and who regards nothing in this world as divorced
from, or other than, God.

"Purity" suggests a single, uncontaminated, element or quality. "Purity of heart," therefore, is an undeviating regard to God
alone, who has become the center and focus of all one's thoughts,
words and actions. Only by such purity of heart is the mind of man
readied and prepared for the perfect concentration of mind which is

known as contemplation.

> The mind of man is of two kinds: pure and impure.
> It is impure when in the grip of worldly desire, and pure
> when free from such desire. ... If men thought of God as
> much as they think of the world, who would not attain liber-
> ation? [17]

Contemplation, the third stipulated precondition, is the result of mental purity, and the open gateway to the experience of the Eternal. It is not attained by allowing the mind to dwell on sense-pleasures, nor by the calculating of philosophers, nor by the proud and complacent; it is attained by the mind that dwells solely and intently on God, who knows its own darkness, and longs solely and purely for the light of clear vision.

> When a wise man has withdrawn his mind from all
> things without, and when his spirit has peacefully left all
> inner sensations, let him rest in peace, free from the move-
> ment of will and desire. ... For it has been said: There is
> something beyond our mind which abides in silence within
> our mind. It is the supreme mystery beyond thought. Let
> one's mind and subtle spirit rest upon that and nothing else.
>   ... When the mind is silent, beyond weakness and
> distraction, then it can enter into a world which is far beyond
> the mind: the supreme Destination. ... Then one knows the
> joy of Eternity.
>   ... Words cannot describe the joy of the soul whose
> impurities are washed away in the depths of contemplation,
> who is one with the Atman, his own Self. Only those who
> experience this joy know what it is.
>   ... As water becomes one with water, fire with fire,
> and air with air, so the mind becomes one with the infinite
> Mind and thus attains Freedom. [18]

If we are to know that Freedom, say the authors of the Upanishads, we must leave behind the world of speculation and philosophizing, and enter into the devout life of grace, purity of heart and contemplation. Thus, they assure us, with a full trust in His loving guidance, with a sincere and naked surrender of all thoughts not of God, and all actions not in His service, and finally in the constant flow of the mind to Him in the intimacy of silent contemplation, we shall enter the depths of our being, and know the glory of our own eternal Self.

When first one discovers these exalted thoughts in the Upanishads, one is startled and wonderstruck that such sublime thoughts
were penned so many hundreds of years ago -- long before anyone in
the West had come near to such heights of knowing. We discover that
the knowledge of the Spirit is not dependent upon the so-called
"progress of civilization," but has always been the same for all
humanity in every age.

In the annals of spiritual knowledge, the testimonies of the
rishis who authored the Upanishads may perhaps be equalled, but they
have never been, nor will ever be, surpassed. They have the last as well
as the original say in spiritual knowledge. All that has been said since
regarding the Source, nature, and final Goal of man is but so many
footnotes to the Upanishads; for, in them, the furthest reaches of
knowledge have been explored. They have reduced all existence to
One, the final number beyond which there is no more reduction. And
they have shown the path whereby this supernal knowledge may be
attained. Whatever came after the Upanishads, in the way of spiritual
knowledge, is only the echoing cries of those who have rediscovered
the same Truth, by the same path, and have raised their voices to sing
the same joyous song.

KAPILA

The seers who authored the Upanishads had known in themselves the great Unity, and had declared for all to come thereafter that
the soul of man and the Lord of all creation were one and the same;
Tat twam asi! was their repeated cry: "Thou art That!" And more,
"All this universe is That!"

"But how," the uncomprehending mind questions, "can this
be so? How can the Unmoving be identical with the incessantly
fluctuating universe? How can this world of transient phenomena,
where all things and beings are born, suffer and die, be identical to
the God who is said to be formless, unchanging, and eternally One?
And how is it possible to reconcile that eternal Self with what we
experience as our separate transient selves existing in the world? Are
there two selves, or is our personal self merely an illusion that we are
experiencing in this world of birth, suffering, and death?"

"It cannot be understood through reasoning or subtlety of

intellect," reply the sages of the Upanishads; "only those who see It in the depths of contemplation know the secret." And yet, still, the uncomforted mind strives to grasp it with the intellect, and those sages who have seen It continue in their steadfast endeavor to describe It, in order to provide to those who have not seen It some idea of just what It is like.

One such sage, named Kapila, who lived around the 8th or 9th century B.C.E. in the northeastern part of India, after realizing in himself the Truth of existence, made a valiant and brilliant attempt to explain the mysterious Unity-in-duality to the satisfaction of those who had not known It. Like all attempts before or since, it failed to accomplish its purpose, and mainly served only to foster more misconceptions and misinterpretations. Still, it is a perfectly true and simple description from the vantage-point of one who has seen the Truth, and for that reason, Kapila's beautifully formulated description of Reality has lived on for centuries and centuries, providing the foundation and framework for description by the many seers of the Truth who came after him.

Kapila's explanation of Reality came to be known as the philosophy of *Samkhya*, a word which, like *Veda*, means "knowledge" or "wisdom." To designate the Eternal, Kapila used the word, *Purusha*; it is a word which had appeared previously in the Vedas to mean the universal Self, or "Person." And to designate the creative Energy which manifests as the phenomenal world, he used the word, *Prakrti*. *Prakrti* is identical with *Prthivi*, the earth-Mother of the Vedas. It is *Prakrti* which appears as atoms, molecules, and all the sentient and insentient world composed of the elements.

These two, *Purusha* and *Prakrti*, are what we today might call "spirit" and "matter," except that *Prakrti* is more than what we regard as matter; it is the substance of all forms, including thought-forms, dream-images, and the individual psyche. It is everything that is experienced as "the world" -- on both the subtle and gross levels. *Purusha*, on the other hand, is the Eternal, the unmanifested Essence, the unstained and unchanging Consciousness. It is the light of conscious Awareness which not only illumines but allows us to perceive the world of *Prakrti*.

Those who have known the experience of Unity realize these two to be complementary aspects of one indivisible Reality; but, as both of these aspects of the One possess mutually exclusive qualities, it is necessary -- in order to differentiate them by quality -- to give them

separate and distinct names. This division of names and qualities
gives the impression of an ultimate duality; but that is an impression
due merely to the nature of language. These two must, in language at
least, remain apparently distinct simply in order to explain their unity.
And that unity is realized only in the transcendent "vision" of the
mystic, who knows them to be, beyond all doubt, inseparably One.

Kapila's categorization and analysis of the two aspects of
Existence, *Purusha* and *Prakrti,* had a vast influence on later thinkers, yet many who had not experienced that Unity for themselves
corrupted his vision into a Dualistic philosophical system wherein the
two came to be regarded, not as complementary aspects of the One,
but as two eternally separate and irreconcilable Principles at odds with
one another. It was just such a dualistic view which was also espoused
by the followers of Zoroaster in Persia, and later by the Manichaean
Gnostics. It seems there has never been a scarcity of unenlightened
men and women at the ready in this world to corrupt the words of the
enlightened to fit their own pitiably childish views. Today we see the
same delusion upheld by those who see existence as an eternal
struggle between Jehovah and Satan.

While these two terms, *Purusha* and *Prakrti*, may appear
foreign to the Western mind, we must recognize that Kapila's conception of Reality is the essence of all mystical philosophy, past and
present. We find it echoed, at least implicitly, in the conceptions of
Reality formulated by all the mystics and teachers of spiritual life.
This, for example, from the Bible, expresses a distinction between "the
Father" and "the world":

> Love not the world, neither the things that are in the
> world. For all that is in the world -- the lust of the flesh, the
> lust of the eyes, and the pride of life -- is not of the Father, but
> of the world. [1]

Similarly, in the earlier Upanishads, these two aspects of the
One, corresponding to *Purusha* and *Prakrti*, were not referred to by
name, but were merely inferred:

> The Immortal is veiled by the world. The Spirit of
> Life is the Immortal. Name and form are the world, and by
> them the Spirit is veiled. [2]
> Behold the glory of God in the universe and all that
> lives and moves on earth. Leaving the transient, find joy in
> the Eternal. [3]

But in the later Upanishads, written after the time of Kapila, such as the *Svetasvatara*, the Samkhya terminology is used:

> *Prakrti* is changing and passing; but *Purusha* is
> eternal. ... By meditation on Him, by contemplation of Him,
> and by communion with Him, there comes in the end destruct-
> ion of earthly delusion. [4]

In the same Upanishad, the author refers to the names used by the older Vedic tradition for these two to show that they are synonymous terms:

> With Maya, His mysterious power, He made all
> things, and by Maya the human soul is bound. Know there-
> fore that *Prakrti* is Maya , and *Purusha* is Rudra (Shiva), the
> ruler of Maya. All beings in our universe are contained in
> His infinite splendor. [5]
> ... He is the Eternal among things that passs away,
> pure Consciousness of conscious beings, the One who fulfills
> the prayers of many. By the wisdom of Samkhya and the
> practice of yoga (contemplation), a man knows the Eternal;
> and when a man knows the Eternal, he is free from all fetters.[6]

The great contribution which Kapila made to philosophical thought was to define and examine in unprecedented detail the nature and qualities of each of the two aspects of Reality, so that the mind could easily distinguish between them. *Prakrti*, he tells us, is the undifferentiated field of Energy which transmutes itself into the elements that make up the entire world of forms. The primary process of this transmutation is described by Kapila as a self-division into three separate modes of Energy which he calls *gunas* (strands). These correspond to what scientists today would call "positive," "negative," and "neutral" energy-charges. Kapila calls them *rajas, tamas,* and *sattva.* They are the three "strands" which, woven together, constitute the fabric of *Prakrti*; and which, by their incessant interaction, form the manifold universe, including all sentient and insentient beings.

We experience these three modes of energy in the following ways: *rajas* as passion, restlessness and assertive activity; *tamas* as dullness, lassitude and inertia; and *sattva* as clarity, refinement of intellect, and tranquility. *Sattva, rajas,* and *tamas* are constantly alternating, which accounts for the changes we experience in mood and functional ability. Thus, *Prakrti,* composed of the three *gunas,* is both the cause and the substance of the entire vast range of experiential phenomena which we call "the world." Yet, while this transient and ephemeral drama of thought, form and movement goes on, there is a steady, unchanging and eternal Consciousness which remains ever-aloof as the Witness of the drama; that is *Purusha*. *Purusha* is the universal Self, the light of Consciousness, which illumines *Prakrti* and which, standing distinguishably separate from *Prakrti,* exists as the unchanging witness-consciousness in every individual being.

All suffering, according to Kapila, is simply the result of forgetfulness of one's true Self, or *Purusha*, while identifying with the ever-changing world of *Prakrti*, and thereby being caught up in the play of light and shadow, believing that to be one's self. And the means of deliverance from suffering is, first of all, to distinguish between the two, and to cease to identify with *Prakrti*. Since *Prakrti* is a mere display, intrinsically transient, it is, in the final analysis, unreal. The real is *Purusha*, the eternal, unchanging Self. Kapila condenses this philosophy into four principle "truths":

1.   That from which we want to be delivered is pain.
2.   Deliverance (liberation) is the cessation of pain.
3.   The cause of pain is the lack of discrimination between
        Prakrti and *Purusha*.
4.   The means of deliverance is discrimination [between these
        two]. [7]

In other words, according to Kapila, all suffering in this life is the result of wrong identification: identifying with *Prakrti* instead of *Purusha*. Suffering is inherent in *Prakrti*, but does not exist in *Purusha. Purusha* is our eternal, and therefore real, Self. When we discriminate between them, we realize that all suffering belongs only to *Prakrti,* and cannot touch our true Self. It is this vision of Kapila's which, as we shall see, provided the framework for that great spiritual masterpiece, the *Bhagavad Gita.*

THE BHAGAVAD GITA

Sometime between the 10th and 5th centuries B.C.E., the great epic classic, the *Mahabharata*, was written by an unknown poet or poets. It told the story of a great war between two rival clans of ancient India, and was no doubt based in part on ancient historical events. Throughout its complex fabric of moral tales within tales, it wove the philosophical precepts of Kapila's Samkhya. By this time, the culture of India had become completely permeated and greatly influenced by Kapila's vision and terminology.

Within the marvellous poetic drama of the *Mahabharata* is found the *Bhagavad Gita,* "The Song Of God." It is a philosophical dialogue, written by some illumined sage of the time (and attributed to the legendary sage, Vyasa), which offers the most comprehensive and definitive expression of the Samkhya philosophy ever written. While it forms a segment of the *Mahabharata* story, it is also a separate and complete work in itself. We can only surmise that it was written by an independent seer, in such a way that it would fit comfortably into the *Mahabharata* story as a philosophical discussion between two of its characters, in order to assure it a place in that immortal work. Indeed, since the time of its composition, it has become the Bible of India, and one of the most sacred of holy books for students of philosophy and religion throughout the world.

In the first chapter of the *Gita*, we find Arjuna, a warrior of the Pandava clan, on the battlefield with Krishna, his chariot-driver, who happens also to be an incarnation of God. Krishna, who is only incidentally Arjuna's cousin and the king of Dwarka, represents, throughout this dialogue, the Divine Spirit in man; he is literally "the driver of the chariot" of the body. And the dialogue begins between Arjuna and Krishna as a dialogue between man and his indwelling Spirit, or Self. Arjuna, faced with the task before him, of battling to the death against those whom he has known from childhood as friends and relatives, faces the battle of life which all men face; and he feels overwhelmed and utterly despondent. "Letting fall his bow and arrows, he sank down in his chariot, his soul overcome by despair and grief." [1]

But Krishna, the voice of the Eternal in him, prods him from his weakness and dejection, by reminding him of his unconquerable Soul. He brings to Arjuna's mind the remembrance that all this world is but a drama, a play of opposites, wherein heat and cold, pleasure and pain alternate, but can never touch the eternal Soul of man. "He dwells in these bodies, beyond time, and though these bodies have an end in time, He remains infinite and eternal. Therefore, great warrior, carry on your fight." [2]

This dialogue, though set on a battlefield and forming an integral part in the story of the great war between the two factions, the Pandavas and the Kauravas, is quite evidently intended as a parable of man's struggle to understand the world and to realize the Divine in himself. It is the perennial battle of life: the struggle between the darkness of ignorance which sees only the frightening appearance of the world, and the light of wisdom which sees the eternal Spirit in and behind all appearance. Krishna, the light of wisdom, explains to Arjuna the truth of the Spirit and exhorts him to take up his arms once again and to struggle in the awareness of his own eternal Soul. He begins to teach him the wisdom of Samkhya and the path of yoga.

Samkhya, as we have seen, is the knowledge of *Prakrti* and *Purusha*, and the discrimination between the two; and yoga is the effort to realize the eternal Truth through the practice of serenity, steadfastness, meditation and contemplation on the Self. Says Krishna: "When your mind, confused by the apparent contradictions of the scriptures, becomes steady in contemplation of the Divine, then the goal of yoga is yours." [3] Through Samkhya, Krishna tells him, he will learn to understand his true Self; and through yoga, the practice of contemplating that Self, he will attain the direct realization of Truth. These two, says Krishna, go hand in hand; understanding leads to practice, or application, and the application of knowledge leads to realization.

Samkhya is the path of knowledge, what Krishna calls *jnan yoga*, "the yoga of knowledge"; and the application of this knowledge in thought, word and deed is the path of action, or *karma yoga*. We are all bound to act, Krishna reminds Arjuna; there is no way to escape from the world of action. But through knowledge, a man learns that he exists beyond *Prakrti* as the eternal *Purusha*, the constant Self, who remains unstained by the actions which he must perform in this world:

> All actions take place in time by the interweaving of
> the *gunas* of *Prakrti*, and the deluded man thinks that he is the
> doer of the actions.
> But the man who knows the relation between the

gunas of *Prakrti* and actions understands that actions are only
gunas acting upon other *gunas,* and that he is not their slave. [4]

In other words, the man who identifies with actions, thinking
he is only the body and mind, is entirely swayed by the desire for
pleasures of the body and mind, and suffers through this wrong
identification; but one who identifies with the Eternal, the *Purusha*, is
not swayed by these desires, and thereby remains free of the suffering
that accompanies this mistaken identification.

In the Fourth chapter, Krishna strips away the last vestiges of
pretense in this thinly disguised parable, and openly declares that his
character represents the *Atman*, the Divine Self in all men. He is the
Avatar, the manifestation of God, appearing within His own drama in
order to give concrete utterance to the unspoken wisdom that teaches
itself from within all men. By this literary device, he becomes the
voice, not of Krishna, the king of Dwarka, but of the all-pervading, all-
inclusive God. "By whatever path men love Me," he tells Arjuna, "by
that path they come to Me. Many are the paths of men, but they all in
the end come to Me." [5] By "Me," he refers, of course, to the one
supreme Self of all.

Krishna, now speaking as the Divine Reality, explains to
Arjuna that, while He acts in the world (as *Prakrti*), He is ever beyond
action (as *Purusha*). He works, but He is ever beyond work, in the
freedom of eternity. And He asks Arjuna to perform all his actions in
the same spirit, understanding that he must continue to do actions for
the good of all, while remaining aware that he is entirely unaffected
by his actions. In this way, says Krishna, you will remain unattached
to and unaffected by the success or failure of your actions. You will
enjoy the peace and freedom of your eternal Self even while engaging
in actions.

Arjuna is not yet clear on this point, however, and he questions Krishna further, just as all men deliberate with themselves on the
facts of life and how they must behave in accordance with the Truth.
Krishna explains to Arjuna that it is not action that is to be renounced,
but wrong identification that is to be renounced; for it is wrong
identification which causes a man to be attached to desire for the fruits
of his actions:

> When a man knows himself to be Brahman, his reas-
> on is steady, and all delusion is gone from him. When pleas-
> ures come, he is not moved; and when pain comes, he is un-

moved.
        He is not bound by things without; within himself he
enjoys happiness. His soul is one with Brahman, and so he
enjoys eternal bliss. [6]

This perfect state is attained through understanding and
through practice. "Such a man is a yogi," says Krishna; "he is one
with Brahman and lives in Brahman." [7]
Krishna then explains to Arjuna the practice of yoga, by
which the realization of his unity with Brahman is to be attained. Now
that Arjuna has learned the renunciation of attachment and desire, he
is ready to learn the path of meditation. Says Krishna:

        When the mind of the yogi is in peace, focused on the
Self within, and beyond all restless desires, then he experiences
Unity.
        His mind becomes still, like the flame of a lamp
sheltered from the winds.
        When the mind rests in the prayerful stillness of
yoga, by the grace of the One, he knows the One, and attains
fulfillment.
        Then he knows the joy of Eternity; he sees beyond
the intellect and the senses. He becomes the Unmoving, the
Eternal. [8]
        ... In this experience of Unity, the yogi is liberated,
delivered from all suffering forever. ... The yogi whose heart
is still, whose passions are dissolved, and who is pure of sin,
experiences this supreme bliss and knows his oneness with
Brahman. [9]

Krishna then goes on, in the Seventh chapter, to describe the
ways that He (the supreme Self) appears in this world:

        I am the fragrance of the earth and the light of the fire;
I am the life of all beings, and the austerity of the yogis.
        ... I am the intelligence of the intelligent, and the
beauty of all things beautiful.
        ... I am the strength of the strong, ... and the purity of
the pure. [10]

And yet again, Krishna reminds us that while all these exist in Him,
He remains ever beyond all manifestation:

        The three gunas comprising Prakrti come from Me,
but I am not in them; they are in Me. The whole world is

under the delusion of My Maya (appearance) and know not Me,
the Eternal. This Maya of Mine is difficult to penetrate, but
those who know Me go beyond My Maya. [11]

Here again, the author is presenting that most difficult of
truths to comprehend: that the universe is the "appearance" of God,
His *Prakrti*, or *Maya*, and not God Himself. The world is His "glory," but it is merely an appearance; He exists beyond His appearance, as the pure Absolute:

> I am hidden by My veil of Maya, and the deluded
> people of the world do not know Me, the Beginningless, the
> Eternal. [12] ... But the man of vision and I are one. His Self
> is Myself, and I am his sole trust.
>   At the end of many lives the man of vision comes
> to Me. "God is all," this great man declares. But how rarely
> is such a man found! [13]

Krishna then explains to Arjuna how the world (His Maya)
evolves into appearance and "involves" back into Himself. The 'day'
of world-manifestation lasts for hundreds of thousands of years, and
alternates with the 'night' of dissolution:

> When that 'day' comes, all visible creation arises from
> the Invisible; and when the 'night' of dissolution comes, all
> creation disappears. [14]

Such a cyclic beginning and ending of the universe of appearance is no mere theory; in the experience of Unity, this recurrent
creation and dissolution is seen quite clearly. From the standpoint of
Eternity, it occurs in the blinking of an eye; it is like the breathing in
and breathing out of *Prakrti*; but from the viewpoint of time and
mortals, it is a cycle that takes millions of years to complete. Only
now, the scientists who study the motions of the heavens are beginning
to surmise from their observations that this is the case, but to one who
has seen it and experienced it, there is not the slightest doubt about it.

In the experience of Unity, when one knows his eternal Self,
this expansion and dissolution of the universe is recognized as only an
appearance. It is like a thought-production that exists for awhile, and
then is withdrawn. The eternal Self is not affected in the least by it:

> ... Beyond this appearance and dissolution of the

world, there is an invisible, higher, eternal Principle. And
when all things in the world pass away, THAT remains forever. [15]

THAT remains pure and infinite, an eternal Consciousness,
beyond all manifestation or non-manifestation. "This invisible and
supreme Self," says Krishna, "is everlasting. ... This is My highest
Being." [16] As a further explanation of how the cycle of universal
creation and dissolution is a function of *Prakrti*, and not of *Purusha*,
the Unchanging, Krishna continues:

> At the end of the 'night' of time, all things return to
> My Prakrti; and when the new 'day' of time begins, I bring
> them again into manifestation.
> Thus, through My Prakrti, I bring forth all creation,
> and all these worlds revolve in the cycle of time. But I am not
> bound by this vast display of creation; I exist alone, watching
> the drama of this play. I watch, while Prakrti brings forth all
> that moves and moves not; thus the worlds go on revolving.
> But the fools of the world know Me not; ... they know not the
> supreme Spirit, the infinite God of all.
> Still, there are a few great souls who know Me, and
> who take refuge in Me. They love Me with a single love,
> knowing that I am the Source of all.
> They praise Me with devotion; ... their spirit is one
> with Me, and they worship Me with their love. They worship
> Me, and work for Me, surrendering themselves in My vision.
> They worship Me as the One and the many, knowing that all
> is contained in Me. [17]

This is the sublime theme that one hears throughout the *Gita*,
in which knowledge, action, love and contemplation, all are synthe-
sized in one vision. To love God is to dwell on Him. For what else is
love but the constant flow of thought and desire toward the object of
love? In the *Gita*, we find the summit of universality, an all-
embracing concern for every tradition, every temperament, every
degree of comprehension. For those who require a tangible form of
God for worship, the adoration of the loveable Krishna is offered; for
those who seek Him in the world through good works, the path of
karma yoga is proffered; for those who are determined to wend their
way to Him through understanding and Self-knowledge, the path of
jnan yoga is opened wide; and for those who, having understood, and
whose actions are ever directed toward Him, and whose love is solely

for Him, the path of meditation and contemplation is the royal road, the *raja* yoga, which leads to union with Him. Of such devotees, Krishna says:

> Their thoughts are on Me, their life is in Me, and
> they give light to all. They speak always of Me, and in Me
> they find peace and joy.
>   To those who focus their minds on Me, who worship
> Me with their love, I give the yoga of vision whereby they
> come to Me. [18]
>   Give Me your mind and give Me your heart; give Me
> your offerings and your adoration. Thus, with your soul
> focused solely on Me as your supreme Goal, truly, you shall
> come to Me. [19]

Throughout every chapter of the *Gita*, there is this inter-weaving of love, action, knowledge and contemplation, harmonized to comprise the full tapestry of the life of the spirit. No one single thread of this finely-woven fabric is emphasized or exalted above another, but all facets and needs of the human spirit are equally represented and interrelated. We find precisely the same message in the *Gita* as was found in the Upanishads; but whereas the Upanishads shine as a single bright beacon of pure white light, the *Gita* is refract-ed into a spectrum of living color and brilliant detail.

When Arjuna begs Krishna to reveal to his eyes the vision of His manifold splendor, Krishna consents, granting to him a divine eyesight whereby he can view the infinite creative effusion of God:

> If the light of a thousand Suns suddenly arose in the
> sky, that splendor might be compared to the radiance of the
> supreme Spirit. And Arjuna saw in that radiance the whole
> universe in its infinite variety, standing in one vast Unity as
> the body of God. [20]

In this vision, Arjuna sees all the worlds and all the gods and demons and peoples of the universe rising up from the one Source and then being devoured by It. Overwhelmed by this vision, and trembling in awe and terror, Arjuna bows before Krishna, and cries out:

> Adoration unto Thee who art before me and behind
> me! Adoration unto Thee who art on all sides, O God! All-
> powerful God of immeasurable might, Thou art the Destin-

ation of all, and Thou art all! [21]

Then, when Krishna had once again resumed his human form, he explained to Arjuna that His vision is not given to the religionists with their reverance for rituals and legal formulas, nor to the self-torturers, nor to those pious people who imagine that devotion consists merely of the dutiful giving of alms; but only to those who long for God with true love in their hearts:

> Only by love can men see Me and know Me, and
> enter into Me.
> He who works for Me, who loves Me, whose su-
> preme Goal is Me, free from attachment to all things, and
> with true love for all creation, he, truly, becomes one with
> Me. [22]

The author of the *Bhagavad Gita*, who put these words into the mouth of Krishna, seems never to tire of repeating his explanation of the primal duality-in-unity; for once again he makes Krishna say:

> Prakrti is the source of all material things; it is the
> creator, the creating, and the creation. Purusha is the Source
> of consciousness. ... The Purusha in man, united with Pra-
> krti, experiences the ever-changing conditions of Prakrti.
> When he identifies with the ever-changing, he is whirled
> through life and death to a good or evil fate. But the Purusha
> in man is ever beyond fate. ... He is the supreme Lord, the
> supreme Self.
> That man who knows that he is the Purusha, and
> understands the changing conditions of Prakrti, is never
> whirled around by fate, wherever he may be. [23]

This theme of *Purusha* and *Prakrti* is so crucial to the under-standing of Reality and the spiritual life that it is explained again and again throughout the *Gita*. In chapter Thirteen, Krishna attempts this explanation in a novel way, by introducing two new terms. Here, *Prakrti* is referred to as *kshetra* ("the Field"), and *Purusha* is referred to as *kshetrajna* ("the Knower of the Field"). "Whatever is born in this world," says Krishna, "comes from the union of the Field and the Knower of the Field." [24] But when a man knows that he is the eternal Knower, the experiencer of the Field, and not the Field alone, he knows his eternal freedom:

> He who knows that he is, himself, the Lord of all,
> and is ever the same in all, immortal though experiencing
> the Field of mortality, he knows the truth of existence.
> And when a man realizes that the Purusha in him-
> self is the same Purusha in all, he does not hurt himself by
> hurting others. This is the highest knowledge. He who sees
> that all actions, everywhere, are only the actions of Prakrti,
> and that the Purusha is the witness of these actions, he sees
> the Truth.
> ... Those who, with the eye of inner vision, see the distinc-
> tion between the Field and the Knower of the Field, and realize
> that the Purusha is free of Prakrti, they attain the Highest. [25]

As we shall see in later chapters of this book, the conception of these two Principles of existence is a perennially recurring one, not only in the religious and philosophical literature of India, but in every mystical tradition throughout the world, in every time. And, in nearly every tradition in which these two Principles appear, the eternal, imperishable Principle is universally characterized as Male, the Father; and the Principle of creative energy, out of which is formed the world of matter, is universally characterized as His Female consort, the Mother. Even today, in our own culture, we say that it is our "Father" in heaven who is our Source and Governor; but it is "Mother Nature" who feeds us and nourishes us.

These same appellations of gender are applied by the ancient seers of India to the two complements of Reality. The very word, *Purusha*, means "the Man"; and *Prakrti*, like *Prthivi* before, is a noun of the female gender, as is *Durga, Maya* and *Shakti*. They are synonymous terms, though stemming from disparate traditions; and each represents the Goddess, the great Mother-Womb of all creation. It is not surprising, therefore, to see that the author of the *Gita* has Krishna say:

> Wherever a being may be born, Arjuna, know that
> My Prakrti is his Mother, and I [Purusha] am the Father who
> gave him life. [26]

The suggestion that we are born of the union of *Purusha* and *Prakrti*, as a child is born of the union of a father and mother, may seem only an extension of a simile; but the Samkhya philosophy means by this "union" something more literal than figurative. These two are really one Reality. *Prakrti* and *Purusha* are merely abstractions designed to separate out these two aspects of the One in order to understand It in Its fullness. Their "union" is in fact a "unity"; they overlap, as it were, like superimposed images on a photographic film. We say at times that *Purusha* is "within" *Prakrti*, or that God is "within" Nature; but that is only a figure of speech. They are locked in an embrace so absolute that they have never been, nor ever can be, separated. Our existence is their interlocking existence. It is in this sense that we are born of their union.

The author of the *Bhagavad Gita* has, through his character, Krishna, stated this truth in many ways to Arjuna, the disciple. But in the Fifteenth chapter, in which Krishna speaks of *Prakrti* and *Purusha* as "the perishable" and "the Imperishable," he states in an unequivocal manner that the ultimate Reality (the supreme Self) is a Unity which, containing within Itself both of these complementary aspects, supercedes them both:

> There exists two Principles in this world: *kshara*
> (the perishable) and *akshara* (the imperishable). The im-
> perishable is the Unchanging, the Eternal. But the highest
> Reality is something else; It is called *Paramatman* (the su-
> preme Self). It is *both* the Eternal *and* that which pervades
> and sustains all this universe. [27]

When one experiences the mystical vision of Unity, he experiences not merely *Prakrti*, the undifferentiated world-energy, nor merely *Purusha*, the unmanifested Absolute; he experiences the one Reality which is both of these at once. It is called *Paramatman*, "the supreme Self." Here is seen no distinction between *Prakrti* and *Purusha*, the perishable and the imperishable; the ONE contains no such division. By transcending *Prakrti*, one realizes the eternal *Purusha*, but in that realization, *Prakrti* and *Purusha* no longer have any separate, independent, existence. They are one.

This great Unity cannot be easily explained; that is why It must be experienced to be known. It is eternal and unchanging, yet It appears as the phenomenal world of change. It is only as a means of explaining Its two aspects that the names, *Prakrti* and *Purusha*, are invented. In fact, the creative Energy, of which this body and all this universe is composed, is just as imperishable and eternal as the one Consciousness which supports it. They are the same; and in this one Imperishable, there is no differentiation between Energy and

Consciousness, *Prakrti* and *Purusha*.

Nothing at all ever perishes -- except the images and forms which *Prakrti* constructs of herself. And because we identify with the perishable body-form, we make a distinction between the perishable body and the "spirit" within us; we regard this body as the vessel or abode of the "spirit." But when the realization of the ONE dawns, then one looks about in awe, declaring, "O my God, even this body is Thine own!" And then one asks, "Which the Imperishable, which the abode?"

> Because I am beyond the perishable, and even beyond the imperishable, in this world and in the Vedas I am known as "the Supreme."
> One who, with a clear vision, sees Me as "the Supreme," knows all there is to be known; his soul is merged in Me.
> I have revealed to you the most secret teaching, Arjuna. He who has realized it has realized the Truth, and his task in this world is done. [28]

To one who knows his own supreme Self, there is no longer a witnessing subject and an acting object, no longer a *Purusha* and a *Prakrti*. All his actions are the actions of the ONE. He can no longer say, "*He* guides me," or "*He* does everything through me." His breathing is God's, his work is God's; there are no longer two. "He is the only ONE in all, but it seems as if He were many." [29]

In the Eighteenth and last chapter, Krishna reiterates and sums up all that he has taught to Arjuna, with a special emphasis on the nature, necessity, and goal of all man's works. It is a message of relevance to every man, but most especially to those who would learn the secret of spiritual harmony and happiness in this world. It is the message of *svadharma*.

Dharma is, of course, translated as "duty," but *svadharma* is not simply the duty to perform works in the world, but the necessity of performing one's own special God-given duty. It is not often easy to know exactly what one's *svadharma* is. Is it simply to work at that occupation which brings the greatest material gain? No. Nor is it simply the serving of others. Rather, it is the serving of God, the Self, who is the indwelling, guiding, joy of man. No matter what a man might do in this world, no matter how respectable or charitable or unselfish, if it is not his *svadharma,* he will be miserable; he will feel frustrated, unfulfilled and dissatisfied. This is especially true for the sincere aspirant to Truth, for he will feel most keenly the disharmony between his spirit and his actions.

Oftentimes, however, there are great obstacles, great temptations, in the way of performing one's *svadharma*. Those whose *svadharma* is to do the work of God know this well. The necessities of the body, the pressures of society, and the loneliness and effort involved in following our *svadharma* are often troublesome obstacles to the following of our God-ordained path. Who cannot imagine how difficult was the path ordained for a Jesus or a Buddha, or for the author of the *Bhagavad Gita*? To follow their *svadharma* required great sacrifice and surrender of all that men regard as good and wholesome in this world. Yet it is to the great benefit of the world that they chose to surrender all else in order to perform their *svadharma*. For them, having known their eternal Identity, there was no other course but to share that knowledge with all humanity. No other duty could possibly hold sway over them. Had they denied or suppressed their *svadharma*, how miserable, how wretched a life would they have had -- even if they had been surrounded with all luxuries and wealth!

It is by this a spiritual man knows his *svadharma*; if his soul is happy and delighted in its performance, and if the very thought of diverting from that path makes him sick at heart and despondent, he may be sure that it is his *svadharma*.

> It is not right to leave undone the holy work which
> ought to be done. Such a surrender of action is a delusion of
> darkness. And if a man abandons his svadharma out of fear of
> pain, truly, he has no reward. [30]

The reward of performing the work appropriate to one's own *svadharma* is the peace and joy of God. By renouncing all other concerns but the performance of the work God has ordained for you, you will feel and know His confirmation within you.

> A man attains perfection when his work is worship of
> God, from whom all things come and who exists within every-
> one.
> Greater is your own work, even if it is meager, than
> the work of another, even if it is great. When a man does the
> work that God gives him, no sin can touch him.
> And a man should not abandon his work, even if he
> cannot achieve it in full perfection; because in all work there is
> some imperfection, as in all fire there is some smoke. [31]
> ... It is better to perish in your own work, than to

flourish in another's. [32]

In earlier chapters, Krishna has already taught Arjuna the way that a man should work:

> Set your heart upon your work, but never on its reward. Work not for a reward; but never cease to do your work. [33] ... When a man surrenders all desires that come to the heart, and by the grace of God finds the joy of God in himself, then his soul has indeed found peace. [34]
>
> The man who has found the joy of the Spirit and in the Spirit has his satisfaction and his peace, that man is beyond the law of karma (actions and rewards). He is beyond what is done and not done. He is beyond the world of mortal beings. In freedom from the bonds of attachment, do, therefore, the work to be done; for the man whose work is pure attains indeed the Supreme. [35]
>
> Therefore, offer to Me all your works and rest your mind on the Supreme. Be free from vain hopes and selfish thoughts, and with inner peace fight your fight. [36]

The *Bhagavad Gita* has stood the test of time, and is so beloved among men of all nations because its author was steeped in wisdom, a wisdom that is applicable to the seekers of God, the lovers of Truth, at every level of understanding. The devotee finds in it the summit of devotion; the intelligent find in it the heights of wisdom; the servant of God finds in it the supreme path to victory; and in it the yogi reads the secrets of inner union.

Whoever the great sage was who wrote it, he was a man of truly universal and all-embracing wisdom. He had attained both the height and breadth of Self-knowledge; he knew the supreme Reality, both at Its Source and in Its manifestation. And his guidance, the sharing of his knowledge in the *Bhagavad Gita*, is now and for all time a source of life and joy for all who have the good fortune to read it. When a book is truly inspired and filled by the grace of God, it shines so brightly into the hearts and minds of men that it becomes universally revered as a holy receptacle of God's word. Such a book is the *Bhagavad Gita*, "the Song of God"; it is a never-failing wellspring of the water of life for all thirsty travellers on the road to Truth.

THE TAOIST SAGES

The vision of the Eternal was not confined merely to those living in India and the Middle East; we also find a few in ancient China who had experienced an identical realization, and spoke of the same infinite and eternal Principle underlying the manifested world. However, That which the Indian sages called "Brahman" or "Purusha," what some others call "God," the Chinese sages called "Tao" (pronounced *Dow*). We must not imagine, as some ignorant people do, that because the languages of various countries are different that there is a difference also in the absolute Reality connoted by these languages. "Taoism" is simply the Chinese name for the one perennial philosophy of all mystics of all lands.

It is often seen that those who have only a cursory knowledge of mystical philosophy become confused by the many different terms used to connote the Absolute by peoples of differing languages, and fail to penetrate beyond linguistic differences to grasp the common significance of words like "Brahman," "Purusha," "Tao," "Godhead," etc. But, just as, in various languages, the words, *pani, jal, agua, eau,* and *water*, all signify one common reality, so do the above words of various linguistic origins connote one common invisible Principle. All of the mystics of whatever time or cultural tradition have experienced the same one, indivisible, Reality; yet, because language is infinitely variable, they have called this One by various appellations.

As we shall see, the sages of Taoism experienced and described the same mystical vision which has been described by all other mystics; and have described the same mystical philosophy which goes by the name of "Vedanta" in India, and by so many other names in other lands. As the 15th century Islamic saint, Dadu, put it, in a statement used as the epigraph to this book, "All the enlightened have left one message; it is only those in the midst of their journey who hold diverse opinions."

Taoism traces its roots in China to sages living as far back as 3000 B.C.E.; but we know of those ancients only from hearsay recorded much later. It was not until the 6th century B.C.E. that the precepts of Taoism were presented in a written form by that most famous of Taoists, Lao Tze, who is said to have been born in 601 B.C.E. We know of his life only the barest of details. It seems he served for some time as the Curator of the Imperial Library at K'au, and was therefore a learned man. In later life, he found the burden of his duties and the decadence of city life incompatible with his spiritual needs, and he decided to withdraw from his duties and the city environs to a more peaceful existence in the countryside.

On his journey from the city, he rested for a short while at the pass of Hsien-ku, where he stayed with the Keeper of the pass, a Yin Hsi, who was himself a student of the spiritual life. Before Lao left to continue his journey, Yin Hsi persuaded him to leave for his instruction some writings on the spiritual path, and so Lao wrote a short book of maxims for him. It is this book which has come down to us as the *Tao Teh Ching*. That is the last we hear of Lao's life; it is not known what became of him or where he died, but later reports state that he lived to a ripe old age.

Lao's little book, the *Tao Teh Ching*, is one of the major classics of Taoism. The word, *Tao*, in its title, refers to the Eternal aspect of reality -- what we have already spoken of as Brahman, or Purusha. *Teh* is Its power of manifestation, identical with Maya or Prakrti. And the word, *Ching*, simply means "book." So, we may interpret the title of the book as "The Book of The Eternal and Its Power of Manifestation." Its simple and somewhat cryptic axioms regarding the Spirit, and the way that a man who has realized It lives his life, has become a favorite introduction to the spiritual life for peoples of both East and West. To the beginning student, its apparent vagueness makes it easily digestible, yet as one learns to understand it more thoroughly, its vagueness disappears, and it reveals itself as a profound and explicit metaphysical guide.

Another great Taoist sage is the venerable Chuang Tze, who lived in the 3rd century B.C. E. Very little is known of his life either; we have only the briefest of biographical information in a 'History' written in the 2nd century B.C.E. by Sze-ma Khien, which states that Chuang Tze was born in the kingdom of Wei, and held some sort of position in the city of Khi-yuan. He grew up in the same part of China as Lao Tze, and had thoroughly studied and understood the writings of his great predecessor. At some time during his life, Chuang attained the realization of the Self, the vision of Truth, and began writing books explaining what he had realized. According to Khien's History, King Wei, having heard of Chuang Tze and perhaps having read some of his books, sent a messenger to Chuang with a quantity of silver and the offer of a position as chief minister at the king's court. Chuang Tze, reportedly, only laughed, and sent back this word:

> A thousand ounces of silver would be a great gain to
> me, and to be a high nobleman and minister is a most honor-
> able position. But have you not seen the victim-ox for the
> ceremonial sacrifice? It is carefully fed for several years, and
> robed with rich embroidery that it may be fit to enter the Grand
> Temple. Then, when the time comes for it to do so, it would
> prefer to be a little pig, but it cannot get to be so. So, go
> away, and do not soil me with your presence. I would rather
> amuse and enjoy myself in the midst of a filthy ditch than to
> be subject to the rules and restrictions in the court of a king.
> I have detemined never to take such an office, but prefer the
> enjoyment of my own free will.[1]

Chuang Tze, like Lao Tze, had seen the one Existence, and he lived his life in dedication to the freedom and joy of the Eternal. In his writings, he told of his vision, and his spiritual knowledge. What Lao Tze said in a cryptic and terse manner, Chuang Tze explained often in a lengthy, detailed manner, and sometimes in metaphorical and satirical stories. He wrote large volumes in clear, explanatory prose to clarify what had only been hinted at by Lao Tze. Much of what we know today as "Taoism" is derived from the combined writings of these two seers.

The understanding of the one Reality expressed by the authors of the Upanishads and the *Gita* is expressed in a remarkably similar manner by Lao Tze and Chuang Tze. This should not be surprising, however, since everyone who is graced with the transcendent vision experiences the same eternal Unity. What Lao Tze and Chuang Tze saw and wrote about is precisely what Kapila and the Upanishadic seers and all other mystics have seen and wrote about. Their language is different, but their meaning is the same. As Chuang Tze says, "Words are used to express meaning. When you understand the meaning, you can forget about the words."

Lao Tze explains, in his *Tao Teh Ching*, that the eternal Reality is a Unity which contains two aspects: the unmanifest *Tao,* and *Teh,* Its Power of manifestation. The *Tao* is the Absolute, devoid of all qualities; nothing can be predicated about It, since It is beyond name and form. Says Lao:

> Before heaven and earth existed, there was something
> unformed, silent, alone, unchanging, constant and eternal; It

could be called 'the Source of the Universe.' I do not know Its
name and simply call It "Tao." [2]
    ... The Tao that can be spoken of is not the absolute
Tao. That Nameless [Tao] is the Father of heaven and earth;
that which is named [Teh] is the Mother of all things. [3]

Here we have the perennial vision of the mystic; the realization
of the two-in-One. The unmanifested Source Lao refers to as the
Father of all; and Its Power of world-manifestation he calls the Mother
of all things. The two are the same One in Its dual aspects of
Unmanifest and manifest. They are not really separate; they are
inextricably One. But, in order to describe the One in both Its aspects,
they must be given separate names:

> These two are the same; they are given different
> names in order to distinguish between them. Together,
> they constitute the Supreme Mystery. [4]

Chuang Tze, from his own experience of Unity, corroborates
what Lao Tze had said. In one of his stories, he puts these words in
the mouth of Lao Tze, when he is asked, "What is the Tao?"

> If you want to know the Tao, said Lao, give a bath to
> your mind; wash your mind clean. Throw out all your sage
> wisdom! Tao is invisible, hard to hold, and difficult to de-
> scribe. However, I will outline It for you: The visible world
> is born of the Invisible; the world of forms is born of the
> Formless. The creative Energy [Teh] is born from Tao, and all
> life forms are born of this creative Energy; thus all creation
> evolves into various forms.
> ... Life springs into existence without a visible
> source and is reabsorbed into that Infinite. The world exists in
> and on the infinite Void; how it comes into being, is sustained
> and once again is dissolved, cannot be seen.
> It is fathomless, like the Sea. Wondrously, the cycle
> of world -manifestation begins again after every completion.
> The Tao sustains all creation, but It is never exhausted.
> ... That which gives life to all creation, yet which is, Itself,
> never drawn upon -- that is the Tao.[5]

If we read for "Tao," *Brahman* or *Purusha*, and read for
"creative Energy," *Prakrti* or *Maya*, we see that the vision of the
mystics is ever one. Lao Tze, in his own inimitable style, explained
Tao and *Teh* in this way:

The Tao is an empty cup, yet It is inexhaustible; It is the fathomless Fountainhead of all things. [6]

That which gave birth to the universe may be regarded as the Mother of the universe. [7]

The Womb of creation is called the Mysterious Female; it is the root of heaven and earth. [8]
The myriad objects of the world take form and rise to activity, but I have seen THAT to which they return, like the luxuriant growth of plants that return to the soil from which they spring. [9]

That ONE called Tao is subtle, beyond vision, yet latent in It are all forms. It is subtle, beyond vision, yet latent in It are all objects. It is dark and obscure, yet latent in It is the creative Power of life [Teh]. [10]

From the ancient days till now Its manifestation has never ceased; it is because of this [Teh] that we perceive the Father of all. It is the manifestation of forms that reveals to us the Father. [11] The Tao is never the doer, yet through It everything is done. [12]

The Tao fathers, and the Teh brings everything forth as the world of form, time, and space. [13]

Lao and Chuang extrapolate from this knowledge of the Tao the correct life for one who knows It. Thus, Tao is not only the Unmanifest, It is also the guiding Path for the sage to whom It is revealed. the Tao is both the Source of the universe and the eternal Soul of man; It is his life and the Way by which he lives. He lives as the Tao beyond the world, while living as the Teh in the midst of it. He identifies with and rests in the Eternal, even while living and acting in the temporal, ephemeral, world:

He who holds to the Eternal [Tao] while acting in the transient [Teh] knows the primal Source from which all things manifest. [14] Therefore, the sage may travel all day, yet he never leaves his store of provisions. [15] He who remains aware of the Male [Tao], while living as the Female [Teh], is a guide to all the people. [16]

The noble man dwells in the Foundation of the form, and not in the form; he dwells in the fruit, and not in the flowering; thus he holds to the one, and ignores the other. [17]

Therefore, he is not vulnerable to weapons of war; the horns of the buffalo cannot touch him; the claws of the tiger cannot rip him; the sword cannot cut him. Why? Because he is beyond death. [18]

As the Eternal, the Tao, gives birth to all things, "yet does not contain them," the sage, doing likewise, "does nothing, yet all things are accomplished." Says Lao:

> My teaching is very easy to understand and very easy
> to practice; yet no one understands it and no one practices it;
> [it is this:] the sage wears a tattered coat [Teh] and carries jade
> [Tao] within his breast. [19]

Since the whole universe appears from the Unmoving, the Unchanging, by imitating or adopting the way of the universe, a man carries on his life in the most perfect manner. By retaining his center of inactivity, his center of changelessness, all his actions take place effortlessly of themselves. And, because he holds to the Unmoving, his energy is not dissipated, his mind is clear, and all that he does is done of a concentrated power and efficiency, and with great clarity of mind. Says Lao:

> Reach far enough toward the Void, hold fast enough
> to the Unmoving, and of the ten-thousand things, none can
> resist you. [20]

And Chuang Tze says:

> I guard my awareness of the One, and rest in harmony
> with externals. ... My light is the light of the Sun and the
> moon. My life is the life of heaven and earth. Before me is
> the Undifferentiated [Teh], and behind me is the Unknowable
> [Tao]. Men may all die, but I endure forever. [21]
> Keep correct your form, concentrate your vision, and
> the heavenly harmony will come to you. Control your mind,
> concentrate your attention, and the Spirit will reside in you.
> Teh is your clothing, and Tao is your sanctuary. [22]

In the experience of Unity, one learns the nature of Reality, and at the same time, learns the nature of one's own mind; for, in an inexplicable way, the two are integrally related. The mind, one discovers, creates thoughts and ideas in a way similar to the creation of waves on an ocean; they consist of contrary motions, so that for every wave, there's a trough; for every motion, an equal and opposite motion. For example, if we love, in that very motion is contained its opposite, hatred. Or if we experience peace, its corollary, mental agitation, is waiting to manifest. Every movement of the mind contains its opposite, just as does the movement of a pendulum; thus, all that we think and experience mentally is but a play of self-produced opposites. As Lao Tze put it:

> When people recognize beauty,
> Ugliness is also recognized.
> When people recognize good,
> Evil is also recognized. [23]

It is only when this alteration, this dual motion of the mind, is stilled, that we can experience that pure Consciousness which is the source of all thought.

In the very same way, the physical world is produced by the universal Mind. It is produced by just such a movement of contrary impulses. It is, from this perspective, a mere mirage; for every form that we see is but an image produced by the vibratory motions of the elementary Energy. And when that cosmic Mind becomes stilled, the world-manifestation ceases, and Consciousness rests in Itself. Then, once again, It remanifests the universe. In a continuous cycle, of world-manifestation and de-manifestation, that one Consciousness lives forever, unmoved, unchanged.

In a previous chapter, we saw how Kapila described this world-manifestation as a play of the *gunas* of *Prakrti*, which consist of two opposing motions, and a state of neutrality resulting from the balancing of the two. Lao Tze and Chuang Tze also recognize the nature of the creative Energy to be constituted of just such opposing movements; they are called by them *yang*, the positive, and *yin*, the negative. The balance of these two opposites is called the "natural" state. Here is how Chuang Tze describes this manifestory process:

> In the beginning, even nothing did not exist. There
> was only the Tao. Then something unnamed which did not
> yet have form came into existence from the Tao. This is Teh,
> from which all the world came into being. Things had not yet
> received their forms, but the division of the *yang* (positive)
> and the *yin* (negative) Principles, which are intimately related,
> had already appeared. This vibratory motion constitutes all
> creation. When the *yang* and the *yin* become active, all
> things come into being. It is in this way that Teh created all
> forms. [24]

This cosmology is, of course, identical to Kapila's if we substitute "Purusha" for *Tao*, "Prakrti" for *Teh*, and "rajas" and "tamas" for *yang* and *yin*. For Kapila, the balancing of rajas and tamas begets sattva, the state of repose, wherefrom one could enter into the realization of Purusha, the Eternal. For the two Chinese sages, the balancing of *yang* and *yin* begets the "natural" state of repose, wherefrom one might enter into Tao, the Eternal. The words are different, but the meaning is the same.

"The nature of water," said Chuang Tze, "is that it becomes clear when left alone, and becomes still when undisturbed. [25] Likewise, the wise man rests in silence, and allows the mind to become pure. In this way the mind reverts to its root, its Source. "To return to the root is repose," said Lao Tze; "it is called 'going back to one's Origin." Going back to one's Origin is to discover the Eternal. And to know the Eternal is to be enlightened. [26]

"When water is still," says Chuang, "it becomes so clear that a man can see every hair of his beard in it. ... If water is clear when it is still, how much more so the human spirit! When the mind of the sage is calm, it becomes the mirror of the universe wherein he can see everything." [27]

> Repose brings good fortune. Without inner repose,
> your mind will be galloping about, even though you are sit-
> ting still. Withdraw your senses within and cease all activity
> of the mind.
> Concentrate your will. Let your ears cease to hear;
> let your mind cease to imagine. Let your spirit be blank,
> passively receptive. In such receptivity, the Tao is revealed. [28]

Lao Tze offers similar advice:

> The wise man shuts his senses, closes all doors, dulls
> his edges, unties all knots, softens his light, calms his turmoil
> -- this is called the attainment of unity with the One. [29]

In yet another passage from the *Tao Teh Ching*, Lao repeats this advice, in a slightly different way:

> If you would reveal your original Self, if you would
> attain union with your true Being, give up your ego, restrain
> your desires. [30] By renouncing of desire, one sees the Secret
> of all life; without renouncing of desires, one sees the world of
> manifested forms.

> Searching within for the ultimate Mystery of this
> mysterious life, one enters the gateway wherein is found the
> great Secret of all life. [31]

In just a few simple words, Lao Tze gives the whole of mystical knowledge, and the path to the experience of it. His message is the message of all who have seen the Truth, the Secret of life: "Blessed are the pure in heart, for they shall see God." For only those who have understood the illusory nature of the world and have erased from their hearts all concern or desire for what it has to offer, can turn their hearts and minds wholeheartedly to the Source of the world. It is a simple matter of attention; so long as thoughts continue to be focused on the world of name and form, the mind is not free to dwell singly and purely on the Source of all this manifestation.

> He who holds fast to the Tao is able to manage very
> well in the world, for he knows how, from the beginning, all
> things manifest from the Tao. [32]
> Thus the sage manages things without acting; teaches
> the Truth without words. The world continues to arise before
> him, but he does not reject it. He knows he is the Life of all
> things, but he does not own any of them. Therefore, he con-
> tinues to act, but he remains unattached to his actions. His
> work is accomplished, but he lays no claim to it. The work
> is done, but he does not identify with it. Thus, his strength
> is never depleted. [33]

How much this sounds like the teaching of Krishna in the *Bhagavad Gita* regarding the path of karma yoga! If we search the words of Lao Tze and Chuang Tze, we realize that they taught all the aspects of yoga: karma (action), bhakti (devotion), jnan (discriminitive knowledge), and raja (contemplation). Jnan yoga, the discrimination between the real and the unreal, the Eternal and the non-Eternal, is very well represented by Chuang and Lao Tze:

> The pure man sees the One as One and the many as
> One. So long as he sees the Unity, he is God; when he sees
> the distinctions, he is man. What marks the pure man is the
> ability to distinguish between the human and the Divine. [34]
> Do not ask whether the Tao is in this or in that; It
> is in all being. It is for this very reason that we apply to It
> the title of "Supreme," "the Highest." All that It has made is
> limited, but It is, Itself, unlimited, infinite.
> The Tao is the source of the activity of universal

manifestation, but It is not this activity. It is the Author of causes and effects, but It is not the causes and effects. It is the Author of universal manifestation and dissolution, but It is not the manifestation or dissolution. Everything proceeds from It, and is governed by It; It is in all things, but is not identical with things, for It is neither divided or limited. [35]

     Only he who can see the Formless in the formed arrives at the Truth. [36] He rejoices in THAT which can never be lost, but endures forever. [37]

The precepts of Lao Tze and Chuang Tze and all the later seers of the Tao are in perfect accord with the teachings of all men of spiritual vision. Theirs is but another expression of the perennial wisdom that stems from the mystical vision of Unity. They report what they have seen, and they offer advice on the means to attain that vision, and how to live in this world in accordance with it. They are not mere Quietists, as some would have it, but are illumined sages who had experienced the truth of which they speak, and offer their insights as a guide to those who would follow in their footsteps. And their words, for all these centuries, have served to bring solace and understanding to countless generations of seekers after Truth.

THE BUDDHA

In the 6th century B.C.E. the main center of Indian civilization was in the Ganges plain, or the 'middle country,' from what is
now Delhi eastward to Bhagalpur. From June to September, during
the monsoon season, a river that is only a couple hundred feet wide in
the preceding hot season becomes two miles wide. The Ganges,
having its source in the melting snows and glaciers of the Himalayas,
never dwindles away; for that reason, the surrounding plain is always
fertile. And during the cooler winter months, from October to
January, the Spring-harvested crops of wheat, barley, and linseed and
mustard, for their oil, are grown in abundance.

During that time long ago, the land was far more fertile and
the forests far more extensive than today. Surrounding the villages
were the cultivated fields; further outward were the pastures, and
beyond them were the forests, deep and lush. Accounts of the time
speak of the forests as places of easy retreat, where mango, banana,
date, jack-fruit, and coconut trees were in bloom, and the banyan,
palmyra, acacia and ebony trees housed the wild and colorful birds
and monkeys.

The town of Kapilavastu (named for Kapila), in the kingdom
of Koshala, lay just due north of Benares, and just west of the great
capital city of Shravasti, containing 57,000 families. It was positioned
along a major trade route from Shravasti to Rajagriha, the capital city
of the neighboring Magadhan kingdom. It was therefore a center of
business and trade, and also a place of much activity, culture, and
entertainment. Then, as now, cities were distinguished from the
country villages by their sophistication and diversity of life-styles. It
was here, in Kapilavastu, that Siddhartha of the Gautama clan, who was
to become known as "the Buddha," was born to Suddhodana and his
wife, Maya, around 586 B.C.E.

Suddhodana was the elected ruling citizen of the small
republic of Shakya of which Kapilavastu was the capital. He was a
wealthy aristocrat, and lived in a sumptuous and elegant home, where
he raised his son, Siddhartha, amid the splendor and wealth which his
position provided. When Siddhartha was but sixteen, he was married
to the princess, Yashodara; and by her he had a son, named Rahula.
But this life of comfort, wealth and pleasure was not to last. At the age
of twenty-nine, Siddhartha, who was of a philosophic turn of mind,

having studied many doctrines and having reflected on the perplexities of life and death, resolved to quit the home of his father and the company of his wife and child, to enter into a life of solitude in the forests, where he might resolve his questions in the supreme inner knowledge of which the sages of old had spoken.

From that time, he became a homeless wanderer, one among many of the monks, ascetics and solitary hermits who frequented the forests and riversides. He met, during his wandering, many brother-monks, *sannyasins*, and would-be teachers; and he experimented with many different practices, including austere penances and discursive reasonings; but he felt as empty, as unfulfilled, as before.

After six years of study and wandering, Siddhartha had become intensely focused on the attainment of his goal of knowing the ultimate Truth. And so, one day, he took his seat beneath a peepul (Bo) tree on the banks of the Nairanjana river, near Uruvela, the present city of Bodh-Gaya, and resolved to meditate there, and not to leave his place until he had attained what he had come to the forest to attain.

Then, one morning, just before dawn, like a flash, enlightenment came. According to the *Dhammapada*, which was written much later, Siddhartha exclaimed at that time:

> Looking for the Maker of this temple (referring to his body), I have run through a course of many births, not finding Him; and painful is birth again and again. But now, Maker of this temple, Thou hast been seen; Thou shalt not construct this temple again. All Thy rafters are broken, Thy ridge-pole is sundered; the mind, approaching the Eternal, has attained *nirvana* [the extinction of the illusion of selfhood]. [1]

In that transcendent experience of Unity, which the Buddha refers to as *nirvana*, he knew himself to be the one Consciousness who is manifesting as the entire universe. All forms, though transient, he knew as his own, with no division anywhere. Yet, when his mind returned to its normal state, once again he was associated with a particular form within the transformative world, called *samsara*, "the ocean of phenomenal appearance." As he sat beneath the Bo tree, Siddhartha reflected on what he had seen in that revelation, and perhaps mused within himself thusly:

> From this state of limited consciousness, I appear once again to be a separate form within *samsara*; but from the

state of expanded awareness, all of *samsara* is a manifestation of myself. I am a single, undifferentiated Mind, yet I shine forth, like the radiant beams of the Sun, as a universe of countless living beings, all made of my light. All beings are united in me, for I am their consciousness, their form, their very being. Never are there any separate selves; that is only an illusion produced by the limiting of consciousness. All are but players in the outflowing radiance of the one Being. These transient forms live but for a moment, but I, the One, live forever. Though I appear as many, I am forever One, forever serene."

'Yet, who would believe such a story?' he wondered. 'It is so implausible, so utterly fantastic and radical a revelation, so completely opposite to what men believe, that no one, unless they too had seen it, would be able to give any credence to it at all.' Siddhartha realized that this transcendent knowledge could never be adequately communicated by words, but was attainable only through such dilligent effort as he himself had put forth. According to a later Buddhist text, called the *Agama Sutras*, he deliberated within himself at this time, questioning the wisdom of attempting to teach such knowledge:

> My original vows are fulfilled; the Truth I have attained is too deep for the understanding [of men]. A Buddha alone is able to understand what is in the mind of another Buddha. In this age of the five-fold ignorance, all beings are enveloped in greed, anger, folly, falsehood, arrogance, and flattery; they have few virtues and have not the understanding to comprehend the Truth I have attained. Even if I revolve the wheel of Truth [by teaching it], they would surely be confused and incapable of accepting it. they might, on the contrary, misinterpret it, and thereby fall into evil paths, and suffer therefore much pain. It is best for me to remain quiet and enter [once again] into nirvana. [2]

In the same vein, another Buddhist text has Siddhartha reflecting at this time:

> Why should I attempt to make known to those who are consumed with lust and hate This which I've won through so much effort! This Truth is not a truth that can be grasped; it goes against the grain of what people think; it is deep, subtle, difficult, delicate. It will be cloaked in the murky ignorance of those slaves of passion who have not seen It. [3]

All those who have experienced this amazing revelation of the true nature of Reality have recognized the impossibility of expressing to others what they had come to know, and have held serious doubts as to the wisdom of speaking of it at all. Chuang Tze, the Chinese sage of the 3rd century B.C.E., for example, debated with himself on this same quandary, and wrote:

> Great truths do not take hold of the hearts of the
> masses. And now, as all the world is in error, how shall I,
> though I know the true path, how shall I guide? If I, while
> knowing I cannot succeed, still attempt to force success, this
> would be but another source of error. Better, then, to desist
> and strive no more. *Yet, if I do not strive, who will?* 4

Siddhartha, pondering on these questions in his forest retreat, apparently reached the same conclusion, and, armed with a firm decision to serve as a guide to suffering mankind, set out on his illustrious teaching career. To many hundreds of generations there- after he would be known as *the Buddha*, "the enlightened"; the *Tathagata*, "the attainer of Truth"; the *Shakya-muni*, "sage of the Shakyas."

The Buddha, having grown up in an environment where the Vedantic mystical tradition had been subverted by the priestly class, saw around him only a ritualistic religion presided over by an unenlightened brahmin priesthood. He had seen how the talk of "God" by the unenlightened led men to a false understanding of the Divine Reality, and fostered a philosophical Dualism between man and God; and he determined, therefore, to explain the knowledge of Unity in a way radically different from his Vedic predecessors. He would eschew the old traditional terms for the One, such as "Brahm- an," "Shiva," "Purusha," etc.; for when one spoke of "the know- ledge of God," a duality was implied between the knower and the object of knowledge, which was not in fact the case. The very nature of language is such that it relies for meaning upon the normal subject- object relationships. But, in the experience of Unity, there is no such separation. Thus, simply by naming It, that Unity is misrepresented.

In the eyes of the Buddha, it was just such objectifications of the Reality in terms such as "Shiva," "Vishnu," etc., which fostered a mistaken notion of the Truth, and perpetuated the present degen- erative state of religion. For this reason, he refused to apply any

name at all to the transcendent Reality; he preferred to refer to the
experience of the eternal Unity, rather than apply to It an objective
noun. The experience of Unity he named *nirvana*, a word which
signifies "extinction," or "non-being." What was extinquished in
this experience was the false sense of a separative ego, and hence the
subject-object relationship. Though misinterpretation was unavoid-
able in any case, the Buddha felt that the term, *nirvana*, was less likely
to misrepresent his meaning than those many objectified nouns which
had been for so long used to signify the one Reality.

He was keenly aware of the inability of language either to
express the Truth or to effect Its realization. He had seen how little
true knowledge was obtained by those proud brahmin scholars who
continually discussed and debated every fine point of metaphysical
doctrine. As for himself, the Buddha would refuse to engage in any
metaphysical discussions at all, insisting that all such harangues were
worthless to effect enlightenment, and that if one sincerely wished to
know and understand the nature of Reality, it was necessary to engage
oneself seriously in the practice of meditation and inner reflection.

When asked by the idly curious such questions as, "Is the
universe eternal or non-eternal? Is it finite or infinite? Is the soul real
or unreal?" the Buddha would reply:

> Such questions are not calculated to profit, and are not
> concerned with the attainment of Truth; they do not lead to the
> practice of right conduct, nor to detachment, nor to purification
> from lusts, nor to quietude, nor to tranquilization of the heart,
> nor to real knowledge, nor to insight into the higher stages of
> the path, nor to nirvana. This is why I express no opinion on
> them. [5]

It is, perhaps, this reluctance on the part of the Buddha to
describe the Reality in objective terms, or to engage in metaphysical
discussions, which has led many to view the Buddhist and Vedantic
perspectives as irreconcilably antagonistic, when, in fact, they are
identical. We are accustomed by unenlightened scholars and partisan
religionists to think of Vedanta, Taoism, Buddhism, and the other
"isms," as separate and distinct religious philosophies; but they are,
in fact, but different names for the one perennial philosophy of the
mystics. Having originated independently in different lands and
different times by different seers, each of these "isms" possesses its
own ideosyncratic language, its own literary heritage; yet the message

of the mystics remains undeviatingly the same. All true mystics have accentuated the need for that personal enlightenment or realization by which the true nature of Reality becomes self-evident. And all have stressed that this enlightenment is attainable, not through much learning, alms-giving, or through following the precepts of ritualized religion, but only through devotion to and contemplation of one's own essential Being.

Shortly after his enlightenment, and his subsequent decision to share his wisdom with other sincere seekers of Truth, the Buddha journeyed to a large deer park near Benares, where many of his fellow monks congregated. And there he addressed his brothers, explaining to them that excessive asceticism, scriptural recitations, sacramental offerings, and other such practices were as futile to the attainment of freedom from suffering as were the opposite extremes of revelry, and the wanton gratification of the senses. He spoke to them of a 'Middle Path' by which one could approach true knowledge and a harmonious life. Like Kapila before him, he offered no religious platitudes, no fanciful gods, but spoke to his hearers of "what pain is, and the method by which one may reach the cessation of pain."

And when he spoke to them, the gathered monks recognized his attainment of enlightenment, and herded around him to listen to his teaching, his Sermon. The Buddha's Sermon at Benares was the first of many to follow; and it contains for his followers the same profound meaning that the Sermon on the Mount holds for followers of Jesus. It contains in brief form the entirety of the Buddha's message, the authentic version of which we may only assume has been passed down to us, as the Buddha wrote nothing himself. What we possess of his teachings were handed down orally until they were committed to writing in the 2nd century B.C.E., nearly 300 years after his death.

Sitting before the gathering of monks, the Buddha began his Sermon by saying:

> Whatever is originated will be dissolved again. All
> worry about the self is vain; the ego is like a mirage, and all
> the tribulations that touch it will pass away. They will van-
> ish as a nightmare vanishes when a sleeper awakes. [6]

This first statement of the Buddha's that "whatever is originated will be dissolved again," is particularly obvious to anyone in the 20th or 21st century who is familiar with the findings of modern physics regarding the nature of matter. All matter, we know, is constituted of one undifferentiated Energy, which 'condenses' or integrates into different congregate forms which then disintegrate once again, only to take on new forms. This statement of the Buddha's is true on all levels of reality, from the microcosmic to the macrocosmic, but here it is intended to refer to the ephemeral nature of the individual body and personality.

Bodies originate, and must one day be dissolved; therefore, "all worry about the self is vain," says the Buddha. He had seen the Truth, and knew that the sense of an individual self, or ego, was an illusion, a mirage, and that all the troubles and worries that afflict one during the course of a life vanish when that false sense of ego vanishes.

One whose mind awakes to the realization that it is the one Mind, and is not in any way affected by the manifestation or de-manifestation of forms within this world of *samsara*, sees this world as a kind of dream. And just as one no longer fears the evil monsters of a dream once he awakes and realizes that he is the dreamer, the awakened Buddha can never again be drawn to identify himself with the body or mental images that exist only in the world of *samsara*.

> He who has awakened is freed from fear; he has
> become a Buddha; he knows the vanity of all his cares, his
> ambitions, and also of his pains. [7]

From the time we are infants and discover this body and mind that manipulates us and in turn is manipulated by us, we feel certain that this body and mind is ourself, is who we are. That identification becomes so strongly rooted in us, that never once do we doubt that we are this particular mind and body limited in space and time, and any suggestion to the contrary strikes us as bizarre and absurd. But, say the seers, the Buddhas, it is merely a case of mistaken identity; that which is born, thrives for awhile, and then decays, is not who you are. You are the one Mind of the universe, which merely witnesses all this world of changing forms, but is never affected by it. You are the Eternal, but you see this transient world of forms and think, "This is me!" It is like a man who, dreaming that he is being roasted alive, suffers the pain from the heat of the imagined flames; or like a man who is frightened by a snake which, on closer inspection, turns out only to have been a piece of rope.

> It sometimes happens that a man, when bathing in
> the river, steps upon a wet rope and imagines that it is a
> snake. Terror will overcome him, and he will shake with fear,
> anticipating in his mind all the agonies caused by the serpent's
> venomous bite.
> What a relief does this man experience when he sees
> that the rope is no snake. The cause of his fear lies in his
> error, his ignorance, his illusion. If the true nature of the rope
> is recognized, his tranquility of mind will come back to him;
> he will feel relieved; he will be joyful and happy. This is the
> state of mind of one who has recognized that there is no self-
> hood (ego), and that the cause of all his troubles, cares, and
> vanities is a mirage, a shadow, a dream. [8]

Here, in his first Sermon, the Buddha gives the essence of his teaching, and the teaching of all the seers. It should be apparent, of course, that the "selfhood" to which the Buddha here refers is not the Self (*Atman*) of the Upanishads, which is synonymous with the Eternal, but is the false sense of self, the ego. When the Truth is realized, the false idea of an individual self is dissolved, like the idea of the snake which is really a rope. Then it is seen that, in reality, no separate self exists or ever existed; it is a mirage, a mistaken inter-pretation of one's own awareness, which is really the immortal and eternal Self, the Absolute. Only that One is real; It is the Self of the universe, the universal Being which manifests as all beings, all things. It is the knowledge of this Self which is the source of the joy and happiness of the enlightened.

> Happy is he who has overcome his ego; happy is he who
> has attained peace; happy is he who has found the Truth. [9]

Some, when they hear of the Truth from one who has seen It, immediately recognize it as the truth, and are overjoyed to learn of It. But some others who hear of It, say, "How unconvincing, how unappetizing!" To them, the Buddha says:

> Have confidence in the [eternal] Truth, although you
> may not be able to comprehend It, although you may suppose
> Its sweetness to be bitter, although you may shrink from It at
> first. Trust in the Truth. ... Have faith in the Truth and live
> [in accordance with] It. [10]

Sooner or later, we must acknowledge that what keeps us from the enjoyment of peace, of happiness, of freedom, is the sense of

selfhood, the false ego, by which all pain, all suffering, comes to us. It
is the mistaken identification with the transient that must eventually
cause us much sorrow.

> [The illusion of] self is a fever; self is a transient
> illusion, a dream; but Truth is sublime, Truth is everlasting.
> There is no immortality except in [the eternal] Truth. For
> Truth alone abides forever. [11]

The Buddha explained his message as the way to the cessation of suffering. He did not promise heavenly rewards, or a place at
the right hand of the Lord, nor did he claim that he was sent from
God; he claimed only that his was the way to the cessation of suffering:

> He who recognizes the existence of suffering, its
> cause, its remedy, and its cessation, has fathomed the four
> noble truths. He will walk in the right path. [12]

Here, the Buddha introduces his formula of the "four noble
truths":

1. There is suffering; i.e., humans suffer.
2. There is a cause of suffering; namely ignorance.
3. There is a remedy to suffering; namely enlightenment.
4. The cessation of suffering results from the destruction of ignorance.

If we pay close attention to the words of the Buddha's Sermon in the above passage, his message is clear and unequivocal: the
cause of all suffering is the ignorance by which we believe we are an
individual self, limited to a particular body and mind. This ignorance is inherent in existence, and has no cause or beginning. Yet it
can be dispelled, and thus ended, by the realization of Truth. In this
sense, it is both real and unreal; while it exists, it is experienced as real,
and when it is dispelled, it is recognized to be unreal, non-existent --
like the snake in the rope. Release from suffering, then, is attained by
the direct realization of our eternal Being. To understand this is to
possess the right understanding:

> Right understanding will be the torch to light the way
> of one who seeks to realize the Truth. Right aims will be his
> guide. Right speech will be his dwelling-place on the road.

His path will be straight, for it is right behavior. His refreshments will be the right way of earning his livelihood. Right efforts will be his steps; right thinking his breath; and peace will follow in his footsteps. [13]

In this metaphor of the Buddha's, in which he likens the moving of a man's awareness toward enlightenment to a man walking toward his destination, he outlines the right means by which a man reaches to the realization of Truth. "Right" simply means that which is conducive to success. This "eight-fold path" of the Buddha reiterates, in its own way, the yogas of the *Bhagavad Gita*: jnan, bhakti, karma, and raja. As a man is a thinking, speaking, acting and contemplating being, all facets of his nature must be coordinated toward the attainment of his goal.

Following naturally from right knowledge, is the second means, right aims, which is to say, the aspiration to know the Truth, to renounce all other pursuits which might detract from the single-minded pursuit of one's goal. Without such unflagging determination, and utter disregard for all the trouble, opposition, and deprivation encountered, a man cannot hope to attain to it. The Buddha's "right aspiration" is really not different from the *Gita's* "devotion to Truth." Devotion to the Truth, or God, is devotion to the Eternal in oneself; aspiration toward the attainment of *nirvana* is also devotion to the Eternal in oneself. The mental restraint, renunciation of self (ego), and inward attentiveness required by the one is the same as that required by the other. They are, in aspiration, practice, and result, identical. Only the words are different.

The third means, right speech, is merely an extension of right thinking; it is that speech which is truthful, sincere, and cognizant of the oneness of all beings. Untruthful speech betrays an untruthful mind, and is entirely incompatible with the mind's attainment of the ultimate Truth. Never, in a million years, will untruthfulness lead to the Truth. "Truth," says the Mundaka Upanishad, "is the way that leads to the region of Truth. Sages travel therein free from desires and reach the supreme abode of Truth."

The fourth means, right action, is also simply an extension of right thought. That action which is inspired by and leads to the awareness of Truth, is the right action. It is action that stems from peace of mind, and whose result is peace of mind. Whatever defiles and disturbs the quiet awareness of Truth cannot be right action. This

"right action" of the Buddha may be compared to the karma yoga of
the *Gita* . It is action whose sole aim is the awareness and promotion
of Truth. It is action that stems not from egoistic desire, but from the
awareness that all this world of *samsara* and all beings in it are
identical in the one Mind. Such actions flow forth naturally as
expressions of service to the One in all.

The fifth means, right livelihood, may be viewed in the same
way that Krishna, in the *Bhagavad Gita*, viewed the necessity of
following one's own *svadharma*. Men of differing stations in life are
obliged by their differing aspirations to differing livelihoods. The
livelihood of the householder is in accordance with his aspirations; the
livelihood of the student is in accordance with his aspirations, and the
livelihood of the realized sage is in accordance with his aspiration.
For one, the "right" is not the same as the "right" for another. What
conduces harmoniously to one's aspirations is the right livelihood.
For the spiritual seeker, that work which is conducive to the meditative
life is the "right" livelihood; and for the sage who has no aspiration
but to share his knowledge to relieve the suffering of the world, the
need for livelihood is not so great; he accepts what comes to him in
the course of his mission.

Right effort is the sixth means, and it follows from right aspiration. If right aspiration is determination to attain enlightenment,
right effort is the application of that determination. The conquest of
the sense of selfhood requires great effort. It is the most difficult of
all battles. According to the *Dhammapada*, "If one man conquers in
battle a thousand men, and if another conquers himself, the second is
the greatest of conquerors." [14] Lao Tze, the great Chinese sage, said
this as well: "He who conquers others may be strong, but he who
conquers himself is stronger." [15] To conquer oneself is, in effect, to
reduce oneself to nothing. For, as the Buddha tells us, that self is not
only an illusion, but an obstacle to the realization of Truth. Only
when it is reduced to nothing, shall we find that greater Self which is
the one all-pervading Reality, the Buddha-Mind, the Truth.

The seventh means, right mindfulness, or recollection, is the
mental aspect of right effort. It means the continual watchfulness of
the mind over itself. The pure mind is itself *nirvana*; the illusions that
continually becloud its surface serve only to obscure the Truth. Right
mindfulness is therefore the retention of the pure mind. It might just
as well be spoken of as surrender of the separative will, for it is just
that will which obscures the awareness of Unity. Jesus of Nazareth

taught the surrender of the will to God; the Buddha taught the surrender of the will to Truth. Who can find any difference between them? That to which the will is surrendered is the one pure Mind. Right mindfulness is simply the retention of the pure Mind.

Right concentration is the eighth and final means; it is an extension or intensification of right mindfulness, which can only be achieved during times of silent meditation. It is the final step toward the threshold of *nirvana*. What is the object of the mind's concentration? Itself. Let it become still and concentrated, and it reverts to its original, pure Mind, state. In this state is all knowledge, all peace, all satisfaction. It is this utter one-pointedness of mind which lifts it to its ultimate state, that state in which it knows itself as the one Mind of the universe.

The Buddha's message is so clear and straightforward that, to the wise, it needs no further clarification or elucidation. But there has been, over the years, no dearth of clarification; for it is the delight of all who have attained the knowledge of Truth to speak of It. Many brilliant followers of the Buddha, who lived much later, have offered their own insights into the Truth and Its attainment. Among these, was an enlightened sage of the 2nd century of the Current Era, called Ashvagosha, whose poetic work, *Buddha-Karita,* tells, in a picturesque fashion, the life of the Buddha. Ashvagosha also wrote a Mahayana treatise called, "The Awakening Of Faith," in which he offered his insights into the nature of Reality. Like Kapila, the author of the *Bhagavad Gita*, and so many others, Ashvagosha attempted to explain the two, absolute and relative, aspects of the one universal Soul, or Self:

> In the one Soul we may distinguish two aspects. The one [aspect] is the Soul-as-Absolute (*Tathata*); the other is the Soul-as-relative-world (*samsara*). Each in itself constitutes all things, and both are so closely related that one cannot be separated from the other.
> What is meant by "the Soul-as-Absolute" is the oneness of the totality of things, the great all-inclusive Whole.
> ... This essential nature of the Soul is uncreate and eternal. Therefore all things in their fundamental nature are not nameable or explicable. They cannot be adequately explained in any form of language. ... They possess absolute sameness. They are subject neither to transformation nor to destruction. They are nothing but the one Soul, for which "Absolute" is simply another designation.

> The Soul-as-the-relative-world comes forth from the
> Womb of the Absolute; but the immortal Absolute and the
> mortal relative world coincide with one another. Though they
> are not identical, they are not two. [16]

It should be evident that, in this explanation by Ashvagosha, these two, *Tathata* and *samsara* , are precisely those same two aspects of Reality described in earlier chapters as Brahman & Maya, Purusha & Prakrti, Shiva & Shakti, Tao & Teh, etc. They "coincide," as Ashvagosha says, in the experience of *nirvana*.

Another great sage of the Mahayana Buddhist tradition was Nagarjuna, who lived in the late 2nd century C.E. He too placed great emphasis on the understanding of these two aspects of Reality, insisting, in his "Discourse On The Middle Way," that:

> The Buddha's teaching rests on the discrimination
> between two aspects of Reality: the Absolute and the rela-
> tive. Those who do not have any adequate knowledge of them
> are unable to grasp the subtle and profound meaning of Bud-
> dhism. [17]

Yet, in the same Discourse, he acknowledged the fact that, "*samsara* is an activity of *nirvana* (in this sense, the Absolute) itself; not the slightest distinction exists between them."

It is only from the viewpoint of the enlightened that *samsara* and *nirvana* (or *Tathata*) no longer appear as two. One who has seen the Truth sees only oneness everywhere. He knows himself to be that One who exists eternally, beyond all manifestation of *samsara*; yet he knows also that *samsara* is his own appearance, a play of changing forms on the one ocean of Existence. When a man awakes to *nirvana*, behold! Suddenly he knows himself as the Absolute, the one eternally pure, unblemished Consciousness. And there, also, shining forth from him is the world of *samsara*, with all its creatures and objects. Like a movie shown on a screen, or like a fantasy-image on one's own mind, the two exist at once. It is ONE, but It has these two aspects.

Those who have seen It realize better than anyone the impossibility of explaining this duality-in-unity to those who have not experienced It, yet they realize, too, that nothing can be said about enlightenment without referring to It. Here, on this same subject, is the master, Padma-Shambhava, who took his Buddhism to Tibet in 747 C.E., and wrote a book entitled, "The Yoga Of Knowing The Mind, And Seeing The Reality, Which Is Called Self-Realization." In it, he wrote:

> Although the wisdom of nirvana and the ignorance of
> samsara illusorily appear to be two things, they cannot truly
> be differentiated. It is an error to conceive them as other than
> one. [18]

Those, like the Buddha, who have realized the Truth, tell of It to others and outline a path to that realization as a way of explaining what happened to themselves and describing the pattern of their progress to it. They are practical scientists who say, in effect, 'This is what happened to me, and these are the mental refinements that lead to it. You too, by doing likewise, will reach the same inner realization.' When we examine the testimonies of those many who have described their experience of Unity and their progress to it, we have to be struck by the remarkable agreement evidenced in all their testimonies. Their lives, their methods, their enlightenment, reveal so undeviating a sameness, so compelling a unanimity, that we must be convinced ot the universality of their experience, and the universality of the path to it. We must come to the conclusion that the Truth is one, that the way is clear, and that the choice is our own.

The Buddha continued to live and teach his disciples for forty-five years, moving about from place to place, proclaiming his wisdom to the people around Benares, Oudh, and Bihar. He established a monastic Order, and accepted as gifts from his householder devotees many groves and monasteries where his liberating knowledge could be taught. He died at the age of eighty in 486 B.C.E. at Kusinagara, the present city of Kasia, in northern Gorakhpur. His last words to the disciples who gathered around him were: "All constituted forms pass away. Dilligently work out your own salvation."

≈≈

II. Mystics Of
The Greco-Roman Era

THE PRE-SOCRATIC GREEKS

Pythagorus

While Lao Tze was meditating on the Tao in his mountain solitude in China, and while the Buddha was teaching his path to *nirvana* in northern India, a young man by the name of Pythagorus (570-490 B.C.E.) from the Greek island of Samos, was studying the mystical knowledge of the Indians and Egyptians in the town of his birth. In Pythagorus' youth, the port city of Samos had close commercial ties with Egypt and the community of Indians who lived in Memphis, Egypt. His biographer, Iamblichus, states that Pythagorus travelled widely, studying the teachings of the Egyptians and Assyrians, and journeyed also to Persia, where he no doubt learned much of his geometry, including the quadrature of the hypoteneuse, which formula came to be known by his name, though it seems to have been known to the Indians since Vedic times. Eventually, he settled in Croton, in southern Italy, where he established his religious society.

Of Pythagorus' personal life and authentic teachings little is known for certain. He left no writings, and what we learn of his teachings comes almost entirely from his critics and commentators who lived long after him, such as Diogenes Laertius, Plutarch, Porphyry and the Church Father, Hippolytus. Judging, however, from the power and scope of the philosophy which bears his name, and the immensity of his influence, it is safe to assume that he was not only an advocate of mystical philosophy, but had experienced first-hand That whereof he spoke. Though there is no evidence to show that he actually attained "the vision of God," from his reputation and legacy, it would not be unreasonable to call him 'one of the first of the great mystics of the West.'

Pythagorus seems to have introduced to the Western mind a truly Monistic philosophy, and in particular, the concept of a Unity (Monad) self-divided into a higher, eternal principle, characterized as Male, and a lower, creative principle, characterized as Female. Says Hippolytus, in his *Refutation of All Heresies:*

> Pythagorus declared the originating principle of the
> universe to be the unbegotten Monad and the generated duad ...
> And he says that the Monad is the Father of the duad, and the
> duad the Mother of all things that are begotten. ... For the

duad is generated from the Monad, according to Pythagorus;
and the Monad is Male and primary, but the duad Female [and
secondary]. [1]

He stated further that the creation produced by the duad, or
"Mother," consisted of two kinds, or levels; one, the physical level,
which includes the "material" world, and the other, a subtle, or
psychic, level which includes all the individualized souls, various
spirits, and mental realms. Plato, in his *Phaedo*, states as a Pythagorean doctrine that the soul is but temporarily encased in the body,
and transmigrates from birth to birth in this world, which is not its true
and final home. For Pythagorus, contemplation of the Eternal was
man's highest calling. When asked, "What are men born for?" he
replied, "To gaze on the heavens." According to him, when the soul
is perfected, purified from its subjugation to the material body, there
would be no further need of rebirth. Thus, it appears that the
philosophy of Pythagorus, if not entirely derived from Indian sources,
was certainly in perfect agreement with that of the Upanishadic seers.

The Pythagoreans formed a widespread and influential
religious cult, which lasted for a number of centuries; they did not kill
or eat meat, and lived a life of seclusion, study, and meditation. They
no doubt resembled the monastic Orders of Buddhism which were
forming at the same time in another part of the world. However, there
seems also to have been a great deal of interest, passed on from
Pythagorus to his followers, in the occult symbology of numbers, and
in secret rites of initiation. Perhaps it was because of these sidetracks
that Pythagoreanism degenerated, becoming known primarily as a
"mystery cult," and eventually faded from view.

Today, Pythagorus is known in the schoolrooms of children
as "the father of geometry," but he was much more; certainly he was
a sage, perhaps even a saint. The truth about him remains to this day
a mystery, and his mystical teachings are long forgotten; still, the
apparently great influence he had upon his time reveals the respect he
commanded, and the extent to which the mystical philosophy of the
East had permeated the Western world of his time.

Heraclitus

Meanwhile, in Ephesus, lived a man "lofty-minded beyond all other men," according to that historian of philosophers, Diogenes Laertius. His name was Heraclitus (540-480 B.C.E.). He was born an aristocrat, a prince, but he renounced all political activities, and ceded his title and properties to his brother. He became a recluse, living in the mountains, "making his diet of grass and herbs." Becoming ill from this diet, he returned to the town of Ephesus, where he lived for a time in a cowshed, and shortly died of his ailments. [2]

His book, *On Nature*, was written in brief epigrammatic statements about the one Reality, which few could understand. According to his biographer, he deliberately made it obscure so that none but adepts should approach it. But there were some who understood, and called it "a guide of conduct, the keel of the whole world, for one and all alike." [3] Diodotus called it "a helm unerring for the rule of life." [4] Apparently, king Darius of Persia also greatly admired this book, and wrote to Heraclitus, requesting that he come to Persia to instruct him regarding Greek philosophy. Darius promised him honor and a life of luxury. But Heraclitus wrote back, politely declining the offer. One appreciative scholar of the time wrote about Heraclitus' book: "Do not be in too great a hurry to get to the end of this book by Heraclitus the Ephesian; the path is hard to travel. Gloom is there and darkness devoid of light. But if an initiate by your guide, the path shines brighter than sunlight." [5]

Heraclitus, like Pythagorus, was a contemporary of the Buddha, but it does not seem that Heraclitus had any contact with Eastern thought, as did Pythagorus and, later, Socrates; but came to his views through his own reflection and experience. While he died ignominiously and in obscurity, he had a great influence on other thinkers of his own time and later. Epicharmus of Syracuse (fl. 485 B.C.E.) and Parmenides of Elea (fl. 475 B.C.E.) were greatly influenced by him. They continued the philosophical tradition of mystical knowledge which he propounded, as did Melissus of Samos (fl. 440 B.C.E.), Empedocles of Acagras (fl. 450 B.C.E.) and Anaxagorus of Clazomenae (fl. 460 B.C.E.). The writings of these authors exist today, however, only in fragments thanks to the anti-pagan zeal of the later Christians.

In a time of polytheism and superstition, Heraclitus' writings were unique; he explained the universe, not as a creation of a God who was separate from it, but as a manifestation of forms within the Whole, which is, Itself, God. This manifestory Power of God he called "Logos," a common Greek word used variously to mean "thought," "reason," "idea," or "theory." What he intended by this term becomes clear when we examine the philosophy of Heraclitus, not as a rational construction, but as an attempt to explain what he had experienced in the mystical vision of Unity. The Logos is that principle of universal manifestation which is co-existent and co-eternal with the one Mind; it is that which the seers of India have called *Prakrti* or *Maya*.

In his own way, Heraclitus tried to explain that the appearance of the many is really the Thought (*Logos*) of the one Mind; and for that reason, is a conscious manifestation of that One, which is, Itself, Consciousness. Man, himself, is a manifestation of the Logos, and, for that reason, can discover the Logos within himself. The Logos is his source, his ruler, and his very being. And, says Heraclitus, it is only through the conquest of egotistical pride, and dedication to the one Self in the silence of contemplation, that one is able to know the "hidden Unity."

Following is a reconstruction of Heraclitus' thought, based on existing fragments from his book, *On Nature* :

> I have explained the Logos, but men are always in-
> capable of understanding it, both before they have heard it, and
> after. For, though all things come into being in accordance
> with the Logos, when men hear it explained -- how all things
> are made of it, and how each thing is separated from another
> according to its nature -- they seem unable to comprehend it.
> The majority of men are as unaware of what they are doing
> after they wake from sleep as they are when asleep. [6] ...
> Everyone is ruled by the Logos, which is common to
> all; yet, though the Logos is universal, the majority of men
> live as if they had an identity peculiar to themselves. [7] ...
> Even when they hear of the Logos, they do not understand it,
> and even after they have learnt something of it, they cannot
> comprehend; yet they regard themselves as wise. [8]
> Those who believe themselves wise regard as real
> only the appearance of things, but these fashioners of false-
> hood will have their reward. [9] Though men are inseparable
> from the Logos, yet they are separated in it; and though they
> encounter it daily, they are alienated from it. [10] What intelli-

gence or understanding do they have? They believe the popular orators, and are guided by the opinions of the populace; they do not understand that the majority of men are fools, and the wise few. [11]

Of all the wise philosophers whose discourses I have heard, I have not found any who have realized the one Intelligence which is distinct from all things, [12] and yet pervades all things. [13] That Intelligence is One; to know It is to know the Purpose which guides all things and is in all things. [14] Nature has no inherent power of intelligence; Intelligence is the Divine. [15] Without It, the fairest universe is but a randomly scattered dust-heap. [16] If we are to speak with intelligence, we must found our being on THAT which is common to all... For that Logos which governs man is born of the One, which is Divine. It [the Divine] governs the universe by Its will, and is more than sufficient to everyone. [17]

One should not conjecture at random about the Supreme [Truth]. [18] The eyes are better witnesses to the truth than the ears; [19] but the eyes and ears are bad witnesses for men if their souls cannot understand. [20] You could not in your travels find the source or destination of the soul, so deeply hidden is the Logos. [21] [But] I searched for It [and found It] within myself. [22] That hidden Unity is beyond what is visible. [23] All men have this capacity of knowing themselves, [24] [for] the soul has the Logos within it, which can be known when the soul is evolved. [25] What is within us remains the same eternally; It is the same in life and death, waking and sleeping, youth and old age; for, It has become this world, and the world must return to It. [26]

The best of men choose to know the ONE above all else; It is the famous "Eternal" within mortal men. But the majority of men are complacent, like well-fed cattle. [27] They revel in mud; [28] like donkeys, they prefer chaff to gold. [29]

[The Eternal is attained only by those who seek It with all their desire;] for if one does not desire It, one will not find the Desireless, since there is no trail leading to It and no path. [30] Such a man is satiated with things seen, and kindles his inner light during the night. While living, he is like a dead man; while awake, he is like a man asleep. [31] But such men, the best of men, are one in ten thousand. [32]

You needn't listen to me; listen to the Logos [within]. When you do, you will agree that all things are One. [33] This ordered universe, which is the same for all, was not created by any one of the gods or by man, but always was, is, and shall be, an ever-living Flame that is first kindled and then quenched in turn. [34] [The universe bursts forth and then is reabsorbed, yet its Source is ever-living, like a Sun that never sets;] and

who can hide from that which never sets? [35] [That eternal Intelligence in man] is forever beyond change; [36] [It is God.]
To God all things are beautiful, good and just, but men see
some things to be just, and others unjust. [37]

One should understand that the world appears by the
opposition of forces; order exists in the world by this play of
contraries. [38] We would never have heard of "right" if we did
not know of "wrong;" [39] whole and not-whole, united-
separate, consonant-dissonant, -- all these are interdependent. [40]
[But] in the One, above and below are the same, [41] [just as]
beginning and end are one in the circumference of a circle. [42]
That which is in conflict is also in concert; while things differ
from one another, they are all contained in the most beautiful
Unity. [43]

[Yet the philosophers cannot understand this;] they do
not understand how that which contains dfferences within It is
also in harmony, how Unity consists of opposing forces within Itself, just as the strings of a bow or a lyre [produce harmony by being pulled by opposing forces.] [44]

[When one's mind becomes stilled, the one Intelligence is experienced separate from the appearance;] just as a
mixture of wine and barley-mean separates when it is not
stirred. [45] [The impulses of the mind must be stilled;] though
it is difficult to fight against impulse. [The impulses of desire
arise, but] whatever the mind wishes, it purchases at the ex-
pense of the soul. [46] [Such desires feed on pride and arrogance,
and] it is a greater task to quench one's own arrogance than it
is to quench a raging fire. [47] Pride is the greatest hindrance to
the progress of the soul. [48] Moderation is the greatest virtue,
and wisdom is to speak the truth and to act in accordance with
nature, while continuously attending to one's own Self. [49]
[A man should see to his own character,] for a man's character
is his destiny. [50]

Heraclitus' words read as fresh and clear today as when they
were written. His wisdom is as timeless as that of Lao Tze, the
Buddha, and all those others who have directly known the Truth. He
was the first of the Western seers to explain, as Lao Tze did, the
dualistic nature of the mind which perceives only in pairs of contraries, and the coincidence of contraries experienced in the mystical
"vision." (Nicholas of Cusa was to elaborate more fully on this
mystical observation, as we shall see in a later chapter.)   But
Heraclitus' most significant contribution to the thought of subsequent authors of mystical philosophy was his establishment of the
word, "Logos," as a term for the effusive Energy, or creative Power,

of God which manifests as the phenomenal universe. Though only these few fragments of his work remain, he is justly remembered and honored to this day as one of the earliest and wisest of the seers of Western antiquity.

Xenophanes

Contemporary with Heraclitus lived another sage named Xenophanes (570-475 B.C.E.). He was a native of Colophon, but was banished, it is said, to Sicily, where he continued to teach his mystical philosophy. He is said to have lived to a very old age, and little more is known of him. The one small fragment of his writing that is left to us indicates that he had known the one God of which he speaks:

> God is one, greatest among gods and men, in no way like mortals, having neither body nor mind. He sees as a Whole, perceives as a Whole, hears as a Whole. ... He remains ever stationary, unmoving; for there is no necessity for Him to go here and there on different occasions. Without acting, He makes all things vibrate by the impulse of His Mind.
> ... Homer and Hesiod have attributed to the gods all manner of shameful and reproachful acts...; but truly, the gods did not reveal all things from the beginning [as these two have suggested]; rather, it is only by long seeking that mortals may discover the Highest. [51]

It was dangerous in those days, of course, to speak against the state-supported religious mythology derived from Hesiod and Homer. But, as we have seen, there were even then, as always, a few great souls who had experienced the mystical "vision," and had known the simple reality of the One from whom all this world is produced. Such sages, in speaking of what they knew, have always had to bear the enmity of the unenlightened majority, and have often been forced, like Heraclitus, to seek seclusion, or, like Xenophanes, to flee the wrath of the ignorant, or, like Socrates a few years later, to pay with their lives for their unyielding devotion to truth.

SOCRATES AND HIS SUCCESSORS

Babylon fell in 538 B.C.E., and Cyrus founded the Persian Empire. In 510 B.C.E., his successor, Darius, made the Indus Valley a part of his empire; and in 480 B.C.E., Darius' son, Xerxes, invaded Greece. In that great Persian war, chronicled by Herodotus, the Greeks successfully repelled the Persians; and there-after, Athens came to prominence as a great power. The fifty years between 480 and 430 B.C.E. constituted the "golden age" of Greece; and it was during this time that the martyred sage, Socrates, lived.

Socrates

Socrates (469-399 B.C.E.) was born to Sophroniscus, a sculptor, and Phaenarete, a midwife, in the deme, or suburb, of Athens called Alopece. In all probability, he was a journeyman stone-cutter to his father in his youth, but we know nothing of it. As a young man, Socrates became an armed infantryman in the Athenian army, and served for at least ten years in the field during the Peloponnesian war. In Plato's *Symposium*, Alcibiades, who served in the war with Socrates, praises him, and tells of his extraordinary powers of endurance during a bitter cold winter at Potidaea, and of his gallant demeanor in battle at Delium, where he stood his post from dawn to the following dawn without moving from his spot -- apparently deeply absorbed in contemplation. Later, Socrates married Xanthippe, who turned out to be a shrew who constantly badgered Socrates about his improvident ways; and by her, or perhaps, as some say, by a second wife, he had three children, two of whom were fathered rather late in his life.

Socrates was not an unlearned man; he was familiar with philosophers both ancient and contemporary. He knew the writings of Heraclitus, Pythagorus, and his contemporary, Anaxagorus, who was prosecuted around 450 B.C.E. And it seems probable that he had at least some knowledge of the philosophy professed by the men of India and Persia who lived in the city. Indian soldiers had taken part in the Persian invasion of Greece, and Greek soldiers and officials were also serving in India by that time. There was, in fact, a good deal of intercourse between India and Greece during the lifetime of Socrates; and in Athens there were a number of brahmin philosophers with whom Socrates is said by Aristoxenus (ca. 330 B.C.E.) to have had frequent meetings. Thus, the mystical philosophy of Unity propounded by the Upanishads was spoken of in the intellectual circles of his time, and no doubt contributed somewhat to his own thought.

It would be a mistake, however, to regard Socrates as a mere product of his philosophical learning, or as a representative of a particular school of thought. Socrates, through his long habit of virtue and self-examination, and his extreme detachment from bodily externals, had learned to contemplate the eternal Truth for long periods of time. In this way, he came to realize the one Mind, the one "Good," by which he became an enlightened and holy man. It was from this pure knowledge that all his teachings sprang; not from learning. And, although Socrates lived in a time when to speak of unpopular ideals was to court disaster, he believed he was led by God to teach what he had known in the streets and marketplaces to all who would listen to him. And so he became a gadfly philosopher, stinging his fellow Athenians with his eloquent reasonings, ever guiding them toward virtue and truth.

In the mornings, Socrates would be found strolling on the promenades, and later in the day at the agora of Athens, which was the commercial center of the city as well as the location of the offices of government. Because so many sophists and self-styled teachers were to be found there, it also became an open market of philosophical discussion. But Socrates was no ordinary teacher; he did not offer to explain to men the nature of the universe, or the way that the world was created; his one intent was to teach men the proper conduct of man whereby they might be led to know for themselves the highest Good, the unchanging Truth. Xenophon, an admirer of Socrates, said that he offered men the hope that, "if only they disciplined themselves, they would become truly noble men. Yet he never promised or taught this; rather, because he clearly was truly noble, he made his companions hope to become like him by imitatiing him." [1]

Socrates was a sage before anyone had any set notions of what a sage should be like, or even what constitutes sagacity. He was short, stocky, balding, with a pudgy nose, and was extremely jovial, eager to converse with whomever showed interest in following along. His conversations inevitably led to a consideration of what is the highest Good, and how a man might live so as to attain to it. Socrates had found in himself that highest Good, and he knew that it was That alone which was the purpose and foundation of all man's actions; and that otherwise there was no stable or reliable foundation for morality, or for judging the rightness or wrongness of any action or motive.

But he was no preacher, nor was he one to reveal everything he knew just like that. He led each of his listeners by just so much of a string of reason as each could comfortably follow, until they were led at last to agree to conclusions to which, theretofore, they would never have agreed. He was so gentle, so extremely kind, that even the meanest sycophant was brought by him to new levels of under-standing simply by following the Ariadne-thread of logic by which he was led out of the dark labyrinth of confusion and into the clear light of truth. For Socrates, a "philosopher" was just what the word implies, "a lover of wisdom"; and wisdom meant the following of truth. To everyone who met him and spoke with him, it was evident that Socrates had obtained something very like wisdom, that he knew something that elevated him far beyond the level of ordinary men, and made him holy.

Had Socrates lived in India, he would have been regarded as a "Guru"; or had he lived in Persia some centuries later, he would have been known as a "Pir." Whatever we may call him, he was one of that small band of perfected men who are intimate with God, and who remain on earth to teach others of the path to blessedness. Like others in a similar position, Socrates was greatly misunderstood in his own time -- and very often he himself was the cause; for he liked to obscure his own merits and his own knowledge of God, or "the Good," as he liked to say. He had rather question others, and by his skilled questioning, lead the young men who gathered 'round him to give birth within themselves to a new insight, a clearer understanding, of the truth. In this, he regarded himself as a sort of midwife, aiding in the birth of wisdom in the souls of his charges.

If pressed, Socrates pretended ignorance of divine know-ledge; he was cautious, not only on account of the danger of incurring the wrath of powerful people who were always eyeing him suspi-ciously, but as a means of encouraging his listeners, as fellow voyagers, to set sail with him on the search for truth. He was so humble, so genial, so lovable, that no one but the very proud and vengeful could find the least fault in him. Yet, with all that, he was a man of uncompromising honesty and virtue, guided incessantly from within by his "guiding spirit." Little wonder that his devoted followers saw in him the model of human perfection.

He seemed, like all true spiritual teachers, to speak in one way

to his casual listeners, and quite another way with his intimate
disciples. Out on the promenades, he would never pretend to any
knowledge of the one Source of the universe; he was fond of letting
all the public know that his only wisdom lay in knowing his own
ignorance. But when he was alone with the young men who were his
closest and most discerning students, he explained the highest vision
to them, and by figures and allusions he sought to explain to them
what it was like. One of his most famous such allegorical references
to the vision of "the Good" appears in Book VII of Plato's *Republic*.
There, Plato depicts Socrates in a conversation with Glaucon and
Adimantus explaining his famous 'Analogy of the Cave,' in which he
portrays allegorically the difference in perception between one who
has seen the Source of all manifestation and those who see only the
appearances of appearances.

Socrates asks his listeners to imagine a dark underground cave
where men are sitting chained, with their backs to a fire, before which
are paraded all sorts of figures, so that the shadow-projections of these
figures are shown on a wall before the eyes of the chained men. The
men chained do not see the actual figures moving behind them, but
only the shadows playing on the wall before them; and this they
regard as the true reality. Next, Socrates asks his listeners to imagine
the state of one who, breaking free from his bonds, was to look
'round and discover the fire and the figures and realize that his
previous estimate of reality had been very superficial and inadequate.
Then, says Socrates, suppose that this newly-freed man was to wander
upward, out of the cave altogether, and reach the light of day, and
discover the very Sun which is the source of that light; imagine his
delight and freedom compared to his previous state! "But then
imagine once more," says Socrates, "such a man suddenly coming
out of the Sunlight to be replaced in his old situation, would he not be
certain to have his eyes full of darkness?"

"To be sure," answered Glaucon.
"And if there were a contest, and he had to compete in
measuring the shadows with the prisoners who had never
moved out of the cave, while his sight was still weak and
before his eyes had become steady, ... would he not be ridicu-
lous? Men would say that up he went and down he came
without his eyes, and that it was better not even to think of
ascending; and if anyone tried to free another and lead him up
to the light, let them only catch the offender, and they would

put him to death."

"No question," he said.

"This entire image you may now apply, Glaucon, to the previous argument. The prison house is the world of sight, the light of the fire is the Sun, and you will not misapprehend me if you interpret the journey upward to be the ascent of the soul into the intelligible world [of the Spirit], according to my poor belief, which at your desire I have expressed -- whether rightly or wrongly God knows. But whether true or false, my opinion is that in the world of knowledge, the realm of "the Good" appears last of all and is seen only with an effort. And, when seen, It is also understood to be the universal Cause of all things beautiful and right, Father of light and Lord of light in this visible world, and the immediate Source of reason and truth in the intelligible world; and to be the Power on which he who would act rationally either in public or private life must have his eye fixed."

"I agree," said Glaucon, "as far as I can understand   you."

"Moreover," [said Socrates,] "you must not wonder that those who attain this height are unwilling to descend to human affairs; for their souls are always hastening into the upper world where they desire to dwell..." [2]

Thus did Socrates describe, in veiled terms, the state of his own consciousness; and thus did he prophecy the fate his contemporaries held in store for him.

In 405 B.C.E., after the Pelopponesian war and the Athenian defeat by Sparta, Athens was racked by internal civil war, and only in 403 B.C.E. settled back into her previous democratic government. A few of the perpetrators of this seditious war, who were among the famous "thirty" who had attempted to seize the government, had previously been frequent visitors to Socrates; and though he had no connection whatsoever with the political activities of these men, in the minds of some, Socrates was, as their previous mentor, the inspirer of their deeds. It was under such volatile circumstances that Socrates was brought to trial in 399 B.C.E. on charges of "disrespect for the gods whom the state recognizes, of introducing new divinities, and of corrupting the young." The penalty demanded was "death."

It was a private citizen, a self-righteous poet by the name of Meletus, who brought charges against Socrates, and who was supported in his suit by Anytus, a wealthy statesman, and another by the name of Lycon. In the courts of Athens at that time, any man could bring charges against another, and take him to court; which suit would be heard by a large jury made up of citizens drafted to serve in that capacity.   It is this trial and the subsequent condemnation and execution of Socrates which are the subject of some of the most exquisite and ennobling literature possessed of man.   Socrates, himself, wrote nothing, but his student, Plato, became his voice; creating some of the greatest works of Western philosophy ever made, Plato told the story of his beloved Socrates, immortalizing his life and his words in his recorded dialogues.

Socrates gave a beautiful speech in his own defense which is immortalized in Plato's *Apology*; in it, he points out that it is not Meletus, nor Anytus, who are his persecutors, but the jealousy and fear of the entire populace. "They have been fatal," says Socrates, "to a great many other innocent men, and I suppose will continue to be so; there is no likelihood that they will stop at me." [3]

Here is a portion of that speech of Socrates to his judges:

> Suppose, then, that you acquit me, and pay no attention to Anytus, who has said that either I should not have appeared before this court at all, or, since I have appeared here, I must be put to death, because if I once escaped, your sons would all immediately become utterly demoralized by putting the teaching of Socrates into practice. Suppose that, in view of this, you said to me, 'Socrates, on this occasion we shall disregard Anytus and acquit you, but only on one condition, that you give up spending your time on this quest and stop philosophizing. If we catch you going on in the same way, you shall be put to death.' Well, supposing, as I said, that you should offer to acquit me on these terms, I should reply: 'Gentlemen, I am your very grateful and devoted servant, but I owe a greater obedience to God than to you; and so long as I draw breath and have my faculties, I shall never stop practicing philosophy and exhorting you and elucidating the truth for everyone that I meet. I shall go on saying, in my usual way, "My very good friend,you are an Athenian and belong to a city which is the greatest and most famous in the world for its wisdom and strength. Are you not ashamed that you give your attention to acquiring as much money as possible, and similarly with reputation and honor, and give no attention or thought to Truth and understanding, and the perfection of your soul?" And if any of you disputes this and professes to care about these things, I shall not at once let him go or leave him; no, I shall question him and examine him and test him; and if it appears that, in spite of his profession, he has made no real progress towards goodness, I shall reprove him for neglecting

what is of supreme importance, and giving his attention to
trivialities. I shall do this to everyone that I meet, young or
old, foreigner or fellow-citizen; but especially to you, my
fellow-citizens, inasmuch as you are closer to me in kinship.

This I do assure you, is what my God commands;
and it is my belief that no greater good has ever befallen you
in this city than my service to my God; for I spend all my
time going about trying to persuade you, young and old, to
make your first and chief concern not for your bodies nor for
your possessions, but for the highest welfare of your souls,
proclaiming as I go, "Wealth does not bring goodness, but
goodness brings wealth and every other blessing, both to the
individual and to the state." Now, if I corrupt the young by
this message, the message would seem to be harmful; but if
anyone says that my message is different from this, he is
talking nonsense.

And so, gentlemen, I would say, 'You can please
yourselves whether you listen to Anytus or not; and whether
you acquit me or not, you know that I am not going to alter
my conduct, not even if I have to die a hundred deaths.' [4]

The jury, made up of Athenian citizens, nonetheless found
Socrates guilty as charged; and, perhaps offended by his offer to pay
a mere one-hundred drachmas as a fine, handed down the death
penalty to him. Socrates, before they led him away, had this to say:

You too, gentlemen of the jury, must look forward to
death with confidence, and fix your minds on this one belief,
which is certain: that nothing can harm a good man either in
life or after death, and his fortunes are not a matter of indifference to the gods. This present experience of mine has not
come about accidently; I am quite clear that the time had come
when it was better for me to die and be released from my distractions. That is why my sign [his guiding spirit] never
turned me back.

For my own part, I bear no grudge at all against those
who condemned me and accused me, although it was not with
this kind intention that they did so, but because they thought
that they were hurting me; and that is culpable of them. However, I ask them to grant me one favor. When my sons grow
up, gentlemen, if you think that they are putting money or
anything else before goodness, take your revenge by plaguing
them as I plagued you; and if they fancy themselves for no
reason, you must scold them just as I scolded you, for neglect-
ing the important things and thinking that they are good for
something when they are good for nothing. If you do this, I

shall have had justice at your hands, both I myself and my
children.

Now it is time that we were going, I to die, and you
to live; but which of us has the happier prospect is unknown
to anyone but God. [5]

It was necessary, however, for Socrates to wait nearly a month
in jail before his execution, due to the occurrance of a holiday
commemorating the ancient tribute of young men paid to king Minos,
and during which no executions were allowed. So, while he awaited
the return of the ships from Delos marking the end of the holiday,
Socrates spent his time with his friends and disciples who were allowed
to visit with him in his cell. At last, the day of execution arrived; a cup
of hemlock was brought to him by a guard, and Socrates
unhesitatingly took and drained the cup. Phaedo, who narrates the
story of Socrates' last hours in Plato's *Phaedo*, tells what happened
after that:

Up till this time most of us had been fairly successful in keeping back our tears; but when we saw that he was
drinking, that he had actually drunk it, we could do so no
longer; in spite of myself the tears came pouring out, so that I
covered my face and wept broken-heartedly -- not for him, but
for my own calamity in losing such a friend. Crito had given
up even before me, and had gone out when he could not re-
strain his tears. But Apollodorus, who had never stopped
crying even before, now broke out into such a storm of passionate weeping that he made eveyone in the room break down,
except Socrates himself, who said: "Really, my friends, what a
way to behave! Why, that was my main reason for sending
away the women, to prevent this sort of disturbance; because I
am told that one should make one's end in a tranquil frame of
mind. Calm yourselves and try to be brave."

This made us feel ashamed, and we controlled our
tears. Socrates walked about, and presently, saying that his
legs were heavy, lay down on his back -- that was what the
man [the guard] recommended. The man kept his hand on
Socrates, and after a little while examined his feet and legs;
then pinched his foot hard and asked if he felt it. Socrates said
no. Then he did the same to his legs; and moving gradually
upwards in this way let us see that he was getting cold and
numb. Presently he felt him again and said that when it
reached the heart, Socrates would be gone.

The coldness was spreading about as far as his waist
when Socrates uncovered his face -- for he had covered it up --
and said (they were his last words): "Crito, we ought to offer a

cock to Asclepius. See to it, and don't forget."

"No, it shall be done," said Crito. "Are you sure that there is nothing else?"

Socrates made no reply to this question, but after a little while he stirred; and when the man uncovered him, his eyes were fixed. When Crito saw this, he closed his mouth and eyes.

Such, Echecrates, was the end of our comrade, who was, we may fairly say, of all those whom we knew in our time, the bravest and also the wisest and most upright man. [6]

Here is what his contemporary admirer, Xenophon, had to say of Socrates after his death:

> Of all who knew Socrates and what he was like, all those who seek virtue even now continue to long for him, for he was the most helpful in aiding them in their quest for virtue. To me, as I describe what Socrates was like, he was so reverent that he could do nothing without counsel from the gods; so just that he never hurt anyone at all, but aided all who dealt with him; so self-controlled that he never chose pleasures in place of something better; so prudent that he never erred in distinguishing what was better from what was worse, and he never needed another's counsel, but was independent in his decisions about good and evil, and skilled in testing others, showing them their mistakes, and urging them toward virtue and true nobility. He seemed to be what the noblest and happiest man would be. And if anyone is not satisfied with this, let him compare the character of other men with what I have described, and then let him judge. [7]

Socrates was a true and devoted "son" of God; he had known the eternal Truth of the universe, but like the hypothetical 'liberated man' in his parable of the Cave, he was constrained to show men the way out of darkness in very cautious and considered ways. To many, the figure of Socrates remains a mystery, but to the knowers of God, his teaching and the manner of his life are clear as crystal, and he is dearly beloved; for only those who have trod the same path and realized the same Truth can know how pure was his soul and how wonderful his task in life and in death.

Here are a few selected quotes from Socrates as preserved by his disciple, Plato:

> The Ruler of the universe has ordered all things with a view to the excellence and preservation of the whole; and

each part, as far as may be, does and suffers what is proper to
it. And one of these portions of the universe is thine own,
unhappy man, which, infinitesimal though it be, is ever striving towards the whole; and you do not seem to be aware that
this and every other creation is in order that the life of the
whole may be blessed; and that you are created for the sake of
the whole, and not the whole for the sake of you. [8]

As for the sovereign part of the human soul, we
should consider that God gave it to be the Divinity in each
one, it being that which, inasmuch as we are a plant not of an
earthly but a heavenly growth, raises us from earth to our
brethren in heaven.
When one is always occupied with the cravings of
desire and ambition which he is eagerly striving to satisfy, all
his thoughts must be mortal, and, as far as it is possible to become such, he must be mortal every whit, because he has
made great his mortal part. But he who has been earnest in the
love of knowledge and true wisdom, and has exercised his intellect more than any other part, must have thoughts immortal
and divine. If he attains Truth, in so far as human nature is
capable of sharing in immortality, he must altogether be immortal. And since he is ever cherishing the divine power, and
has duly honored the Divinity within, he will be supremely
happy. [9]

The true lover of knowledge is always striving after
Being -- that is his nature; he will not rest at those multitudinous particular phenomena whose existence is in appearance
only, but will go on -- the keen edge will not be blunted, nor
the force of his passion abate until he have attained the knowledge of the true nature of all essence by a sympathetic and
kindred power in the soul. And by that power, drawing near
and becoming one with very Being, ... he will know and truly
live and increase. Then, and only then, will he cease from his
travail. [10]

The immortality of the soul is demonstrated by many
proofs; but to see it as it really is -- not as we now behold it,
marred by communion with the body and other miseries -- you
must contemplate it with the eye of reason in its original purity; and then its beauty will be revealed. [11] ... When a person
starts on the discovery of the Absolute by the light of the
reason only, without the assistance of the senses, and never
desists until by pure intelligence he arrives at the perception of
the absolute Good, he at last finds himself at the end of the
intellectual world... [12]

Of that Heaven which is above the heavens what earthly poet ever did or ever will sing worthily? It is such as I will describe; for I must dare to speak the truth, when Truth is my theme. There abides the very Being with which true knowledge is concerned; the colorless, formless, intangible Essence visible only to mind, the pilot of the soul. ... Every soul which is capable of receiving the food proper to it rejoices at beholding Reality. ... She beholds Knowledge absolute, not in the form of generation or of relation, which men call existence, but Knowledge absolute in Existence absolute. [13]

To find the Father and Maker of this universe is most difficult, and, to declare Him, after having found Him, is impossible. [14]

A man must have knowledge of the Universal, formed by collecting into a unity by means of reason the many particulars of sense; this is the recollection of those things which our soul once saw while following God -- when, regardless of that which we now call being, it raised its head up towards true Being. And therefore the mind of the philosopher alone has wings; and this is just, for he is always, as far as he is able, clinging in recollection to those things in which God abides, and in beholding which, he is what He [God] is. And he who employs aright these memories is ever being initiated into perfect mysteries and he alone becomes truly perfect. But since he stands apart from human interests and is rapt in the Divine, the vulgar deem him mad and do not know he is inspired. [15]

He who would be dear to God must, as far as is possible, become like Him. Wherefore the temperate man and the just is the friend of God, for he is like Him.
And this is the conclusion -- that for the good man to ... continually hold converse with God by means of prayers and every kind of service, is the noblest and the best of things, and the most conducive to a happy life. [16]

This is that life above all others which man should live, ... holding converse with the true Beauty, simple and divine. In that communion only beholding Beauty with the eye of the mind, he will be enabled to bring forth, not images of beauty, but Reality [Itself]; ... and bringing forth and nourishing true virtue, to become the friend of God and be immortal, if mortal man may. Would that be an ignoble life? [17]

Socrates' Successors

Since Socrates wrote nothing, we must rely primarily on the *Dialogues* of his student, Plato (d. 347 B.C.E.) for a formulation of his teachings. But Plato was not a mystic like his master; he was a thinker. And, as so often happens when one who has not "seen" attempts to convey the teachings of a seer, a great deal is lost, and a great deal of speculation and outright misinterpretation becomes added to the original teachings. We see this same phenomenon occurring much later with the remolding of the teachings of Jesus by Paul and others of his unillumined disciples.

Plato elaborated from the mystical teachings of Socrates a full-fledged metaphysical philosophy. How much of it he invented on his own is impossible to say; but it is *his* name which is rightly attached to the metaphysical system he taught at his Academy. Plato sought to describe in detail the manner and means whereby the Divinity manifests the phenomenal world through Its universal Ideas. According to him, these Ideas have their own subtle forms independent of what we know as material forms, yet which produce and support the forms of the material world. He held that all particular forms, thoughts, and acts approach perfection only insofar as they approach fidelity with those original Ideal forms. It was a notion born, not of vision, but of imaginative speculation; yet it was a notion which seemed to answer some important questions, and which fired the imagination of later philosophers as well. It offered an explanation of God's methodology which could be comprehended by the mind of man; yet, in that very attempt to fit the magical manifestory-Power of God into words comprehensible to man, all but the slightest resemblance to Reality was lost.

Plato was succeeded, indirectly, by Aristotle (384-322 B.C.E.), who revolted against many of Plato's concepts, and founded his own school, the Lyceum, where he taught doctrines at yet a further remove from the mystical vision of Socrates. It is not our aim here to go into the details of the philosophies of these two men; suffice it to say that, while both upheld the idea that it was possible to attain union with and supramental knowledge of Divinity, neither had actually done so. Both, constitutionally, were thinkers, philosophers, systematists; and the names of both remain to this day synonymous with 'the epitome of intellectual attainment.'

The works of both Plato and Aristotle are magnificent monuments to the power and achievement possible to the human intellect. They analyzed and argued and deduced with a fine-tuned logic and perspicacity that has awed and inspired generations of thinkers down through the years; but while they thought much, they never came to *know*. Their lifelong efforts never brought them to the ultimate vision of Truth. It has often been said that the narrow mountain path of the mystic's ascent begins where the philosopher's broad highway leaves off. And this is true, for once that road of intellectual discrimination has led one to infer the divine nature of one's own being, one has reached its furthest access and arrived at the point of departure. From that point on, the road leads only in circles.

From there, the leap (facilitated by grace) must be made to a steeper and less-travelled path of inner devotion if one is to reach the summit of knowledge. The brave sojourner on this path walks quite alone, yet he is moved by an inward grace which lures him on by whisperings and carresses of love, inspiring in him a burning desire for the meeting with his Beloved at his journey's end. That summit, which is God, is hidden from the philosophers and known to the pure in heart. If one is to become a truly wise man, one must come (by His grace) to know God. For in that knowledge is true certainty and wisdom which sheds its light on all mankind, while those who presume to teach philosophy without that God-revealed knowledge, however well-meaning their endeavor, succeed, for the most part, in engendering only doubt and confusion in the world.

ZENO OF CITIUM

Zeno (333-261 B.C.E.) was not a Greek, but a Semite, a Jew from Phoenicia. He came to Athens as a young merchant, bringing a cargo of Tyrian (purple) die, and stayed to study philosophy. Plato's Academy was still flourishing, and Aristotle's Peripatetics, the Pyrrhics, Cynics, Skeptics and Epicureans were all philosophizing in Athens at this time. Zeno studied with various schools for twenty years, and then began to teach on his own. His favorite spot for teaching his philosophy was a portico or porch (*stoa* in Greek), where he spoke so often he became known as "the Stoic." But he lived in a time of Athenian decadence; students of philosophy were made up almost entirely of an elegant elite, who were cultivated, wealthy, and isolated from the reality of the practical world. The golden age of Greece was long past; Alexander had recently died, and his generals were vying for leadership. It was a time of great unrest and demoralization, a time when the wisdom of sages past was calcified in formalized doctrines to be taught in schools.

As Zeno left no written works, it is difficult to say with certainty whether or not he was a genuine mystic; but the Greek Stoics who claimed him as the originator of their teachings, including Cleanthes, Chrysippus and Posidonius, taught what must certainly be regarded as "mystical philosophy." It is impossible to say, without any personal claims to enlightenment on their part, whether they borrowed the whole of their cosmology from earlier mystical philosophers such as Heraclitus, Socrates, Empedocles and Anaxagorus, or whether any of them actually had direct knowledge of the Truth. There is no doubt that their teachings were very much in keeping with the truths realized by the mystics, but it is possible that those teachings represented mere philosophical positions, rather than realized truths; tenets of faith, rather than certainties of knowledge.

The Stoics regarded the universe as a manifestation of the divine Logos, a manifestation in which "all things are bound together with one another." Chryssipus, a follower of Zeno, asserted that "no particular event, not even the smallest, can take place otherwise than in accordance with universal Nature and its laws." While this precept is definitely in keeping with the mystic's vision, to many, the strict determinism which this position implied was unacceptable. And when others, including the Epicureans and Aristotelians, sought to preserve the notion of chance and spontaneity in Nature, the Stoics postulated "hidden causes" to account for what appeared to be chance occurrances, much as Einstein was later to do against the indeterminists, Bohr and Heisenberg.

While the fragmentary writings of the Stoics are facinating for their adaptation and rationalization of mystical thought, they seem to represent intellectually adopted, rather than mystically perceived, truths; and the lives of the Stoics themselves seem rather the lives of professional philosophers than of sages. Nonetheless, they offered an extremely sophisticated presentation of the mystical philosophy of unity, and were greatly responsible, during their time, for the popularization and dissemination of the perennial wisdom of the mystics.

PHILO JUDAEUS

The death of Alexander in 323 B.C.E. marked the end of the glory days of Greece; and with his death, the port-city of Alexandria in Egypt, which he founded and which bears his name, became, under the Ptolemys, one of the greatest cities in all the Mediterranean world. It was, for several centuries thereafter, the recognized center, not only of shipping and commerce, but of culture, learning and philosophy as well.

Under the Ptolemys, the Museum Library of Alexandria grew to contain more than 700,000 scrolls, and included all the great classical works of antiquity. In 272 C.E. the main library was destroyed by the Roman Emperor Lucius Aurelianus, but much of the collection of classical works was saved by removing it to the nearby Temple of Serapis. In 391 C.E., under the Roman Emperor, Theodosius, the Christians, wishing to obliterate all centers of pagan (non-Christian) learning and culture, burned the remaining collection of classical literature, accomplishing the virtual elimination of all recorded thought of the remote past. It is for that reason that today we possess only scraps and pieces of scattered lines from the great mystics and philosophers of antiquity, along with bits of hearsay by later chroniclers who were, for the most part, indifferent or antipath-etic to them.

During Alexandria's more illustrious period, however (from the 3rd century B.C.E. to the first few centuries of the Current Era),

the city was a booming center of culture, a teeming metropolis, a true
"melting pot" of the civilized world. There, in peaceful co-existence,
lived Greeks, Romans, Egyptians, Syrians, Indians and Jews. The Jews
of Alexandria had originally been brought to Egypt as prisoners by
Ptolemy I (323-283 B.C.E.); a century later, they were freed by
Ptolemy Philadelphus and allowed to become a part of Alexandrian
society. Thereafter, they flourished and prospered, assimilating the
predominantly Greek culture to the point of writing and speaking
Greek, even in their synagogues. It was during this time that the
Hebrew Bible was translated into Greek (the Septuagint version), as so
few Jews any longer understood Hebrew.

It was in this mixed climate of Greek, Roman, and Jewish
culture that Philo Judaeus (20 B.C.E. to 40 C.E.) was born. During
his lifetime, one out of every ten citizens of Alexandria was a Jew, and
Philo was a member of one of the most wealthy and prominent of
Jewish families. His brother was the manager of the city's Jewish
export trade, and Philo, himself, was one of the respected leaders of
the Jewish community selected to lead a delegation of their people to
the Emperor, Caligula, in Rome. What more we know of him we learn
through his writings.

Philo was undoubtedly familiar with the tradition of Heraclitus and the Stoics, for he made ample use of their term, "Logos," to
explain his philosophy. But Philo spoke not merely as a philosopher; rather he spoke from his own experience of "the vision of
God." He wrote in Greek, and knew Greek philosophy well --
especially that of Plato; but he was foremost a Jew with rabbinical ties,
and was fiercely dedicated to reconciling Greek philosophy with
Judaism by showing that they were but two expressions of an identical
world-view.

His primary endeavor was to explain what he had come to
know in the vision of Unity, but this task was greatly compounded by
the fact that he was loyal to the Jewish scriptural tradition, a tradition
which did not believe in a God who could be "seen"; certainly not in
one with whom man could be united. Jews then, as now, relied heavily
on the sanctity of the ancient scriptures, believing them to be the
highest and final word on God's revelation to man. Philo had then to
first reconcile the Hebrew scriptures with what he had seen, to explain
away much of the anthropomorphism and dualism as mere allegory,
and to show that the God of Abraham and Moses was the same as the
Absolute of the Greek philosophers.

Much of what Philo wrote is almost unreadable today, not so much because of the difficulty of comprehending his theology, but because of the shere bulk of his work, and the many far-fetched interpretations he offers of the words and events of the Hebrew Bible. For example, according to Philo, the word, "Israel," as used in the Bible, when God tells Moses, "Israel is my first-born son," [1] refers not to the nation, but to those who have seen God. And "the people of Israel" refers to "those who are members of that race endowed with vision." In his eagerness to translate the cultural mythology of the Hebrews into a viable philosophy, he makes many such fantastic interpretations, and, contrary to his intentions, succeeds only in leaving his readers less convinced than before. Nonetheless, if we search deep into Philo's rambling exegesis of Hebrew scripture, we can find some of the most profound and authentic statements of the perennial mystical philosophy ever written.

Philo was an authentic "seer" of the Truth; and, in an attempt to unravel the knotted threads of confusion woven by both Greek and Jewish scholars, he expounded his vision as best he could, utilizing the terminologies of both Greek and Hebrew tradition. Like all seers before and since, he explained that the unitive Reality, experienced in the contemplative state, is both transcendent and immanent. In Its transcendent aspect, It is ever-one, unmoving, un-changing; and in Its immanent aspect, It is the active, creative principle, which manifests as the universe of form and substance. The transcendent and absolute aspect he calls "Pure Being"; and, borrowing from Heraclitus and the Stoics, he calls the active, manifestory-Power by the name, "Logos":

> That aspect of Him which transcends His powers can-
> not be conceived of at all in terms of place, but only as pure
> Being; but that power of His (the Logos) by which He made
> and ordered all things ... pervades the whole and passes through
> all the parts of the universe. [2]

The Absolute, or "pure Being," is, of course, the primary Reality; It is the pure Consciousness in which the manifestory-Power, the Logos, inheres -- similar to the way in which the power of thought inheres in the human consciousness. Like many seers before him, Philo characterizes these two aspects of the One as masculine and feminine:

> The supremely generic is God, the next is the Logos

of God; [3] ... That which comes after God, even if it were the
most venerable of all other things, holds second place, and was
called feminine in contrast to the Creator of the universe, who
is masculine, ... [4]

Philo explained that the God of the Hebrew scriptures is the
same as the immovable Absolute of which the Greek philosophers
spoke. The world is also God (*Theos*), he states, in that it is a manifestation of His Thought, or Logos. "The Logos," he explained, in
terms familiar to his Jewish readers, is "the first-born of God"; it is
that which "was conceived in God's mind before all things [were
formed], and is that which manifests as all things." [5] It is this, says
Philo, that is described in the Hebrew scriptures as the "Word" of
God, the "Wisdom" [*Chokmah*] of God, and the "Spirit" of God;
all of these, he says, are synonymous terms for the "Logos."

The Logos, Philo also points out, is the same as the totality of
"Ideas," of which Plato spoke, and the same as the *logoi spermatikoi*
of the Stoics, and the same as the "angelic powers" spoken of in the
rabbinical mythologies. Had he known of the writings of the Indian
sages, he might have added that the divine Logos is the same as what is
meant by the terms, *Prakrti, Maya,* and *Shakti.* It is co-equal and co-
eternal with the absolute God; is, in fact, identical with Him, being His
own creative Power by which the world of form comes into being and
of which it is constituted. The Logos, says Philo, flows out from God
as "a breath of His own Divinity"; the soul of man, therefore, is " a
part of [the one] great divine and blessed Soul ..., a part not separated
from its Source, for no part of the Divine is truly cut off so as to exist
apart; it is only an extension." [6]

This truth of the Divine Identity of the soul is clearly apprehended in the mystical vision; but no matter how well or how often the
Reality experienced in contemplation is described, It remains unknown and a matter for speculation to those who have not directly
perceived It. Philo made it clear that one could actually "see" and
experience God for oneself. He made a distinction between the
knowledge which was simply a formulation of the mind, derived from
the evidence of the senses, and that knowledge (*gnosis*) which was
directlly obtained in the transcendent vision of God. The first, he
says, is derived "from created things, as one may learn of a substance
by watching its shadow"; [7] the second is obtained when the mind,
"having risen above and beyond creation, obtains a clear vision of the

uncreated One, so, from oneness with Him, to apprehend Himself and also His shadow, which is the Logos and the world created by It." [8]

Like others who have been graced with the vision of Truth, Philo loved to speak of It, and to show others the way to It. Despite the censure of traditional Jews, Philo could not help proclaiming that God could actually be seen and known in all certainty, and that it is the highest victory of the soul to attain that vision. Here are a few illustrative selections from his writings:

> God is high above place and time ... He is contained by nothing, but transcends all. *But though transcending what He has made, nonetheless, He filled the universe with Himself.* (My italics.) ... When, therefore, the God-loving soul searches into the nature of the Existent, he enters on a quest of That which is beyond matter and beyond sight. And out of this quest there accrues to him a great boon -- to comprehend the incomprehensible God. [9]

> He who is escaping from God flees to himself; [but] he who escapes from his own mind flees to the Mind of the universe, confessing that all things of the human mind are vain and unreal, and attributing everything to God. [10]

> He who has completely understood himself renounces himself completely, when he has seen the nothingness of all that is created. [11]

> ... Without Divine grace it is impossible to leave the ranks of mortality; [but] when grace fills the soul, it is possessed and inspired, ... and hastens to that most glorious and loveliest of visions, the vision of the Uncreated. [12]

> The soul, stirred to its depths and maddened by heavenward yearning, [is] drawn by the truly Existent Being and pulled upward by Him. [13]

> ... It is the characteristic of him who would see God not to leave the holy warfare without his crown, but to persevere till he reaps the prize of victory. And what victory garland more fitting or woven of rarer flowers than the clear and unalloyed vision of Him who IS. It is a worthy conflict that lies before the striving soul: to win eyes for the clear vision of Him Whom alone it is worth man's while to see. [14]

> ... Go up, then, O soul, to the vision of Him who IS -- go up quietly, mindfully, willingly, fearlessly, lovingly [15]

... [for] to know God is the highest happiness, and immortal
life. [16]

    ... It is worth more than all wealth, private or public.
For if the sight of elders or holy teachers, rulers or parents,
moves one to reverence and modesty and zeal for a pure life,
how great a support for virtue in our soul shall we find, who
have learnt to pass beyond all things created, and to see That
which is uncreated and divine, the highest good, the greatest
Joy; nay, to speak the truth, That which is greater than the
greatest, more beautiful than the greatest beauty, more blessed
than the most blessed, more joyful than the joyfulest; aye,
more perfect than any words such as these [can tell]. [17]

Philo is generally recognized by modern scholars as a major
thinker of his day, but the depth and scope of his wisdom is, alas, little
appreciated. He formulated, in every particular, the perennial philosophy of mysticism as clearly and unequivocally as a Plotinus, a
Shankara, or an Eckhart. Yet the wisdom of Philo has made little
mark upon the world; his mystical knowledge has been, through the
centuries, little regarded. The profundity of his vision is perhaps too
deeply buried in the verbiage of his prolific works, and too obscured
by his overwhelming determination to rationalize the anthropomorphism of the Judaic scriptures and to see mystical symbolism in merely
historical narratives. It seems that, in his desire to reconcile the Judaic
scriptures with Greek philosophy, he succeeded only in alienating his
fellow Jews by his catholicity, and his fellow philosophers by his
Jewish orthodoxy. Ironically, his greatest influence was upon neither
of these factions, but upon a religious sect which, during his lifetime,
was just in the process of being born.
    While the traditional Jews of his time and after found little use
for Philo's mystical thoughts, and frowned upon them, the Christian
Fathers and the Gnostics of the 1st and 2nd centuries of the Current
Era found in them the basis for their theology; wholeheartedly
adopting his vision of the two-in-One, they established upon it their
own Christian creed. John, the author of the Fourth Gospel of Christ,
written about 90 C.E., began his work with these words:

    In the beginning was the Logos; the Logos was with
God, and the Logos *was* God. ... All things were made by the
Logos; without him nothing was made. It was by him that all
things came into existence. [18]

JESUS OF NAZARETH

By the end of the 1st century B.C.E., while Greek culture was still widely influential, the entire Mediterranean world was under Roman rule. The mystical philosophy of unity had been thoroughly expounded and re-expounded by the Roman Stoics, and the unitive vision had also been well represented by the Brahmin and Buddhist emissaries living in Greece, Rome and Alexandria. But, while it is one thing to hear of and understand the unity of all existence, it is quite another to actually realize it in oneself. The former is the province of the philosophers and theologians; the latter is the province of the saints and sages.

In Judea, in the early years of the Current Era, during the Roman occupation of that land, there lived in the town of Nazareth in the region of Galilee, a young Jew by the name of Joshua bar Joseph, known as *Jesus* by the Greeks, who was to become just such a saint. He was a carpenter by trade, but from his early youth he had felt a strong urge to understand the mysteries of life, and had studied both the Hebrew scriptures and those books of other traditions which he could find. Around the age of twenty-eight (when the planet Saturn returns to its natal position, and a young man becomes turned to his life's work), Jesus became strongly drawn to spiritual devotion; his mind became filled with a new and subtle understanding of God, and consequentially a sweet thrilling love for God filled his heart.

The world of his people was in great foment and political upheaval, and while he was not unaware of the tyranny of the Roman state and the various rebel factions striving for liberation from its yoke, his mind was more concerned with a different kind of liberation. He felt deeply that peace and goodwill among men was something that could only be obtained by a personal attunement with peace and love in the heart of each individual man. The answer to the suffering of man was not in attempting to forcefully change society from without, but lay rather in the transformation of the mind and the heart from within. Antagonism and warfare only seemed to lead to more of the same, and to the increasing of bitterness in the heart; but the true happiness and peace of man could be found only within himself, through dedication to the satisfying love of God, by which a man might manifest in himself the presence of God on earth.

It was a time of great trouble and bitterness for his people, and everywhere men were shouting for revolution and bloodshed; but there were also many whose understanding was like his own. In religious communities and spiritual brotherhoods, they lived the contemplative life of prayer, study and service, engaging in the inner warfare of the soul, and endeavoring to become perfect, loving, and increasingly aware of God's joyful presence within. Some were known as Essenes, others called themselves Gnostics ("Knowers"); and there were yet others who lived alone in the wilderness outside the cities, following the contemplative life and teaching those who would listen that man's true salvation in this life lay in the inner communion with God, and the conformation of one's life to His will of love.

One such solitary teacher was a man named John, who was known as "the Baptist," for his practice of baptizing aspirants to the inner life in the river Jordan. He preached the necessity of an inner transformation which began with a true, heartfelt remorse for one's own past wickedness; for, he said, it was only in the spirit of repentance that a man could purify his heart and be prepared in humility to approach God in inner prayer.

Jesus, listening to the preaching of this man on the banks of the Jordan, understood the truth of what he said, and went forward to accept the symbolic baptism into a new life of the spirit. And when he was baptised by John, who had accumulated by his austere and devout lifestyle a divine power of influence, Jesus felt such a thrill of joy, such an opening of his consciousness, that it seemed the very heavens had opened up to reveal the living presence of God. God's grace flooded his entire body and mind, and that grace was revealed to his inner eye in the form of a white dove entering his heart with a great fluttering and showering of light.

From that time forward, Jesus was inspired with a new delight in God, and a fervent desire to draw near to Him and to know Him within himself. And he felt a great need to be alone in order to focus all his mind on the Lord who had so bountifully graced him with vision and inward joy. So he took himself into the solitude of the desert wilderness outside the city. Filled with certainty that God was drawing him to yet clearer vision, he swept away all concern for his own bodily welfare and went alone into the rocky wastelands, to pray and to seek the clear vision of God within himself.

During one star-filled night, deeply drawn into a silent prayer of longing, Jesus suddenly became awake to a clear, still awareness; his mind was lifted beyond itself into a pure, eternal, Consciousness. He had become one with the Mind of the universe. In that exalted awareness, there was no longer a Jesus and his God, but a one, all-pervading, Reality which had no division in it at all. He had entered what he was later to call, "the kingdom of God," and knew himself as the one Being existing in all. He knew the unsurpassably joyful truth that he was, and had always been, the one Existence that lives in every single form on this earth, animating them all as by a magic projection of Himself onto a universal screen. He was the eternal Soul of all, appearing as all, yet beyond all, unaffected by the play of all these infinite forms. Gone were all illusions; gone was all suffering and confusion; he was eternally present, yet eternally free, eternally unchanging and untouched by the fortunes or misfortunes of the world.

By morning, Jesus had come back to his limited self, but the knowledge of his infinite and eternal Self still flooded his mind, and he bathed in the intoxicating afterglow of that knowledge. He had been released of every delusion, fear, and source of pain that man is subject to in this world. 'Had anyone else ever experienced such a state?' he wondered. The ancient prophets of Israel had said nothing of such an experience! Compared to what he had seen, the scriptures were like the babbling of children. 'Am I the only one to have known this incredible Truth?' he wondered; 'Dear God, am I the messenger, the Messiah, whom the people await?' Such were undoubtedly the thoughts that swirled through Jesus' mind on that day.

It is unlikely that a young laboring-class Palestinian of those times, raised and educated in the Jewish tradition, would have had a great deal of access to the small body of mystical lore then existing. The books of the Jewish prophets bore little in the way of insightful testimonies of the mystical experience; and without some acquaintance with Vedantic, Buddhist, Platonic or Pythagorean doctrines, Jesus would have been ill-prepared for the startling revelation that came to him on that fateful night. With no knowledge of those others before him who had experienced such an enlightenment and had known their eternal Identity, Jesus could scarcely avoid the conclusion that he was uniquely endowed, that he was indeed the one chosen to be the Messiah whose mission on earth had been prophesied for centuries in the holy literature of his people. He had been shown beyond a shadow of a doubt that he was an embodiment of the Father, that his eternal Identity was the infinite Source of all existence. 'How shall I not speak of this saving knowledge?' he asked; 'How shall I not take on the role of Messiah, and announce the Truth to everyone who will hear?'

Jesus remained in the wilderness for several days more, exulting in the knowledge and joy which flooded his mind, and praising God for His wondrous gift; and then he made his way back to the city of Jerusalem. After refreshing himself, he went to the great temple of the city, and, climbing to the top of it by the stairs, he looked out over the housetops and the people moving in the streets with an awed, yet troubled, vision. 'I am all these objects and beings,' he thought; ' yet I am forever beyond all appearances. Who will believe such a thing? I, myself, would not believe it if I had not experienced it for myself! Such knowledge came to me only through the grace of God -- so what can I think to teach to others? Better if I were to end this life now, to cast myself from this parapet, and return at once to my eternal home.' But he realized that he had no choice; he had received a mandate, an assignment, to play out his role on this earth as a revealer of the truth to others. There was no way to turn away from this, his God-ordained destiny.

Soon after, Jesus began visiting his old comrades, and speaking to them of what he had realized in the wilderness. The radiance on his face and the certainty of his words had a profound effect upon them. Some believed that, indeed, he might well be the Messiah; others only wondered at the strange delusion of the young carpenter from Nazareth whom they had known previously as a good, level-headed, young man. And as Jesus went about teaching his friends and those he met, many, having heard of his holy transformation, came to see him out of curiosity; others, believing he had been graced by God, came to be blessed or cured of their illnesses. And, in a short time, Jesus had become a notorious celebrity in the city; to some, an illumined teacher, to others, an inspired healer and prophet, and to some scornful onlookers, a pretentious scalliwag and nuisance.

But Jesus continued to teach what he knew to be the truth, heedless of how others viewed him. One day, after announcing that he would give a sermon on the nearby hill, called the Mound of Olives, he climbed to the top of that hill and spoke to the people who had gathered to hear him. He explained, in his gentle but commanding way, of how he had experienced the kingdom of God, and of how they too could know that infinite realm: "The kingdom of God is not far away in the heavens," he told them; "it is near, it is at hand, within your very selves. Those of you who truly long for Him, sorrow for Him, in the emptiness and poverty of your hearts, will surely be blessed with His vision. The kingdom of God belongs to those who become as little children before God. Those who sorrow for Him will be comforted; those who thirst for Him, and purify their hearts for the beholding of Him, will have their thirst quenched and their hunger satisfied.

"The purification of the heart," he told them, "consists firstly in the heartfelt repentence for past wrongs done, and the determination to root out all unrighteousness, all deeds and thoughts which go counter to your love for all as embodiments of yourself. When your heart has become pure, and your mind becomes utterly dependent upon and fully surrendered to Him, you will see God. If you understand that all men are God's own, you will not stir men against one another, but will make peace between men. Such peacemakers are the true sons of God.

"But do not thnk such a task is easy," he warned them; "there are many who will not understand, and they will persecute you. But endure; for those who are persecuted because of their devotion to truth, will yet enjoy the reward of heavenly joy. Be happy to endure the persecutions of men, for your reward is in the perfection of your soul, by which you will be drawn nearer and nearer to the realization of God."

And he explained to them that it was not his intention to alter the ancient Jewish faith, or the laws of Moses, but rather to bring them to their fulfillment, their culmination, in the direct realization of God. It is not merely the letter of the law which is to be obeyed as a sort of imposed duty, he told them, but rather the laws are to be followed as a means of purifying the heart and the mind; for it is the mind and heart which must be purified in order to experience the kingdom of God.

Like the Buddha in far-off India, Jesus had been born into a religious tradition which taught only the preliminary stages of the religious life, and had lost sight of the ultimate purpose and goal of those practices. It was because the purpose and reason of a pure life was forgotten or unknown, that so many of his people had begun to doubt the wisdom of the moral laws; for, without an understanding of their purpose and fulfillment, such laws make little sense to men. Without understanding the ultimate purpose of the remembrance of God, and the restraint of the mind and senses, who would undertake the struggle and hardship of a spiritual life?

"Prayer," said Jesus, "is not meant for the appproval of men, but for the ascent of the mind to the awareness of the presence of God. It is to Him and for Him alone that prayer is to be directed, for He is the goal and reward of prayer." And he taught them the way to pray to God: "Regard Him as your beloved Father; remember Him every moment by singing His name in your heart; and when you pray to Him in solitude and silence, ask Him to open His kingdom to you. Say to Him: 'Our Father, who art beyond the earth and the heavens, holy is Thy name. Let me enter into Thy kingdom, if it be Thy will, for Thy will is done here on earth as well as in heaven. Grant us this day our daily bread, and forgive us our past sins, as we forgive those who have sinned against us. Lead us, not into temptation, but to freedom from all evil thoughts, so we may enter into Thy eternal kingdom and know Thy power and Thy glory.'

"If you truly love God," said Jesus, "your mind will be with God, and if you love the world, your mind will be with the world. Your mind cannot go in two directions at once, but goes singly to that which you most love." And, remembering his own experience in the wilderness, he told them, "If a man truly loves God, and is filled with the divinely-inspired longing for Him, such a man need not concern himself about what he will eat or wear. If God draws him to the knowledge of Himself, no harm can come to him; he will not starve or go naked. Does not God know the needs of His own, and supply them with everything? Seek first and foremost the kingdom of God, and all the rest will be taken care of. You need not concern yourself to supply your future needs, for each day God will be near at hand to guide you and provide for you.

"It is our own minds we must be concerned with," said Jesus, "if we would know God. Of what use is it to look to correct others when what is needful is the correction of our own wayward minds! It is only by the perfection of our own souls that we can come to the threshold of the kingdom of God. And if your desire for Him is sufficient, His door will be opened, and you will see Him face to face. Knock, and He will open His door to you; seek Him and you will find Him.

"Yet do not imagine that it is an easy road to God. No; the path to Him is strait and narrow, difficult to tread. It is as narrow as the edge of a sword, and there are few who attain the goal. But I have known Him, and I can show you the way. Not all of you who call yourselves my followers will reach His kingdom, but only those who truly follow the will of God within themselves. Not merely by pretending to follow a teacher's words can that vision be obtained, but only by those who sincerely strive to reach Him with all their hearts."

And when he had finished, the people listening to Jesus were astounded, for they could tell by what he said that he had truly attained to God, and that he spoke not merely from a learned know-ledge, but with the authority of one who had actually experienced the Truth for himself.

Later, when Jesus was alone with a few of his most ardent disciples, he spoke to them more particularly of the nature of God and of man. "You have read in the Psalms," he said to them, "that man is the son of God; and it is true, we are born of God, and we are truly God in essence, and so we are His own. When I say that I am the son of God, understand that what is meant is that I am of the Father and am in the Father. He is in me and I am in Him. Truly, I and the Father are one. When you have realized the Truth, you too will know your oneness with God. Yet, as beings on earth, we are 'sons' of God, for all this world is born of that one eternal Father in whom we live and move and have our being.

"Some of you will understand, and make your way to the vision of God; others will not. My words I plant in your hearts as seeds; and if that seed is planted in fertile ground, it will spring up into life, but if it is planted in rocky soil, it will die without bearing fruit. The vision of God is like a hidden treasure; some will renounce all other pursuits to find it, while others, though they hear of it, will not seek it, and will not find it." And all of the disciples who heard his words vowed to nourish and cultivate them in their hearts.

Jesus then travelled with a few of his disciples to the sea-coast cities of Tyre and Sidon, and to other villages about the region, teaching and blessing the people he met. But when at laast he returned to the great city of Jerusalem, and began speaking there, he was increasingly confronted by the many rabbis and orthodox Jewish citizens who were offended by his teachings. They were jealous to guard their own authority and their own hallowed traditions, and Jesus seemed to pose a threat to both. But more than that, what Jesus taught threatened their values, their very conception of life's purpose and duty. God was to be worshipped in the synagogues, and to be remembered for His blessings; but to seek to know God was more than they were prepared to do. This 'other-worldliness' which Jesus taught seemed cowardly and unworthy of "real" men, in their eyes, and they feared that their children would be corrupted by it, ruining all chances of their worldly success. Furthermore, that an unlettered and obviously impractical man like Jesus should claim a direct knowledge of God was preposterous and against all the teachings of the prophets of their religion.

Thus, Jesus was faced with the perennial challenge of the mystic-teacher: how to explain to those already established in their own learning, and convinced of their own wisdom, that there existed a knowledge and a wisdom above and beyond their own. The learned and degreed men of position were scarcely willing to listen to this young and impoverished vagabond, for they were, after all, the wisest and most learned men of the community, and it was they who were the teachers, the authorities. How it hurt their pride to be contradicted and taught by this young, naive, nobody!

Jesus quickly saw that it was impossible to pour new wine into vessels already filled to overflowing with their own proud learning and unyielding convictions. He preferred to teach only those who approached him humbly with openness and eagerness to learn; nonetheless, he was often faced by those closed-minded men who received his pearls of wisdom, not with a pure intent toward knowledge, but with a rancor born of resentment and egotistical pride. They gave no true consideration to his words, and sought no true understanding, but maliciously sought only to refute him. They challenged him, not with reason, but with quotations from scriptures which they had learned. And, spurred by a contempt born of injured pride, they plotted amongst themselves to censure and discredit him. Wherever Jesus went to speak, he met with the growing hostility of such men. They were scholars, rabbis, and respectable men of position; and they planned among themselves to put an end to Jesus' mystical talk and his claims of Godhood.

Though Jesus had by now a presentiment that he would be arrested and probably killed by these men, he was entirely surrendered to God's will and to whatever destiny he had to face. And so the time came when he was accused, arrested, and tried by the orthodox Jewish leaders, who insisted that the Roman Procurator, Pontius Pilate, crucify him in the manner that was customary in those days for insurgents against the state. The Procurator, in order to appease these respected religious leaders and maintain harmony with the Jewish community he ruled, carried out their wishes; Jesus was tortured and executed in a particularly cruel manner at the instigation of his own people. But, instead of putting an end to his teachings, the death of Jesus served rather to inspire a popular religious movement which quickly grew to proportions beyond the wildest dreams of his persecutors.

Many legends grew around the heroic figure of Jesus, and within a very short time he was exalted by his followers to the status of "Only-begotten Son of God." In the literature that told of his life and death, written thirty to fifty years after he died on the cross, he had become much more than a sage or saint; he was the very person of God Himself, come down to deliver the world. Jesus had been humiliated, tortured, and utterly destroyed by the men of the world, and even while free of their persecutions, he suffered their rejection and lived as an outcaste, with scarcely a place to lay his head. Yet, to the wise, he was a mirror of God on earth, having shown, in his words and in his life, the arduous path of unyielding love. It is because of his life and teachings that, among all the sages, seers, and holy men whom the world has known, Jesus stands honored at the forefront. If any man ever deserved the title, "Son of God," it is he. For, as the personification of the Love which is God, he was the very instrument and voice of the Father of us all.

THE EARLY CHRISTIANS AND GNOSTICS

During the first few centuries following the death of Jesus, the entire Mediterranean world, from Rome to Tunis, from Athens to Alexandria, experienced a widespread outbreak of popular religious sects; Christians, Gnostics, Manichaens, Hermetics, Stoics and a host of other religious sects competed with one another for the ear of the populace. And since this period of religious fervor derived so much of its fundamental idealogy from the Greek heritage of mysticism, it is worthwhile to trace, briefly, the influence of mystical thought during these formative years on the theology of two of these religious sects: the Christians and the Gnostics.

The Early Christians

What we know today as the religion of Christianity began with a handful of Apostles, some of whom had actually been disciples of Jesus, and some who, like Paul of Tarsus (d. ca. 60 C.E.), had learned about Jesus and his teachings only after his martyrdom. During that first century after Jesus' death, the Apostles travelled far and wide, extolling Jesus as the greatest of teachers, a Savior who had taught the message of the soul's salvation through devotion to God. Despite prolonged persecutions and martyrdoms, the little band of Christians grew, thanks in great measure to the zealous leadership of Paul, a convert from orthodox Judaism, who was convinced that Jesus was, literally, the Son of God.

By the second century of the Christian era, hundreds of Christian communities flourished throughout the Mediterranean world, and the talents of the learned among them were put to the task of formulationg a coherent religious philosophy, a Christian theology, which would convincingly establish the divine origin of Jesus, the Christ (*Christos*, Greek for Messiah). It was necessarily a time for the building up of a bulwark of dogma by which the philosophical and theological position of Christianity would be clearly enunciated, so as both to unite all elements within the Christian community and to weed out those opinions deemed inconsistent with, and therefore heretical to, the "official" interpretation of the life and teachings of Jesus.

The Christian community had, among its more vocal proponents, a number of learned philosophers and theologians during this time, including Justin Martyr (d. ca. 165 C.E.), Clement of Alexandria (d. ca. 215 C.E.), and Origen (182-251 C.E.), all genuinely devout and earnest men. They seem not to have been mystics, however; they had not, themselves experienced God directly, but were interested primarily in rationalizing the Christian tenet of the divine authority of Jesus. Being well-learned also in the philosophical tradition of the Greeks, they were at pains as well to explain their theology in terms recognizable to the "pagan" world. As a means of accomplishing this, they adopted the Greek concept of the Logos, and asserted that Jesus was none other than the divine Logos of God.

Let us look for a moment at the progression of ideas and events which led to the whole-hearted adoption of this conception by the Christian Church. The idea first appears in the opening paragraph of the Fourth Gospel written about sixty years after the death of Jesus by the evangelist known only as John. John undoubtedly had some familiarity with the concept of the Logos, probably from Philo, and perhaps from Stoic sources as well. He began his Gospel with these words:

> In the beginning was the Logos; the Logos was with God, and the Logos *was* God.
> ... All things were made by the Logos; without him nothing was made. It was by him that all things came into existence.
> ... What came about in him [the Logos] was life, and the life was the light [of God] in man. The life shines in the darkness [of world-manifestation], but the darkness did not understand it. [1]

All this is in keeping with the mystical perception of duality-in-Unity enunciated by mystics of every time and place. John then goes on to assert that the Logos became Jesus of Nazareth:

> And the Logos became flesh and lived among us ...
> as the only-begotten son of his father. [2]

This statement, that the Logos became flesh in the person of Jesus, is also inarguable, as it is the Logos, the creative Energy of God, which has become flesh in the person of every creature on earth; and the phrase, "only-begotten son" is a designation for the Logos which goes back to Philo. But John seems to imply that Jesus was more than simply another manifestation of the Logos, that he was, indeed, the creative Energy itself. It was this very suggestion which gave immediate rise to a widespread movement among 2nd century Christians to regard Jesus as a special and unique manifestation of God, through whom the very Godhead lived and acted upon earth for the upliftment of humanity. But let us take a moment to recall the meaning of the term "Logos," as it had been traditionally used up to that time.

The Logos, as we have stated before, is synonymous with Prakrti, Maya, Shakti, and all those other terms which have been used over the centuries to denote the manifestory aspect of the transcendent Absolute. It is the Absolute in Its projected aspect of manifestory Power, or Energy, which appears to our eyes as the world of form. These two, the absolute Consciousness and Its projected Energy are one and inseparable, just as a mind and its thought are one and inseparable. Thus, Nature is God's Thought, or Logos, and is replete with Divinity, is nothing but Divinity; and is as much one and synonymous with God as the radiance of the Sun is with the Sun itself. The term, "Logos," had long been understood in this way, and it was in this way that it was understood and explained by Christians as well, such as Athenasius, Patriarch of Alexandria (293-372 C.E.):

> Was God, who IS, ever without the Logos? Was He, who is light, ever without radiance? ...God is, eternally; then, since the Father always is, His radiance also exists eternally; and that is His Logos. [3]
> ... For, as the light [of the Sun] illumines all things within its radiance, and without that radiance nothing would be illumined, so the Father wrought all things through the Logos, as by a hand. And He did not speak in order that some subordinate might hear, understand what the speaker wanted, and [then] go perform the task. This is what happens in human affairs. But the Logos of God *is* creator and maker; he *is* the Father's will. [4]

Athenagorus (2nd century C.E.), who wrote an Apology of Christianity to the Roman Emperor, Marcus Aurelius, also asserted the eternal co-existence and oneness of God, the Father, and His world-emanation, which he calls "the Son":

> If ... you ask what is meant by the Son, I will state briefly that he is the first product of the Father, not as having been brought into existence (for from the beginning, God, who is the eternal Mind has the Logos in Himself, being from

eternity instinct with Logos); but inasmuch as the Logos came
forth to be the Idea and energizing power of all material things. [5]

Tertullian (150-225 C.E.), another of the early Church Fathers, expressed the same idea in more simplified terms:

> The Spirit is the substance of the Logos, and the Logos
> is the activity of the Spirit; the two are a Unity (*unum*). [6]

These remarks by the early Church Fathers are identical with
the declarations of all the mystics who have, over the centuries, described their experience of the two complementary aspects of Reality.
But they went on, from this conventional observation, to formulate a
rather startling tenet of faith: that the Logos, the very manifestory
Power of God, took on a personality of its own, and lived on earth as
the man known as Jesus of Nazareth.   Here is how this idea was
expressed by one of the most influential of the early Church Fathers,
Ireneus, the bishop of Lyons (ca. 130-200 C.E.):

> The Logos existed in the beginning with God, and
> through him all things were made. He was always present
> with the human race, and in the last times, according to the
> time appointed by the Father, he has been united with his own
> handiwork and become man, capable of suffering.
> ... He was incarnate and made man; and then he
> summed up in himself the long line of the human race, procur-
> ing for us a comprehensive salvation, that we might recover in
> him what in Adam we had lost, the state of being in the image
> and likeness of God. [7]

At a later date, Athenasius, the Patriarch of Alexandria, added
some clarifying remarks to that, in order to explain how the Logos
could be working entirely through the person of Jesus while at the
same time manifesting the entire universe:

> The Logos was not confined solely within [Jesus']
> body; nor was he there and nowhere else; he did not activate
> that body and leave the universe emptied of his activity and
> guidance. Here is the supreme marvel. He was the Logos and
> nothing contained him; rather he himself contained all things.
> He is the whole creation, yet in his essential being he is dis-
> tinct from it all, while he is in all things in the activities of
> his power, ordering all things, extending over all things his
> universal providence, quickening each and every thing at once,
> containing the universe and not contained by it, but in his

Father alone existing wholly and entirely.
    So also when he was in the human body he gave that
body life; and at the same time he was of course giving life to
the whole universe, and was present in all things; and yet
distinct from and outside the universe. And while being recognized from his body, he was also manifest in his working in
the universe. [8]
    ... Though he was God, he had a body for his own,
and using it as an instrument, he became man for our sakes. [9]

Not everyone among the Christian priests and intellectuals
agreed with this idea, however; some found all this a bit fanciful and
illogical, and resisted the movement to declare that Jesus was God
incarnate. A hot debate ensued among the clergy, and eventually the
Emperor, Constantine, himself a zealous Christian partisan of the
'incarnation' theory, called a universal Council of the Church, which
took place in 325 C.E. in the town of Nicaea. It was attended by 318
bishops, who, after all the arguments were presented, decided
overwhelmingly (with Constantine's happy approval) to regard Jesus
as the Logos, and to adopt the following Creed:

    We believe in one God, the Father almighty, maker
of all things visible or invisible; and in one Lord Jesus Christ,
the Son of God, begotten ... not made, being of one essence
(*homoousion*) with the Father ... who, for us men and our
salvation, came down and was made flesh, was made man,
suffered, rose again the third day, ascended into heaven, and
comes to judge the quick and the dead. [10]

Thus a formalized Christian theology was born, declaring
Jesus to be identical with the Logos, the creative Power of God. Nor
was this the first time, or the last, that a great mystic and teacher was
deified by his followers. Many times throughout history, others
besides Jesus have been declared by their followers to have been
similarly divine "incarnations" of the Godhead; among them,
Krishna, Zoroaster, Mahavira Jina, Gautama Buddha, Mani, Jnaneshvar, Meher Baba, and Ramakrishna. Each of these great religious
teachers hoped with all their hearts to convince mankind that the
realization of God which they had experienced was possible to all
men, and that such realization would open to them a new life of
freedom and joy.
    Whether we believe or disbelieve in the special status of these

illustrious teachers, whether we do or do not attribute divine authority to their utterances, the truth they taught remains eternally valid and relevant to all mankind. For the message of Jesus, Krishna, Buddha, and all other seers of God is the same: 'Strive to realize God in yourself! Then you will know the joyful truth that you and the Source of the universe are one.'

The Gnostics

Contemporary with the growth of the Christian movement, during the first few centuries of the Current Era, there existed throughout the Mediterranean world a number of religious sects referred to as *Gnostics*. The Gnostics claimed to represent the eso-teric tradition of mystical knowledge (*gnosis*), and while many of them embraced and infiltrated the Christian community, they stood opposed to the authority of the orthodox (Catholic) Church, regard-ing themselves as representative of the "true" interpretation of Jesus and his teachings.

Originating, apparently, among dissident Jews, and grounded in Jewish mythology, the Gnostics drew from a number of widely diverse mystical traditions, including Indian, Persian, Greek and Egyptian. And, while some of their peculiar ideas were vehemently attacked and declared heretical by representatives of the established Church, the Gnostics served nonetheless to stimulate the formulation and clarification of early Christian theology by many of the early Church Fathers.

It is impossible to briefly and categorically assess Gnosticism as a whole, for in the period between the 1st and 4th centuries, such a wide variety of beliefs and creeds were subsumed under the name, "Gnostic," that they cannot all be treated collectively or summarily. Suffice it to say that among the Gnostics, as among any religious group, there were perhaps some genuine mystics, or *knowers*, and undoubtedly a great many unenlightened who superimposed upon the declarations of the true mystics their own fantacies and mis-conceptions. We find, therefore, in the literature of Gnosticism, as in nearly all bodies of religious literature, an occasional instance of true mystical knowledge, and a preponderant body of pretentious and uninspired mythology.

That it was not only possible but incumbent upon men to attain direct knowledge of God was a basic tenet of all who professed

Gnosticism, as their name implies; however, the literature produced by
the Gnostics reveals, not surprisingly, that there were many more who
sought this knowledge than had actually attained it. If one is to
comprehend the vast literature of the Gnostics, therefore, one must be
prepared to find but a few gems of genuine mysticism here and there
amidst the inevitable and overwhelming excrudescence of superimposed speculations by those who were mere theologians and
mythologizers.

Among the Gnostic hymns, prayers, and expository declarations by the anonymous mystics who claim to have attained the
vision of God, is this, from the Mandean tradition (ca. 2nd century):

> From the place of light have I gone forth; from thee,
> bright habitation ...; an *Uthra* (angel or spiritual guide) from
> the House of light accompanied me ... and he turned upward the
> eyes in my head so that I beheld my Father and knew Him. [11]
> From the day when we beheld Thee, from the day when
> we heard Thy word, our hearts were filled with peace. We be-
> lieved in Thee, Good One; we beheld Thy light and shall not
> forget Thee. [12]

And this Hermetic prayer (2nd century C.E.):

> Saved by Thy light, we rejoice that Thou hast shown
> Thyself to us whole; we rejoice that Thou hast made us gods
> while still in our bodies through the vision of Thee.
> Man's only thank-offering to Thee is to know Thy
> greatness. We came to know Thee, O Light of human life; we
> came to know Thee, O Womb impregnated by the seed of the
> Father ...
> In adoration of Thy grace, we ask no other grace but
> that Thou shouldst preserve us in Thy knowledge (*gnosis*) and
> that we shall not stumble from the life so gained. [13]

It was common, at that time, to speak of the experience of the
absolute Godhead as "the Light," and to refer to the state of normal
awareness within the manifested world as "darkness." We see this
same terminology used by the Gospel author, John, as well. Here, as
illustration, is a prayer from the Gnostic book, *Pistis Sophia* (3rd
century C.E.), by one who had "seen" the Light of God, and now
once again finds himself returned to the "lower" world of obscurity
and darkness:

> O Light of lights, in which I have had faith from the

beginning, hearken now to my repentence. Deliver me, O
Light, for evil thoughts have entered into me. ... I went, and
found myself in the darkness which is in the chaos beneath,
and I was powerless to hasten away and to return to my place,
for I was afflicted. ... And I cried for help, but my voice did
not carry out of the darkness; and I looked upwards so that the
Light in which I had faith might come to my rescue. ... And I
was mourning and seeking the Light that I had seen on high.
... Now, O Light of lights, I am afflicted in the darkness of
chaos... Deliver me out of the matter of this darkness, so that
I shall not be submerged in it. My strength looked up from
the midst of the chaos and from the midst of the darkness, and
I waited for my Spouse, that He might come and fight for me,
and He came not. [14]

Such a sense of alienation, upon descending from the vision
of God, is certainly understandable. The mystic feels that he has
fallen from his true home, his eternal identity, and now must dwell in
exile in a world ignorant of its true Source. Compared to the state of
awareness in which he knew himself to be the eternal Light of pure
Being, the state of existence in the manifested world is a place of exile,
a place dimmed by the darkness of ignorance; and he longs to return
to that absolute state of Godhood which he has known to be his true
Self. Yet never does he imagine that he is, even for a moment,
actually separated from that eternal Selfhood; for he has seen, with a
clarity and certainty far surpassing all worldly clarity or certainty, that
all this world is God's, and that there is no other but He.

Unfortunately, however, the words of the mystics are often
misinterpreted by the ignorant, who imagine that the "Light" and the
"darkness" are two separate and irreconcilable realms, each governed by its own deity, one good, one evil. It is just this foolish sort of
Dualist view which the unillumined theorists among the Gnostic
community created, and which pervades much of the later Gnostic
literature, consisting of endless cosmological mythologies and quasi-
Biblical allegories.

Up until recent times, the bulk of our knowledge about the
Gnostics was derived from the anti-Gnostic writings of the early
Church Fathers, especially Ireneus and Hippolytus (d. ca. 235). But
since the find of fifty-one Gnostic books at Nag Hamadi in Egypt in
1945, and their belated publication thirty years later, we possess
numerous first-hand accounts of the Gnostic views during the 2nd and
3rd centuries. These have, for the most part, only tended to confirm

the harsh judgements made against them during those centuries by the Church Fathers and others, including the (pagan) mystic, Plotinus. It is now clear that the greater portion of that discovered Gnostic literature represents a tradition counter to the true "gnosis," or revelatory knowledge, and is a corruption of the authentic teachings of the mystics, as perennial perhaps as the mystical view itself.

How this corruption, or degeneration, took place can be illustrated by taking as a starting point an example of the clear expression of authentic mystical philosophy, such as this, attributed to Simon Magus (1st century C.E.), and preserved by Hippolytus:

> There are two aspects of the One. The first of these is the Higher, the Divine Mind of the universe, which governs all things, and is masculine. The other is the lower, the Thought (*epinoia*) which produces all things, and is feminine. As a pair united, they comprise all that exists.
>
> The Divine Mind is the Father who sustains all things, and nourishes all that begins and ends. He is the One who eternally stands, without beginning or end. He exists entirely alone; for, while the Thought arising from Unity, and coming forth from the divine Mind, creates [the appearance of] duality, the Father remains a Unity. The Thought is in Himself, and so He is alone. Made manifest to Himself from Himself, He appears to be two. He becomes "Father" by virtue of being called so by His own Thought.
>
> Since He, Himself, brought forward Himself, by means of Himself, manifesting to Himself His own Thought, it is not correct to attribute creation to the Thought alone. For She (the Thought) conceals the Father within Herself; the Divine Mind and the Thought are intertwined. Thus, though [they appear] to be a pair, one opposite the other, the Divine Mind is in no way differrent from the Thought, inasmuch as they are one.
>
> Though there appears to be a Higher, the Mind, and a lower, the Thought, truly, It is a Unity, just as what is manifested from these two [the world] is a unity, while appearing to be a duality. The Divine Mind and the Thought are discernible, one from the other, but they are one, though they appear to be two.
>
> [Thus,] ... there is one Divine Reality, [conceptually] divided as Higher and lower; generating Itself, nourishing Itself, seeking Itself, finding Itself, being mother of Itself, father of Itself, sister of Itself, spouse of Itself, daughter of Itself, son of Itself. It is both Mother and Father, a Unity, being the Root of the entire circle of existence. [15]

This brief explanation of the mystically perceived duality-in-Unity is, without doubt, the clearest and most comprehensible such explanation ever written; yet, crystal clear as it is, there are few, it seems, who are capable of grasping its meaning. It is important to an understanding of this, and other such characterizations of the Absolute and Its creative Power as Male and Female, to realize that such descriptions are merely poetic representations of what is *experientially perceived* in the mystical vision. Such descriptions are admittedly inadequate to the experience itself, for which no language or metaphor is truly apt; but these remarks of Simon Magus, a contemporary of the apostle, Peter, represent the best that language can approximate to that ineffable knowledge revealed in the transcendent vision.

In the vision of God, the mystic experiences, through himself, the absolute Godhead. It is not separate from himself, but *is* who he is; he experiences and knows *as* the Godhead. He is the eternal, motionless, Consciousness; utterly alone, without a second. Yet, *from* him, he is aware of the outflow of power, a radiance, which may be likened to that of the Sun's rays, or to that of a heart's love, which is projected as the multitudinous universe of animate and inanimate forms. From the vantage point of eternity, he experiences also the withdrawal of this radiation, much as a breath is indrawn following its expiration. From his absolute vantage point, he watches the cyclic manifestation and de-manifestation of the universe. How is it possible to describe to others such an experience? He knows that the Godhead and Its creative Power are one, yet he must differentiate between them; for the one is single, formless, and eternally constant, while the other appears as a multiplicity of form and is transitory. The Godhead he calls the "Father"; Its emanating manifestory Energy he calls the "Mother" -- yet he knows, with a certainty that is possessed by no other, that they are one Being, one God, one and only one Reality.

When his mind descends from this "vision," he is cut off, as it were, from that pure Awareness; he is returned once more to his worldly existence in time and space; but the knowledge of Oneness, the knowledge of his identity with the Godhead is retained. And the conviction is firmly established in his heart that he can never be separated from That from which nothing can ever be separated. His worldly form and all forms that can be perceived he recognizes as the projection of God. He lives in a world that is imaged forth from God; and he walks in that world as God, the eternal Self of all, and views all creation as his own dream-world, his own play, knowing that he is

ever-secure, ever-alone, ever-still, the ever-conscious Fountainhead of
his own drama.

It is this state of *gnosis* which the Upanishads refer to as
"Liberation" (*moksha*) and which the Gnostics called "Release" or
"Salvation" (*apolytrosis*). The Gnostic sect of the Valentinians declared: "The cognition of the ineffable Greatness is itself the perfect
salvation... To us suffices the knowledge of universal Being; this is the
true salvation." [16]   It is a liberation and release from the ignorance of
one's true nature, a release from the slavery of fear, passion and error
which those ignorant of their true, eternal Identity must unwittingly
endure.

Another marvellous example of the expression of mystical
vision among the Gnostics which Hippolytus has preserved is this,
attributed to Valentinus (ca. 160 C.E.):

> The Father existed alone, unbegotten,without place,
> without time, without counsellor, and without any conceiv-
> able qualities ..., solitary and reposing alone in Himself. But
> as He possessed a generative Power [the Mother, Logos, Pra-
> krti, etc.], it pleased Him to generate and produce the most
> beautiful and perfect that He had in Himself, for He did not
> love solitude. He was all love, but love is not love if there
> is no object of love. So the Father, alone as He was, project-
> ed and generated [the world]. [17]

We find, however, that the Valentinians, like many of the other
followers of Gnosticism, soon distorted the concept of duality-in-
unity, and transformed it into a duality-in-duality. Following in the
tradition of Persian Zoroasterism (from the 6th century B.C.E.), the
Gnostic scriptural authors translated the two complementary aspects of
Reality into two independent and irreconcilable principles. Some, like
the followers of Marcion (ca. 140 C.E.) or Mani (216-276 C.E.),
declared that the two were eternally independent and antagonistic
principles, one the power of Good and Light, the other the power of
Evil and Darkness; and that the world was solely the product of the
Evil and Dark force. Others, like the followers of Simon Magus and
Valentinus, rightly viewed the Power of world-manifestation as an
"emanation" of the Absolute, but hypostacized that creative
Principle, and attributed to it a "will" independent of and rebellious
to its original Source. The result is that Gnosticism, in many of its
forms, came to assert a philosophy of Dualism, viewing the world, not
as an expression or manifestition of God, but as wholly separate from

God, and diametrically opposed to Him.

It would seem that, for all their talk of "gnosis," many of the authors of the Gnostic Gospels were frauds who had not actually experienced the revelation of Truth of which they so glowingly spoke; for it is impossible to behold that vision without apprehending the singularity of Existence, the fundamental unity of God and His creative Power. Indeed, the Gnosticism of the 2nd and 3rd centuries provides us with a clear example of how the mystical philosophy expounded by the authentic seers is invariably corrupted and distorted by deluded pretenders to mystical knowledge. It is the perennial hallmark of ignorance to see division, conflict, alienation, just as it is the hallmark of the mystic to have attained the realization of unity, harmony, and integration.

The true mystic -- however grievously he may suffer, however longingly he may yearn for a return to his original pristine state, reunited in awareness with the Godhead -- can never, even for a moment, declare this world to be separate and divorced from God. If he has truly known God, he knows that this entire universe is the manifestation of God's will, and is replete with Divinity. He could never assert the contrary, though his head were battered and bleeding; and never, ever, could he assert, as do the pseudo-Gnostics, that this world is the creation of a second, and evil, Creator, whose will is antagonistic to its Origin and Source.

The true mystic and sage, Plotinus, writing in the 3rd century of these pretenders to gnosis, stated the matter most clearly:

> The one Divine Mind, in Its mentation, thinks Itself;
> the object of Its thought is nothing external; Thinker and
> Thought are one, unchangeably the same. [18]
> How could anyone say that [this world] is not a clear
> image, beautifully formed, of the Divine? ... Such a one could
> neither have fathomed this world nor have had any vision of
> that other [the Divine Mind]. [19]

But, of course, not all of the Gnostics were of that type. One of the authentic mystical traditions which historians now include under the heading of "Gnostic" is the Hermetic tradition. Up until the 17th century, when a Greek scholar named Isaac Casaubon (d. 1614 C.E.), corrected their dating, the body of writings called the *Corpus Hermetica* was considered to be of a very ancient origin. They are purportedly the writings of Hermes (the Egyptian Thoth, identified with Mercury), who is usually given the title, "Trismegistus" (thrice-great). He was said to be a great mystic and prophet, descended from Atlas and Prometheus, who lived only shortly after Moses (ca. 1200 B.C.E.). This ancient geneology was believed to be accurate even by such Christian notables as Lactantius and, later, Augustine. It is now clear, however, that the writings attributed to Hermes Trismegistus were written during that mystically prolific period from the 1st to the 3rd centuries of the Current Era. Therefore, they must be regarded as a portion, though a distinct one, of the Gnostic movement of that time.

In its Greek form, the *Corpus Hermetica* was known and widely influential during those early centuries, but fell into obscurity during later centuries, until it was translated from a Greek manuscript into Latin by Marcilio Ficino in 1463. Ficino brought the Hermetic writings into great prominence during the early Renaissance period, still believing it to be the work of a pre-Christian and pre-Socratic Egyptian sage of great antiquity. The diverse body of writings known as *Hermetica* is divided into two main books: *Asclepius* ("On The Divine Will") and *Poimander* ("On The Power And Wisdom Of God"). They vary in content from purely mystical theology to the lore of magic and astrology. It is not within our province to examine here the astrological and magical elements of the *Corpus Hermetica*, but the mystical portions, among the most noteworthy writings of this period, deserve extensive quotation. The dialogues between God and Hermes and between Hermes and his son in *Poimander* are some of the most beautiful and authentic mystical utterances ever written.

Unlike the degenerate forms of Gnosticism, in which a Dualistic cosmology is asserted, the Hermetic writings are predominantly Monistic, and based on genuine mystical vision. In the *Poimander*, Hermes experiences God as an infinite Light, which he describes as "That which is non-polluted, which has no limit, no color, no form, is motionless, naked, shining, which can only be apprehended by Itself, the unalterable Good, the Incorporeal." That infinite Light is the Divine Mind (*Nous*), which speaks to Hermes, telling him, "This Light is I, Myself, thy God, .. and the luminous Word (*Logos*) issuing from Me is the Son of God." [20]   This characterization of the creative Power of God as "the Son" is also mentioned in *Asclepius* :

> The Lord and Creator of all things, whom we have
> the right to call God, ... made the second God [the Logos]
> visible and sensible... He made him first, and alone, and
> one only; and he appeared to Him beautiful, and most full

of good things; and He hallowed him and altogether loved
him as His own Son. [21]

As we have seen, the designation of God's creative Power as
God's "only begotten Son" did not originate with the early Christians, but was a designation popular since Philo; and is merely another
analogical attempt to differentiate the creative Impulse of God from
the primal Essence, universally designated as the "Father" of all. The
"Son" is that hypostacized Power which, in many other traditions, is
called the "Mother"; but, of course, these designations of gender are
figurative only, being merely arbitrary symbols of That which is
beyond all gender. They represent the mystic's attempt to portray,
with anthropomorphic symbols, the bond of relationship existing
between the primal Source and Its projective Power.
   The Divine Mind, continuing to speak to Hermes, explains
how It manifests the world through Its Logos:

> The eternal [Logos] is the Power of God, and the
> work of the eternal [Logos] is the world, which has no begin-
> ning, but is continually becoming by the activity of the
> eternal [Logos]. Therefore, nothing that constitutes the world
> will ever perish or be destroyed, for the eternal [Logos] is im-
> perishable. All this great body of the world is a Soul, full of
> intellect and of God, who fills it within and without and
> vivifies everything.
>   Contemplate through Me [the Divine Mind], the world
> and consider its beauty. ... See that all things are full of light.
> See the earth, settled in the midst of all, the great nurse who
> nourishes all earthly creatures. All is full of Soul, and all be-
> ings are in movement. Who has created these things? The
> one God, for God is one. You see that the world is always
> one, the Sun, one; the moon, one; the divine activity, one;
> God, too, is one. And since all is living, and Life is also one,
> God is certainly one. It is by the action of God that all things
> come into being...
>   ... All that is, He contains within Himself like
> thoughts: the world, Himself, the All. Therefore, unless you
> make yourself equal to God, you cannot understand God; for
> like is not intelligible save to the like. Make yourself grow to
> a greatness beyond measure; by a leap [of intellect], free your-
> self from the body; raise yourself above all time, become
> Eternity; then you will understand God.
>   Believe that nothing is impossible for you; think
> yourself immortal and capable of understanding all, all arts, all
> sciences, the nature of every living being. Mount higher than

the highest height; descend lower than the lowest depth. Draw
into yourself all sensations of everything created, fire and
water, the dry and the moist, imagining that you are everywhere, on earth, in the sea, in the sky; that you are not yet
born, in the maternal womb, adolescent, old, dead, beyond
death. If you embrace in your thought all things at once -- all
times, places, substances, qualities, quantities -- you may
understand God.

       Say no longer that God is invisible. Do not speak
thus, for what is more manifest than God? He has created all
only that you may see it through the beings. For that is the
miraculous power of God, to show Himself through all beings.
For nothing is invisible, not even the incorporeal. The
intellect makes itself visible in the act of thinking; God makes
Himself visible in the act of creating. [22]

In yet another dialogue, this time between Hermes and his son,
Tat, the identity of God, man, and the world is further elucidated:

       HERMES: The intellect, O Tat, is drawn from the
very substance of God. In men, this intellect is God; and so
some men are gods and their humanity is near to the Divine.
When man is not guided by intellect, he falls below himself
into an animal state. All men are subject to Destiny, but
those in possession of the Logos, which commands the intellect from within, are not under it in the same manner as others.
God's two gifts to man of intellect and the Logos have the
same value as immortality. If man makes right use of these, he
differs in no way from the immortals.

       The world, too, is a god, image of a greater God.
United to Him and performing the order and will of the Father,
it is the totality of life. There is nothing in it, through all the
duration of the cyclic return willed by the Father, which is not
alive. The Father has willed that the world should be living so
long as it keeps its cohesion; hence the world is necessarily
God. How then could it be that, in that which is God, the
image of the One, there should be dead things? For death is
corruption, and coruption is destruction, and it is impossible
that anything of God could be destroyed.

       TAT: Do not the living beings in the world die, O
father, although they are parts of the world?

       HERMES: Hush, my child, for you are led into error
by the appearance of the phenomenon. Living beings do not

die, but, being composite bodies, they are dissolved; this is not death but the dissolution of a mixture. If they are dissolved, it is not to be destroyed but to be renewed... Contemplate then the beautiful arrangement of the world and see that it is alive, and that all matter is full of life.

TAT: Is God then in matter, O father?

HERMES: Where could matter be placed if it existed apart from God [who is infinite]? Would it not be but a confused mass, unless it were ordered? And if it is ordered, by whom is it ordered? The energies which operate in it are parts of God. Whether you speak of matter or bodies or substance, know that all these are the energy of God, of the God who is all. In the All there is nothing which is not God. Adore this teaching, my child, and hold it sacred. [23]

This teaching is, indeed, the perennial teaching of all mystics; we find it in the Upanishads, in the words of the Buddha, Jesus, and all others who have seen the unitive Truth of all existence. And while these teachings, attributed to Hermes Trismegistus, are not as ancient as once believed, they are nonetheless remarkable for their brilliant clarity, depth of knowledge, and uncompromising wisdom. Many times, throughout the course of history, they have been rediscovered, re-examined, and re-appreciated; and, even today, they weild great facination for students of mystical theology. However, we still know very little about the real Hermes -- if he existed at all, and nothing of the 2nd century author who wrote such magnificent examples of the perennial philosophy under his name. We cannot even be certain of whether he was an Egyptian, Greek, or Jew. But we are grateful for his testimonies, and count him among the greatest and wisest of the seers of God, whose teachings have served to illumine countless generations along the way.

PLOTINUS

The perennial philosophy which began in Greece with Heraclitus, Pythagorus, and Socrates, became, in the Rome of the first few
centuries of the Current Era, a full-fledged religious tradition. This
"religion" had no ecclesiastical organization, or zealous pros-
elytizers; yet it produced some of the most devoutly religious literature created during those times. It had not the fervent appeal of
Christianity's proclaimed "Savior," nor the long heritage of divine
appointment claimed in Jewish historico-religious narratives; but was
rather a sane and sober religion of simple devotion to the one Divine
Principle which was both transcendent to and immanent in all His
creation.

It was the hallmark of these "pagan" religionists to view all
earlier mythical and cultic religious manifestations as so many figurative expressions of the one perennial urge toward Divinity, so many
poetical renderings of the one common Truth. This broadly tolerant
and conciliatory view was best expressed by the historian, Plutarch (ca.
100 C.E.), who said:

> There is one divine Mind which keeps the universe in
> order and one providence which governs it. The names given
> to this supreme God differ; he is worshipped in different ways
> in different religions; the religious symbols used in them vary,
> and their qualities are different; sometimes they are rather
> vague, and sometimes more distinct. [1]

A contemporary of Plutarch, and one of the most exemplary
representatives of the perennial philosophy in 1st century Rome, was
the freed-slave, Epictetus (50-120 C.E.), who is usually regarded as a
Stoic but who was equally inspired by Socrates whom he held as his
model. Despite his devout and holy views, however, it is difficult to
find any explicit references to the mystical "vision" of God in his
Discourses; his pre-eminent concern, like Socrates', was to guide men
to the awareness of the Divinity within them through the development
of virtue, right understanding, and spiritual strength.

During the 2nd century C.E., there lived in Rome a teacher
called Maximus of Tyre (ca. 150 C.E., a man of whom little is known,
but who spoke eloquently and passionately of the mystical life. Here,
in the following passage, he summarizes the ultimate attainment of

man, and the means to that attainment:

> The eye cannot see God, words cannot name Him,
> flesh and blood cannot touch Him, the ear cannot hear Him;
> but within the soul That which is most fair, most pure, most
> intelligible, most ethereal, most honorable, can contemplate
> Him becaause it is like Him, can hear Him because of their
> kinship.
>   ... The soul holds herself erect and strong, she gazes
> at the pure light [of the Godhead]; she wavers not, nor turns
> her glance to earth, but closes her ears and directs her eyes and
> all other senses within. She forgets the troubles and sorrows
> of earth, its joys and honors, its glory and its shame; and sub-
> mits to the guidance of pure reason and strong love. For
> reason points out the road that must be followed, and love
> drives the soul forward, making the rough places smooth by
> its charm and constancy. And as we approach heaven and leave
> earth behind, the goal becomes clear and luminous -- that is a
> foretaste of God's very self. On the road we learn His nature
> better; but when we reach the end, we see Him. [2]

By the end of the 3rd century C.E., Christianity, though still in
its birth-throes, was gathering wide popular support; the great Greek
philosophers were merely a distant memory, and the last of the great
Roman Stoics, the Emperor, Marcus Aurelius (121-180 C.E.), had
long since passed away. The ancient civilizations were in a period of
decline. In Rome, the revolt of Maximus (ca. 235 C.E.) marked the
beginning of an endless series of civil and foreign wars, domestic
calamities, plagues and famines, which depopulated and impoverished
the empire, and put an end to culture, learning, and philosophy, along
with the elite who had the leisure to pursue them.

In this unhappy period of transition, Plotinus (205-270 C.E.)
stood alone to represent the supreme knowledge of Unity. He was
born at Lycopolis (the modern city of Asyut) in upper Egypt, and
lived for some time at Alexandria. We are told by his biographer,
Porphyry (237-304 C.E.), that at the age of twenty-eight, Plotinus
made a decision to follow the life of philosophy. He read and heard
the teachings of many philosophers, but found no one he wished to
take as his mentor until he heard the teachings of Ammonius Saccus,
who was known as "the God-taught." After hearing one of Ammonius' lectures, Plotinus said to a friend, "This is the man I've been
looking for."

Ammonius, and another of Plotinus' major influences, Nu-

menius, were both well learned in the Persian and Indian philosophies, and taught a sort of Platonized Vedanta. After studying for eleven
years with Ammonius, Plotinus, having heard so much of the
philosophy of the East, decided he would like to learn more of the
Persian and Indian thought first-hand. With this object in mind, he
joined up with the invading forces of Emperor Gordian which were
enroute to Persia. He got as far as Mesopotamia, when the Emperor
was assassinated, and the expedition was halted. Plotinus managed to
escape to Antioch and then to Rome, where he arrived in the year 245
C.E.

For the next twenty-five years, Plotinus taught his philosophy
in Rome. His lectures were free and open to the public, and he lived
solely on the favors of his wealthy students and patrons. He taught
from his own mystical experience, but he framed his thoughts often in
terms familiar to students of Plato; and for that reason he became
labeled in much later times as "the founder of neo-Platonism." This
is an unfortunate misnomer, however, for it tends to detract from the
fact that Plotinus' message was founded, not so much on any one
tradition, but on his own personal realizations.

Plotinus, like Socrates, had attained the realization of the
absolute Reality, and was solely intent on expressing what he had
directly perceived in the "vision" of Unity. Yet, since he and Socrates had experienced a common unitive Reality, it is only natural that
Plotinus would utilize familiar terms which had been used previously
in the Socratic dialogues of Plato. It should be remembered that the
mystic writes in order to put into rational verbal form what he has
experienced, and he utilizes the verbal symbols and terms of
preceding mystics, not in a dogmatic fashion, but solely in order to
draw upon familiar terminologies to make clear his own vision, and to
show its consistency with the vision of those who preceded him.

Plotinus' philosophy of Unity is identical to the Upanishadic
philosophy also, yet, though he was no doubt familiar with Indian
thought, it would be a mistake to infer therefore that he borrowed his
own philosophy from those sources. For it is only natural and to be
expected that one person, having experienced the Unity, will describe
It in terms similar or identical to another who has experienced It. For
Plotinus, philosophy was not a mere game of ideas put forward as a
convincing hypothesis; he had experienced, through contemplation,
the ultimate unitive Truth, and spoke from his experience in order to
explain It to others. We need not, therefore, be astonished that his

words agree with those of all others who have experienced that same interior revelation.

Plotinus found corroboration for his philosophy, not only in the utterances of Socrates and the Upanishadic seers, but in the writings of a number of other ancient philosophers as well. In his classes, his students were required to read the commentaries of Severus, Cronius, Numenius, Caius and Atticus, as well as the works of Aspasius, Alexander of Aphrodisias, and Adrastus. Said Plotinus, "We must believe that some of the ancient and blessed philosophers also discovered the Truth; and it is only natural to inquire who of them found It, and how we may obtain a knowledge of It." [3]

In the first ten years of his life in Rome, Plotinus wrote nothing, but by the time Porphyry had become his follower in 263 C.E., he had completed twenty-one treatises. In answer to the questions of his later students, he wrote thirty-three more, which were circulated without titles among his closest followers. And, after Plotinus' death, Porphyry gathered these fifty-four treatises together into a book of six sections, containing nine treatises each; hence the title, *Enneads* ("Nines"), by which Plotinus' book is known.

In his meetings with his friends and students, Plotinus would explain in an imaginative and compelling manner the truths of the spiritual life. Says Porphyry: "When he was speaking, the light of his his intellect visibly illumined his face; always of winning presence, he then appeared of still greater beauty; a slight moisture gathered on his forehead, and he radiated benignity." [4] "Plotinus," said Porphyry, "lived at once within himself and for others; from his interior attention he never relaxed unless in sleep. And even that he kept light by often touching not so much as a piece of bread and by constantly concentrating upon the thought within. [5] ... He was gentle, and always at the call of those having the slightest acquaintance with him. After spending twenty-six years at Rome, acting, too, as arbiter in many differences, he had never made an enemy of any citizen." [6]

Plotinus taught and wrote and discussed questions with his devoted students, but most of his time was spent in solitary contemplation, leading his soul to union with its divine Source. Porphyry states that, during the time he knew him, Plotinus attained that exalted state of awareness four times. When, in his later years, he became gravely ill, suffering from malign Diphtheria, Plotinus retired to the estate of a nobleman disciple in Campania. A friend who visited him there, reports that Plotinus, weak and scarcely able to speak, whispered,

"I am striving to give back the divine in me to the divine in all."   He died soon thereafter at the age of sixty-six.

In his writings, Plotinus traces the evolution of the individual soul from the primal ONE, the unchanging Godhead, and shows how, by the process of involution, it returns back to that state of oneness. Having realized that primal Unity in himself, he describes that state from which all manifestation originates:

> Time was not yet; ... it lay ... merged in the eternally
> Existent and motionless with It. But an active princible there
> ... stirred from its rest; ... for the One contained an unquiet
> faculty, ... and it could not bear to retain within itself all the
> dense fullness of its possession.
> [Like] a seed at rest, the nature-principle within, un-
> folding outwards, makes its way towards what appears a multi-
> ple life. It was Unity self-contained, but now, in going forth
> from Itself, It fritters Its unity away; It advances to a lesser
> greatness. [7]

The student of mystical cosmology may find it interesting to compare the above words of Plotinus with the Song of Creation from the Rig Veda, quoted on pages 24-26, and with the quote from Chuang Tze on page 68; in both cases, the words are slightly different, but the meaning is the same.

It is just here, in the description of the One which becomes two, without becoming two, that we confront an incomprehensible and inexplicable mystery. If the Absolute, the Godhead, is eternally unmoving, unchanging Unity, how can we say at the same time that It gives birth to a second, active, principle through which, and in which, the entire universe is formed? It is beyond rational explication; we can only say they are "complementary" aspects of the same one Reality. They are two (in appearance), but they are one (in Truth).

The First Principle, the unchanging Absolute, Plotinus calls simply, "the One"; sometimes he refers to It as "the All-Transcending," or "the First," or "the Unity." Its active principle or aspect, Plotinus refers to as "Mind" (*Nous*). These two are, of course, our old friends, Brahman and Maya, Purusha and Prakrti, Shiva and Shakti, Theos and Logos. These two make up the one Reality; there is nothing else but these two aspects of the One, who, in combination -- one superimposed on the other -- make up the living universe. And if we say that the first is the "Spirit" and the second the "form," it is only by way of a concession to the compartmentalization of thought;

for they can never really be separated, any more than the Sun's
radiance can be separated from the Sun. Plotinus, using this very
analogy, explains how the divine Mind (i.e., Logos) comes into being
from the transcendent Unity:

> It is a circumradiation produced from the unaltering
> Supreme, as the brilliant light encircling the Sun is ceaseless-
> ly generated from that unchanging substance. [8]

Just as the Sun's light and warmth exist in its radiance, the
light of life and consciousness exists in the divine "Mind" (Plotinus'
term for the creative Energy) which manifests the universe. Or, we
might say, by way of a further analogy, that, just as the consciousness
of a dreamer is the consciousness and animating power of the
multitude of beings populating a dream, so is that one unaltering
Consciousness the consciousness and animating power of the universe.

In man, that primal Consciousness is experienced as Soul.
Though each individual possesses that same awareness which we call
Soul, because of the difference in experiences, circumstances and
choices, each one evolves in a unique manner; and each man regards
his "soul" as unique and separate from other souls. But, in fact, there
is only one Soul; it is one universal Consciousness which appears as
multitudinous souls. (Recall the Upanishadic dictum: "Atman is none
other than Brahman.") Here is Plotinus' explanation of that truth:

> There is one identical Soul, every separate manifest-
> ation being that Soul complete. The differentiated souls issue
> from the Unity and strike out here and there, but are united at
> the Source much as light is a divided thing on earth, shining
> in this house and that, and yet remains one. One Soul [is] the
> source of all souls; It is at once divided and undivided. [9]
> ... Diversity within the ONE depends not upon
> spatial separation, but sheerly upon differentiation; all Being,
> despite this plurality, is a Unity still. [10]
> ... The souls are apart without partition; they are no
> more hedged off by boundaries than are the multiple items of
> knowledge in one mind. The one Soul so exists as to include
> all souls. [11]

What then of matter? That, says Plotinus, is also manifested by
the "Thought" of the divine Mind. But, whereas in the Vedantic
conception, the world-manifestation produced by the principle cor-

responding to the divine "Mind," namely *Maya*, is also called *Maya;*
in Plotinus, the "Thought" produced by the divine Mind is
categorically differentiated from the "Mind" itself, and is called the
"Logos." In the terminology of Plotinus, therefore, it is the Logos,
whose source is the divine Mind, which is manifesting as the phe-
nominal world of matter. Again, it must be said, they are not separate; they are intermingled. Man becomes aware of the Soul, however,
only by a transfer of his awareness away from the material
manifestations, and even beyond the intellectual manifestations, of the
divine Mind:

> [The Soul] is to be reached by him who, with the
> nature of the lover, is a born philosopher, suffering the pangs
> of love for beauty, yet not held by material loveliness, but
> rather fleeing from that to things whose beauty is of the
> Soul. [12]
> ... He that has the strength, let him arise and with-
> draw into himself, foregoing all that is known by the eyes,
> turning away forever from the material beauty that once made
> his joy. [13]

If the Soul is to be realized, says Plotinus, it must be returned
to its original stillness, uninvolved in the manifestations of the divine
Mind -- including both the gross physical manifestations and the
subtle manifestations of the individual mind:

> What is meant by the purification of the soul is
> simply to allow it to be alone. [It is pure] when it keeps no
> company, entertains no alien thoughts; when it no longer sees
> images, much less elaborates them into veritable affections. [14]

Thus, in order to realize the one eternal Source from which all
creation evolves, we must turn back that process, and retreat from the
sensible universe of form to the soul, and from thence to the divine
Mind (i.e., Nature, Prakrti, etc.) which produced it; and from that to
the absolute Consciousness from which that activating principle arose:

> [Once we know our own soul,] rising still higher, we
> sing the divinity of the Mind [which produced it], and above
> all these, the mighty King of that dominion (the Absolute),
> who, while remaining as He is, yet creates that multitude, all
> dependent on Him, existing by Him and from Him. [15]
> ... In advancing stages of contemplation, rising from
> contemplation of Nature, to that in the soul, and thence again

to that in the divine Mind, the object contemplated becomes progressively a more and more intimate possession of the contemplating being, more and more one with them.

   ... In the divine Mind itself, there is complete identity of knower and known, no distinction existing between being and knowing, contemplation and its object, [but] constituting a living thing, a one Life, two inextricably one. [16]

When one reaches that stage of inward contemplation where the divine Mind is realized as constituting one's own being, one exclaims: "O my God, even this body is Thine own!" Then one knows that he is a part of the one divine Mind, and has no existence apart from it. But, as one's vision becomes more clear, as the soul strains to see, it realizes that beyond that manifesting Mind is an unchanging, eternal Consciousness which is its true, unaltering, Self:

   The All-Transcendent, utterly void of multiplicity, is Unity's Self, independent of all else... It is the great Beginning, wholly and truly One. All life belongs to It. [17]

   ... The One is, in truth, beyond all statement; whatever you say would limit It; the All-Transcendent has no name. [18]

   ... [It] is That which is the truly Existent. ... It is the Source from which all that appears to exist derives that appearance. [19] ... Everywhere one and whole, It is at rest throughout. But, ... in Its very non-action It magnificently operates and in Its very self-being It produces everything by Its Power. [20]

   ... This Absolute is none of the things of which It is the Source; Its nature is that nothing can be affirmed of It -- not existence, not essence, not life -- It transcends all these. But possess yourself of It by the very elimination of [individual] being, and you hold a marvel! Thrusting forward to This, attaining, and resting in Its content, seek to grasp It more and more, understanding It by that intuitive thrust alone, but knowing Its greatness by the beings that follow upon It and exist by Its power. [21]

On knowing That, everything is known; the seeker will have seen the ultimate Truth of all existence. But It is not "seen" as something separate from himself; rather he knows It as "I." He knows, "I am the One existence; all this is myself":

   In this state of absorbed contemplation, there is no longer any question of holding an object in view; the vision is

such that seeing and seen are one; object and act of vision have
become identical. [22]

    ... There, our Self-seeing is a communion with the
Self restored to purity. No doubt we should not speak of "seeing," but, instead of [speaking of] "seen" and "seer," speak
boldly of a simple unity. For in this seeing we neither see,
nor distinguish, nor are there, two. The man is changed, no
longer himself nor belonging to himself; he is merged with
the Supreme, sunken into It, one with It; it is only in separation that duality exists. This is why the vision baffles telling; for how could a man bring back tidings of the Supreme as
something separate from himself when he has seen It as one
with himself? [23]

    ... This is the life of the gods and of godlike men,
liberation from the alien that besets us here, a life taking no
pleasure in the things of earth, a flight of the alone to the
Alone. [24]

But how is this inward journey to be undertaken? How does
one set about it? And what is required for the attainment of the Goal?
Plotinus, like all other seers before him, maps out the pathway by
which he himself travelled, and comments on each stage and pathmark
along the way. Here, in his own words, is a summary of his advice to
all wayfarers on that inward journey:

    Withdraw into yourself and look. And if you do not
find yourself beautiful yet, act as does the creator of a statue
that is to be made beautiful; he cuts away here, he smoothes
there, he makes this line lighter, this other purer, until a love-
ly face has grown upon his work. So do you also; cut away
all that is excessive, straighten all that is crooked, bring light
to all that is in shadow; labor to make all one glow of beauty
and never cease chiseling your statue until there shall shine out
on you from it the godlike splendor of virtue, until you shall
see the perfect goodness established in the stainless shrine. [25]

    ... We dare not keep ourselves set towards the images
of sense, or towards the merely vegetative, intent upon the
gratifications of eating and procreation; our life must be pointed towards the divine Mind, toward God. [26]

    If anyone seeks any other pleasure in the life of the
godly, it is not the life of the godly he is looking for. [27]

    He who is to be wise and possess happiness must
draw his good from the Supreme, fixing his gaze on THAT,
becoming like to THAT, living by THAT. He must care for
no other goal than THAT; all else he will attend to ... not in
expectation of any increase in his established felicity, but

simply in a reasonable attention to the differing conditions surrounding him as he lives here or there. [28]

To place happiness in actions is to put it in things that are outside virtue and outside the Soul; for the Soul's expression is not in action but in wisdom, in a contemplative operation within itself; and this, this alone, is happiness. [29]

... Even the desire for God is to be desired as a good. To attain [God] is for those who will take the upward path, until, passing on the upward way all that is other than God, each in the solitude of himself shall behold that lone Existence, the Detached, the Unmingled, the Pure, THAT from which all things arise, toward which all look, the Source of life, of thought, and of being. [30]

We ought not to question whence it [the experience of Unity] comes; there is no whence, no coming or going in place; it either appears [to us] or does not appear. We must not run after it, but we must fit ourselves for the vision and then wait tranquilly for it as the eye waits on the rising of the Sun which in its own time appears above the horizon and gives itself to our sight. [31]

Suppose the soul have attained; the Highest has come to her, or rather has revealed Its presence; she has turned away from all about her and has made herself apt, beautiful to the utmost, brought into likeness [with the Divine] by the preparings and adornings known to those growing ready for the vision. She has seen that Presence suddenly manifesting within her, for there is nothing between, nor are they any longer two, but one; for so long as the Presence remains, all distinction fades. It is in this way that lover and beloved here [in this world], in a copy of that [Divine] union, long to blend their being.

... Once There, she will trade for This nothing the universe holds -- no, not the entire heavens; for there is nothing higher than This, nothing more holy; above This there is nowhere to go. All else, however lofty, lies on the downward path; she knows that This was the object of her quest, that there is nothing higher. [32]

... Without that vision, the soul is unillumined; but illumined thereby, it has attained what it sought. And this is the true Goal set before the soul: to receive that light, to see the Supreme by the Supreme; ... for That by which the illumination comes is That which is to be seen, just as we do not see the Sun by any other light than its own.

How is this to be accomplished?
Let all else go! [33]

This is Plotinus' final word on the means to the attainment of that supernal vision: "Let all else go!"   Whether we call this by the name of "dedication," "devotion," "purity of heart," "singleness of mind," "renunciation," or "detachment," it is the word of all the seers of God in responce to the question, "How is It attained?"   But who can let all else go? How does one find the courage to turn away from the world to focus all one's attention on the divine Source within? It cannot even be attempted unless one is inspired from within by His grace. For it is that One Himself who puts such a desire into the heart; it is He who attracts like a magnet the soul to its own awakening, to contemplation, just as it is He who reveals Himself as the one Soul of all.

We may object to this idea, saying that our own free will precludes such an apparently determinist view; but as Plotinus points out:

> Even though the 'I' is sovereign in choosing this or
> that, yet by that choice it takes part in the ordered Whole.
> Your personality does not come from outside into the univers-
> al scheme; you are a part of it, you and your personal dispos-
> ition. [34]

We *do* have free-will, as Plotinus is quick to assert; yet *He* is the One who is living, desiring and acting as us, albeit at a remove from Himself. Even our despair, our longing, our faithlessness, is contained within Him, and "all is one ordered Whole." It is He who draws the heart towards Himself, for He is doing everything as us. When His light shines within us, only then are we attracted to it, as a moth to a flame; otherwise we flutter about, searching for truth and beauty and joy in the shadows, catching only shadows.   When the Divine in us stirs us, then the soul becomes, in Plotinus' words, "filled with a holy ecstacy; stung by desire, it becomes Love."

> When there enters into it a glow from the Divine, the
> soul gathers strength, spreads true wings, and, however dis-
> tracted by its proximate environment, speeds its buoyant way
> to something greater; ... its very nature bears it upwards, lifted
> by the Giver of that love. ... Surely we need not wonder that
> It possesses the power to draw the soul to Itself, calling it
> back from every wandering to rest before It. From It came
> everything; nothing is mightier. [35]

Thus, we see that Plotinus, like all true knowers of God, like the author of the *Gita*, like Jesus, Buddha, and the others, reveals the royal path to Truth as an intermingling of grace, purity, knowledge, devotion and contemplation. He represents that pure tradition of mystical philosophy which is the expression of the eternal and perennial vision of Truth, unalloyed by any sectarian considerations or ties. Perhaps it is because of this independence from popular religious movements that his name is so little known by the general populace, but by those who are able to recognize and appreciate the singular purity of his vision, he is honored and reverenced, and numbered among the greatest and wisest of the teachers of men.

≈≈≈

III. Mystics Of
The Early Middle Ages

DIONYSIUS

The designation "Early Middle Ages" is used by scholars for that period of time between the 4th and 10th centuries of the Current Era. It was a time during which the various religious traditions of the world were relatively isolated from one another, each existing in its own vacuum, as it were. In the West, Christianity had become so much a part of the cultural and political heritage, that the Church became almost indistinguishable from the state. Orthodoxy, in religion as well as in politics, was the safest course; still, there appeared, during this time, a number of daring thinkers, philosophers, and theologians, such as Augustine (354-430), Boethius (480-524), and Eriugena (810-877). But these men, though capable of occasional mystical glimpses, fall short of being included among the pre-eminent mystics of the world.

The declarations of the mystics differ from the exclusively philosophical and theological reasonings of such intellectuals in that they are derived solely from direct experience, and are put forward as a means of expressing the truths realized in that experience rather than as speculations based on authority or reason. And since it is only the very few who reach to the height of direct experience of God, the mystical writings which appear in the early Middle Ages are also very few.

One of the best examples of genuine mystical thought produced during this time is found in a series of writings which came to light in the early 6th century, and which produced a great effect on all subsequent Christian theology. This collection of writings was attributed to Dionysius, the Areopagite, a figure who is mentioned only briefly in the New Testament book, *Acts of the Apostles* (17:32), as a follower of Paul in Athens. This collection consists of four treatises: *The Divine Names, Mystical Theology, The Celestial Hierarchy,* and *The Ecclesiastical Hierarchy,* along with several letters addressed to various Apostolic figures. All were regarded, up until the 16th century, as genuine and authoritative, and greatly influenced the thought of such men as Maximus the Confessor (580-662), who wrote a Commentary on them; John Scotus Eriugena (810-877), who translated them from the original Greek to Latin; Hugh (1096-1141) and Richard (1123-1173) of St. Victor; Saint Bernard (1091-1153), Bonaventura (1221-1274), and Thomas Aquinus (1225-1274), as well as many lesser notables of the Church.

It was determined in the 16th century, however, and corroborated by scholars of later centuries, that these writings could not possibly have been by Dionysius of the 1st century, owing to their use of terms which came into prominent usage only much later, and were therefore spurious. It is now supposed that they were written at some time around the end of the 5th century, perhaps by a Syrian monk who had some familiarity with the Plotinian tradition through Proclus (410-485), and who, no doubt, chose to use the name of an Apostolic figure as a means of assuring permanence to his work. To Christians, the fact that it was not Dionysius, the Areopagite, who wrote these mystical works, might present a serious impediment to considering their author a genuine representative of Christian mysticism; nonetheless, regardless of who the author really was, he not only greatly influenced Christian thought for over a thousand years, but he was and remains an able spokesman for the perennial philosophy of mysticism.

It was the intention of the author calling himself Dionysius, the Areopagite, to explain, as best he could, the nature of the transcendent Reality which he had experienced, and which the Greek philosophers called "Being," or "the Good," and which the Jews called "Yahveh." That God could not be seen as an object of perception by the eyes, and could not be known by the intellect, the author -- whom we shall call Dionysius for convenience sake -- firmly maintained. However, he explained, God could be experienced in rapt contemplation when the mind transcended all perceptions of images and all knowledge as we commonly know it, and entered into a perfect union with God, participating in His being, and knowing through His knowing:

> He is super-essentially exalted above created things,
> and reveals Himself in His naked Truth to those alone who
> pass beyond all that is pure or impure, and ascend above the
> topmost altitudes of holy things, and who, leaving behind
> them all divine light and sound and heavenly utterances,
> plunge into the Darkness where truly dwells, as the Oracles
> declare, that ONE who is beyond all. [1]
> That divine Darkness is the unapproachable light
> in which God dwells. Into this Darkness, rendered invisible

by its own excessive brilliance and unapproachable by the
intensity of its transcendent flood of light, come to be all
those who are worthy to know and to see God. [2]

We pray that we may come unto this Darkness
which is beyond light, and without seeing and without knowing, to see and to know That which is above vision and above
knowledge. [3]

The Absolute, which he calls, "divine Darkness," is beyond
telling, says Dionysius, for,

The higher we soar in contemplation, the more limited become our expressions of that which is purely intelligible;
even as now, when plunging into the Darkness which is above
the intellect, we pass not merely into brevity of speech, but
even into absolute silence, of thoughts as well as of words...
and, according to the degree of transcendence, so our speech is
restrained until, the entire ascent being accomplished, we become wholly voiceless, inasmuch as we are absorbed in Him
who is totally ineffable. [4]

... We maintain that He is neither soul nor intellect;
nor has He imagination, opinion, reason or understanding; nor
can the reason attain to Him, nor name Him, nor know Him;
neither is He darkness nor light, nor false nor the true; nor
can any affirmation or negation be applied to Him, for although we may affirm or deny the things below Him, we can
neither affirm nor deny Him, inasmuch as the all-perfect and
unique Cause of all things transcends all affirmation, and the
simple pre-eminence of His absolute nature is outside of every
negation -- free from every limitation and beyond them all. [5]

We may approach God, says Dionysius, by either of two ways:
the way of affirmation (*via affirmativa*), or the way of negation (*via
negativa*). By the way of affirmation, we start from the intellectual
understanding of the universal First Cause and proceed downward to
affirm the Divinity in all created things; by the way of negation, we
start from the perception of created things, and, by the process of
elimination, negating and negating (*neti, neti*), we proceed upward,
until finally we reach the All-Transcendent, the Godhead. It is only
this second way, the way of negation, says Dionysius, that can truly
lead us to the vision and knowledge of God. For, while God is,
indeed, manifested as the phenomenal world, this manifestation is not
God, in essence, but His "appearance"; though projecting Himself as
the world, He remains ever as the Unmanifest, the Transcendent, the

Absolute:

> ... While He possesses all the positive attributes of
> the universe, yet, in a more strict sense, He does not possess
> them, since He transcends them all; ... [6]

Therefore, in his treatise on *Mystical Theology*, Dionysius
advises his fellow-presbyter, Timothy, to whom his treatises are
(ostensibly) addressed, to follow the *via negativa* in order to reach by
way of contemplation the supramental knowledge of the transcendent
God:

> ... Do thou, dear Timothy, in the dilligent exercise
> of mystical contemplation, leave behind the senses and the
> operations of the intellect, and all things sensible and intellect-
> ual, and all things in the world of being and non-being, that
> thou mayest arise by unknowing towards the union, as far as
> is attainable, with Him who transcends all being and all know-
> ledge. For by the unceasing and absolute renunciation of thy-
> self and of all things, thou mayest be borne on high, through
> pure and entire self-abnegation, into the superessential radiance
> of the divine Darkness. [7]

It is by this method, says Dionysus, that

> ... we ascend from the particular to the universal conceptions,
> abstracting all attributes in order that, without veil, we may
> know that Unknowing which is enshrouded under all that is
> known and all that can be known, and that we may begin to
> contemplate the superessential Darkness which is hidden by
> all the light that is in existing things. [8]

It is by this method that the "incomparable presence" of God

> ... breaks forth, even from that which is seen and that which
> sees, and plunges the mystic into the Darkness of unknowing,
> whence all perfection of understanding is excluded, and he is
> enwrapped in THAT which is altogether intangible and nou-
> menal, being wholly absorbed in Him who is beyond all, ... [9]

Of that ONE who is beyond all, Dionysius speaks only in
negative terms, for He is beyond all qualities and beyond all that one
could possibly predicate of Him:

> He is neither number nor order; nor greatness nor

> smallness; nor equality nor inequality; nor similarity nor dis-
> similarity; neither is He still, nor moving, nor at rest; neither
> has He power nor is power, nor is light; neither does He live
> nor is He life; neither is He essence, nor eternity nor time; nor
> is He subject to intelligible contact; nor is He science nor
> truth, nor a king, nor wisdom; neither one nor oneness, nor
> godhead nor goodness; nor is He spirit according to our under-
> standing, nor a son, nor a father; nor anything else known to
> us or to any other of the beings or creatures that are or are
> not; ... [10]
>
> ... He suffers no change, corruption, division, priv-
> ation or flux; none of these things can either be identified with
> or attributed to Him. [11]

Nevertheless, of course, if we are to speak of that one Source at all, we must use such words as "God," "Being," etc. And, to signify that Power of God, by which He, the Unmanifest, becomes manifest, we must also invent a multitude of similarly inadequate names. Shall we call it God's "Will," His "Word," His "Maya," His "Thought?" Or should we speak of it as His "emanation," His "projection," His "superimposition," His "illumination," or what? All of these are, of course, but a few of the many terms by which mystics have attempted to convey some idea of what it is like; but none of them may be taken as concise, for words can be evocative at best when used to signify so unique and incomparable a process as that of the Divine whereby He manifests Himself phenomenally as "the world."

In the last analysis, words are but symbols agreed upon to denote particular recognizable things, qualities, etc. A word-symbol can have meaning only to those who have known or experienced that which it symbolizes. In the case of those who have not experienced in the contemplative state that "emanation" or "radiation" of the world-appearance from the supreme Consciousness, they have no means of comprehending what is meant by those words except in the context of their own limited experience, according to which these words are interpreted to mean the same as they would when applied to the phenomenon of light or some other like physical perception.

The analogy of light radiating from the Sun is often used by mystics to describe the "radiation" of the world-appearance from God; but it must be remembered that this is an analogy only, and, though perhaps the best possible, it is an imperfect one. That "radiation" is of a kind utterly unique, and its like is not to be found in anything in the heavens or on earth. That is why it is so difficult for minds unillumined to grasp how it could be that God projects the universe from Himself, yet lives in and as His projection; how it is Himself and yet is other than Himself; how He remains actionless and unmanifest, while acting and manifesting.

We have seen how the word, "Logos," has been used to represent the manifestory-power of God, but Dionysius uses, instead, the word, "Providence," for that mysterious power by which God, while remaining forever beyond all motion and manifestation, never abandoning His absolute Unity, projects Himself as the living universe of movement and form:

> Providence, in going forth to all, yet remains imman-
> ent within itself and stays in a condition of motionless same-
> ness, forever standing fixed, without departing from Itself...
> It will be clear to anyone who interprets divine things in a
> divine way that the cause of the being and well-being of all
> is also Providence, going forth to all, existing in all and about
> all; that it is both [constituent] in all things and transcendent,
> in no way a something within anything, but excels the whole,
> being eternally the same, as Itself, remaining stable within It-
> self, always having the same condition, never becoming
> external to Itself or departing from Its own abode and motion-
> less immanence. And even in effecting Its vast and entire pro-
> vidences, proceeding to all beings, It remains immanent in
> Itself, eternally standing and yet moving, yet neither standing
> nor moving, but as one might say, possessing Its providential
> activity in Its immanence and Its immanence in Its providence,
> both according to and yet transcending nature. [12]
> ... For this Light can never be deprived of Its own
> intrinsic unity, and although in goodness, as is fitting, It
> becomes a manyness and proceeds into manifestation for the
> upliftment and unification of those creatures who are governed
> by Its Providence, yet It abides eternally within Itself in
> changeless sameness, firmly established in Its own unity. [13]

All this creation is God's own Self, a manifest projection of His own being, from Him, in Him, and to Him; and He is realized and felt within the soul as the source of all love-yearning, which draws Himself back to Himself. Says Dionysius:

> Why do the sacred writers speak of God sometimes as
> Yearning and Love, and sometimes as the Object of these
> emotions? In the one case, He is the Cause and Producer and
> Begetter of the thing signified; in the other, He is the Thing

signified Itself. Now the reason why He is Himself on the one
hand moved by the quality signified, and on the other causes
motion by it, is that He moves and leads onward Himself unto
Himself, Who is the only ultimate Beauty and Good -- yea, as
being His own Self-revelation and the bounteous Emanation of
His own transcendent Unity. The motion of yearning [is] ...
pre-existent in the "Good, and, overflowing from the Good,
once again returns to the Good. [14]

But the question arises, "If God is the ultimate Good, and all
this universe is Himself in manifestation, whence comes this thing
called 'evil'?" In his treatise on the *Divine Names*, Dionysius points
out that what we call evil is no more than unawareness, or ignorance,
brought to an active level, and which, like all nescience, has no positive
existence, but is rather a lack, an absence. Evil, says Dionysius, must
not, therefore, be thought of as a real and positive force, but rather as
an absence of the Good. This is no mere trick of language; it is the
considered opinion of all true mystics, including the Buddha, Jesus,
Plotinus and Shankara.

The ignorance of the child is vanished in the man; and where
can we say that it went? It went nowhere; for it never was as a real
entity, but was a mere absence or deprivation of knowledge, as darkness is but the absence of light. Indeed, the process of evolving
toward light or knowledge diminishes and eventually dispels darkness
or ignorance, thereby revealing its non-existence. Likewise, says
Dionysius, the procession toward the Good reveals the non-existence
of evil; it has but an ephemeral and illusory appearance of reality.
And when the perfect Light, the absolute Good, the supreme Knowledge, is attained, all darkness, all evil, all ignorance, is seen to be truly
non-existent.

Even those who seem to be "devils," says Dionysius, derive
their existence from the Good,

and are naturally good, and desire the Beautiful and Good in
desiring existence, life, and consciousness, ... And they are
called evil through the deprivation and the loss whereby they
have lapsed from their proper virtues. Hence they are evil only
insofar as they lack [true] existence; and in desiring evil, they
desire non-existence. [15]
    ... Even so, we say that the air is darkened around us
by a deficiency and absence of the light; while yet the light is
itself always light and illumines the darkness. Therefore, evil
inheres not in the devils or in us, as evil, but only as a defi-

ciency and lack of the perfection of our proper virtues. [16]
... Thus evil has no being, nor any inherence in
things that have being. Evil is nowhere *qua* evil; and it arises
not through any power but through weakness. [17] ... In a
word, evil is weakness, impotence, and deficiency of
knowledge... [18]

It is the Good, the perfect Source and Goal of all beings, says
Dionysius, toward which all men strive, for which all men yearn, and
which all men love. And it is that very inborn love and yearning
which leads all men ultimately to Itself. For that love, that yearning, is
Himself, from Himself, and to Himself. And as that love-longing, He
leads all creatures to the ultimate awareness of the one perfect Good,
their own divine Self.

What the ancient author who called himself Dionysius wrote
then is as true and relevant today as it was when written nearly fifteen
hundred years ago. And so it is with the writings of all the mystics,
for, having experienced the timeless Truth of all existence, their
revelations are also timelessly true. While we know nothing of the life
and circumstances of the author of this small collection of writings,
penned under the name of Dionysius, we may easily infer from what
he says that he was a holy and wise man, and a member of that elite
corps of souls who have been graced with entrance into the Godhead,
and privileged to speak in praise of the eternal Truth for the benefit of
all God's children.

NARADA

Dionysius held that the love of God is God's own activity
within man that serves to draw him to the intimate embrace of union
with Himself. And he was certainly not the first, nor the last, to
observe that devotional love is a gift of God's grace, a sweet breeze of
heavenly joy sent to incite the ardent soul, and is awakened in the
hearts of those whom God would draw to Himself. We have no way,
of course, of tracing the beginnings of devotional love; it has resided
inherently in man since the beginning of time, and has been extolled
as the primary pathway to the unitive experience by thousands of
mystics throughout history.

Before the names of Varuna and Indra were coined, before
Baal, Ra, and Jehovah were called upon by name, before the first

uttered word, this love arose in man -- who then searched for a word to express the hidden Object of his love. The beauty of nature, the sympathy with other creatures, the mystery of the heavens, all stir the primitive heart to love. And that love restlessly searches for the Artist who painted all this beauty, who planted this sympathy in our hearts, and who is concealed behind the mystery of the heavens. It is this love which is the primary religious impulse of all primitive peoples, overlaid as it may be with an infinite variety of conceptual interpretations.

The songs of the Vedas, the Hymns to Amen-Ra, the Hebrew Psalms, all are expressions of that same love for the hidden Creator. And from the very earliest of times, there were those who, finding within themselves the intoxicating joy of this divine love, unparalleled by any worldly love, gave free rein to it, dwelling solely on God, and thereby came to discover within themselves the secret of all existence. This religion of love is the only religion that has ever been; however, mistaking their invented names and rules for the true coin, men have created countless counterfeit religions and fought with one another over the centuries over their invented words and their phantom religions.

It would be foolish to claim that the religion of love was born in this place or that, at this time or that; for beyond about 2500 B.C.E. our search into the past meets with utter obscurity. How many sages, how many glorious souls delighting in divine love, may have lived in those ancient days when the world was young we shall never know. We are able only to see the full-grown tree of devotional love in a later, post-literate, age; its sprouting and its seedling-growth are forever lost to us.

In the land of India, by the time of the Upanishads, the relig-ion of love was a deeply-rooted and sturdy oak. In the Kena Upani-shad, for example, Brahman is referred to as *Tatvanam*, "That which is to be loved." "He should be loved," says its author, "for one who loves the Lord is loved by all." And in the *Bhagavad Gita*, the path of devotional love, or *bhakti*, is fully praised as the highest path to God: "I am the same in all beings," says Krishna, "and My love is ever the same. Those who worship Me with devotion exist in Me and I exist in them." [1]   But perhaps one of the best-known of ancient Indian writings which focuses singularly on the path of love is a treatise called, *The Bhakti Sutras*, attributed to the legendary sage, Narada.

It is impossible to accurately date this brief devotional text; we cannot even be sure that anyone named Narada ever existed. While his name appears in some of the most ancient of legendary epics, *The Bhakti Sutras*, written under his name, appears, by its style and content, to have been written much later -- probably sometime in the first few centuries of the Current Era. The work itself is important, however, as a representative of that philosophy of divine love which permeated Indian culture from the earliest of times. *The Bhakti Sutras* contains no heady metaphysics; it declares nothing about God at all. Its only concern and object of praise is *bhakti*, for it is *bhakti* which leads to the supreme experience of union, wherein everything about God will be known directly.

The author starts off his book by defining *bhakti* :

> Divine love (*bhakti*) is of the nature of nectar (*amrit*), gaining which, one becomes perfect, divine, and contented; and having gained which, a man has no further desire. [2]
>
> ... It is impossible to describe the nature of divine love precisely; one is in the same predicament as a mute person asked to describe the taste of sugar. That inherent love may arise at any time or in any place within one who is fit to receive it. It has no distinctive characteristics, except that it is free of selfish motive. It is an extremely subtle inner experience of all-pervading Unity.
>
> ... Once that divine love is obtained, one looks only to that, one speaks only of that, and one contemplates only that. It is easily recognized; love requires no proof outside of itself -- it is its own proof. It appears in the form of inward peace and supreme happiness. One who has attained it has no anxiety about worldly struggle; he has completely surrendered himself, the world, and everything to the Lord. [3]

The author, whom we'll refer to as Narada, is unique in that he doesn't bother explaining God or Truth; but goes right to the essence of what constitutes man's greatest joy. He eschews the dry metaphysics of his predecessors, and points directly to the self-evident fact of man's inherent love; and expresses his conviction that it is this love which constitutes man's greatest joy, and leads to the attainment of man's greatest fulfillment in union with God. "Knowing this love," says Narada,

> one becomes intoxicated and enthralled, continually immersed in the inherent bliss of the Self.
> This love is not the same as worldly love; by its very

nature, divine love turns away from all worldly love. By
"turns away," I mean that all one's intention is "turned toward"
God. This leads to union with God, and indifference toward all
else. Union with God is attained by giving up all other supports. [4] [Recall Plotinus' "Let all else go."]

Then, explaining how such one-pointed love is reflected in the
life of man, he says:

> Narada holds that divine love manifests as the dedi-
> cation of all activities to God, complete surrender to Him, and
> extreme anguish in the event of forgetting Him. [5]
> ... The greatest and most blessed of His devotees are
> those who feel one-pointed love for the Lord for His own sake
> alone. When such devotees gather together, and speak of Him,
> their voices choke with emotion, their hairs stand on end, and
> tears stream from their eyes. Such devotees purify not only
> those around them, but the entire world. It is they who make
> holy places holy, who make good deeds good, and who give
> authority to scriptural authority; for they are filled with God.
> ... Their ancestors rejoice, the godlike dance with
> happiness, and the earth itself is revived. Such devotees make
> no distinctions based on class, learning, beauty, family, wealth
> or position; they recognize everything as God's. [6]

He further asserts that the paths of dedicated service,
knowledge and meditation are secondary to *bhakti*, for it is *bhakti*
which inspires and brings into being these various effects. *Bhakti* is
therefore the cause of all efforts undertaken, and is also the goal of all
efforts; i.e., love leads to *parabhakti*, "supreme love." This supreme
love is spoken of in other ancient devotional texts as well, such as the
Devi Bhagavatam, where it is defined in this way:

> As oil poured from one vessel to another flows in an
> unbroken stream, so when the mind in an unbroken stream
> thinks about God, we have what is called *parabhakti*.

And in the *Bhakti-rasayana,* parabhakti is extolled as:

> the highest goal of all man's endeavors; it is uncom-
> parable and unalloyed bliss.

Narada points out that this highest state of the mind, this
attainment of pure and perfect love, is attainable through no means
other than loving:

Some teachers think that knowledge (*jnan*) alone is
the means to attain divine love (*bhakti*); others think that
these two are mutually interdependent. But Narada thinks that
a fruit must come from a tree of the same kind. Therefore, to
attain to supreme love, the only means worthy of acceptance is
love. [7]

Finally, Narada speaks of the several ways of developing that
inner love:

Teachers sing of various methods of obtaining divine
love: one may obtain it immediately by turning away from
the objective world, and giving up all worldly desires; or one
may develop it through continually giving loving service to
humanity; or by listening to and singing forth the praises of
God, even while engaged in the ordinary activities of the
world; or it may be obtained by contact with a great person
(*mahapurusha*) who has love for God; or simply by receiving
a little of God's grace. [8]

... One does not need to avoid the world to attain
divine love, nor is it necessary to avoid the world after attaining it. Actions must undoubtedly continue to be performed; it
is only the desire for the fruits of actions that is to be abandoned.

It is necessary to rid oneself of pride, vanity, and
other related vices. One who has dedicated all his activities to
the Lord should also direct all his feelings of desire, pride,
anger, and so forth, to Him as well. One should love Him as
a servant loves his master, or as a devoted wife loves her
husband, giving constant service to Him. [9]

... One should not engage in theological disputes;
there is room for many differrent viewpoints, and no single
viewpoint is the final truth. One should reflect, instead, on
the means to awaken devotion, and one should engage oneself
in the practice of those means.

It is the Lord alone who is to be loved and adored at
all times with a mind free from external care. To those devotees who love Him and sing His glory, He reveals Himself.
This is the highest path, to love the one absolute, eternal,
Truth. Truly, this divine love is the Highest. [10]

Narada's path of divine love is complete in itself; it requires
no further amplification, no elaborate metaphysical explanations. It
begins from a point beyond the mere intellectual understanding of
who and what the Lord is, and so requires no recapitualation of that

understanding.   Thus, *The Bhakti Sutras* expresses the pure and
simple essence of all religions, the condensation of all philosophies,
the ultimate directive of all spiritual guidance; in a brief and concise
form it reveals the path, the goal, and the way. Says Narada:

> Whoever has faith in these teachings and practices
> them, attains love for God, and realizes his beloved God.
> Truly, he attains that Lord whom all in the world adore. [11]

PATANJALI

The name of Patanjali is invariably associated with the word
"yoga," even though this word was in use long before Patanjali. We
find the word, "yoga," used in the ancient epic literature and in the
Upanishads as well. For example, the *Katha Upanishad* states:

> When the five senses and the mind are still, and the
> reasoning intellect rests in silence, then begins the highest
> path. This calm steadiness of the senses is called yoga. Then
> one should become watchful, because yoga comes and goes. [1]

From this passage it is clear that yoga is regarded as the final
stage of the journey toward God, once the mind and the senses have
been stilled by preceding devotional or purificatory practices. This
same meaning is carried over into the *Bhagavad Gita*, where, in the
Sixth Chapter, Krishna explains to Arjuna its practice:

> Day after day, let the yogi practice the stilling of the
> mind, in a secret place, in deep seclusion, master of his
> thoughts, hoping for nothing, desiring nothing. Let him
> find a place that is pure and a pose that is restful... In that
> place let him rest and practice yoga for the purification of the
> soul; with his mind and vital energy (*prana*) stilled, let him
> be silent before the One.
>   With his soul in peace, and all fear gone, and firm in
> the vow of purity, let him hold his mind steady, focusing his
> intention on Me, the supreme Lord. When the mind of the
> yogi is steady, and finds rest in the Spirit, when all restless
> desires have vanished, then he is a *yukta*, one who has attained
> yoga. ... Then he knows the joy of eternity; he sees with his
> mind far beyond what the senses can see. He remains steady in
> the Truth, unmoving. ... This supreme joy comes to the yogi

whose heart is still, whose passions have found rest; he is free
from all sin, and is one with Brahman. [2]

Yoga, it is clear, cannot be divorced or separated from devotion; no one has ever reached the stage of mental concentration
upon the eternal Self without one-pointed devotion to his Goal,
without the utter determination to fix the mind solely on That to the
exclusion of all extraneous thoughts or interests. Concentration upon
the eternal Self is nothing but devotion; yoga is, therefore, the very
summit and culmination of devotion.

This word, "yoga," is usually defined as stemming from the
Sanskrit root word, *yuj*, from which the English word, "yoke," also
comes, and is said to signify a joining together, a union. (Incidentally, the word, "religion," derived from the Latin, *religare*, has an
identical meaning.) But yoga may not rightfully be said to be a
union, since the Soul (*Atman*) is already eternally identical with the
one Consciousness (*Brahman*). Nor can it truly be said to be a
separation of the soul from the body, since they are but two aspects of
one indivisible Unity. If we say it is an "expansion" of consciousness, we imply that the one Consciousness is not already fully
expanded; and if we say it is a "removal" of ignorance, we find it
impossible to explain just what this ignorance is that has been removed. How then can we define yoga?

Sometime in the first few centuries of our Current Era, a sage
going by the name of Patanjali stated it this way:

> *yogas chitta-vritti nirodha*
> ("Yoga is the restraint of the thought-waves of the mind.") [3]

This statement asserts that the one Consciousness is manifest as
the very mind of man which is incessantly vibrating with thought; and
that when the mind is once again brought to stillness, it is verily the
one Consciousness. Like a candle-flame in a drafty room, the mind is
flickering here and there because of the gusts of thought constantly
moving it; but when all the drafts are sealed off, and the winds cease to
blow, the mind becomes steady and bright, like an unflickering
candle-flame -- and the mind regains its eternal, unitive, state.
"Then," says Patanjali, "a man abides in his own true nature.
Otherwise [while the thought-waves are still arising in the mind], he
remains identified with the thought-waves." [4]

If we accept this definition of yoga, we can perhaps envisualize it figuratively as a mergence of the waves on a lake into the lake itself, or a mergence of the ripples into the calm surface of a pond. This is very close to an apt analogy, for, while it suggests a mergence or "union" of two things, it is clear that the two were never actually separate. Similarly, when the subtle vibrations of the mind are entirely stilled, that mind is itself the absolute Mind, the universal Self.

This word, "yoga," also has a broader meaning; it signifies not only the unitive state, but also the path or means to the attainment of that state. Thus, the *Bhagavad Gita* speaks of "jnan yoga," "bhakti yoga," etc., as the various paths to mergence. These various paths are really only varying aspects of the one broad highway of yoga; devotion, knowledge, meditation and selfless service are simply the actualization of the various facets of one's being on the emotional, intellectual, spiritual and physical levels, toward the goal of unitive awareness. And while these various "yogas" may be spoken of individually, they may not be separated in fact; for they are interdependent, and, in the final analysis, integral.

Yoga did not originate with Patanjali, or even with the Upanishads -- as witness the yogic posture of the Shiva prototype on the seal from Mohenjo-daro; but it is Patanjali who formulated the coherent set of precepts known as *The Yoga Sutras*, in which the path of yoga is explicitly defined and systematized. Utilizing the familiar terms of Kapila, he outlined his metaphysicas along the lines of the traditional Samkhya view:

> The Purusha is pure Consciousness; but though pure,
> it appears as the mind. Prakrti exists only because of, and for
> the sake of, Purusha. Purusha appears as Prakrti only so that
> He may experience Himself [as a subject and object]. It is
> only when Purusha becomes incognizant of His real nature
> that Prakrti exists. When this incognizance is removed,
> Purusha knows Himself to be alone, independent and free.
> And the way to dispel or remove this incognizance is to
> practice the uninterrupted awareness of the Self. [5]

As we can see, Patanjali's philosophy does not deviate in the slightest from that of Kapila or the author of the *Bhagavad Gita*, or that of the Upanishadic sages. Patanjali made no real contribution to mystical philosophy; he merely formalized it, by framing a systematic outline of its progressive stages. He begins with the preliminary requisites of "austerity, study, and dedication of the fruits of one's work to God." Next, he moves on to the purificatory stage of adherence to moral principles such as truthfulness, non-stealing, refraining from harming others, etc. This is followed by the practice of contentment, mental control, concentration, meditation, and finally, *samadhi*, or absorption in the Self.

Concentration (*dharana*) he defines as "holding the mind fixed on one internal or external object." Meditation (*dhyana*) is a further progression or intensification of concentration, in which there is "an unbroken flow of thought toward the object concentrated upon." And absorption (*samadhi*) is when, "in meditation, the object alone shines forth, without the distortion produced by the mind." This, says Patanjali, "is Liberation (*moksha*). The Self alone shines forth in its own pristine nature, as pure Consciousness."

In the sense in which the word, "yoga," is used to mean a "path" to the unitive state, "the yoga of meditation" is sometimes opposed to "the yoga of devotion." And though they are complementary aspects of the one broad road of yoga, the two approaches differ in some important ways. *Bhakti*, or devotional love, expresses itself in other-directed prayer, while meditation may be said to be the expression of *jnan*, or knowledge. Thus, devotion and knowledge manifest in entirely different ways. The *bhakta* identifies with the ego-mind (the individuality, or *jiva*), and carries on a prayerful dialogue with the Supreme, until, becoming fully concentrated on his Lord, he becomes entirely stilled and surrendered to God. Then he is able to experience that "union" in which he knows himself to be the one all-pervading Reality, the universal "I" who is the Source and Witness of all individuality.

The *jnani*, on the other hand, identifies with the Witness, the pure Consciousness, and attacks the task from the other side, concentrating his awareness entirely on the universal Self from the start. By so doing, he silences the ego-mind at its root, and becomes still. In the *jnani's* meditation on the Self, there is no prayer, no clamoring of the ego-mind; there is only the continuous awareness of the witnessing Self. Thoughts, as they begin to arise out of consciousness, like bubbles rising to the surface of a pond, are witnessed at their source; and, as the awareness is not given to thoughts but is concentrated on the witnessing Self, thoughts, unfueled by attention, simply fade and disappear. Thus, one reaches, by the front door, as it were, the awareness of the all-pervading Self. It can be seen, therefore, that meditation and prayer cannot be practiced simultaneously, but they are both necessary and complementary, and should not be regarded as mutually exclusive paths.

Throughout the ages, many different methods of meditation have been recommended, yet in nearly every mystical tradition certain basic elements are invariably prescribed: (1) a beneficial posture, such as the "lotus posture" (*padmasana*); (2) a gaze fixed on the object of concentration; and (3) an inner attention upon a single word or phrase (*mantram*), which may be a name of God or perhaps simply the natural sound of *sah-ham*, as the breath is inhaled and exhaled. The posture allows the freest flow of the body's subtle energy-current, helping to lift the consciousness to a plane above the body and mind; and the focusing of the gaze, and concentration upon a *mantram,* displaces the play of thoughts and allows the awareness to be reassigned to the witnessing Self.

The benefits of such meditation are manifold; it brings calm and stability to the mind, and a sense of peaceful well-being; and it enables the awareness to reach the threshold of Self-realization -- the same experience known through devotion as "the union with God." When one experiences, through meditation, that one's true, constant identity is above and beyond thought, beyond the individual body and soul, one ceases to identify with these ephemera, and begins to identify with the witnessing Consciousness, and to view one's own thoughts, feelings, and daily activities from a vantage point that is detached and supremely secure.

The approach to God-realization advocated by Patanjali is one that is much more appealing to the *jnani* than to the *bhakta*. But these two designations, as mentioned before, are not at all exclusive of one another, but are complementary -- each being appropriate to one or the other aspect of our dual-sided nature. Some, *jnanis* by temperament, prefer to identify with the eternal Self; others, *bhaktas* by nature, identify with the separative ego, and relate to the eternal Self as a child to a father, or a lover to a beloved. There are some who recognize the validity of both these paths, and practice now one, now the other, according to the inspiration of the moment, without feeling the least contradiction in so doing.

TANTRA

The word, "Tantra," seems to have been derived from the Sanskrit root, *tan*, meaning "to expand." It appears as early as the 4th century B.C.E., in a work called the *Apastamba-Srauta Sutra*, where it is used to signify any ritual procedure containing a number of aspects. Kautilya, in the 3rd century B.C.E., used the word in the sense of 'fundamental canons of a system of thought.' But by the early centuries of the Current Era, the word, *Tantra*, had come to be associated with a distinct metaphysical view complete with its own unique terminology. It is a metaphysic based on mystical experience, and is essentially identical to the viewpoint of Vedanta, Samkhya and Yoga. It is, indeed, yet another expression of the age-old and perennial vision of a primal and essential Unity self-divided into Male and Female principles.

Since the earliest utterings of man, the primal Unity, experienced by the mystic, has been characterized as dual-faceted; one aspect being transcendent, the other immanent as the world; one absolute, the other relative; one eternally unchanged, the other a panoply of movement. And since earliest times these two aspects have been designated Male and Female: the Absolute, the supreme Consciousness, is the Father, the male sovereign and Lord; His creative Energy, which gives birth to the universe, is the Mother-power, the bountiful Goddess, queen Maya. Put in less figurative terms, the constant Awareness, which is realized in the experience of Unity to be the one eternal and indivisible Reality, is also realized to be the very One who projects His own living light in the form of the universe. That light is not separate from Himself, nor does it, in fact, go out from Him; but in order to speak of it at all, it is necessary to differentiate it from the constant Awareness, the unchanging Absolute. Thus, the primal Awareness is spoken of as "He"; and the light that forms the mutable world is called "She." But they are never two. He is the universal Mind; She is His Thought. He is the Speaker; She is the Word. He is the Seed; She is the Tree. They are complementary aspects of one indivisible Reality.

It is not very difficult to see how these two purely abstract principles came to be represented by artists and poets since primitive times as two independent objects of worship, humanized according to the characteristics described by the sages. "He" was the remote, unapproachable, Absolute, and was therefore portrayed by the Dravidian peoples of ancient India as a totally indrawn ascetic, a naked yogi, seated in perpetual contemplation of eternity atop the icy peaks of Mount Kailas. He sat on the ground with his long, untended hair piled on his head, a cobra draped 'round his neck, and his face and body covered with the ashes of the world, which, in his own mind, he had reduced to nothing. In his hands he held a trident and a conch; his mount was the great white bull, Nandi; and his symbol was the phallus-shaped stone, called the *lingam* .

Such an hyposticized representation of the absolute Being has existed in India since the most ancient of times, long before the Aryan invasion; and over the centuries, "He" has been called by many different names. In Vedic times, he was referred to as *Pashupati* ("Lord of *pashus*, or sentient creatures); when associated with the angry and destructive forces of nature, he was *Rudra*. One of Rudra's epithets was *Shiva*, meaning "auspicious" (even today, in India, a great rain-storm is considered "auspicious"); and eventually, *Shiva* came to be the name for God most prominently used among the Dravidian peoples. Frequently, Shiva, himself, is referred to by such epithets as *Mahadev,* "the great God," or *Maheshvar*, "great Lord."

Simultaneous with the early development of this God-symbol among the rural populace consisting mostly of the aboriginal races of India, was the similarly symbolic representation of the one God among the Aryan population as *Vishnu*. Vishnu, one of the names for God appearing in the Vedas, was pictured as a golden-robed sovereign who lived in splendor in the heavenly realm of Vaikuntha. It was he who became incarnated as Krishna, the cow-herd boy who later became the great king and sage of Dwarka in the *Bhagavad Gita,* and also as Rama, the brave warrior-king of the epic, *Ramayana*.

Shiva and Vishnu, though obviously dissimilar in characteristics, are both symbols of the one Godhead. Shiva represents the qualities of eternity, detachment, immovability; while Vishnu stands as a symbol of the power, glory and sovereignty of the one all-governing Lord. From both the predominantly Dravidian Shaivites and the predominantly Aryan Vaishnavites, a vast body of mythology arose around both these symbols as their ritual worship spread throughout the land of India, and as many temples and statues (*murtis*) were built commemorating one or the other of these two representations of God. But, of course, the poets and artists had not forgotten the Female aspect of Reality. The *shakti*, or manifestory-power of God, was symbolized as the female counterpart to the male deity. The consort of Shiva, his *shakti*, was *Sati* (feminine form of *Sat*, or "Truth"), the beautiful nymph-like daughter of king Daksha, whose seductive charms moved Shiva to awake from his profound contemplative state. In yet another mythological representation, She was called *Parvati*. As the hypostacized and deified Power of Shiva, She was also called *Durga, Kali,* or *Ambika*. She too was represented by statues, and worshipped in temples devoted to her alone. She was usually depicted as many-armed, displaying both her beneficent and her destructive aspects, holding out one hand in a gesture of gentleness and compassion, while in another she wielded a sword. She was garlanded with skulls, and daubed with blood, as she rode forth astride a ferocious lion or tiger.

For those who preferred the Vishnu-personification of God, the Female principle was the goddess, *Lakshmi*, also known as *Shri*. She was the source of all wealth and good fortune. She was the jewel-bedecked Mother who granted to her children whatever boons they asked of her. It was she who took the form of Radha, the paramour of Krishna; and Sita, the faithful wife of Rama. While Shiva's female counterpart was associated more prevalently with the angry, destructive, aspects of nature, and was pictured as a blood-thirsty she-demon, Vishnu's consort was the compassionate and gracious bestower of gifts, and was pictured as the epitome of feminine beauty and grace (*Figure 9*).

Between the 1st and 5th centuries of the Current Era a vast body of mythological literature was written about these two pairs of gods. Hundreds of stories were written to describe their lives and exploits, and, mingled with these stories were the philosophical explanations of the abstract principles which they represented. These philosophical mythologies were all the rage, as they reached to the non-intellectual populace in a way that purely didactic treatises could not. They were called by the generic name of *Puranas;* there was the *Vishnu Purana,* the *Shiva Purana,* the *Shakti Purana,* the *Bhagavat Purana* (which told the legends of Krishna), a *Skanda Purana*, and many, many others.

By this time and probably long before, there were large magnificent temples dedicated to Shiva all over the country. Some of the grandest were the Badrikashrama and Somnath temples in the north, Vishvanath temple at Benares, Nakulishvar temple at Calcutta and Rameshvaram temple in the south. Great yogis of the time, such as the illustrious Gorakshanath and Manikka-vachakar, sang the praises of Shiva, and imitated Him in their outer appearance and appurtenances. Temples and *murtis* dedicated to Vishnu in the form of Rama and Krishna also dotted the country in every town and city. The spread of the Puranic legends aroused devotion to one or another of these "gods" in the hearts of the simple populace, and every facet of their lives became permeated with devotion to these legendary beings, who represented, of course, the one Divinity.

Shakti, too, had her own temples, and her own worshippers. According to Farquhar, the medieval historian, the period ranging from 500 to 900 C.E. was called "the Shakta period," a time in which Shakti worship became widely prevalent throughout India. But even as early as the 2nd century it is apparent that She was the object of a widespread cult. In the *Mahabharata* (2nd-3rd century C.E.), She is described as Durga, and prayers are offered to Her. And in the *Markandeya Purana,* compiled during the Gupta period (ca. 4th century), Mahadevi, the great Goddess, is treated quite extensively in one complete book of thirteen chapters, called the *Devi Mahatmyam* ("Praise of the Goddess"). There She is described as identical with Purusha's Prakrti, Vishnu's Maya, and Shiva's Shakti. She is also referred to as *Chiti*; i.e., pure Consciousness, a manifested aspect of the Absolute. The *Devi Bhagavata Purana* is entirely devoted to Her; there She is referred to as *Mahashakti, Mahalakshmi, Mahakali,* and *Mahamaya.*

The great Goddess also appears in the *Agni Purana, Bhaga-vat Purana, Vishnu Purana,* and others of this genre. In the 8th and 9th centuries, lesser Puranas were written in sole dedication to the Goddess; these were the so-called *Upa-Puranas:* the *Devi Purana, Kalika Purana,* and *Mahabhagavata Purana.* Here, as a representative sample, is how She is described in the *Vishnu Purana*:

> Shri, the bride of Vishnu, the mother of the world, is eternal, imperishable. As He is all-pervading, so also is She. ... Vishnu is the meaning, She is speech (*Vac*). Vishnu is consciousness; She is intellect. He is Goodness; She is devotion. He is the Creator; She is the creation. Shri is the earth; Hari (Vishnu) is the substratum. The God is utter stillness; She is surrender.
>
> ...Lakshmi is the light; and Hari, who is the All and the Lord of all, is the lamp. She, the mother of the world, is

the creeping vine; and Vishnu, the tree around which She
clings. ... He, the bestower of blessings, is the bridegroom;
the lotus-throned Goddess is the bride. ... Govinda (Vishnu)
is love; and Lakshmi, his gentle spouse, is [the] pleasure [of
love]. But why go on listing the ways in which they are present? It is enough to say, in a word, that of gods, animals and
men, Hari is all that is called male; Lakshmi is all that is
termed female. There is nothing other than these two. [1]

It was by such figurative language that the mystic's profound
vision of a unitive duality was conveyed to the populace. In art, the
one self-divided Reality was sometimes portrayed as a god and
goddess locked in a passionate embrace. In some medieval sculptures,
Shiva is portrayed as a corpse (dead to the world), with Shakti, in the
dreadful form of Kali, sitting on him in an act of sexual union, or
dancing in abandon on his outstretched body. What the Chinese
symbolized in the Yin-Yang circle, which is both divided and
undivided, the Indians preferred to represent as male and female
joined in a loving union (*Figure 10*).

Some of the most beautiful and erotic representations of this
union were sculpted by the Buddhists in the 9th century, and are in
evidence to this day in the caves of Orissa and at Khajuraho. Many
Tibetan figurines of the same period, which are called *Yab-Yum*
(Father-Mother), also represent in erotic copulative poses these two
principles of the one Reality (*Figure 11*). The inseparability of these
two is expressed in the statues of Shiva as *Ardhanarishvara,* a being
who is half male, half female (*Figure 12*). The predominant picto-
graphic symbol of this duality-in-unity, however, has been since pre-
Aryan times, the *lingam* in the *yoni*, a symbol found in almost every
Indian temple, comprised of a stone phallus symbol accompanied by
a base in the form of the female sex organ. The two together form a
recognizable symbol of the complementarity of the two inseparable
aspects of the One.

We are now ready, after this long preamble, to understand the
expansive development of Tantra during this same period. Tantra is
the yoga of the union of Shiva and Shakti. Of course, they are
already one, but in order to *experience* this unity, certain practices are
prescribed whereby the illusory and separative ego is dispelled and the
awareness of the eternal unity dawns within. Where the Upanishadic
philosophy leaves off, spiritual practice, or *sadhana*, begins; and it is
this *sadhana* which is the province of the Tantric scriptures.

From the earliest times, the Tantric *sadhana* has co-existed with the Vedantic philosophy in the mainstream of Indian spiritual teaching. But only around the 5th or 6th centuries was it disseminated in literary form; thereafter, the principles of Tantra are to be found in nearly every subsequent piece of spiritual literature, and in the teachings of India's saints and sages. If the Vedanta represents the exoteric teaching, the Tantra represents the esoteric teaching; it is the guide to the culmination of the spiritual journey begun with the comprehension of monistic philosophy.

Some of the earliest of the literary expressions of Tantra were the *Apabhramsa dohas* and the *Charyagitis* of the Siddhas, and the Yogic texts of the Nathas, such as that of Gorakshanath. In Kashmir, a number of Tantric writings appeared in the 7th and 8th centuries which are called *Agamas*, regarded by their proponents as divinely inspired scriptures. As they extol the Absolute by the name of Shiva, they are also known as *Shaivagamas*. They contain the precepts of what is now known as Kashmir Shaivism. Among these scriptural writings are the *Shiva-sutras* of Vasugupta, the *Shiva-drshti* of Somananda, the *Tantraloka* of Abhinavagupta, and the *Pratyabijna-hrdayam* of Kshemaraj. Immensely popular, these Tantric texts were immediately copied both in Sanskrit and in the regional Dravidian languages such as Telugu, Tamil, and Kanarese.

By the 8th century, Tantrism was widely taught by Brahmin and Buddhist teachers alike. In 747 C.E., Padma Shambhava, a professor at the Buddhist university of Nalanda, took the Tantric philosophy to Tibet where he founded his monastery; and around the same time a Mahayana Buddhist in Bengal was publishing his *Hevajira Tantra*. Shankaracharya, the great exponent of *advaita* (non-dualistic) Vedanta, is also said to have written at least two Tantric works, the *Sundaryalahari*, and the *Prapancha-sara*. In the 10th century, while a Shaivite yogi was writing his Tantric works, the *Kalika Purana* and the *Rudrayamala*, a Jain monk of Aysore was writing his *Jvalini Tantra*. Today, the treatises on Tantra by the representatives of various religious sects are too numerous to mention.

While Tantra is primarily a *sadhana,* that is to say, a prescribed system of practice, nonetheless, in order to understand the reasoning behind the *sadhana,* it is necessary to understand not only Tantra's metaphysics, but its conception of the psycho-physical nature of the human body as well. It is the teaching of Tantric yoga that the Shakti, which is the universal creative force manifesting as all sentient and insentient beings, is the projected "Power" or "Will" of Shiva, the pure Absolute:

> He knows the true Reality who sees the entire uni-
> verse as the play of the supreme Shakti of supreme Shiva [2]
> ... Throughout all these forms, it is the Lord alone;
> He illumines His own nature. In truth, there is no other cause
> of all manifestation except His Will (Shakti) which gives ex-
> istence to all worldly enjoyment and liberation as well. [3]
> ... In truth, there is no difference between Uma
> (Shakti) and Shankara (Shiva); the One consists of two
> aspects; of this there is no doubt. [4]

Such statements reveal that the Tantric metaphysic is identical to the Vedantic view and to that of all its mystically inspired predecessors. What is unique in Tantrism, and what constitutes its most significant contribution to mystical thought is its conception of man's subtle psycho-physical nature. Like all mystical philosophies, Tantra recognizes that man's essential being is identical with the ultimate Being; i.e., Shiva. But, according to the Tantric scriptures, man remains ignorant of his Godhood and identified with the body and mind, so long as the Shakti residing in him remains unawakened and unevolved.

According to the Tantric scriptures, Shakti exists in man in an involuted state, whose purpose it is to evolve toward the realization of its identity with Shiva. This Shakti resides in man in a concentrated state in the subtle body, at a location corresponding to the perineum (shown in diagrams as being at the base of the spine). To differentiate this involuted Shakti-within-man from the all-inclusive Shakti, it is called *Kundalini-Shakti* ("the coiled energy"). This *Kundalini* energy can be compared to a watch-spring which is involuted to a state of potential release, and which, according to its own timing, acts as the evolutionary force which eventually brings all mankind to a complete expansion of consciousness. When, however, it is activated (awakened), by any of several methods, it becomes quickened, rapidly increasing its activity, and leads a person to enlightenment within one lifetime.

The Tantric seers say that the subtle body is composed of a complex network of subtle nerve-filaments (*nadis*) through which the life-force, called *Prana-Shakti,* flows. This *Prana-Shakti* (called *Chi* by the Taoists of ancient China) is the current, as it were, which operates to enliven the body and mind and to regulate the functions of the internal organs.   When the involuted *Kundalini Shakti* is aroused, it infuses the *Prana* current with a newly intensified potency, by which the evolutionary process is greatly accelerated.

The *Prana-Shakti* normally flows evenly through two main *nadis* which parallel either side of the spinal column; these are called *Ida* (on the left) and *Pingala* (on the right).   But when the *Kundalini-Shakti* is activated, this current finds its way through a subtle middle passage, called the *Sushumna*.   Within this central *nadi,* through which the activated *Prana* current flows, there are six ascending nerve-plexuses, called *chakras* ("wheels").   It is the purpose of the awakened *Kundalini* energy to cleanse and purify the *nadis,* which in unregenerate man, are clogged and constricted by immoderate living, and to pass through each of the *chakras* as it ascends from the base of the spinal column to the crown of the head. Its final goal is the seventh nerve-plexus at the top of the head, called *Sahasrar* (the thousand-petalled lotus), where *Kundalini-Shakti* is said to attain its union with Shiva.   When this occurs, a person experiences the Absolute, the Godhead:

> As long as the Prana does not flow in the Sushumna
> and enter the Sahasrar, ... as long as the mind does not become
> absorbed in the Self, so long those who talk of spiriual know-
> ledge indulge only in boastful and false prattle. [5]
> ... The rush of bliss that ensues upon the meeting of
> the Pair, the supreme Shakti and the Self above, is the real
> joining; all other joinings are mere copulation. [6]

The *Kundalini-Shakti* is ordinarily in a dormant, regulated-function state; only when it becomes awakened, or activated, does it begin its accelerated work.   This awakening is said to be achieved by several different methods: one may awaken the *Kundalini* forcefully through the regimen of postures (*asanas*) and breathing techniques (*pranayama*) prescribed by *Hatha-Yoga*; through intense devotion to God; through concentration of the mind upon the inner Self; through the practice of chanting or reciting the *mantram* given by a qualified Master (*Sadguru*); or simply by coming in contact with and receiving the graces of one who has already accomplished the full ascendency of the *Kundalini-Shakti*.   Such a person, who is in the state of enlightenment and capable of transmitting *Kundalini-Shakti* from his own accumulated fund, is called the *Guru*; and the transmission of his grace in the form of Shakti is called *Shaktipat.* According to the Tantric *shastras,* or scriptures, such a Guru is able to thus awaken the dormant *Kundalini* of those he deems prepared for it, by a mere glance, a word, a touch, or simply by his very thought or will. Such an "initiation" by the *Guru* is regarded as synonymous with receiving the grace of God:

> The learned men of all times always hold that the descent of grace does not have any cause or condition, but depends entirely on the free will of the Lord. [7]
> ... From his transcendent station, the Lord in the form of the Guru frees one from all bondage. [8]
> ... The Guru is the means [to enlightenment]. [9]
> ... Initiation [by the Guru] is the first ladder to the terrace of Liberation. [10]
> ... The touch of the hand of the Guru destroys the impurities of the world and converts the base metal [of the disciple] into gold. [11]

When the *Kundalini-Shakti* is thus awakened, certain initial symptoms occur. They are evidenced physically, mentally, and emotionally. Physical symptoms include internal body heat, involuntary shaking of the spine and limbs (*kriyas*), and the spontaneous occurance of *asanas* and vocal productions. Physical pain may be experienced at the base of the spine, or one may experience alternating heaviness and lightness of the body, or a stimulation of the sexual glands, or merely a great increase in vitality. One may also have the sensation of a darting, or crawling, energy rising up the spine, or experience the movement of the activated *Prana-Shakti* moving about in various parts of the body.

It is said that when a person's Shakti is operating in the lower three *chakras* -- *Muladhar, Svadhisthana,* and *Manipura* (corresponding to the coccyx, the sex organ and the navel) -- sleep, sex, and food are their main concerns. But when the *Kundalini-Shakti* reaches the heart-center, the *Anahat chakra,* one begins to feel intense devotion and longing for God. As the *Kundalini-Shakti* rises higher to the throat region, the *Vishuddha chakra,* then one begins to hear different inner sounds and taste inner nectars; and at the forehead, the *Ajna chakra,* one sees delightful lights and visions. When the Shakti reaches the crown of the head, the *Sahasrar,* the individual consciousness merges into super-consciousness, and the aspirant reaches *samadhi,* the pure awareness of the transcendent Self:

From the element earth in the Muladhara,
To the element fire in the Svadhisthana,
To the element water in the Manipura,
To the element air in the Anahata,
To the element ether in the Vishuddha,
To the element of mind in the Ajna,
You travel, O Mother, to keep your secret rendezvous
With your Lord in the thousand-petalled lotus, Sahasrar. [12]

>   ... When the bliss of Consciousness is attained, there
> is the lasting acquisition of that state in which Consciousness
> is one's only Self, and in which all that appears is identical
> with Consciousness. Even the body is experienced as identical
> with Consciousness. [13]
>   ... Awareness of the perceiver and the perceived is
> common to all beings. But with Self-realized yogis it is
> different; they are aware of them as one. [14]

Thus, the whole purpose of the Tantra scriptures is to elucidate the means whereby one may experience the union of Shakti and
Shiva, and thus know the transcendent Unity in *samadhi*. This Tantric
sadhana takes many forms, from the ritualized worship of Shiva and
Shakti (with flowers and fruit offerings, etc.) to austere yogic
practices, to the actual sexual union of male and female practitioners
in the symbolic enactment of the transcendent union of the God and
Goddess. This last, however, is a degenerate form of Tantra, known
by the name of *Vamachara,* or "left-hand path," to distinguish it
from the "right" (*Dakshina*) or pure Tantric path. It was just this
degenerate form of Tantra which led Kumarila, in the 6th century
C.E., to write that Tantra was "only for the degraded, the uneducated,
the fallen, and the infirm, and is fraught with much danger." The
"pure" form of Tantric *sadhana* aims at transforming the individual
through a harnessing of his inherent energy (*shakti*), and by a
concentrated confinement of that energy within, forcing it to rise
Godward. It is the focusing of this psychic energy which is the entire
purpose of Tantric *sadhana*; and the goal of this *sadhana* is Self-
realization.

In the Tantric, as well as the Vedantic, view, Self-realization is
synonymous with Liberation. "Liberation," said the Shaivite sage,
Abhinavagupta, "is nothing else but the awareness of one's own true
nature." He was stating in effect what Jesus of Nazareth had said

many centuries previous: "You shall know the Truth, and the Truth shall set you free." Always we are Consciousness. That is our continually undeviating Reality. We are the Witness of the play of our own Shakti which is forming this entire universe. It is the *knowing* of this, the direct realization of the Self, which constitutes the soul's liberation. For the Self, of course, there is no liberation; the Self is always free. It has never been bound. It is only our "illusory" self, our limited soul-identity, that experiences bondage and liberation:

> Though in reality there is no bondage, the individual
> is in bondage as long as there exists the feeling of limitation
> in him. ... In fact, there never has been any veiling or cover-
> ing anywhere in reality. No one has ever been in bondage.
> Please show me where such bondage exists. Besides these two
> false beliefs, that there is such a thing as bondage and such a
> thing as an individual mind, there is no bondage for anyone
> anywhere. [15]
> ...The individual soul (*jiva*) is Shiva; Shiva is jiva.
> When in bondage, it is jiva; freed from bondage, it is Shiva. [16]
> ... The knowledge of the identity between the jiva and
> Shiva constitutes liberation; lack of this knowledge constitutes
> bondage. [17]

The eternal Self is always free; yet so long as we are unaware of that freedom, we are bound. Liberation is therefore a state of awareness. So long as we are aware of the ever-free Self, we are entirely unconditioned by external circumstances or states of the mind. For, one who has realized that Self possesses a certainty, a permanent underlying confidence, that can never be erased, and which allows him to retain an inner peace and joyfulness regardless of circumstances of destiny or the transient fluctuations of the mind:

> The yogi who knows that the entire splendor of the universe is
> his, who rises to the consciousness of unity with theuniverse,
> retains his Divinity even in the midst of various thoughts and
> fancies. [18] ... This entire universe is a sport of Consciousness.
> One who is constantly aware of this is certainly a liberated
> being (*jivanmukta*). [19] ... The individual who has the cogni-
> tion of identity,   who regards the universe to be a sport and is
> always united with it, is undoubtedly liberated in life. [20]

Such "liberation" is the ultimate goal of all knowledge-seeking. It is the inner freedom which all men seek, a freedom from doubt, from the barbs of worldly misfortune, from the deadly sting of sorrow to which all those ignorant of their true nature must be subject. For one who has attained this liberating knowledge of his eternal Self, neither bodily affliction, nor worldly circumstance, nor even death, has the power to afflict him with fear; he is fearless, (*abhaya*), for he is grounded and established in the unshakeable certainty of his perm- anent immortality and incorruptible bliss.

Figure 9. The Male and Female principles in the form of Vishnu and Lakshmi, Parsvanath Temple, Khajuraho (950-1050 C..E.). The playful eroticism of these figures reflects the intimacy of the Absolute with the relative, the transcendent with the immanent, the Divine with the mundane.

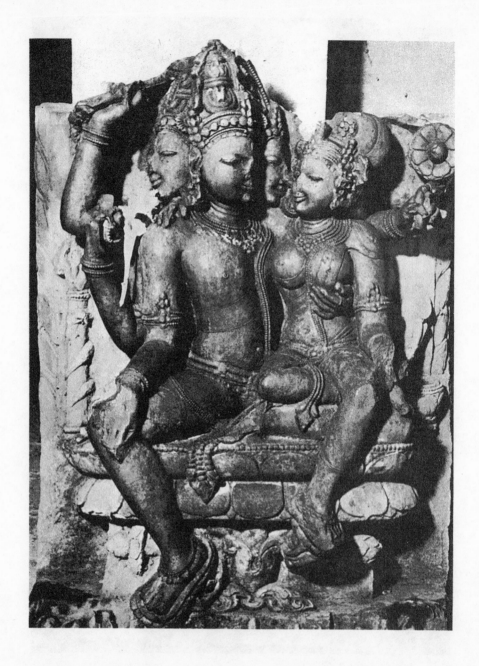

Figure 10. Shiva and his consort as *Purusha* and *Prakrti*; Brahmeshvara temple, Bhuvaneshvara (Orissa province), 11th century C.E. Here the metaphor is mixed: He is represented as both the Creator-Preserver-Destroyer, *and* the transcendent *Purusha* to His creative Power, *Prakrti*.

Figure 11. Adi-Buddha ("original Consciousness") and His Shakti. Tibetan bronze Yab-Yum (18th century C.E.). Locked in an eternal loving embrace, the Absolute and His Power of manifestation create the relationship of subject and object, while remaining forever one. Such images of the God and Goddess are intended to evoke remembrance of the one Mind and Its creative Power of world-manifestation, the undivided One who appears to be two, the nameless Reality as It has been experienced within by countless mystics throughout history.

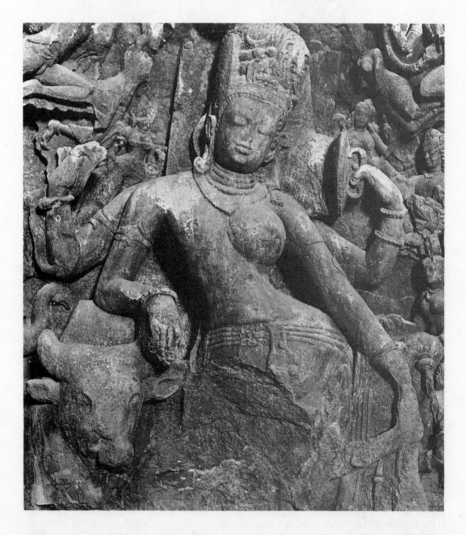

Figure 12. Shiva *Ardhanarishvara*, "The Lord as Male-Female." Relief from the Shiva Cave Temple, Elephanta, India (8th century C.E.). He is both male and female in one, signifying the Unity which is both the subject and the object, the transcendent and the immanent Reality.

SHANKARA

One of the greatest and most influential seers of India is the illustrious *acharya* ("teacher"), Shankara. His life is shrouded, of course, in legend and folktale, and so what dates and events we possess as biographical data are highly suspect. Nonetheless, according to the story passed down to us, it seems that he was born around 686 C.E. at Kaladi in southern India of poor brahmin parents and was recognized as a precociously intelligent and spiritually inclined child at a very early age. By the time he was ten, he is said to have been studying the Vedanta and consorting with the holy men of his village. Around this same time, his father died, and Shankara persuaded his mother to allow him to take up the spiritual life of a renunciant.   Seeking a qualified Master, he approached the sage Gaudapada (whose commentary on the *Mandukya Upanishad* is a classic work of Vedanta) but Gaudapada was by this time quite old, and had vowed to remain solitary, contemplating God. So he sent the young boy to his disciple, Govindapada. Shankara was thus initiated into *sannyasa* (the Order of renunciant monks) by Govindapada and taught the means to realize the Self.

We do not know how long Shankara remained with his teacher, but he seems to have struck out on his own to begin his own teaching career while he was still in his teens. One story tells of his forcing a debate with a well-known scholar named Mandana Mishra at the beginning of his teaching career. When Shankara handily won the debate, Mishra became his devoted follower.

During his brief lifetime, Shankara wrote commentaries on the *Vedanta Sutras* of Bhadarayana, twelve on the Upanishads, and also a number of independent works on the *Advaita* (non-dualistic) Vedanta philosophy -- among the best known of which are the *Vivekachudamani* ("The Crest-Jewel of Discrimination"), *Upadeshasahasri* ("The Thousand Teachings"), and *Atma Bodha* ("The Knowledge of The Self"). He wrote not only philosophical treatises, but several devotional works in Sanskrit metre as well. He did not found the Order of *sannyasa*, but under his influence it was reformed and organized into twelve separate branches; many monasteries were thereafter built, and a tradition firmly established. At the age of thirty-two, his life ended under mysterious circumstances at Kedarnath in the Himalayas.

Shankara did not teach anything new; he took his starting point from the Vedanta philosophy already established in the Upanishads. The rise and spread of Buddhism over a thousand years before had caused among the people a decline of confidence in the Upanishadic tradition; and it was for Shankara to re-establish the essential meaning of those ancient scriptures and to reaffirm their vision of Unity. Having experienced that Unity himself, he was able, through his analytic writings, to explain the philosophy of Vedanta in a clear, concise and organized manner. By his expositions and reformulations, he single-handedly re-established the philosophical basis of the Vedanta, and ushered in a period of renewed vigor and growth within the Vedantic tradition which lasts till this day.

Shankara's little book, "The Crest-Jewel of Discrimination," is undoubtedly one of the clearest and most persuasive accounts of the mystical philosophy ever written. It is cast in the form of a dialogue between a master and disciple, and serves its reader as an unerring guide to enlightenment. This little book, among all the spiritual guides and philosophies ever written, must certainly be regarded, as its title implies, as the crown-jewel of all knowledge, and the consummate pinnacle of its expression. In the field of enlightenment literature, there is nothing to compare with it.

In it, Shankara explains that Brahman, the absolute Reality, alone is real, and that the world is "unreal." It is just this apparent "world-negation" that has caused many to reject Shankara; but it is an unfair judgement, most frequently made by those who have not read him. There are just as many passages in his writings which declare that "the world is nothing but Brahman." Nonetheless, Shankara's apparent rejection of the world has caused much confusion to arise in the minds of those lacking discrimination; a confusion which can be alleviated when it is understood that, in the one instance, he is differentiating between the eternal and non-eternal aspects of Reality, and in the second instance, he is asserting the absolute unity and indivisibility of the non-dual Reality.

Shankara's sole message is that "nothing exists but Brahman." Brahman is the conscious Self (*Atman*) within everyone, and It also constitutes all appearance of diversity. When Brahman is directly realized,then one knows, "I am Brahman; I am the one Consciousness from which all this universe arises." The world itself, including one's own body, is realized to be an image in Brahman's cosmic light-show, an undifferentiated sea of Energy in which vari-

ous separate forms are distinguishable. This light-show, this vast sea
of living Energy, is projected from the Absolute, from Brahman; it is
His own, but it is not Brahman-as-Absolute; it is not the Eternal Self.
Looked at from a different perspective, as nothing else exists but
Brahman, the world too is Brahman. From the first perspective, the
world is illusory; from the second, the world is nothing but Brahman
Itself manifesting in form. Both perspectives are true. The ever-
changing world-appearance shines forth magically from the Ever-
Unchanging Self; it is He, but it is not He. Shankara calls this shining-
forth by the name of "Maya":

> Maya, ... also called the Undifferentiated, is the power
> (*shakti*) of the Lord. She is without beginning; She consists
> of the three *gunas* and is prior to the effects of the *gunas,*
> being the Cause of all. One who has a clear intelligence infers
> Her existence from the effects She produces. It is She who
> brings forth this entire universe.
> Maya is neither real nor unreal, nor both together;
> She is neither identical with Brahman nor different from Him,
> nor both; She is neither differentiated nor undifferentiated, nor
> both. She is most wonderful and cannot be described in words.[1]
> ... Everything, from the intellect down to the gross
> physical body, is the effect of Maya. Understand that all these
> and Maya itself are not the [absolute] Self, and are therefore
> unreal, like a mirage in the desert. [2]

When Shankara says that the world of Maya, the phenomenal
aspect of Brahman, is unreal, he is merely pointing out that its
appearance of multiplicity, of inconstancy, or transiency, is illusory
from the standpoint of the Eternal. And that, by identifying ourselves with the transient appearances, we consequently suffer the
anxieties and pains of desire for, and attachment to, what is merely
ephemeral.

All visible objects, like the body, etc., are merely products of
Maya, and are as evanescent as bubbles, says Shankara. One should
not identify with these, but should know oneself as the Eternal, as
Brahman. One should practice, says Shankara, the awareness: "I am
Brahman; I am without attributes and actions, eternal, without
movement of thought, unstained, changeless, formless, ever-pure and
free. Like space, I pervade everything. I am within and without.
Never affected by the manifestation of forms, I am eternal, unattached,
motionless and pure, the same in all." If this true understanding is

continually kept alive by remembering "I am Brahman," claims Shankara, it will vanquish all the agitations caused by the arising of ignorance, just as medicine vanquishes disease.

We are nothing but the one Reality, says Shankara; and, like It, we consist of these two aspects: the absolute and the relative. We are Brahman, and we are also manifest in form. The one aspect is our permenent, unchanging, Self; the second is a mere appearance, a turbulently fluctuating facade. These two are inextricably mixed, inseparable. We may say that one is "in" the other, but that is only a concession to the relational structure of language. They are, in fact, as intermingled as consciousness and thought, as fire and its light.

Shankara explains that the Self is pure Consciousness, distinct from all products of Maya; viz., the manifested body, mind, intellect, etc.; and is merely a witness to their functions, as a king standing apart, witnesses the activities of his kingdom. And it is because these two aspects, the Eternal and the superimposed manifestation of form, are intermingled that the mind attributes consciousness to itself, and feels, "I am the knower." It is because of the superimposition of the manifested world of form upon the one Self that the false sense of ego arises. Yet, says Shankara,

> ... The Self never undergoes change; the intellect
> never possesses consciousness. But when one sees all this
> world, he is deluded into thinking, "I am the seer, I am the
> knower." Mistaking one's Self for the individual entity, one
> is overcome with fear. If one knows oneself not as the indi-
> vidual but as the supreme Self, one becomes free from fear. [3]

According to Shankara, it is because Brahman, through Its power of Maya, manifests in human form that Brahman-as-man is ignorant of his true nature. The intermingling of the pure Spirit with Its own manifested appearance causes the soul thus formed to con-fuse Itself with the appearance, thus giving rise to the false sense of identity, or ego. Brahman, the conscious Self, is always pure, blissful and eternal; but, deluded by Its imprisonment in appearance (Maya), It believes It is conditioned by thoughts, sorrows and death. It is just this false identification, says Shankara, that constitutes the individual soul (jiva). The individual soul, therefore, has a strange status which is neither real nor unreal. Brahman, its true Identity, is real; but it exists as an individualized soul only by virtue of its false identification:

> The Self is the witness, beyond all attributes, beyond
> action. It can be directly realized as pure Consciousness and
> infinite bliss. Its appearance as an individual soul is caused by
> the delusion of our understanding, and has no reality. By its
> very nature, this appearance is unreal. When our delusion has
> been removed, it ceases to exist. [4]

Like the Buddha, Shankara states that the realization of the
Self reveals the illusory nature of the individualized soul, just as the
perception of a snake disappears when it is realized to be, in fact, a
rope. Like Plotinus, he asserts that there is one Soul which is identical with Brahman. It appears as many due only to the Lord's power
of *Maya* , or nescience (*avidya*):

> Because all selves are essentially non-different, and
> their apparent difference is due to nescience only, the individual
> soul, after having dispelled nescience by true knowledge,
> passes into unity with the supreme Self. [5]
> ... The transmigrating soul is not different from the
> Lord. [6]
> ... Just as the light of the Sun and the Sun are not
> absolutely different, ... so also the soul and the supreme
> Self are not different. [7]

Long previous to Shankara, there had existed a great body of
lore about the transmigration of the soul, according to which the soul
reincarnates again and again in order to reap the fruits of its deeds
(*karmas*). Some asserted that, therefore, the circumstances of this life
are wholly determined by the actions of the soul in its preceding
lifetime. And this led to confusion in the minds of some regarding
the question of whether a soul was responsible for its present
condition in the world, or whether God was responsible.

The"law of karma," which corresponds to the well-known law
of cause and effect, Shankara acknowledged freely; but, he said, if we
understand that it is the ONE who is in charge -- in the past life and
the one's preceding it as well -- then we will not make the mistake of
attributing *causality* to those past actions. The real and only Cause of
the circumstances of this life and past ones is *His* will. In other words,
the past lives do indeed precede this one in a causal chain or
progression, but the original and continuous Cause is the ONE who is
manifesting as man and woman throughout the entire evolution of the
universe. Says Shankara:

> The soul acts, to be sure, but the activity of the soul
> is not independent. It acts itself, but the Lord causes it to act.
> Moreover, the Lord in causing it to act now has regard to its
> former efforts, and He also caused it to act in a former exist-
> ence, having regard to its efforts previous to that existence. [8]

To claim, as some do, that the soul is responsible for its condition in every incarnation is to make the transient soul the ultimate
cause. Yet the soul is ultimately unreal and illusory in relation to the
Consciousness which produces it. Can we say that a character in a
dream is responsible for its acts within the dream? No; for, ultimately, it is the dreamer who alone exists and who is the cause of all
activity taking place in the dream state. Or can we absolve the Sun of
all relationship to its radiating light? Is it reasonable to say that it is
only that radiation that has caused the heat on earth, and that the Sun
is absolved from all causal agency? Certainly not.

The soul is a product of *Maya*; and *Maya*, the "illusory"
manifestation of the entire world of phenomena, is a radiation of
Brahman. Without Brahman, *Maya* does not exist. It is the very
nature of Brahman to radiate this *Maya*, as it is the nature of the Sun
to radiate light and heat. *Brahman* and *Maya* are not two independent entities; it is not reasonable therefore to cite *Maya* as an independent cause, and to release Brahman from all causal agency. To do
so is to fallaciously interpret the conceptual separability of the two
terms, *Brahman* and *Maya*, and to omit to acknowledge their actual
unity. The soul is never apart from the ONE. It is the activity of the
ONE. Indeed, if we see clearly, the whole issue of cause and effect
rests on an imaginary division, for there is only the ONE, without a
second, without a shadow; and since It is both the Cause and the effect,
it is an error to attribute independent causes to various effects.

It is the one Lord, says Shankara, who is doing everything. We,
as souls, progress through the world of *Maya* in strict accordance with
the law of cause and effect (the law of *karma*), to be sure. But we souls
are His manifestation; we are the dream, and He is the Dreamer. All
this is His doing, and His Being. We are products of that one Consciousness, and not different from It. Attribute causality not to the
dream, but to the Dreamer. He is the Cause and the effect; there is
nothing but Himself.

The objection that such a view is fatalistic and erodes the will
to initiative is an unfounded one; for the awareness that one's own
consciousness is the divine Consciousness of the universe does no-

thing to limit initiative. Indeed, it enables one to act from a clearer
and more considered awareness of what is correct action and what is
not, what stems from the illusory ego, and what stems from a divine
will for the greater good of all. "Free-will" is nothing but the will of
God *freed* of the passions and impulses arising from the false ego.
The so-called "free-will" of the murderer or thief is not a "free" will
at all, but one that is constricted and obscured by the false sense of
ego, and its attendant desires.

Shankara, like all those seers of the Self, says that when that
one eternal Self is realized, there is no individualized soul; the soul
exists only on the relative plane, and not at all in the Absolute. For
when the soul realizes the Self, it is no longer the soul; it is the Self. It
has shed all its limiting conditions, and "an embodied soul without
limiting conditions does not exist." [9]   That one Lord is the source
and manifestation of all existence; it is He who has planted ignorance
in our hearts; it is He also who reveals the Truth:

> For the soul which, in the state of nescience, is
> blinded by the darkness of ignorance and hence unable to
> distinguish itself from the complex of effects and instruments,
> that *samsara*-state in which it appears as agent and enjoyer is
> brought about through the permission of the Lord who is the
> highest Self, the governor of all actions, the Witness residing
> in all beings, the Cause of all intelligence; and ... final release
> also is affected through knowledge caused by the grace of the
> Lord. [10]

Shankara has often been accused by his critics of postulating a
separation between the world and God, of regarding the world as
"unreal" and therefore set apart from God as a mere mirage to be
disregarded. Those who have understood his meaning, however,
would never accuse him of seeing the world as apart from God. Like
Kapila, and other true seers, he recognized two aspects of the one
divine Reality, but never regarded these two as separate or independent. In his commentary on the *Vedanta Sutras,* he makes his
position very clear:

> Brahman is apprehended under two aspects: in the one
> aspect [He appears] as qualified by limiting conditions owing
> to the multiformity of the evolutions of name and form; in the
> other aspect, He is the opposite of this, i.e., free from all
> limiting conditions whatever. [11]
> ... As there is non-difference before the production [of

the effect], the effect even after having been produced continues
to be non-different from the cause. As the cause, i.e.,
Brahman, is in all time neither more nor less that that which
IS, so the effect also, i.e., the world, is in all time only that
which IS. But that which IS is one only; therefore, the effect
is non-different from the cause. [12]

And in his *Vivekachudamani* :

The universe is truly Brahman, ... for that which is
superimposed (the universe) has no separate existence from its
substratum (Brahman). Whatever a deluded person perceives
through mistake is Brahman and Brahman alone. The silver
imagined in mother-of-pearl is really mother-of-pearl. The
name, "universe," is superimposed on Brahman, but what we
call the "universe" is [really] nothing but Brahman. [13]

And, again, in his *Atma Bodha* :

The entire universe is truly the Self. There exists
nothing at all other than the Self. The enlightened person
sees everything in the world as his own Self, just as one
views earthenware jars and pots as nothing but clay. [14]

Nevertheless, in the experience of Unity, the "I" is known to
be eternal, unchanging, entirely unaffected by the transient phenomena in the world of form. It is the knowledge of this eternal " I "
which is the object of Shankara's philosophy. His methodology is
one of discrimination (*viveka*), a discrimination between the Self, the
one conscious"I," and all that is not "I"; and the practice of the
continual awareness of that true Self. Instead of taking the position of
a soul worshipping God as though there were really two, says
Shankara, one should take non-dualism as the starting point, and
refuse to identify with the body, mind, intellect, etc. By this practice,
he says, the illusion of the false ego will be dispelled.

Shankara asserts that, when realization comes, it will reveal to
you that you, yourself, are Brahman. Why not, then, he says, instead
of identifying with the unreal ego, and tormenting yourself with
mental agony, start with the awareness "I am Brahman"? What after
all is the difference between one who, identifying with the ego,
eventually surrenders the ego to the divine Self, and one who identifies with the divine Self and thereby silences the ego? The only
difference is that the first is a process of diminishing and finally

annihilating the ego, and the second a process of affirming the Self and annihilating the ego immediately. If you identify with the false ego, you identify with the suffering accompanying its annihilation; but if you identify with the Self, you go from truth to Truth, and from peace to Peace.

But such a practice is not altogether easy; in fact, it requires an intensely focused concentration of awareness, ever on the alert to dispel ego-thoughts as they begin to arise from consciousness. In short, it requires a mind continually in meditation. Unremitting attention to this awareness, says Shankara, is identical to *bhakti*, or devotion; for "the endeavor to know one's true nature is [truly] devotion." It is this concentrated devotion to the Self which constitutes Shankara's methodology:

> That Reality is One; though, owing to illusion, It
> appears to be multiple names and forms, attributes and
> changes, It always remains unchanged. [It is] like gold which,
> while remaining one, is formed into various ornaments. You
> are that One, that Brahman. Meditate on this in your mind.[15]
> ... Seated in a solitary place, free from desires and
> with senses controlled, one should meditate free of thought on
> that one infinite Self. [16]

Shankara's "method" is intended to be as applicable subsequent to Self-realization as it is prior to that experience. His way of the practice of knowledge (*jnan-abhyasa*) is true for the seeker and true for the adept as well. For, as he says:

> Even after the Truth has been realized, there remains
> that strong, beginningless, obstinate impression that one is
> the agent and experiencer... This has to be carefully removed
> by living in a state of constant identification with the supreme
> Self. Sages call that cessation of mental impressions, "Liber-
> ation."
> ... As the mind becomes gradually established in the
> Self, it proportionately gives up the desire for external objects.
> When all such desires have been eliminated, there is the un-
> obstructed realization of the Self. [17]

When a man knows the Truth, he knows beyond all doubt, " I am the Self, and all this universe is my manifestation." He realizes that his only previous error was to regard himself as small, limited to a particular body and mind. This is the liberating knowledge of which Shankara sings in all his works. Listen to his sage advice to one who would attain this knowledge:

> The fool thinks, "I am the body"; the intelligent man thinks, "I am an individual soul united with the body." But the wise man, in the greatness of his knowledge and spiritual discrimination, sees the Self as the only reality and thinks, "I am Brahman." [18]
> ... Utterly destroy the ego. Control the many waves of distraction which it raises in the mind. Discern the Reality and realize "I am That."
> You are pure Consciousness, the witness of all experiences. Your real nature is joy. Cease this very moment to identify yourself with the ego.
> You are the Self, the infinite Being, the pure, unchanging Consciousness, which pervades everything. Your nature is bliss and your glory is without stain. Becaue you identify yourself with the ego, you are tied to birth and death. Your bondage has no other cause. [19]
> ... When the vision of Reality comes, the veil of ignorance will be completely removed. So long as you perceive things falsely, your false perception distracts you and makes you miserable. When your false perception is corrected, misery will also end. For example, you see a rope and think it is a snake. As soon as you realize that the rope is a rope, your false perception of a snake ceases, and you are no longer distracted by the fear which it inspired. Therefore, the wise man who wishes to break his bondage must know the Reality. [20]
> ... Teachers and scriptures can stimulate spiritual awareness. But the wise disciple crosses the ocean of ignorance by direct illumination, *through the grace of God.*
> Gain experience directly. Realize God for yourself. Know the Self as the one indivisible Being, and become perfect. Free your mind from all distractions and dwell in the consciousness of the Self.
> This is the final declaration of Vedanta: Brahman is all; [It is] this universe and every creature. To be liberated is to live in the continual awareness of Brahman, the undivided Reality. [21]

DATTATREYA

Shankara extolled the recognition of one's eternal identity as the highest attainment of man; he held that the constant awareness, " I am Brahman," "I am Shiva," "I am the Self," is the true and perfect state of enlightenment, the ultimate freedom. But it is a state beyond that of ordinary men, known only to those who have actually realized the truth of their eternal identity, and thus attained absolute knowledge and unwavering certainty.

Such a perfectly enlightened sage was the legendary Datta-treya, who was known as "the Avadhut." In Indian mythology, he was said to be an incarnation of Vishnu, born to the sage Atri and his chaste wife, Anasuya; but as to whether such a person actually lived and what were the factual details of his life we know nothing at all. *Avadhut* is a generic term for those enlightened sages of India who wander about, naked and free of all attachment to the world; and Dattatreya was apparently the embodiment of this ascetic ideal.   The song (*gita*) in Sanskrit verse, called the *Avadhut Gita,* which is attributed to him, is certainly one of the purest expressions of the unitive awareness of the Self ever written.

The actual date of authorship of the *Avadhut Gita* is unknown, but, judging by its terminology and style, it appears to have been written, not in the millennia prior to the Current Era, as legend would have it, but sometime around the 9th or 10th centuries of our Current Era. This does not, of course, preclude the possibility of an oral transmission to that point in time. Its theme is the same as that of the Upanishads, the *Bhagavad Gita,* and that of all illumined seers: the Self. It speaks, not of the soul or of God, but speaks rather from the experiential awareness in which that subject-object relationship no longer exists. It is a song of the final, unltimate, and irreducible Reality known as "I."

Dattatreya's song has had many forerunners and many re-affirmations over the centuries; yet, of all the many such declarations of the knowledge of the one Self, none is more eloquent and compelling, none more convincing and illuminating, than this. Whoever the author of the Avadhut's Song might have been, there is no doubt that he was a great teacher, one truly established in the certainty of his supreme Identity. It is not only the profundity and genuineness of his vision, but the poetic beauty of his Song as well that has made it a source of joy and inspiration to his grateful readers over the years.

The *Avadhut Gita* teaches by the method of repetition: the message is unvarying; only the words are slightly different in each chapter. It is a method which serves to instill in us, not merely the message of the Avadhut, but his awareness. By reading and absorbing the meaning of his Song, we are privileged to share in some measure his exalted and uncompromising vision. By reading or reciting only a few verses, our mind is immediately lifted to a realm of immeasurable calm and certainty. A few more verses, and we've become immoveable, invincible, unruffled, secure once more in the recalled awareness of the eternal Self which, somehow, we had forgotten. Simply by filling our mind with his Song, we are able to absorb some of the freedom and exultation of its author's consciousness, and taste a little of the sweet nectar of our own intrinsic bliss.

The Song of the Avadhut consists of seven chapters (eight in some versions, but the eighth is spurious in my estimation), written in flawless Sanskrit verse, so perfect in rhythm and symmetric beauty that they seem to have been formed by some superhuman mind. In the following translation of the First Chapter of his Song, I have retained the form and sense of Dattatreya's verses, if not their original rhythm and beauty:

The *Avadhut Gita*: Chapter One [1]

1. Truly, it is by the grace of God
   That the knowledge of Unity arises within.
   Then a man is released at last
   From the great fear of life and death.

2. All that exists in this world of forms
   Is nothing but the Self, and the Self alone.
   How, then, shall the Infinite worship Itself?
   Shiva is one undivided Whole!

3. The five subtle elements that combine to compose this world
   Are as illusory as the water in a desert mirage;
   To whom, then, shall I bow my head?
   I, myself, am the stainless One!

4. Truly, all this universe is only my Self;
   It is neither divided nor undivided.
   How can I even assert that it exists?

I can only view it with wonder and awe.

5.   What, then, is the heart of the highest truth,
        The core of knowledge, the wisdom supreme?
        It is, "I am the Self, the formless One;
        By my very nature, I am pervading all."

6.   That one God who shines within everything,
        Who is formless like the cloudless sky,
        Is the pure, stainless, Self of all.
        Without any doubt, that is who I am.

7.   I'm the infinite and immutable One;
        I'm pure Consciousness, without any form.
        I don't know how, or to whom,
        Joy and sorrow appear in this world.

8.   I have no mental karma, either good or bad;
        I have no physical karma, either good or bad;
        I have no verbal karma, either good or bad.
        I'm beyond the senses; I'm the pure nectar of the knowledge
        of the Self.

9.   The mind is formless like the sky,
        Yet it wears a million faces.
        It appears as images of the past, or as worldly forms;
        But it is not the supreme Self.

10.   I'm One; I'm all of this!
        Yet I'm undifferentiated, beyond all forms.
        How, then, do I regard the Self?
        As both the Unmanifest *and* the manifest world.

11.   You, also, are the One! Why don't you understand?
        You're the unchanging Self, the same within everyone.
        You're truly illimitable; you're the all-pervading Light.
        For you, how can there be any distinction between the day
                        and the night?

12.   Understand that the Self is continuous Being,
        The One within all, without any division.
        The "I" is both the subject and the supreme object
                ⸺ of meditation;
        How can you see two in That which is one?

13.   Neither birth nor death pertain to you;
        You have never been a body.

It is well-known that "All is Brahman";
The scriptures have stated this in various ways.

14.   You are *That* which is both inside and outside;
        You're Shiva; you're everything everywhere.
        Why, then, are you so deluded?
        Why do you run about like a frightened ghost?

15.   There's no such thing as union or separation
        For me or for you.
        There is no me, no you, no manifold world;
        All is the Self, and the Self alone.

16.   You can't be heard, or smelled, or tasted;
        You can't be seen, or sensed by touch.
        Truly, you're the ultimate Reality;
        Why, then, should you be troubled so?

17.   Neither birth, nor death, nor the active mind,
        Nor bondage, nor liberation, affects you at all.
        Why then, my dear, do you grieve in this way?
        You and I have no name or form.

18.   O mind, why are you so deluded?
        Why do you run about like a frightened ghost?
        Become aware of the indivisible Self.
        Be rid of attachment; be happy and free!

19.   Truly, you're the unchanging Essence of everything!
        You're the unmoving Unity; you're boundless Freedom.
        You have neither attachment nor aversion;
        Why, then, do you worry and succumb to desire?

20.   All the scriptures unanimously declare
        That the pure, formless, undifferentiated Reality
        Is the Essence of all forms.
        There is absolutely no doubt about this.

21.   All forms, understand, are only temporary manifestations;
        The formless Essence eternally exists.
        Once this truth is realized,
        There's no more necessity to be reborn.

22.   The one Reality is ever the same;
        This is what all wise men say.
        Whether you embrace or renounce desires,
        The one Consciousness remains unaffected.

23.   If you see the world as unreal, can that be the experience
           of Unity?
        If you see it as real, can that be the experience of Unity?
        If it's seen as both real and unreal, can that be the experience
           of Unity?
        To see everything as the One is the true state of Freedom.

24.   You are the pure Reality, always the same;
        You have no body, no birth and no death.
        How, then, can you say, "I know the Self"?
        Or how can you say, "I don't know the Self"?

25.   The saying, "That thou art,"
        Affirms the reality of your own true Self.
        The saying, "Not this, not this,"
        Denies the reality of the five composite elements.

26.   The Self is the identity of everyone;
        You are everything, the unbroken Whole.
        The thinker and the thought do not even exist!
        O mind, how can you go on thinking so shamelessly!

27.   I do not know Shiva; how can I speak of Him?
        I do not know Shiva; how can I worship Him?
        I, myself, am Shiva, the primal Essence of everything;
        My nature, like the sky, remains ever the same.

28.   I am the Essence, the all-pervading Essence;
        I have no form of my own.
        I'm beyond the division of subject and object;
        How could I possibly be an object to myself?

29.   There's no such thing as an infinite form;
        The infinite Reality has no form of Its own.
        The one Self, the supreme Reality,
        Neither creates, nor sustains, nor destroys anything.

30.   You are that pure and unchanging Essence;
        You have no body, no birth, no death.
        For you, how could there be such a thing as delusion?
        How could delusion exist for the Self?

31.   When a jar is broken, the space that was inside
        Merges into the space outside.
        In the same way, my mind has merged in God;
        To me, there appears no duality.

32.   Truly, there's no jar, no space within;
        There's no body and no soul encased.
        Please understand; everything is Brahman.
        There's no subject, no object, no separate parts.

33.   Everywhere, always, and in everything,
        Know this: the Self alone exists.
        Everything, both the Void and the manifested world,
        Is nothing but my Self; of this I am certain.

34.   There are no divine scriptures, no world, no imperative
                    religious practices;
        There are no gods, no classes or races of men,
        No stages of life, no superior or inferior;
        There's nothing but Brahman, the supreme Reality.

35.   The subject and object are unseparated and inseparable;
        That undivided One is you.
        When this is so, when no "other" exists,
        How could the Self be objectively perceived?

36.   Non-duality is taught by some;
        Some others teach duality.
        They don't understand that the all-pervading Reality
        Is beyond both duality and non-duality.

37.   There is no color or sound to the one Reality;
        It has no qualities at all.
        How can one even think or speak of That
        Which is far beyond both mind and speech?

38.   When you know all this universe of forms
        To be as vacant as the sky,
        Then you'll know Brahman;
        Duality will forever cease to be.

39.   To some, the Self appears as "other";
        To me, the Self is "I."
        Like undivided space, One alone exists.
        How, then, could the subject and object of meditation
                    be two?

40.   Nothing of what I do or eat,
        Or give or take,
        Exists for me;
        I'm Purity itself, beyond birth and death.

41. Know that the whole of the universe is without any form.
Know that the whole of the universe is forever unchanging.
Know that the whole of the universe is unstained by its
        contents.
Know that the whole of the universe is of the nature of God.

42. You are the ultimate Reality; have no doubt about this.
The Self is not something to be known by the mind;
The Self is the very one who knows.
How, then, could you think to know the Self?

43. Maya? Maya? How can it be?
A shadow? A shadow? It doesn't exist.
The Reality is One; It's everything.
It's all-pervasive; nothing else exists.

44. I have no beginning, middle, or end;
I have never been, nor will ever be, bound.
My nature is stainless; I'm Purity itself.
This I know as a certainty.

45. To me, neither the elemental particles
Nor the entire universe exists;
Brahman alone is everything.
Where, then, are the castes or the stages of life?

46. I always recognize everything
As the one indivisible Reality.
That undivided One constitutes the world,
The Void, all space, and the five elements.

47. It's neither neuter, nor masculine, nor feminine.
It possesses neither intellect nor the power of thought.
How, then, can you imagine that the Self
Is either blissful or not blissful?

48. The practice of yoga will not lead you to purity;
Silencing the mind will not lead you to purity;
The Guru's instructions will not lead you to purity.
That purity is your Essence; It's your very own
        Consciousness.

49. Neither the gross body, consisting of five elements,
Nor the subtle body, exists;
Everything is the Self alone.
How, then, could the fourth state (*samadhi*) or the other

three states (waking, dreaming, deep sleep) exist?

50.   I am not bound, nor am I liberated;
I'm Brahman, and nothing else.
I'm not the doer, nor am I the enjoyer;
I do not pervade anything, nor am I pervaded.

51.   If water and water are mixed together,
There is no difference between one and the other.
It is the same with matter and spirit;
This is very clear to me.

52.   If I've never been bound,
I can never be liberated.
How could you think that the Self
Is restricted to formlessness or imprisoned by form.

53.   I know the nature of the one supreme Being;
Like space, It extends everywhere.
And all the forms that appear within It
Are like the [illusory] water of a desert mirage.

54.   I have neither Guru nor initiation;
I have no discipline, and no duty to perform.
Understand that I'm the formless sky;
I'm the self-existent Purity.

55.   You are the one Purity! You have no body.
You are not the mind; you're the supreme Reality.
"I'm the Self, the supreme Reality!"
Say this without any hesitancy.

56.   Why do you weep, O mind?
Why do you cry?
Take the attitude: "I am the Self!"
Drink the supreme nectar of Unity.

57.   You do not possess intelligence, nor do you possess
          ignorance;
Nor do you possess a mixture of these two.
You are, yourself, Intelligence --
An Intelligence that never ceases, never strays.

58.   I'm not attained by knowledge, or *samadhi,* or yoga,
Or by the passage of time, or the Guru's instructions;
I'm Consciousness Itself, the ultimate Reality.
Like the sky, though I change, I am ever the same.

59.   I have no birth, no death, and no duties;
I've never done anything, either good or bad.
I'm purely Brahman, beyond all qualities.
How could either bondage or liberation exist for me?

60.   If God is all-pervading,
Immovable, whole, without any parts,
Then there is no division in Him at all.
How, then, could He be regarded as "within" or "without"?

61.   The universe is the 'shining forth' of the One,
There is no split, or division, or separate "aspects."
The idea of "Maya" is itself the great delusion;
Duality and non-duality are merely concepts of the mind.

62.   The world of form and the formless Void:
Neither of these exists independently.
In the One, there is neither separation nor union;
Truly, there is nothing but Shiva alone.

63.   You have no mother, or father, or brother;
You have no wife, or son, or friend.
You have no attachments or non-attachments;
How, then, do you justify this anxiety of mind?

64.   O mind, there is neither the day [of manifestation] nor the
            night [of dissolution];
My continuous Light neither rises nor sets.
How could a wise man sincerely believe
That the formless Existence is effected by forms?

65.   It is not undivided, nor is It divided;
It experiences neither sorrow nor joy.
It is not the universe, nor is It not the universe;
Understand that the Self is eternally One.

66.   I'm not the doer, nor am I the enjoyer;
I have no karma, either present or past.
I have no body, nor are all these bodies mine.
What could be "mine" or "not-mine" to me?

67.   In me, there is no impurity such as attachment;
There is no bodily pain for me.
Understand that I'm the Self; I'm Unity.
I'm vast as space, like the sky above.

68.   O mind, my friend, what's the good of so much speaking?
        O mind, my friend, all of this has been made quite clear.
        I've told you what I know to be true;
        You're the ultimate Reality. You're unbounded, like space.

69.   It doesn't matter where a yogi may die;
        It doesn't matter how he may die.
        He becomes absorbed in the Absolute,
        As the space within a jar becomes absorbed [in the outer
                space when the jar is destroyed].

70.   Whether he dies near a holy river,
        Or in an outcaste's hut;
        Whether he is conscious or unconscious at his death,
        He merges into Freedom, into Unity, alone.

71.   All duties, wealth, enjoyments, liberation,
        All people and objects in the world as well;
        Everything, in the eyes of a yogi,
        Is like the [illusory] water in a desert mirage.

72.   There is no action,
        Either present, future, or past,
        Which has been performed or enjoyed by me.
        This I know, without any doubt.

73.   The Avadhut lives alone in an empty hut;
        With a pure, even mind, he is always content.
        He moves about, naked and free,
        Aware that all this is only the Self.

74.   Where neither the third state (deep sleep) nor the fourth
                state (samadhi) exists,
        Where everything is experienced as the Self alone,
        Where neither righteousness nor unrighteousness exists,
        Could bondage or liberation be living there?

75.   In that state (samadhi) where one knows nothing at all,
        This versified knowledge doesn't even exist.
        So, now, while I'm in the state of samarasa, *
        I, the Avadhut, have spoken of the Truth.

76.   It is pointless to differentiate between the Void and the
                world-appearance;
        It's pointless to speak of "the Real" and "the unreal."
        One Self, self-born, exists alone;
        This is what all the scriptures declare.

In this composition by Sri Dattatreya
Called The Song of The Avadhut,
This is the First Chapter,
Entitled, "The Instruction On The Wisdom Of the Self."

*   *samarasa* : Literally, "same taste"; the state of awareness just
         this side of *samadhi*, in which the world of forms is per-
         ceived as a unity, all things being recognized as the one Self.

MILAREPA

Tibet, that mysterious world high up in the Himalayan mountains, has borrowed much of its religious tradition from India, which it borders.   From very early times, the mythology and philosophy of India found its way into the highlands of Nepal and Tibet, and, in a curious mixture with peculiarly Tibetan mythologies of a more primitive culture, formed a Totemistic religion called *Bon*. When Buddhism began to infiltrate Tibet in the 2nd and 3rd centuries of the Current Era, Bon was slow to give way; but by the 9th century, after the coming of Padma-Shambhava and other Buddhist monks, whose esoteric teachings were flavored with much from the Yogic and Tantric traditions, Tibetan Buddhism began to take on a settled character of its own, with its own sects and sub-sects.

Tibetan Buddhism was therefore compounded of the shamanism of Bon, the mythology of the Vedas, the non-dualism of the Upanishads, the ideals of the Buddha, and the disciplines of Yoga and Tantra. One of the more esoteric of the sects which flourished in the 9th and 10th centuries was the Karguptya line, descended from the great Buddhist yogi, Tilopa. And in the 11th century there was born a yogi of surpassing greatness who was to fuel the fire of Buddhist faith, and invigorate the Karguptya teachings, as no other man before or since has done. His name was Jetsun Milarepa.

Jetsun Mila (later to be known simply as Milarepa, meaning, "Mila, wearer of cotton garments") was born to Mila-Sherab Gyaltsen ("Mila, the Trophy of Wisdom") and his wife, Karmo-Kyen ("White Garland"), in mid-August of 1052, at Kyanga-Tsa, in the province of Gungthang on the Tibetan frontier of Nepal (about 50 miles due north of modern Katmandu, the capital of Nepal). Milarepa's father was a wealthy and industrious trader, and a man of some influence in his village. He owned a large piece of land, with a luxuriously spacious house, and he and his family were highly respected and honored in the community. He died when Milarepa was but seven years old, leaving his vast estate, including herds of cattle and horses, farmlands and granaries, to his son. He had stipulated that all was to be held in trust for Milarepa and cared for by an uncle and aunt until the child came of age.

The uncle and aunt, however, treated Milarepa, his mother, and his younger sister, Peta, very badly, forcing them to labor hard and long in the fields, with only meager earnings, and to live in great poverty and distress. And when the time came, after a number of years, for Milarepa and his mother and sister to receive the father's legacy, the uncle and aunt who had been entrusted with the property, refused to give it over. They had many sons and relatives, and were able, by their sheer numbers, to enforce their will upon Milarepa and his hapless family.

Milarepa's mother, Karmo-Kyen, was in such a distressed and enraged state of mind due to the perfidy of her husband's relatives that she sold what little she possessed in order to send Milarepa to a Guru who could teach him the art of black-magic, so that he could bring curses down upon the wicked uncle and aunt who had robbed them, and bring destruction to their whole family. She threatened to kill herself if Milarepa did not agree to carry out her plan. And so, the young Milarepa travelled to a village called Yarlung-Kyorpo, where he became a student of a famous black-magician called Lama Yungtun-Trogyal ("Wrathful and Victorious Teacher of Evil").

The Lama taught Milarepa everything he knew, and then sent him after one year to someone more versed in the arts of destruction - - another master of the black arts called Khulung Yonton-Gyatso, in the valley of Tsongpo. Here, Milarepa learned what he needed to destroy his arch-rivals. And thereupon, he caused by his incantations the death of thirty-five people, all sons and friends of the wicked aunt and uncle, by bringing down upon them the house in which they had gathered for a wedding feast. After that, he caaused a hail-storm to destroy the grain crops of the entire village.

After thus consummating his mother's revenge upon those who had mistreated them, Milarepa felt great remorse for his deeds, and undertook to find a Teacher who would teach him the path of religion, so that he could free himself from the evil deeds he had committed. With this objective in mind, he travelled, with his old Guru's blessings, to Rinang to see a famous Lama of the Ningma Buddhist sect. This Lama told him to go to a monastery called Dowo-Lung ("Wheat Valley") in the province of Lhobrak, where he would find his destined Guru, a disciple of the famous Naropa, called Marpa, the Translator.

Marpa was called "the translator," for his many translations of traditional Buddhist and Tantric scriptures which he had person-ally brought to Tibet after a long search in India. He was a Lama; that is to say, a Guru, but he was not a monk. He was married, and lived the life of a normal householder. He was the favored disciple of Naropa, who had been a disciple of Tilopa, the founder of the Karguptya school of Tantric Buddhism in the mid-tenth century. Tilopa had claimed that his doctrines were transmitted to him by the celestial Buddha, called Dorje Chang (*Vajra Dhara* in Sanskrit).

When Jetsun Milarepa went to Marpa, his arrival had been expected, due to a dream in which it was revealed to Marpa that a great disciple was coming to him, one who would become the bearer of the banner of Buddhist teaching in Tibet, and who would be celebrated throughout the world. Marpa, however, aware that Milarepa had accumulated many sins due to his black-magic practices which had first to be expiated before he could attain enlightenment, put Milarepa to many severe tasks and trials, and dealt with him very harshly, feigning on many occasions indifference or anger toward him. Marpa withheld his oft-promised teachings from Milarepa, while for years Jetsun was made to build stone houses in different locations and according to various plans, which then, on one pretext or another, he was required to tear down again. He had to convey the building-stones from great distances on his back, causing him to suffer from numerous bloody pus-oozing sores over the extent of his back.

Many times, Milarepa despaired of ever gaining the teach-ings which would lead him to enlightenment. But throughout his trials, he had the sympathy and encouragement of Marpa's wife, Damena, who nursed him and cared for his needs. On one occasion, Milarepa, through a plot hatched by Damena, pretended to leave Marpa, in despondency of ever receiving the precious teachings of his Guru, only to be beaten and kicked by Marpa, who saw through the pretense.

After much such ill-treatment, and in utter frustration, Mila-repa set out to find another Guru, and stayed for a time with one of Marpa's chief disciples, Ngogdun-Chudor, to whom he had falsely represented himself. But in time, Marpa learned of his whereabouts, and sent for him. Marpa then confided to Milarepa that all his apparent mistreatment of him had been for his own benefit. He had known, he said, that Milarepa was a worthy disciple who would one day bring him fame, but he had to bring him to utter despair nine separate times to expiate the sins of his past and to enable him to be fit to attain enlightenment in this lifetime. However, he had succeeded in so doing only eight times, interrupted in his last attempt by Milarepa's escape. Now, said Marpa, he would indeed attain enlightenment, but he would have to undergo yet more suffering in the attempt.

Relieved to know that his Guru had treated him so badly, not out of contempt, but out of concern for his welfare, Milarepa now began a new period in his *sadhana*. He was duly initiated into monkhood by Marpa, and received from him the holy teaching. Thereafter, Milarepa lived in a cave for eleven months practicing intense meditation, while his Guru provided him with food and other essentials. At the end of this period, Marpa, who was now quite old, travelled to India to see his own Guru, Naropa; and after receiving his instructions, returned to pass the mantle of the Karguptya sect to Milarepa.

Milarepa remained several more years with Marpa, meditating in his cave, and practicing the discipline of *Tum-mo*, the awakening of the inner fire to heat his body in the severe cold of the mountains. And when he had attained proficiency in this practice, he approached Marpa, requesting that he be allowed to visit for one last time his old home, to see if his mother and sister were still alive and cared for. Marpa consented, but added that he and Milarepa would never see each other again, as Marpa was nearing the time of his death. He gave thorough instructions to his disciple to remain at his ancestral home for only seven days, and thereafter to take himself to the remote caves in the mountains far from civilization, and there to continue his meditations to attain enlightenment for the benefit of all living creatures. With much show of emotion and tears from Marpa and Damena, Milarepa then set off on his journey to Kyanga-Tsa.

When Milarepa returned to his old home, he found it dilapidated and empty, and learned that his mother had been dead for eight years, and his sister, now a beggar, had disappeared and no one knew her whereabouts. After a short stay, during which he exchanged his family property for a store of barley-meal and other provisions, he retired to a remote cave where he lived for three years on the provisions he had taken with him. Thereafter, his diet was reduced to a soup made of nettles which he found growing in a spring-fed field.

In time, his clothes rotted off, and his body became horribly emaciated. his skin and even his hair turned dark green from the solitary diet of green nettles. But it happened that his long-lost sister, Peta, having heard of his whereabouts, came to the cave to see him, and, appalled at his sad appearance, brought him food and clothing, and nursed him back to health. Yet, despite her entreaties, Milarepa would not give up his resolve to attain full enlightenment. And so he continued to live in caves far from the populace, meditating steadfastly on the *Dharmakaya,* the Absolute.

Milarepa moved from cave to cave in the snowy mountain fastnesses, and, having passed through many inner trials, temptations, and visionary experiences, at last became firmly established in the highest realization of the all-pervading Consciousness. "At last," he said, "the object of meditation, the act of meditation, and the meditator are so interwoven with each other that now I do not even know how to meditate!" He had also acquired an abundance of *siddhis* (super-normal powers), and before long, a number of disciples gathered around the now-famous yogi who had attained Buddhahood. Among his disciples, there were twenty-five accomplished yogis who, themselves, became saints through his blessings; of these, four were women.

Exhorting all his followers to spiritual endeavor, he taught them to abandon all other concerns in order to obtain enlightenment. "I have obtained spiritual knowledge," he told them, "through giving up all thought of food, clothing and reputation. Inspired with zeal in my heart, I bore every hardship and inured myself to all sorts of privations of the body; I devoted myself to meditation in the most unfrequented and solitary places. Thus did I obtain knowledge and spiritual experience; do you also follow in the path trodden by me, and practice devotion as I have done." [1]

Thereafter, Milarepa travelled about from mountain to mountain, community to community, to spread his teachings of enlightenment. Oftentimes, during his travels, he met with proud and learned scholars, who, having attained nothing more than book-learning, were of the opinion that their intellectual knowledge was the highest knowledge to be attained; and they attributed to Milarepa the same base motivations for fame and prestige which they themselves possessed. One such scholar, Geshe (pandit) Tsaphuwa, eager to engage Milarepa in debate, asked him to give an interpretation of some doctrines found in a certain book. Said Milarepa to the Geshe: " I have never valued the mere sophistry of intellectual knowledge, which is set down in books in order to be committed to memory. These lead only to mental confusion, and not to those practices which conduct one to the actual realization of Truth." [2] Then he asked the Geshe to listen to this song:

Obeisance to the honored feet of Marpa the Translator!
May I be far removed from contending creeds and dogmas.
Ever since my Lord's grace entered my mind,
My mind has never strayed to seek such distractions.
Accustomed long to contemplating love and compassion,
I have forgotten all difference between myself and others.
Accustomed long to meditating on my Guru as enhaloed over
my head,
I have forgotten all those who rule by power and prestige.
Accustomed long to meditating on my guardian deities as
inseparable from myself,
I have forgotten the lowly fleshly form.
Accustomed long to meditating on the secret whispered truths,
I have forgotten all that is said in written or printed books.
Accustomed, as I have been, to the study of the eternal Truth,
I've lost all knowledge of ignorance.
Accustomed, as I've been, to contemplating both nirvana and
          samsara as inherent in myself,
I have forgotten to think of hope and fear.
Accustomed, as I've been, to meditating on this life and the
next as one,
I have forgotten the dread of birth and death.
Accustomed long to studying, by myself, my own
          experiences,
I have forgotten the need to seek the opinions of friends and
          brethren.
Accustomed long to applying each new experience to my own
          spiritual growth,
I have forgotten all creeds and dogmas.
Accustomed long to meditating on the Unborn, the
Indestructible, the Unchanging,
I have forgotten all definitions of this or that particular goal.
Accustomed long to meditating on all visible phenomena as
          the Dharmakaya,
I have forgotten all meditations on what is produced by the
mind.
Accustomed long to keeping my mind in the uncreated state
          of freedom,
I have forgotten all conventions and artificialities.
Accustomed long to humbleness, of body and mind,
I have forgotten the pride and haughty manner of the mighty.
Accustomed long to regarding my fleshly body as my
hermitage,
I have forgotten the ease and comfort of retreats and
          monasteries.
Accustomed long to knowing the meaning of the Wordless,
I have forgotten the way to trace the roots of verbs, and the

sources of words and phrases.
You, O learned one, may trace out these things in your books
[if you wish]. [3]

It is said that this very Geshe to whom Milarepa sang this song thereafter poisoned Milarepa out of malicious envy; and Milarepa, aware that his death was approaching soon anyway, accepted it knowingly. Then, as his life was coming to its end, Milarepa called to himself all his devotees and disciples from far and wide, and gave to them his final teachings, which are, in many respects, reminiscent of the last instructions given by Gautama, the Buddha, to his own disciples:

> All worldly pursuits have but one unavoidable and in-
> evitable end, which is sorrow; acquisitions end in dispersion;
> buildings in destruction; meetings in separation; births in
> death. Knowing this, one should, from the very first,
> renounce acquisitions and storing-up, and building, and meet-
> ing; and, faithful to the commands of an eminent Guru, set
> about realizing the Truth. That alone is the best of religious
> observances.
> ... As regards the method of acquiring practical spirit-
> ual knowledge, if you find a certain practice increases your evil
> passions and tends you toward selfishness, abandon it, though
> it may appear to others virtuous. And if any course of action
> tends to counteract your evil passions, and to benefit sentient
> beings, know that to be the true and holy path, and continue
> it, even though it should appear to others to be sinful.
> ... Life is short, and the time of death is uncertain; so
> apply yourselves to meditation. Avoid doing evil, and acquire
> merit, to the best of your ability, even at the cost of life itself.
> In short, act so that you will have no cause to be ashamed of
> yourselves; and hold fast to this rule.
> ... Works performed for the good of others seldom
> succeed if not wholly freed from self-interest. It is difficult to
> meet success in the effort to insure one's own spiritual wel-
> fare, even without seeking to benefit others. If you seek
> another's spiritual welfare before attaining your own, it would
> be like a helplessly drowning man trying to save another man
> in the same predicament. Therefore, one should not be too
> anxious and hasty in setting out to saave others before one
> has, oneself, realized Truth in Its fullness. That would be like
> the blind leading the blind. As long as the sky endures, there
> will be no dearth of sentient beings for you to serve, and your
> opportunity for such service will come. Till it does, I exhort
> each one of you to keep but one resolve: namely, to attain

Buddhahood for the benefit of all living creatures.

... Maintain the state of undistractedness, and distractions will fly away. Dwell alone, and you shall find the Friend.
Take the lowest place, and you shall reach the highest. Hasten
slowly, and you shall soon arrive. Renounce all worldly goals,
and you shall reach the highest Goal. If you follow this unfrequented path, you will find the shortest way. If you realize
Sunyata (the absolute Emptiness), compassion will arise
within your hearts; and when you lose all differentiation
between yourself and others, then you will be fit to serve
others. [4]

Milarepa, in the company of his illustrious disciples and a host
of celestial beings, passed away in his mountain homeland in 1135
C.E., at the age of eighty-four. And from that time to the present, his
life, his unswerving perseverence in the pursuit of enlightenment, his
teachings, and his incomparable songs, have inspired millions of souls
to the attainment of the liberating Truth to which he dedicated his life.

THE CH'AN AND ZEN BUDDHISTS

Buddhism entered China in the first few centuries of the
Current Era, and, for a number of centuries thereafter, vied with
Taoism for popular acceptance. Buddhism eventually prevailed, due
perhaps to the already decadent condition of Taoism, and the massive
proselytizing efforts of the Buddhists. There was really little to
choose between the two, however; for, while the Taoist and Buddhist
terminologies were different, the realization of Truth which each
taught was, of course, the same. In every mystical tradition, the ultimate goal is the attainment of enlightenment, the direct perception of
the one Reality. In ancient India, this realization was called *nirvana,*
or *samadhi*; when Buddhism was transplanted in China, this supramental experience was called, in Chinese, *chien-hsing*, and as Buddhism became established in Japan in later centuries, this experience was
called *ken-sho* or *satori*. The words and the languages are different,
but the experience is the same.

This experience of enlightenment, of the absolute, quiescent,
Source of all existence, is described by one Chinese Buddhist in this
way:

In learning to be a Buddha, and in seeking the essence
of the teaching of our school, man should purify his mind and
allow his spirit to penetrate the depths. Thus he will be able
to wander silently within himself during contemplation, and he
will see the Origin of all things, obscured by nothing.
        ... His mind becomes boundless and formless, ... all-
illuminating and bright, like moonlight pervading the darkness. During that absolute moment, the mind experiences
illumination without darkness, clarity without stain. It
becomes what it really is, absolutely tranquil, absolutely
illuminating. Though this all-pervading Mind is tranquil, the
world of cause and effect does not cease; though It illumines
the world, the world is but Its reflection. It is pure Light and
perfect Quiescence which continues through endless time. It is
motionless, and free from all activity; It is silent, and self-
aware. ... That brilliant Light permeates every corner of the
world. It is This we should become aware of and know. [1]

Many of the early Buddhist philosophers of India called this
absolute, all-pervading Reality, *Dharmakaya,* "the Body of Truth."
Ashvagosha (2nd century C.E.) referred to It as *Sarvasattvachitta,*
"the one pure Consciousness in all." In China, It was called *Hsin,*
"Consciousness"; and in Japan, It was *Kokoro.* According to Ashvagosha, there arises, in this one pure Consciousness, a spontaneous
movement, from which all the phenomenal world is produced; this
aspect of Reality, he calls *ekachittakshana,* "the movement of the one
Consciousness." In Chinese, it is *nien*; in Japanese, it is *nen.* Just see
how many words there are for our old friends, Brahman and Maya,
Purusha and Prakrti, Shiva and Shakti!
        Similarly, in every mystical tradition, the means to the realiz-
ation of Reality is the same; it is an inturning of the mind in search of
its root, its source; we call this process"meditation." In India, the
Sanskrit word for meditation is *dhyana*; in China, it is *ch'an*, and in
Japan, it is *zen.* Ch'an, or Zen, then, is nothing but the practice of
meditation toward the attainment of enlightenment. Enlightenment is
the only goal of Zen; and it is meditation, or contemplation, alone
which leads to it. For this reason, all the Ch'an and Zen masters
incessantly point all sincere seekers of enlightenment to the meditative
life. Here is an example of such pointing, from a Sermon by the
Ch'an master, Szu-hsin Wu-hsin (1044-1115):

        O brothers, to be born as a human being is a rare

event, and so is the opportunity to hear discourses on the
Truth. If you fail to achieve liberation in this life, when do
you expect to achieve it? While still alive, be therefore
assiduous in practicing meditation. ... As your self-reflection
grows deeper and deeper, the moment will surely come upon
you when the spiritual flower will suddenly burst into bloom,
illuminating the entire universe.

   ... This is the moment when you can transform this
vast earth into solid gold, and the great rivers into an ocean of
milk. What a satisfaction this is then to your daily life!
Since this is so, do not waste your time with words or
phrases, or by searching for Truth in books; for the Truth is
not to be found there. ... They consist of mere words which
will be of no use to you at the moment of your death. [2]

This, throughout the centuries, has been the perennial call of
the Ch'an and Zen masters. Their message is not different from that
of all enlightened seers of the One. The early Ch'an masters of
China, having realized the unchanging Absolute, acknowledged the
unity of the One and the many, and grappled for some time with the
expression of this paradox. Reiterating the old truth of the identity of
nirvana and *samsara,* they spoke of the Real, the unreal, and the
unitive way which embraces them both in an undivided awareness.
But the Chinese had their own way of expressing this duality-in-unity,
this unity-in-duality. Here, for example, is a conversation of the
Ch'an master, Ts'ao-shan Pen-chi (840-901) and one of his disciples:

   MONK: "Where is the Reality in appearance?"
   MASTER: "Wherever there is appearance, there is Real-
               ity."
   MONK: "How does It manifest Itself?"
   MASTER: (The master silently lifted his saucer.)
   MONK: "But where is the Reality in illusion?"
   MASTER: "The origin of illusion is the Real."
   MONK: "But how can Reality manifest Itself in
               illusion?"
   MASTER: "Wherever there is illusion, there is the
               manifestation of Reality."
   MONK: "Do you say, then, Reality can never be
               separated from illusion?"
   MASTER: "Where can you possibly find the appearance
               of illusion?" [3]

At another time, this same Ts'ao-shan Pen-chi was asked by a wandering monk,

> "What is your name?"
> "My name is Pen-chi," he answered.
> "Say something about ultimate Reality," demanded
the monk.
> "I will not say anything," [replied Pen-chi].
> But the monk insisted; and Pen-chi said simply,
"It is not called Pen-chi." [4]

The difficulty of expressing the paradoxical nature of the absolute Reality, which is other than, but not other than, Its projected world-appearance is oftentimes illustrated in the utterances of the early Ch'an masters.

Tung-shan Liang-chieh (807-896) said:

I meet Him wherever I go;
He is the same as me,
Yet I am not He.
Only if you understand this,
Will you identify with the *Tathata* (the Truth, the Real). [5]

Ch'an and Zen Buddhism is replete with the recognition of this paradoxicality, and brings this recognition into the most ordinary experiences of life, and the most ordinary of conversations, relying often, not on words, but on wordless symbols to get across their point:

> The Master asked Pai-chang, his disciple, "What will
you teach others?"
> Pai-chang raised his staff aloft.
> The Master remarked, "Is that all? Nothing else?"
> Pai-chang threw his staff on the ground. [6]

Ummon (d. 996), holding up his staff before his disciples, asked, "What is this? If you say it is a staff, you go right to hell; but if it is not a staff, what is it?" And Tokusan (799-865), who was fond of giving blows with a stick to awaken his disciples, also used to ask a similar question of his disciples, and then say, "If you say 'yes,' thirty blows; if you say 'no,' thirty blows."

It is easy to see from these examples that, while the goal of enlightenment is the same in all mystical traditions, and the Truth experienced is always the same, the expression of that Truth is infinitely variable.   What distinguishes the Ch'an and Zen Buddhist traditions from their Indian counterparts is their unique methods of teaching. They trace this "non-verbal" method of the transmission of knowledge to the Buddha himself, who, according to legend, gave his message to the gathered assemblage on the Mount of the Holy Vulture by simply raising aloft a single kumbhala flower which had been given to him by the god, Brahma. Only one disciple in the throng gave evidence of understanding the import of the Buddha's gesture: an old man named Mahakasyapa, who simply smiled in appreciation. With this, the Buddha is said to have immediately turned over the succession of Mastership to Mahakasyapa. From this legendary non-verbal transmission, the Ch'an and Zen Buddhists find a precedent for their own tradition.

The perpetuation of this special tradition is said to have been initiated in China by Bodhidharma, who came from India to China in 520 C.E. His influence is described in a 9th century work called "The Complete Explanation of The Source of Ch'an" by Kuei-feng Tsung-mi (780-841):

> When Bodhidharma came to China, he saw that most
> Chinese students did not grasp the truth of Buddhism. They
> merely sought it through interpretation of textual terminology,
> and thought of the changing phenomena all around them as
> real activity. Bodhidharma wished to make these eager
> students see that the finger pointing at the moon is not the
> moon itself. The real Truth is nothing but one's own mind.
> Thus, he maintained that the real teaching must be transmitted
> directly from one mind to another, without the use of words. [7]

Bodhidharma and his followers rejected the necessity of the long-winded metaphysical formulations of the Indians as a means to enlightenment. They advocated instead a method of evoking an immediate perception of Truth, a sudden recognition of the nature of one's own mind, unfettered by mental formulations or expectations, "a special transmission outside the scriptures; no dependence upon words and letters, a direct pointing to the Soul of man; the seeing into one's own nature and thus the attainment of Buddhahood."

Whenever words are used, whether as tools of analysis, or to construct metaphors and analogies, they must invariably fall short of an adequate representation of the unitive Reality. To many enlightened men, the endless parade of word-pictures and attempted descriptions by the countless millions of seers over the ages appears a futile and self-defeating game. Such a recognition led the early

Chinese and Japanese Buddhists to pursue a method of knowledge-awakening which transcended the impossible demands of language, which directly evoked the immediate Reality, and awakened the mind to its true nature. And over the centuries, this method has gradually become the special hallmark of the Ch'an and Zen Buddhist traditions.

Taking the rejection of metaphysical formulations as their starting point, they began to devise methods whereby they might turn, or startle, a disciple toward the direct perception of his own Self, his own Being. "What is the sound of one hand clapping?" questioned the Master; and the disciple, deprived of a verbalized answer, had necessarily to peer into the silence of his own being for the comprehension of non-duality. Thus, instead of hoping to awaken a disciple to enlightenment through such explanations as Shankara and the Vedantists offer, and thereby leading him to delve into his own mind to experience the Truth, the enlightened seers of China and Japan practiced a non-analytical method of awakening the disciple; a method which causes the disciple to grab directly and immediately, by wordless insight, at the living truth of his own existence.

When Ummon is asked, "What is Zen?" he stares the disciple fiercely in the face, and exclaims, "That's it! That's it!" This method of the famous Ch'an and Zen masters is a method of shock, a startling of the mind in order to suddenly knock away the clouds of verbalized concepts in the mind of the seeker, and awaken him to the immediate reality of consciousness in the here and now. But who can say whether this method is more effective than another? Who can say whether more men and women have been induced to know the Truth for themselves by Shankara's reasonings, or by Jesus' exhortations, or by the words of the *Bhagavad Gita,* or by Ummon's "That's it!" We can only observe that, in China and Japan, the intellectual method was rejected, and the "direct pointing to the Soul of man" was embraced as a method of instruction.

Teaching methods may vary; but the Truth remains one. And no one has ever realized It without an intense and arduous searching for It within themselves. In the last analysis, it is the determination and fitness of the disciple which determines whether he will attain to the clear vision of Truth, and that, after all, is in the hands of God. Perhaps the most a teacher may do is to exhort and encourage a student to apply himself with all his might to the search for Truth within himself. With this purpose in mind, the famous Zen master,

Hakuin (1683-1768), sang:

> Not knowing how near the Truth is,
> People seek It far away, -- what a pity!
> They are like one who, in the midst of water,
> Cries imploringly for a drink of water,
> Or like the son of a rich man
> Who wanders away among the poor.
> ... Those who testify to the truth of the nature of the Self,
> Have found it by reflecting within themselves,
> And have gone beyond the realm of mere ideas.
> For them opens the gate of the oneness of cause and effect;
> And straight runs the path of non-duality ...
> Abiding with the Undivided amidst the divided,
> Whether going or returning, they remain forever unmoved.
> Holding fast to, and remembering, That which is beyond
> thought,
> In their every act, they hear the voice of the Truth.
> How limitless the sky of unbounded freedom!
> How pure the perfect moonlight of Wisdom!
> At that moment, what do they lack?
> As the eternally quiescent Truth reveals Itself to them,
> This very earth is the lotus-land of Purity,
> And this body is the body of the Buddha. [8]

The experience of *samadhi,* or *satori,* is self-revealing, self-illuminating; it effortlessly reveals the unitive Truth, and dispels all doubts. There is no difficulty of understanding involved in it whatsoever. What *is* difficult, however, is the subsequent adjustment to living the rest of one's life with the knowledge thus acquired. It takes a good deal of reflection and getting-used-to in order to recognize only the One in all phenomenal manifestations as well. Such an acquired habitual perspective no longer distinguishes between the Absolute and the relative, but focuses singly on the awareness of Unity. Such a mind takes no interest in pursuing gratification in appearances, but remains unswayed from Unity-awareness by either pleasant or unpleasant circumstances.

It is this adjustment, or resolution, to life on the relative plane which, therefore, claims much of the attention of the enlightened, and which constitutes much of the written material by the Self-realized sages of every mystical tradition. The writings of the early Ch'an Buddhists are particularly replete with declarations concerning this resolution, this final state of Unity-awareness. Though the language and teaching methods of the Ch'an and Zen Buddhists are unique to themselves, the goal of enlightenment and the attainment of a perfect and lasting Unity-awareness is the same for all. In many of the poems and utterances of the memorable saints of the Chinese and Japanese Buddhist tradition, we can hear something of that pure and simple state; we can hear the voice of the unfettered Self, released from all doubt and conflict.

In one of the earliest Buddhist treatises to come out of China, called *Hsin-hsin ming*, "Inscription on The Self of The Self," written by an obscure monk named Seng-ts'an (d. 606), we find an especially illuminating expression of this ultimate awareness. While it represents a movement toward the early China-izing, or simplifying, of Buddhist ideology, it is scarcely distinguishable from the Taoism which preceded it. Its author was, undoubtedly, an enlightened man, and a Buddhist; but he was also a Chinaman with a long heritage of Taoist phraseology. In this perfect gem of wisdom, we can actually see the transformation of Indian Buddhism into something distinctly Chinese, as Buddhism blends into Taoism, and the one perennial philosophy of Unity resurfaces once more; this time, under the name of Ch'an:

> The perfect Tao knows no difficulties;
> It only refuses to make preferences.
> When freed from hate and love,
> It reveals Itself fully and without disguise.

> A tenth of an inch's difference,
> And heaven and earth are set apart;
> If you want to see It manifest,
> Take no thought either for or against It.

> To set up what you like against what you dislike:
> This is the disease of the mind;
> When the profound Truth is not understood,
> Peace of mind is disturbed and nothing is gained.

> [The Truth is] perfect like the vastness of space,
> With nothing wanting, nothing superfluous;
> It is indeed due to making choices
> That the One Reality is lost sight of.

> Pursue not the outer entanglements,
> Dwell not in the inner Void;
> When the mind rests serene in the oneness of things,
> Dualism vanishes by itself.

When oneness is not thoroughly understood,
In two ways loss may be sustained:
The denial of the world may lead to its absolute negation,
While the denying of the Void may result in the denying
of your [true] Self.

Wordiness and intellection --
The more with them the further astray we go;
Away, therefore, with wordiness and intellection,
And there is no place where we cannot pass freely.

When we return to the root, we gain the meaning;
When we pursue the external objects, we lose the purpose.
The moment we are enlightened within,
We go beyond the voidness of a world confronting us.

Transformations going on in an empty world which
            confronts us
Appear real all because of ignorance.
Try not to seek after the Real;
Only cease to cherish opinions.

Tarry not with dualism,
Carefully avoid pursuing it;
As soon as you have right and wrong,
Confusion ensues, and the mind is lost.

The two exist because of the One,
But hold not even to this One;
When the one Consciousness is not disturbed,
The ten-thousand things offer no offence.

When no offence is offered by them, they are as if
            non-existent;
When the mind is not disturbed, it is as if there is no mind.
The subject is quieted as the object ceases;
The object ceases as the subject is quieted.

The object is an object for the subject;
The subject is a subject for an object.
Know that the relativity of the two
Rests ultimately on the oneness of the Void.

In the oneness of the Void, the two are one,
And each of the two contains in itself all the ten-thousand
            things.
When no discrimination is made between this and that,

How can a one-sided and prejudiced view arise?

... In the higher realm of true Being,
There is neither "other" nor "self";
When a direct identification is required,
We can only say, "not two."

In being not two, all is the same;
All that is is comprehended in it.
The wise in all the ten quarters
Enter into this same absolute Awareness.

This absolute Awareness is beyond movement and rest;
One instant is ten-thousand years.
No matter how things are regarded -- as being or non-being,
It is manifest everywhere before you.

... One in all,
All in One --
If only this is realized,
No more worry about your not being perfect! [9]

About one-hundred years later, another Ch'an master, by the name of Yung-chia Ta-shih (d. 713), wrote his *Cheng-tao Ke,* "Song Of Enlightenment," which reiterates, in equally inspiring tones, this same knowledge, this same enlightened state of awareness:

Do you know that leisurely sage who has gone beyond learning, and who does not exert himself in anything?
He neither endeavors to avoid idle thoughts nor seeks after
the Truth;
[For he knows that] ignorance is also the Reality,
[And that] this empty, illusory, body is nothing but the
absolute Reality (*Dharmakaya*).

When one knows the Absolute, there are no longer any
[independent] objects;
The Source of all things is the absolute Self of all the
enlightened.
The five elements are like a cloud floating aimlessly here
and there;
And the three passions are like the foam which appears and
disappears on the surface of the ocean.

When the absolute Reality is known, it is seen to be without
any individual selves, and devoid of any objective

forms;
All past [mental and physical] actions which lead to hell are
            instantly wiped away.
... After the Awakening, there is only vast Emptiness; this
            vast universe of forms ceases to exist [outside of
            one's Self].

Here, one sees neither sin nor bliss, neither loss nor gain.
In the midst of the eternal Serenity, no questions arise;
The dust of ignorance which has accumulated on the
            unpolished mirror for ages,
Is now, and forever, cleared away in the vision of Truth.

... The people do not know where to find this precious jewel
Which lies deep within the creative Power (*Tathagata-garba*);
The activity miraculously performed by the creative Power
            is an illusion and yet it is not an illusion,
[Just as] the rays of light emanating from the one perfect Sun
            belong to it and yet do not belong to it.

Let us be thoroughgoing, not only in inner experience, but
in its interpretation,
And our lives will be perfect in meditation and in wisdom as
            well -- not adhering one-sidedly to Emptiness
            (*Sunyata*) alone.
It is not we alone who have come to this conclusion;
All the enlightened, numerous as the sands of India, are of
            the same mind.

I crossed seas and rivers, climbed mountains, and forded
            streams,
In order to interview the Masters, to enquire after Truth, to
            delve into the secrets of Ch'an;
But since I learned the true path from my Master (Hui-neng:
            638-713),
I know that birth-and-death is not what I need to be
            concerned with.

For walking is Ch'an, sitting is Ch'an;
Whether talking or remaining silent, whether moving or
            standing still, the Essense Itself is always at rest.
Even when confronted by swords and spears, It never loses
            Its way of stillness;
Not even poisonous drugs can perturb Its serenity.

Ever since the realization -- which came to me suddenly --
            that I have never been born,

All vicissitudes of fate, good and bad, have lost their power
              over me.
Far off, in the mountains, I live in a modest hut;
The mountains are high, the shade-trees are broad, and
              under an old pine tree
I sit quietly and contentedly in my monkish home;
Here, perfect tranquility and rustic simplicity reign.

[The sage] neither seeks the Truth, nor avoids the defilements;
He clearly perceives that all dualities are empty and have no
              reality.
And, since they have no reality, he is not one-sided, neither
              empty, nor not-empty.
This is the genuine state of sagehood.

The one Mind, like a mirror, reflects everything brightly,
              and knows no limitations;
It pervades the entire universe in even its minutest crevices.
This world and all its contents, multitudinous in form, are
              reflected in the one Mind,
Which, shining like a perfect gem, has no "outer" or "inner."

If we hold exclusively to Emptiness, we deny the entire causal
              world;
All is then attributed to chance, with no ruling principle,
              inviting evil to prevail.
The same error occurs when one holds exclusively to the
              manifested, denying the Emptiness;
That would be like throwing oneself into the flames in order
              to avoid being drowned in the water.

... The Real need not be adhered to;
As for the non-real, there has never been any such thing.
When both Real and non-Real are put aside, "non-real"
              becomes meaningless.
[Even] when the various means to [the attainment of]
              Emptiness are abandoned,
The eternal Oneness of the sage remains as It has always
              been. [10]

In the ongoing tradition of Ch'an and Zen Buddhism, many
such declarations have been uttered; oftentimes they are but brief and
simple declarations of isolation and profound contentment.   And
oftentimes, when we read the poems of the early Ch'an and Zen
masters, such as this, by P'ang-yun (d. 811):

> How wondrously supernatural,
> And how miraculous this!
> I carry water, and I carry fuel. [11]

Or this, by Pao-tzu Wen-ch'i (10th century):

> Drinking tea, eating rice,
> I pass my time as it comes;
> Looking down at the stream,
> Looking up at the mountain,
> How serene and relaxed I feel indeed! [12]

Or this, by Hsue-tou (950-1052):

> What life can compare to this?
> Sitting quietly by the window,
> I watch the leaves fall and the flowers bloom,
> As the seasons come and go. [13]

... we may fail to recognize the connection of these Oriental Buddhists to their parent tradition, and lose sight of the long, arduous progression of understanding which led to the apparent simplicity of the enlightened Ch'an and Zen masters. Their simple poems may seem far removed from the reasonings of the early Buddhist Fathers on the complementarity of *nirvana* and *samsara*, but they represent the ultimate synthesis of centuries of metaphysics, and the final freedom of those who have realized that synthesis in their ordinary lives. How simple seem these Buddhist sages, yet their very simplicity is the simplicity of the blessed; it stands on the heads of the Buddhas of the past, and reveals a consummation of the struggles of a thousand lifetimes.

THE SUFIS

The religion of Islam was founded in Arabia by Muhammed (d. 632), whose book, the *Quran* or *Koran*, constitutes the final authority and credo for all who claim Islam as their religion. Though Muhammed claimed that the book was inspired by God, whom he calls *Allah*, it contains much that is derived from ancient Jewish and Christian sources. Muhammed set forth in the *Quran*, by the use of many anecdotes and commentaries, a number of moral precepts and social laws which did much to transform a diversified group of lawless nomadic tribes into a united God-fearing nation. And while the *Quran* is essentially a book of moral principle and faith, it contains many statements by Muhammed which may be interpreted as mystical in nature.

Following upon the death of Muhammed, a number of devout mystics belonging to the Islamic faith appeared throughout the Middle East, spreading from Arabia to Egypt, Iraq, Persia, Turkey, and Afghanistan. They came to be known as *Sufis*, from the word for "wool" -- apparently because of the woolen garments worn by these gnostics to set them apart as "knowers" of God. While the mainstream faithful of Islam were busily engaged in the spread of their religion through territorial conquest during the 8th and 9th centuries, the Sufis were teaching the pure love of God, and living an ascetic life aimed at realizing Him in the depths of their souls.

Among the best known and revered of these early Sufis were Hasan al-Basri (d. 728), Rabi'a Adawiyya, the slave-girl of Basra (d. 801), Dhu'n-Nun, the Egyptian (d. 859), Beyizid Bistami, the Persian (d. 874), and Abu'l-Husayn an-Nuri, the Iraqi (d. 907). All were great lovers of God, and each of them greatly influenced the mystical mood of their time. Their love of God took the form of a one-pointed yearning for union with Him, for the "vision of His Face"; and their writings often resembled the arduous outpourings of a lover to his beloved.

For the Sufis, the path of love is the Way by which the soul makes the involute journey to the awareness of her own true identity. And the prayerful songs of love sung by the Sufis are the expressions of the soul's yearning to return in awareness to her eternal Source and Ground. She searches inwardly for her pristine state, her Beloved, her Lord; and subdues herself, dissolving herself, as it were, by reducing her own being to her pristine simplicity and ultimate non-being. She renounces all regard for herself, divests herself of all facination with manifested phenomena, both inner and outer; and, drawn by a one-pointed love and desire for God, is brought at last to silence. Then the illusory duality of soul and God is no more; the awareness of the one Self dawns with supreme clarity, knowing who It has always been, knowing Its eternal freedom and joy.

Such a description of the soul's inner "pilgrimage" makes it appear a simple and clear-cut process, but it is the most difficult accomplishment that can be performed, for the ego-soul does not die without a fight. It wages a tireless and bitter warfare against its own attraction to God, and fights with all the fury and panic of a drowning man struggling to sustain his existence; it incessantly asserts its love of the manifested world and life, and restlessly strives to create a diversion from its path toward God. Torn in two directions, the soul suffers, on the one hand, the agonies of annihilation, and on the other, the painful prolonging of its failure to reach its avowed Goal. Only when it comes at last, by the grace of God, to that point where it surrenders all other objectives for God alone does it become capable of reaching its cherished Goal; divinely inspired by the desire for God alone, it makes that leap into the consciousness of universal Being.

In the writings of the early Sufis, and in particular, those of Dhu'n-Nun, this path of divine love for God, culminating in vision, or *gnosis*, is charted as a path (*tariq*) marked by several distinct advances, or stations. The entering upon the path originates with a call from God and the assent of the individual will to embark on the journey. This "call" is an awakening of the heart which is affected solely by God's grace, serving to draw the wandering soul back to its true home and divine source. This awakening might be precipitated by the meeting with a *Shaikh* (spiritual Master), or through a reading of the words of one of the mystics who had travelled the path of divine love and reached its goal.

The actual journey along the spiritual path begins with the station of Repentence (*tauba*). "Repentence," said Jalaluddin Rumi, "is a strange mount; it jumps toward heaven in a single moment from the lowest place." A man may have led an utterly despicable life prior to the awakening of the soul, but once that awakening takes place, he immediately wipes clean the entire slate of the past, and utterly transforms his own mind and will by the intense remorse he feels for all the little acts of wicked selfishness performed theretofore.

He is filled with shame and regret for every instance of hurt given to another, because his heart is now filled with pity and love for all humanity struggling to find the joy and understanding he has now found through God's grace. Such remembrance of one's own stupidity in the previous state of ignorance is also a great humbler of what pride one might otherwise be tempted to feel in the possession of that grace.

The next station is that of Faith, or Surrender To God (*tawakkul*). The mental agitation resulting from fear for one's own welfare, which may afflict the novice when he chooses to give all his thought to God, is dispelled by the calm rembrance that it is He who has called the soul to Him, and that He will nourish and provide for the body as well. Surrendering all thoughts of his own bodily welfare, he gives everything into the hands of God, and says, "Lead me wheresoever Thou wilt." This attitude was expressed by Jesus to his disciples when he told them to take no thought for the morrow: "Do not worry and say, 'What shall we eat?' or 'What shall we wear?' Your Father in heaven knows that you need all these things. Seek first His kingdom and all these things shall be given to you." This may lead to Poverty (*faqr*), and often does; but if this poverty is necessary to the freedom to contemplate God, so be it. To those who have been thus led to it, this poverty is the true and greatest wealth.

The next station is that of Patient Endurance (*sabr*), a great necessity for the soul called to the contemplation of God. Calm acceptance of the rigors of such a life is necessary to the stability of the soul, which must pass through many ordeals, and many temptations that arise in the mind. Next, and allied with Patient Endurance, is Joy In Affliction (*rida*). When the soul is free to focus its attention on God, it enjoys an inner bliss which cannot be dislodged by any outward occurance, no matter how unpleasant. Its joy is derived from a source entirely untouched by worldly pains or pleasures, and therefore the soul remains unaffected by them, revelling solely in the proximity of the Beloved. The soul, burdened by afflictions, has only to remember God to rise above all earthly pain, and know the healing caress of imperturbable bliss.

However, following that sweet time, comes another, often referred to as "The Dark Night Of The Soul"; the Sufis call it *gabd*. This is a state of dryness and emptiness, when the soul, struggling to become completely selfless, egoless, has not yet reached the ultimate degree of extinction, and suffers the heavy sense of death, with no light of superconscious life yet visible. It is a dry, awful, sense of one's own nothingness, one's own emptiness, which may be likened to the darkness experienced while going through a dark tunnel when the light at the other end cannot yet be seen. The ego-self is withered, dried-up, and all but gone; but the greater Selfhood has not yet revealed Itself. The suffering soul feels great agony in the lack of both worldly and spiritual consolation; and worse, it imagines that it has been damned and relegated forever to its present hell, and thus suffers all the more.

Then comes the revelation of Love and Spiritual Knowledge (*mahabba* and *ma'rifa*). The soul awakens to an incredibly clear awareness that embraces both divine Love and Knowledge. It is an inner realization by the soul that the God it sought is all-inclusive Love, and the soul experiences that Love within itself. It knows that This is the sustaining Power and guide of all its life. And it vows to surrender all else for the sake of being filled throughout life with this perfect Love. With great joy, the soul is refreshed, and sings: "Thou art my God, the sole Father of my being, the sweet breath of Love that lives in my heart; and I shall follow Thee, and live with Thee, and lean on Thee till the end of my days."

This experience of divine Love may be likened to the corona of the Sun; it is fully Light, yet it has a still deeper Source. And this Love, while fully complete, yet yearns for its own source, its own center of radiance; and so, while being the fulfilling Light itself, it is drawn by longing to Itself. Says Rumi: "The hearts of the wise are the nests of love, and the hearts of the lovers are the nests of longing, and the hearts of the longing are the nests of intimacy." The longing of the lover for God is often compared to that of a worldly lover for her beloved. The soul so blessed, or afflicted, with divine Love has no other thought or desire but to reach her Beloved. She weeps sweet tears of love nightly, and calls in her heart for death at her Beloved's feet. Like a moth drawn to a flame, she longs to be annihilated in her Beloved's embrace, and so to enjoy the ultimate intimacy of union with her beloved God.

It is this love-longing which leads to the station of Annihilation (*fana*). This is the profoundly transformative experience previously referred to as *nirvana, samadhi,* or "the vision of God." For, at the moment the ego is extinguished, the eternal and all-pervasive "I" is realized. It is an experience that overturns all previous conceptions of God and the soul. Previously, there was a relationship:

the soul to God, the lover to the Beloved; but now, the ego-soul is no more. The false sense of selfhood which is part of the illusion of phenomenal existence has been erased, and only the Real, the One, exists. What shall we call It? The *Dharmakaya* of the Buddhists? The *Atman* of the Vedantists? The "One" of Plotinus? The Sufis call It *Haqq*, "the Real."

Scholars may imagine that a Buddhist experiences one thing, a Vedantist another, and so forth; but one who has experienced It, whether a Sufi, Christian or Hindu, knows that It is the final Truth, the only One. There are not different Unitys, one for each sect or denomination; there is only one One, and it is That which is experienced by Christians, Buddhists, Hindus and Sufis alike. It should be obvious that, if there is such a thing as Unity, and if It can be experienced, then the experience must be the same for all; since Unity, by its very definition, by its very nature, is one. So what if that One is called by different names in different lands! In every place and in every generation, new terms are ever being invented in the hope of elucidating the knowledge of Unity.

All phenomenal existence comes into being by the power of that One. This makes an apparent two; but it is really only one. The appearance of two is just the result of the "imaginary" juxtaposition of subject and object. But, of course, the subject and the object are the same One. It is this Unity that is realized when the soul reaches the station of *fana*. When the ego-mind is dissolved, having been drawn to its extinction by its own Source, there is no longer a subject-object relationship. There is only the Unnameable, beyond all subject-object predications. It is what has been called by the Sufis, *jam,* or "Unity."

The Upanishadic seers of this Unity declared that, "When one realizes Brahman, he becomes Brahman." "When I died to myself," says the Sufi, "I became the Beloved." "I have ceased to exist, and have passed out of self," said Rabi'a; "I am one with Him and entirely His." It is from the standpoint of this experience of Unity that al-Hallaj declared, *ana'l Haqq,* "I am He"; and Bistami exclaimed, "Glory be to Me! There is nothing under my garment but He." For, after such a revelation, if one is to speak the truth, he can no longer make a distinction between "me" and "Thee." He knows full well that there is no other in all the universe but "I." If he makes the slightest separation between "I" and "Thou," he has forfeited the Truth, and re-established Duality. How strange and baffling, that only moments before, he was a soul on fire with love; and now he is enjoined by the Truth revealed to him to forget about souls and desire for union.

One might imagine this experience of *fana* to be the final station on the Sufi path, but, in Sufism, as in nearly every mystical tradition, there is recognized to be a further, final, station on the journey to perfection. This ultimate summit of spiritual attainment is called Retention of Identity (*baqa*). This is the state of one living continuously in the enlightened awareness of Unity. It is the state of the *jivanmukta* of Vedanta; the state of Buddhahood of the Buddhists; the Beatitude of the Christians; the Sagehood of the Taoists. *Baqa,* the final and ultimate station, is nothing less than the continuous retention of the awareness of Unity throughout one's life; in every moment and breath, to live in the awareness of one's true, all-pervasive, Identity. This is the perfect life of freedom, contentment, and utter surrender of the soul to the will of God within.

We find this state of perfection described by the Taoist, Lao Tze, by the *Bhagavad Gita,* by the Avadhut, by the Christians, Zen Buddhists, and all the enlightened saints of all time; yet all have declared as well that this state is beyond description. "The Way that can be told is not the true Way," said Lao Tze; it would make no sense at all to those unprepared for it by inner experience, and besides, no words can tell just what the life of such a man is like. It must be lived to know it. Such a man may teach, or he may not teach; he may beg for his food or he may labor for it; he may be fat or he may be thin; he may write books or he may appear a simpleton; but the joy is the same. He may be a Sufi or a Jew; he may be a Buddhist or an Avadhut, a Christian or a Sikh, a farmer or a monk; but the joy is the same.

Naturally, it is very difficult for people at a lower station of knowledge to recognize or appreciate the view of one at the highest station, and it is because of this that they so often deride and persecute the saints. On the other hand, one who has reached the final state cannot malign the preliminary stations as incorrect; for it was by the ascension of the path, by way of these very stations, that he arrived at his Goal. Once there, he sees that all the people of the world are at the station on the path where God has placed them. How can he fault their ignorance? If anyone at all can understand him or even hear his voice, it is those at the stations most near to him. The great majority of men are far below him, and must imagine him to be a madman. As

Lao Tze has said, "If it were not the highest Truth, it would not be laughed at by the majority of people."

Within Islam, as within all religious traditions, there are individuals of varying degrees of spiritual experience and understanding, with the mystic standing at the highest degree, opposed at the other end of the scale by those pious and pretentious people whose understanding of spiritual experience is dim. These two contrary elements within any religious tradition tend naturally to conflict mightily with one another; and, in Islam, as elsewhere, this conflict has often resulted in the extreme persecution and martyrdom of the mystics. One of the best known and most often cited examples is that of the martyred Sufi saint, al-Hallaj.

AL-HALLAJ

Husayn ibn Mansur al-Hallaj (858-922) was an Arab, born in the province of Fars, and spent most of his life in the city of Baghdad. He became a disciple of 'Amr al-Makki and also of the famous Sufi teacher, al-Junayd of Persia (d. 910). At some time during his discipleship, al-Hallaj attained the transcendent Unity, and realized his identity to be the Identity of the One. But when he spoke of it, he found that both al-Makki and al-Junayd had no inkling of such an experience, and refused to acknowledge that what al-Hallaj said was true. It seemed to them quite contrary to the teaching of the Prophet, and therefore a dangerous heresy.

Al-Hallaj, around this time, became married to the daughter of a well-known religious teacher; but the girl's father also became turned against al-Hallaj when he began speaking of the unity of his own soul with God. In al-Hallaj's own home, his father-in-law regarded him as "a miserable infidel." It was then he began writing in poetic verse of what he had realized, in order to make known to his fellow Sufis what he had known to be the Truth. He wrote of his search for God by the path of loving prayer, and his eventual experience of Unity, declaring, "I am the Truth," "I am the Reality" (ana'l Haqq); but very few of his writings have survived, due to their being regarded as blasphemous and heretical in his own time.

In his writings, al-Hallaj attempted to explain that his saying, "ana'l Haqq," was not heretical, by comparing his own saying to the similar declarations of Satan and the Egyptian Pharoah in certain mythological stories.   He argued that, whereas the "I" of the Pharoah's saying, "I am your highest Lord," and Satan's "I am the Highest," referred to the personal "I," the ego; his own "I" was an "I" devoid of ego, referring not to the personal self, but to the one "I" of all.   Said al-Hallaj:

> I am He whom I love, and He whom I love is I; we
> are two spirits dwelling in one body. If you see me, you see
> Him; and if you see Him, you see us both. [1]

These words of his were very similar to those of Jesus, who had experienced the same revelation; and they met with a similar response. Both his old friends and teachers, al-Makki and al-Junayd, went to the *ulama,* the guardians of Islamic faith, and accused al-Hallaj of propagating a false and heretical doctrine.

The antagonism mounted against him by the *ulama* became too oppressive, and al-Hallaj was forced to leave Baghdad. He travelled for five years, meeting with other Sufis in Khurasan, and in Mecca. It is said that when he made pilgrimage to Mecca, four-hundred disciples accompanied him. In the year 905, at the age of forty-seven, he took a boat to northern India, where the Muslim empire had already begun to establish itself. He travelled through Gujerat, Sind and the lower Indus Valley, presumably meeting with and teaching the Sufis living there. It is not known how long he stayed in India, nor if he had any intellectual intercourse with the Vedantic teachings, but he seems to have travelled extensively; and to have gone from there north to Khurasan, Turkestan, and Turfan, travelling with trade caravans, and eventually back to Baghdad.

Upon his return to Baghdad, al-Hallaj resumed his teaching and preaching to the people on the life of prayer and intense love of God. He led an ascetic and holy life, and was revered by many. But again, opposition rose up from the orthodox legalists of the city, and al-Hallaj left for two years to remain in Mecca. On his return, the religionists -- in particular, one Muhammed ibn Da'ud -- brought action against al-Hallaj's "heretical" doctrines. Both the Shiites and the Sunnites rallied against him, and, in the year 912, he was arrested and imprisoned. Nearly ten years were to pass before the high judge of Arabia (now Iraq) could be prevailed upon to sign the order for his execution.

Mansur passed those years in prison in prayer and contemplation, sometimes writing of his ecstatic experiences of divine love, and expressing his knowledge of the oneness of God and the universe. Of his last days, the famous Turkish Sufi, Attar (d. 1220), later wrote:

> When al-Hallaj was in prison, he was asked, "What is love?" He answered, "You will see it today and tomorrow and the day after tomorrow." And that day they cut off his hands and feet, and the next day they put him on the gallows, and the third day, they gave his ashes to the wind..." [2]

On the day of his execution, March 26, 922, a great many of the people of Baghdad turned out to see his death; among them many of his old friends, teachers and disciples. It is told that he danced to the gallows, singing praise to God, as though he were going to a wedding festival. Some threw stones at him as he passed, but al-Hallaj had long foreseen and prepared for that day, and was like a bridegroom going to meet his beloved. He had written, in his poetry, of the moth that, drawn to the flame, and caring nothing for its light or its heat, desires only to be merged in that flame. "Happi-ness comes from God," he said, "but suffering is He Himself!" "Slay me, O my trustworthy friends!" he sang; "For in being slain is my life." And, as he approached his executioners, he remarked, "It is now time for the lover to make the One single."

It is reported that his death was long, and deliberately drawn out by his tormentors. First, he was beaten with scourges, and then his hands and feet were cut off; and he was left in that condition to bleed and suffer until the following day when he was hanged. Then, as if to rid themselves of his voice forever, his persecutors severed his head and burned his body, and dumped his ashes in the Tigris. Since that time, however, the name of al-Hallaj has become famous throughout the world, and his perfect love has been extolled in song over the centuries. One admirer, who had also known the experience of *ana' Haqq*, wrote:

> O my friends, you have wreaked your vengeance on al-Hallaj; but it is you who are the losers. What a gentle, perfect soul he was! *"Ana'l Haqq,"* he said. Perhaps if you had listened, you too would have learned to put an end to that ignorance which prevents you from saying *ana'l Haqq*. Far better had you murdered your own sense of pride and selfhood which stands like a cloud between you and your *ana'l Haqq*.
> But you will live in sorrow and struggle and bitter pain, while al-Hallaj is spread throughout space in blissful

joy, all-pervading and sparkling with light. You tried to
silence him, but his words are whispered even by the autumn
winds. The lips of countless millions of sages praise him
still. You cut off his head to wipe the smile from his face,
but his bell-like laughter spreads from shore to shore, and his
laughing eyes twinkle in the clear blue sky. [3]

His words of truth live still; in a modern-day drama on
the life of al-Hallaj by the Egyptian, Abdu's-Sabur, a chorus sings:

We will go scatter in the plough furrows of the
peasants what we have stored from his words ...
We will preserve them among the merchant's goods,
and we will give them to the wind that wanders o'er the waves;
We will hide them in the mouths of singing camel-
drivers who traverse the desert; we will note them down on
papers, to be kept in the folds of the frock; and we will make
them into verses and songs.
Tell us -- what would have become of his words had
he not been martyred? [4]

Thus, al-Hallaj lives on, as did Jesus, in the hearts and minds of
all true lovers of God; and his name is a banner of victory for all who
would declare the saving truth to men.

≈≈

IV. Mystics Of The Late Middle Ages

JEWISH MYSTICISM

By the late Medieval period (11th-14th centuries), the philosophers and theologians of the Western world had become increasingly aware of the long tradition of mystical philosophy dating from the early Greeks and Neoplatonists. This was due primarily to the availability of newly translated manuscripts dating from that earlier era. The late Medieval period, therefore, saw a great resurgence of interest in metaphysics and mystical theology, and many celebrated thinkers emerged during those centuries within the traditions of Judaism, Islam and Christianity.

The beginnings of this resurgent movement may be traced, in particular, to a few Muslim philosophers living in Spain. While most of Europe was under the domination of Christian Catholicism, Spain, bordered by Islamic countries, was conquered by the Arabs in the 8th century and remained under Muslim rule until the late 15th century. In the 10th century, Al-Farabi (ca. 870-950), and several other Arab philosophers, rediscovered the great legacy of Greek thought, particularly in the works of Aristotle and Plotinus (whose writings were misrepresented during Medieval times as "The Theology of Aristotle"), and these were translated into Arabic. In the 11th and 12th centuries, these were reformulated and elaborately commented upon by the Spanish Muslim philosophers, Avicenna (980-1037) and Averroes (1126-1198). These works in turn were translated into Latin by the Christian philosophers, setting the stage for their great influence upon the Scholastics of the 13th century.

Spain had also become the home of a large Jewish population; and in the 11th century those learned Jews who shared in the Arabic culture and language of their Muslim rulers were quick to share also in the new fervor for reconciling ancient religious tenets with the sober logic of the Greek tradition. One such Jew was the great poet and philosopher, Solomon Ibn Gabirol. If we mean by the term, "mystic," one who has experienced his identity with God, and gives witness to that experience, we may only qualifiedly designate Ibn Gabirol a mystic, as he never explicity declares his experience; nonetheless, his more than genuine devotion, his evident intimacy with God, and his influence upon subsequent generations, earns for him a place in the history of mystical thought.

Ibn Gabirol

Solomon Ibn Gabirol (ca. 1021-1058 or 1070) was born in Malaga, in southern Spain, reared and educated in Saragossa, and began composing religious poems at the age of sixteen. He wrote his philosophical works in Arabic, but his poems, of which he wrote over three-hundred, were written in Hebrew. Some of these poems are still part of the liturgy of the Spanish Jews. His main philosophical work is *The Fountain Of Life,* but he wrote, in addition, two ethical treatises, *The Improvement Of The Qualities Of The Soul,* and *The Choice Of Pearls,* along with a book on the Divine Will, which is lost.

The original Arabic manuscript of *The Fountain Of Life* was also lost, but was preserved in a Latin translation (*Fons Vitae*) in the middle of the 12th century by a Christianized Jew, Johannes Hispanus, and the archdeacon of Segovia, Dominicus Gundassalinus. This translation became well-known to Christian Scholastics who assumed that its author was a Muslim, whom they called Avicebron or Avicebrol. This assumption was due to the fact that it was originally written in Arabic, and also because no reference is made throughout the work to Judaism, nor is there a single quotation from Biblical, Talmudic or Midrashic sources.

In its Latin form, this work greatly influenced such Christian theologians as Albertus Magnus, Bonaventure, Thomas Aquinus, and Duns Scotus, all of whom quoted it freely. And it was not until the 19th century that a Jewish scholar, Solomon Munk, discovered that the translation of Ibn Gabirol's work, from Arabic to Hebrew, which had been made by Shem Tob Falquera (1225-1290) under the Hebrew title, *Mekor Hayim,* was identical to the work Christians called *Fons Vitae.* Thus it was discovered that the Muslim, Avicebron or Avicebrol, was none other than the Jewish philosopher, Solomon Ibn Gabirol.

Since the recent translation of, and interest in, the writings of Aristotle and Plotinus, in whose works the stages of the emanation, or manifestation, of the world from the Divine had been so elaborately described, it had become necessary, if one was to formulate an acceptable ontological theory, to explain step by step the progression of manifestation from God to corporeal matter. This Ibn Gabirol attempted to do in his *Fountain Of Life.* But is it possible even to describe how our own conscious minds create from themselves a thought or image? We are in an even more difficult predicament when trying to describe the "emanation," "creation," or "willing" of the world-Thought from the Divine Mind. Philosophers, from Aristotle onward, have labored to explain the process whereby the Thought passes into corporeal form, but it is a futile and unrewarding task. Words may be employed, like *genus* and *species,* and distinctions may be drawn between substance and form, etc.; yet, when all is said and done, we must admit that it remains a mysterious and indescribable occurrence.

Ibn Gabirol, following after the fashion of Aristotle and Plotinus, with whom he was familiar through Arabic translations, tried his hand at such a systematic presentation, and made a remarkable effort, offering many clarifying conceptualizations. Yet, for all his genius and skill, in addition to his apparent first-hand knowledge, his great work, *The Fountain Of Life*, remains a dry and tedious work, holding little appeal for the modern mind. It is an unhappy fact that any attempt to explain the emanation of the world from God must prove futile and unrewarding, no matter how clearly and unmistakably one has "seen" it in the mystical experience. See how many have vainly tried to do so, utilizing such words as "Logos," "Prakrti," "Will," "Shakti," and so many others, to signify the ineffable Power of God by which He casts forth this world-image from Himself, remaining all the while entirely unaltered, eternally and indivisibly One!

To those who have "seen" God, His projection of the universe from Himself is a clear and obvious fact; but to those who have not, the notion that the mutable universe is, in some way, identical with the immutable God must seem an impossible contradiction. Nonetheless, Ibn Gabirol, like so many others who have been granted that "vision" in contemplation, felt the need to explain it in hopes that the intellects of men might grasp some sense of the Divinity inherent in all life, and might likewise be guided toward the communion with God that leads to true knowledge, and the joyous life in awareness of God.

He spoke of the Absolute variously as the "First Essence," or simply as "God"; and God's outspreading radiance of Power, he called the "Divine Will." God, or the Essence, is infinite, eternal, and unchanging, declares Ibn Gabirol. Nothing at all can be predicated of Him, since He is utterly beyond all qualities or attributes, being pure Consciousness, pure Being. His "Will," which Ibn Gabirol repeatedly reminds us is the same as what was meant in earlier times by the words,

"Logos" or "Wisdom," radiates forth from God, and manifests as the world of matter and form. The "Will," he is quick to point out, is co-eternal with God, being His own, but becomes temporal and finite in its manifestation.

Ibn Gabirol argues, in a profusely detailed manner, that all of what we call "matter" is nothing else but that universal Energy, or Will, of God emanating forth from the Divine Essence; that it is "the Power of God which fills everything, exists in everything, and works in everything." [1] All the various forms which this universal "matter" takes, says Ibn Gabirol, only conceal from us the universality of the one Divine Substance by presenting the impression of diversity. It is form which, impressed or superimposed upon the one universal matter, accounts for all diversity within the subtle and gross worlds.

In a manner reminiscent of Shankara, he offers this analogy:

> Consider golden bracelets, [and necklaces] made of
> gold, and put them in place of all existent things. You will
> find them to be different through [their] forms, while you
> will find the matter which underlies them to be one...
> From this [example] you can understand that existent things
> are different through their form, while the matter which
> underlies them is one; for the essence of this matter is not
> different from the essence of these [various] things. [2]

In another passage, equally reminiscent of Shankara, he declares the impossibility of defining or explaining the nature of the Divine Will, or as Shankara called it, "Maya":

> It is impossible to describe the Will. One may only
> approximate its definition by saying that it is a divine Power,
> creating matter and form and holding them together, and that it
> is diffused from the highest to the lowest... It is this Power
> which moves and directs everything. [3]

Like all mystics, Ibn Gabirol asserts that one should see the one all-filling Radiance glimmering in every form in the universe, no longer perceiving things in their separateness and distinctiveness, but as one multiformed, multicolored, spectacle of God's splendor. So that, rising still higher, by the aspiration of the heart and will, one might view the subtler realms of that splendor, until, drawn by love and yearning toward the Source and Master of all splendorous forms, one is drawn by grace into "the Wonder of wonders," the Silence of silences, and knows, with God's knowing, his own true being, the eternal Self of all.

In the dialogue of *The Fountain Of Life*, Ibn Gabirol, as the teacher, instructs the student on the method of this ascent:

> If you wish to form a picture of the [divine] Sub-
> stance, you must raise your intellect to the last [substance]
> intelligible. You must purify it from all sordid sensibility,
> free it from the captivity of nature and approach with the force
> of your intelligence to the last limit of intelligible substance
> that it is possible for you to comprehend, until you are entire-
> ly divorced from sensible substance and lose all knowledge
> thereof. Then you will embrace, so to speak, the whole corpo-
> real world in your being, and will place it in one corner of
> your being. When you have done this you will understand the
> insignificance of the sensible in comparison with the greatness
> of the intelligible. Then the spiritual substance will be before
> your eyes, comprehending you and superior to you, and you
> will see your own being as though you were that substance.
>   Sometimes it will seem to you that you are a part of
> it by reason of your connection with corporeal substance; and
> sometimes you will think you are all [forms], and that there is
> no difference between you and them, on account of the union
> of your being with their being, and the consubstantiality of
> your form and their forms...
>   When you have raised yourself to [awareness of] the
> first universal matter ... and fathomed its shadowy nature, then
> you will see the *Wonder of wonders*. Therefore, pursue this
> dilligently and with love, because this is the purpose of the
> existence of the human soul, and in this is great delight and
> extreme happiness. [4]

However, such flights of mystical instruction are rare in *The Fountain*; for the most part it is a dry, undramatic, philosophical treatise, like those of many another Medieval philosopher, which fails to convince the critical intellect or to inspire the heart. Where Ibn Gabirol soars is in his poetry. There, he paints fervently and lovingly, with imagery from the Bible, the awesome glory of the Divine. He uses such figurative images as "the Throne" of God, "the canopy," "the fire of the soul," etc.; yet his philosophy comes through much more clearly and vividly in his poetry than in his deliberately philosophical prose, proving clearly how much more appropriate is poetry to the portrayal of the Divine than philosophy, how much more evocative the call of the heart than the call of reason.

In one of his longest and best-known songs, called "The Royal Crown" (*Keter Malkhut* in Hebrew), he expresses, in an infinitely superior manner, all that he attempted to say in the more lengthy intellectual formulations of *The Fountain Of Life*. In this poem of forty chapters, or sections, he expresses the incompre-hensibility to the intellect of God's mysterious hidden Essence, which he refers to at times as "the Throne," and he speaks of the creative effulgence of God as "the Will," "the Intelligence," "the Fountain of Life," "Wisdom," or "the Habitation." Here are a few verses from the beginning of that Song:

> Thine are the mysteries, which neither fancy nor imagination can comprehend; and the life, over which dissolution hath no power. Thine is the Throne exalted above all height; and the Habitation concealed in the eminence of its recess. Thine is the existence, from the shadow of whose light sprung every existing thing; of which we said, "under Its protecting shadow shall we live..."
>
> Thou art One, the first of every number, and the Foundation of all structure. Thou art One, and in the mystery of the Unity all the wise in heart are astonished; for they cannot define it. Thou art One, and Thy unity can neither be lessened nor augmented; for nothing is there wanting or superfluous. Thou art One, but not such a One as is numbered; for neither plurality nor change, nor form, nor physical attribute, nor name expressive of Thy nature, can reach Thee...
>
> Thou art Light, and the eyes of every pure soul shall see Thee; for the clouds of iniquity alone hide Thee from her sight... Thou art most high, and the eye of the intellect desireth and longeth for Thee, but the intellect can see only a part; it cannot see the whole of Thy greatness...
>
> Thou art God, who by Thy Divinity supportest all things formed; and upholdest all creatures by Thy Unity. Thou art God, and there is no distinction between Thy Godhead, Unity, Eternity or Existence; for all is one mystery; and although each of these attributes is variously named, yet all of them point to One.
>
> Thou art wise, and Wisdom, which is the Fountain of Life, floweth from Thee; and compared with Thy Wisdom, the knowledge of all mankind is folly. Thou art wise, and didst exist prior to all the most ancient things; and Wisdom was born of Thee. Thou art wise, and hast not learned aught from another, nor acquired Thy Wisdom from anyone else. Thou art wise; and from Thy Wisdom Thou didst cause to emanate a ready Will, an agent and artist as it were, to draw being from

out of the Void, as light proceeds from the eye. Thou drawest
from the Source of light without an intermediary, and produc-
est everything without a means... [5]

In subsequent sections of "The Royal Crown," following a
scheme derived from a combination of Plotinian and Aristotelian
doctrines popular in his day, he speaks of the ten descending
"spheres" of the universal manifestation: from the primal Will, to the
sphere of the fixed stars, the seven planets, and finally the sub-lunar
world, describing as he goes the astrological influences of the planets,
the Sun and the moon. (This description of the ten "spheres" of
existence was to play a great role in the cosmology of the later
Kabbalists, as we shall see.) And then he returns once again to his
theme of the primal Will, or Intelligence, as the material source of all
beneath it, and the mystery of the Absolute, the "Hiding Place," "the
Throne," from whence the Will is born:

> Who can understand Thy tremendous mysteries, when
> Thou didst exalt above the ninth sphere, the sphere of Intelli-
> gence, the inner temple... This is the sphere which is exalted
> above all the highest, and which no imagination can reach; and
> there is the *Hiding Place*, wherein is the canopy for Thy glory.
> O Lord! who can come near to understanding That
> which is above the sphere of the Intelligence, the Throne of
> Thy glory, the glorious dwelling of the *Hiding Place*! There
> is the Mystery and the Foundation; the intellect may reach to
> the Foundation (the Will), but no further, for above this Thou
> art greatly exalted upon Thy mighty Throne, where no man's
> intellect may reach... [6]

For Ibn Gabirol, there is no duality between God and His
world-manifesting Will. It is God alone who exists in all, while He is
beyond all. Yet, for all his Monism, for all his metaphysical profundity, Ibn Gabirol is no mere philosopher; he is at once a fervent
and sincere lover. For the mystic, there is no contradiction here. He
knows that, as a manifestation of God, he is, himself, nothing but God,
but he longs, with the longing of a manifestation for its source, to be
drawn back into that Essence from whence he sprang, and to
experience the infinite joy of his own eternal Being. Thus, while he is
a Monist in thought, he is a Theist in heart -- or, as the Hindu would
put it, a *jnani* and a *bhakta* in one. Here, in one of his songs, Ibn
Gabirol calls out to God with the timeless cry of the soul yearning for
that ineffable presence:

I have sought Thee daily at dawn and at twilight, I have
stretched forth my hands to Thee, and lifted up my
face;
Now my thirsty heart cries out to Thee, like the beggar who
cries at my door for grace.
The infinite heights are too small to contain Thee, yet, if
Thou wilt, Thou mayst make Thy abode in my heart.
Shall my heart not treasure this hope of harboring Thee, or
shall I not entreat Thee till my tongue can call no
more?
Nay, I will surely worship Thy name, till my nostrils no
longer breathe. [7]

And again:

My soul shall declare to Thee that Thou art her Maker,
And shall testify that Thou art her creator, O Lord.
At Thy word, "Be, O soul," she took on existence,
And from Thy Emptiness Thou didst draw her forth as light
from the eye.
It was Thee who didst breathe in her life; I shall proclaim and
affirm this with uplifted hands.
And therefore she shall pour out her thanks and give witness
that she was bidden to do so by Thee.
While yet in the body, she serves Thee as a handmaid;
And on that day when she returns to the land from whence she
came,
In Thee will she dwell, for in Thee is her being.
Whether she sits or rises, Thou art with her the same.
She was Thine before she was born and breathing;
She was nourished by Thee with wisdom and knowledge,
And it is to Thee she looks for her guidance and sustenance,
Grateful to Thee for her water and bread.
She looks only to Thee, and hopes only for Thee.
When she cries out in fear, like a woman in childbirth,
Accept her torn heart as an offering for sacrifice,
And her tattered ribs as an offering for the flames.
Let her pour out her tears as the wine on the altar,
And let the breath of her sighs rise as fragrance to Thee.
At her gate and her doorway, she watches in prayer;
She is burning like flame with her passion for Thee.
She comes before Thee as a servant to his master,
Or as a handmaiden looks to her mistress's eye.
She spreads out her palms, entreating Thy mercy,
And, weeping, waits humbly for pity from Thee.
She calls Thee, for she cannot remain silent;

Like a bird in a net, her one hope is flight.
In the depths of the night, she rises and waits,
For her only task is to praise Thee and Thy works.
She pines for Thee, and entreats Thee, O Lord:
Make the works of her hands as clean and pure as her thought;
Heal her wounds, be her hope and her rescue.
When she draws near Thee, embrace her; look not on her sins.
Behold her afflictions, heark to her weeping;
For, in the realm of Thy Being, she and Thee are alone.
Redeem and restore her, O Lord; attend to her anguish,
When she bemoans her own weakness with sobbing and tears.
... Please don't yield up this child Thou hast raised up to
          manhood, ...
For, truly, the tree's fruit is born of its root;
The saying, "Like mother, like daughter," is true. [8]

Ibn Gabirol became more famous among his Jewish contemporaries for his poetry than for his philosophy, and he is remembered by the Jewish community to this day for his treasury of songs to
God.   It was the Christians, two centuries after his death, who
discovered the philosopher, and who preserved his prose works. Yet
few among either Jews or Christians truly appreciate the depth of his
wisdom and the beauty of his songs. And that is as he would have
wished; for his soul belonged to God, and his words were for Him.

The Kabbala

One can scarcely speak of Medieval Jewish mysticism without
making some mention of the separate and unique phenomenon of the
Kabbala, a word which simply means "the tradition." *Kabbala*
stands for a peculiar movement of Jewish esotericism which arose in
the 12th century, making use of mystical thought to elaborate a
system of secret symbolism, much as the Pythagoreans had done
much earlier. The Kabbalists seem to have borrowed heavily from the
writings of authentic mystics of the past, yet their proclivity was for
mystery and obscurantism, and they veiled their comments in a maze
of symbolism which, they held, could only be grasped by those
initiated into these "higher" mysteries. This highly esotericized
tradition might have been regarded by future generations as only a
curiously bizarre phenomenon where it not for the grain of truth
which exists in the writings of the Kabbalists and which has sufficed to

keep alive a genuine interest in this tradition over the centuries.

One of the earliest known contributions to Kabbalistic thought was a treatise of the Talmudic period (ca. 3rd-6th centuries) called "The Book Of Creation" (*Sefir Yetzirah* in Hebrew). This book asserts that God created the world by means of 32 "secret paths of wisdom," consisting of 10 basic numbers and 22 basic Hebrew letters. The numbers are called "the ten (*sefirot*)," and represent the ten basic principles of reality, as its author saw them: first, the Spirit of God; then the elements of air, water, fire; and then the six extremities of space: North, South, East, West, up, and down. The 22 letters of the Hebrew alphabet were said to be elements of God's Speech or Word which is the source of all existing creation. Thus each letter was regarded as having a mysterious and magic power relating to the various attributes, or creative modes, of God.

The Medieval Kabbalists were to make of the *sefirot* a major tenet of their "system." In Provence, in the 12th century, appeared a book called the "Brightness" (*Bahir*), written by an anonymous author, which interpreted the idea of the *sefirot* in a new way. Very likely influenced by Ibn Gabirol's conceptualization of the ten principles of world-manifestation emanating from God, the author of the *Bahir* described the ten *sefirah* (singular) as the ten principles, or attributes, of God by and through which the manifested world came into being.

Around the same time, in Provence, lived another Kabbalist called Isaac the Blind (ca. 1060-1135), who wrote a number of works similarly describing the manifestation of God in ten distinct stages, or spheres, which he also named the *sefirot*. Borrowing heavily from Plotinian sources and perhaps from Ibn Gabirol as well, he established a distinction between God, the primal Essence, and His Power of manifestation. To the "Essence," of Ibn Gabirol he gave a new name, calling It "the Infinite" (*En Sof*); and the "Will" of Ibn Gabirol he called "the Divine Thought" (*Mahashava*). He held that it is from the Divine Thought that the descending scale of nine subsequent principles emanate, all together making up the *sephirah* of God.

It was Moses de Leon, in his pseudepigraphic work, the "Splendor" (*Zohar*), who carried on the formulations of Isaac the Blind, explaining in a similar fashion the manifestation of the world from the *En Sof*. Moses de Leon, a Castillian Kabbalist, wrote the *Zohar* around 1280, but presented it as an ancient tract from the hand

of a member of the circle of Simeon bar Yohai, a revered figure of the
Talmudic literature, who lived in the 2nd century C.E. Under this
pretence, it managed to have a wide circulation and influence during
Medieval times. De Leon went to great lengths to portray the *Zohar*
as a work of the 2nd century by writing much of it in the Aramaic
language, and by extolling its authenticity in his other writings. So
successful was he in his forgery that it was not until recent times (the
19th century) that the fraud was discovered; up to that time, the *Zohar*
was regarded by many devout Jews as possessing an authority
equivalent to that of the Talmudic scriptures.

In the first chapter of the *Zohar*, the Biblical description of
Creation in the book of Genesis is reformulated to comply with the
mystically perceived projection or emanation of the phenomenal
universe from the Absolute, the *En Sof*:

> In the beginning, when the Will of the King began to
> take effect, He impressed His signs into the heavenly sphere.
> Within the Most Hidden, the Infinite (*En Sof*), a dark flame
> issued forth, like a fog forming in the Unformed.
> Forming the concentric ring of that [first] sphere,
> [this flame was] neither white nor black, neither red nor green,
> of no color whatever. Only after this flame began to assume
> size and dimension, did it produce radiant colors. From the
> innermost center of the flame gushed forth a host of colors
> which spread on everything beneath. Concealed within all was
> the hidden mystery of the Infinite (*En Sof*). [9]

This rather fanciful description is, of course, in keeping with
the general scheme of creation put forward by the philosophers of the
so-called "Neo-Platonic" tradition, including Ibn Gabirol. But, from
this point on, the *Zohar* reveals itself as a *Midrash*, or commentary,
upon the tales of the Jewish Torah, inventing tales of its own to
elucidate the teachings of the ancient prophets. Still, there are a few
metaphysical passages of the *Zohar* in which one may find the clear
statement of the immanence of God in all creation, such as in this
prayer ascribed to Elijah:

> Elijah began to praise God, saying: "Lord of the uni-
> verse! You are One but are not numbered. You are Higher
> than the highest. You are the Mystery above all mysteries.
> No thought can grasp You at all.
> It is You who produced the ten perfections which we
> call the *sefirot*. With them You guide the secret worlds which

have not been revealed, and worlds which have been revealed;
and in them You conceal Yourself from human beings. But it
is You who binds them together and unites them. Since You
are in them all, whoever separates any one of these ten from
the others, it is as if he had made a division in You. [10]

Yet, despite the occasional enunciation of such universal
concepts, the *Zohar* and other similar Kabbalist works tended to
emphasize to a great degree the more esoteric, or occult, elements of
mysticism. Many of the esoteric elements of the Kabbala, such as the
description of the lights seen in contemplation, the disciple's
identification with the spiritual Master, the vision of one's double, and
the correspondence of certain sounds and letters with specific divine
powers, have their counterparts in the esoteric Tantric tradition of
India, and have been attested to by mystics of all traditions. However,
in the *Zohar* and other Kabbalist works, these elements are so
deliberately mystified and so inextricably intertwined with such
specifically Mosaic concepts as the divine appointment of the Jewish
nation, the promise of a coming Messiah, the return of the Jews to
Israel, etc., that they tend to present a bewildering miscellany of racial
history, mythology and doctrine, rather than a coherent mystical
testimony.

The Kabbala, as a whole, from its very beginnings, seems to
have appealed more strongly to those interested in occult arts and
magical sources of power than to the one-pointed devotee whose
interest was solely in the simple loving regard of God. And in later
centuries these magical elements became even more predominantly
the focus of Kabbalist learning. In the late 15th and 16th centuries,
the Kabbala enjoyed a resurgence of interest due to the writings of
certain Christian and Neo-Platonist writers, such as Marcilio Ficino,
Pico della Mirandola, Giordano Bruno, and John Dee, who borrowed
extensively from it to frame their own eclectic occultism in terms of
what they thought was an authentically ancient tradition. But the
dawning scientific era, with its more realistic view of the universe,
demolished the ten spheres of the Kabbalist cosmology, and invalid-
ated those magical formulas based on its spurious conception of the
world.

Today, the Kabbala still holds some interest for those curious
to find in it some clues to the hidden secrets of magic and the occult
"sciences." But, for the simple lover of God, earnestly intent upon
the purification of his own heart and soul for the union with God,

such curiosities have little appeal, and serve only to distract and titilate rather than inspire the mind to greater devotion.

IBN ARABI

Sufism, in the 13th century, produced some of its most prized literature from the hands of some of its most revered saints; among them were: Attar (d. 1220), al-Farid (d. 1235), Ibn 'Arabi (d. 1240), Rumi (d. 1273), and Iraqi (d. 1289). As we shall later see, it was an equally illustrious period in the Christian and Vedantic traditions; indeed, the 13th century saw one of the most saint-filled and spiritually glorious periods in the history of the world. In the Muslim tradition, with which we are now concerned, it was Ibn 'Arabi who, through his philosophical writings based on his vision of Unity, set the tone for his time, and gave new life and understanding to the mysticism of the Sufis.

Muhammed Ali Muhammed Ibn al 'Arabi al-Ta'i al-Hatimi, better known simply as Ibn Arabi (1165-1240), was born into a Muslim family in Murcia, Spain, on the 7th of August, 1165. He was given religious training by his father, and while he was still quite young, his father took him to meet the famed philosopher, Averroes, in Cordoba. It seems the aging Averroes had heard of young Arabi's spiritual proclivities, and had asked to meet him. During this youthful period in Spain, Ibn Arabi also came under the spiritual tutelege of two women, both elderly ladies well-versed in mystical knowledge, to whom he became quite devoted. It is said that the young man used to spend his free hours in the cemetary, where he practiced his meditation on God.

After his education in Seville, Ibn Arabi became married and obtained a position as secretary to the governor of Seville. He was twenty years of age when he was initiated into the Sufi path. It is not known when he became illumined by God's grace and realized the Unity of which he was later to write; but we know that between the ages of twenty-eight and thirty, he travelled several times to Tunis in North Africa, where he visited a number of Sufi *Shaikhs,* and spent much of his time in studying and writing.

In the year 1200, when he was thirty-five, Ibn Arabi was in Morocco, and had a vision telling him to journey to Fez, and then on to Egypt. He travelled through Alexandria and Cairo and finally made his way to the holy city of Mecca. During the period between 1200 and 1206, much of which was spent at Mecca, he wrote a great deal, including portions of his magnum opus, *Meccan Revelations*. And by the time he went to Cairo in 1206, his reputation as a divine had already preceded him. However, the orthodox *mullas* of Islam living there were highly offended by his teachings, and were openly antagonistic to him.

In 1210, he travelled north, and arrived in the city of Konya in Anatolia. There he was welcomed as a great teacher of Sufism, and his influence spread rapidly. He continued to travel about, visiting with celebrated divines, such as Shaikh Suhrawardi (1145-1234) in Baghdad, and eventually settled in Damascus in 1223, where he stayed for the remainder of his life. Having married twice before, he now married a third time in Damascus, and fathered three children; but the children for which he is best remembered are the products of his pen. He wrote *Bezels Of Wisdom* around 1230; and is said to have once remarked that he had written over two-hundred and fifty books during his lifetime.

When reading the books of Ibn Arabi, one cannot help wishing that he had presented his thought in a more simple and direct manner, without the many effusive embellishments of Quranic myth and imagery. As in the case of Philo, whose Jewry gets in the way of his expression and makes it all a muddle, so Ibn Arabi's Islamic heritage gets in the way; and one must tramp through a vast swamp of verbiage to find the occasional gems of clear mystical insight. What he had to say was said in so much more precise a manner by Shankara, in so much more direct a manner by Ashvagosha and S'eng-hsin, so much more poetically by a great number of his own fellow Sufis, and with so much less verbiage by so many who have realized the Truth. But, it is because he represents an early attempt within the Islamic tradition to convey a rational formulation of the vision of Unity that he must be accounted one of the most influential thinkers of Sufism in any history of mystical thought.

We have already seen how the various seers of other traditions have described the experience of Unity in complementary terms, naming the Absolute and Its manifestory-Power by such terms as "Brahman-Maya,""Purusha-Prakrti," "Nirvana-Samsara,""Theos-Logos," and so on; the Sufis also had long framed their conception of the Reality in such complementary terms. Prior to Ibn Arabi, the

martyred saint, Suhrawardi (1153-1191), who died in prison at the age
of thirty-eight (not the Suhrawardi whom Ibn Arabi met in Baghdad),
had written of the manifestation of the world from God in terms
reminiscent of the Christian Fathers' exposition of the Logos:

> The Essence of the First, the absolute Light, God,
> gives constant illumination, whereby It is manifested and
> brings all things into existence, giving life to them by Its
> rays. Everything in the world is derived from the light of His
> Essence, and all beauty and perfection are the gifts of His
> bounty. To attain fully to this illumination is salvation. [1]

Ibn Arabi's contribution to mystical philosophy was his clarification of this concept of complementarity, and his employment of
two distinct terms to distinguish the unmanifest Absolute from the
manifested world of phenomena; (borrowing from al-Hallaj,) he calls
them *Haqq* and *Khalq*. When we experience the Absolute in the
transcendent state of consciousness, says Ibn Arabi, we are experiencing *Haqq*; when we experience the world of multiple phenomena through our senses, we are experiencing *Khalq*. "But," says
Ibn Arabi, "the *Haqq* of whom transcendence is asserted is the same
as the *Khalq* of whom immanence is asserted, although the one is
distinguishable from the other." [2]   Thus, Ibn Arabi's vision and his
doctrine, like that of the other great mystics of all religious traditions,
was one of the essential unity of God and the universe.

For him, the world (*Khalq*) is simply the appearance of God
(*Haqq*). It is simply our limited perspectives as individual perceiving
entities that produces the appearance of multiplicity. "Multiplicity,"
he says, is simply due to the existence of different points of view, not
to an actual division in the one Essence." [3]   And unity simply means
that, "two or more things are *actually* identical but *conceptually*
distinguishable the one from the other; so that, in one sense the one is
the other, while in another sense it is not." [4] "If you regard Him
through Him, then He sees Himself through Himself; but if you
regard Him through yourself, then the unity vanishes." [5]
"[Furthermore,] if you assert that only *Haqq* is real, you limit God [to
transcendence]. And if you assert that only *Khalq* is real, you deny
Him [altogether]. But if you assert that *both* things are real, you
follow the right course, and you are a leader and a master in gnosis."[6]
Elsewhere, he says, in much the same vein:

> Do not distinguish *Haqq*, lest you regard Him as
> separate from *Khalq*. Do not distinguish *Khalq*, lest you
> invest it with non-Reality. Know Him as both particularized
> and unparticularized, and be established in Truth. Be in a state
> of unity if you wish, or be in a state of separation if you wish;
> if the Totality reveals Itself to you, you will attain the crown
> of victory. [7]

In the following passage, Ibn Arabi describes how, when the
mystical vision of unity dawns, it is seen that the One alone exists --
and that It *is* the many:

> When the mystery of the oneness of the soul and the
> Divine is revealed to you, you will understand that you are no
> other than God. ... Then you will see all your actions to be
> His actions and all your attributes to be His attributes and your
> essence to be His essence.
> ... Thus, instead of [your own] essence, there is the
> essence of God and in place of [your own] attributes, there are
> the attributes of God. He who knows himself sees his whole
> existence to be the Divine existence, but does not experience
> that any change has taken place in his own nature or qualities.
> For when you know yourself, your sense of a limited identity
> vanishes, and you know that you and God are one and the
> same. [8]
> ... There is no existence save His existence. ... This
> means that the existence of the beggar is His existence and the
> existence of the sick is His existence. Now, when this is ad-
> mitted, it is acknowledged that all existence is His existence;
> and that the existence of all created things, both accidents and
> substances, is His existence; and when the secret of one part-
> icle of the atoms is clear, the secret of all created things, both
> outward and inward, is clear; and you do not see in this world
> or the next, anything except God. [9]

This vision is universal among the seers. It must be admitted
that Ibn Arabi, by the 13th century, had access to the writings of the
seers of ancient Greece, the Neo-Platonists, the Christian Fathers,
perhaps even of the Vedantists and Buddhists, and certainly of his Sufi
predecessors. However, we mustn't imagine on that account that he
was merely recounting a learned philosophical position. He had
"seen" It, and spoke from his own direct experience, framing his
words in the idiom of his own time and traditional affiliations. "Such
knowledge," he said,

can only be had by actual experience, nor can the reason of
man define it, or arrive at any cognizance of it by deduction,
just as one cannot, without experience, know the taste of
honey, the bitterness of patience, the bliss of sexual union,
love, passion, or desire. [10]

In his writings, Ibn Arabi strove above all to explain the
identity of God and the Self for the benefit of all who sought to
comprehend the Truth. Here are a few of his most penetrating remarks on this theme:

> Know that whenever something permeates another, it
> is assumed into the other. That which permeates, the agent, is
> disguised by that which is permeated, the object. In this case,
> the object is the manifest [universe], and the agent is the Un-
> manifest, the Hidden. [11]

> On Him alone we depend for everything; our depend-
> ence on other things is in reality dependence on Him, for they
> are nothing but His appearances. [12]

> The eye perceives nothing but Him; only He is to be
> known. We are His; by Him we exist, and by Him we are
> governed; and we are, at all times and in all states, in His
> presence. [13]

> Nothing but the Reality is; there is no separate being,
> no arriving and no being far away. This is seen in true vision;
> when I experienced it, I saw nothing but Him.

> When my Beloved appears, with what eye do I see
> Him? With His eye, not with mine; for no one sees Him
> except Himself. [14]

> It is none other than He who progresses or journeys
> as you. There is nothing to be known but He; and since He is
> Being itself, He is therefore also the journeyer. There is no
> knower but He; so who are you? Know your true Reality.
> ... He is the essential Self of all. But He conceals it by [the
> appearance of] otherness, which is "you." [15]

> If you hold to multiplicity, you are with the world;
> and if you hold to the Unity, you are with the Truth. ... Our
> names are but names for God; at the same time our individual
> selves are His shadow. He is at once our identity and not our
> identity... Consider! [16]

> In one sense the Reality is creatures; in another sense,

It is not. ... Whether you assert that It is undivided or divided,
the Self is alone. The manifold [universe] exists and yet it
does not exist. [17]

Therefore, know your Self, who you are, what is your
identity. ... Consider well in what way you are *Haqq*, and in
what way *Khalq*, as being separate, other. [18]

He who knows himself knows his Lord; ... indeed,
He is his very identity and reality. [19]

As for the theorists and thinkers, and the scholastic
theologians, with their talk about the soul and its properties,
none of them have grasped the Reality; such speculation can
never grasp it. He who seeks to know the Reality through
theoretical speculation is flogging a dead horse; ... for he who
seeks to know It by any means other than the one proper to It,
will never grasp It. [20]

If men knew themselves, they would know God; and
if they really knew God, they would be satisfied with Him and
would think of Him alone. [21]

IRAQI

A younger contemporary of Ibn Arabi, the celebrated Sufi
poet, Fakhruddin Iraqi (1213-1289), was born in the village of
Kamajan, in Persia (present day Iran). According to legend, he was
famous in his region for his religious devotion by the time he was
eight years old; and by the age of seventeen he was giving lectures on
the scriptures to his schoolmates. As the story goes, he was drawn to
the Sufi path when a group of wandering dervishes passed through the
town, and he happened to hear their plaintive songs of divine love.
Iraqi immediately left his studies behind, and went off with the Sufi
band, wandering throughout Persia and into India.

In the city of Multan, in India, he met the Shaikh, Baha'uddin, of the Suhrawardiyya Order, and became his disciple. Not long
thereafter, he married the Shaikh's daughter, by whom he had a son,
Kabiruddin. For twenty-five years Iraqi lived in Multan under the
munificent protection and guidance of his master, Baha'uddin. Iraqi
was, by nature, a poet; and during his years at Multan he wrote a

number of devotional songs; but his great masterpiece of poetry, the *Lama'at*, or "Glimpses," which has brought him everlasting fame, was written some years later, in Anatolia (Turkey).

In 1268, when Iraqi was fifty-five, his old master, Baha'uddin, died, and passed the succession of the Order to him. However, there was much discontent and turmoil over this change of leadership, not only within the Order, but among the political factions of the area as well; and Iraqi decided it would be best to leave Multan. So, along with a few loyal friends, he journeyed by sea to Oman, on the coast of Arabia. There, he was received as a celebrity, and was soon made the chief Shaikh of the district. But Iraqi was not content to remain in Oman; instead, he set out for Mecca, and from there to Damascus, and onward north to Anatolia, to the city of Konya.

Konya was the city in which Ibn Arabi had spent some years of his life, and where Sadruddin Qunawi (d. 1274), Ibn Arabi's chief disciple, now lived. It was also the home of the famous Sufi, Jalaluddin Rumi, about whom we shall hear more later. Iraqi quickly became the intimate friend of both of these revered Sufis, but most especially of Qunawi, who had a great influence on him intellectually. Qunawi, as mentioned, was the principal disciple of Ibn Arabi in this area; and he was also very actively engaged in the dissemination of Ibn Arabi's teachings, attempting to popularize the philosophy of unity taught him by his master. It was this philosophy which was to become the foundation and rationale of Iraqui's most exquisite poetry, the loom upon which he would weave a tapestry of unparalleled beauty.

Ibn Arabi had been not only the teacher of Qunawi, but had also become his step-father by marrying Qunawi's widowed mother; in addition, Ibn Arabi had bestowed on Qunawi the successorship of his lineage, and Qunawi was now the chief Shaikh of the city of Konya. He gave frequent lectures and wrote books explaining the mystical and metaphysical precepts of Ibn Arabi, and had a number of gifted, and later distinguished, disciples himself. His lectures on Ibn Arabi's *Bezels Of Wisdom* and *Meccan Revelations* were attended by Iraqi, who became thoroughly facinated and inspired by the study of these works. Each day, after the lectures of Qunawi, he would, in a state of inspired joy, set down a few verses of his own, illustrating Ibn Arabi's teachings, and at last collected them in a book, which he called *Lama'at,* which may be translated as "Flashes," or "Glimpses" of insight.

When he showed his little book to Qunawi, the great Shaikh, after reading it, pressed it reverently to his eyes, and exclaimed, "Iraqi, you have captured the secret essence of Ibn Arabi's thought; your *Lama'at* is the very heart of his words!" Ibn Arabi, though a true mystic, had been of a metaphysical turn of mind; he labored at great length to thoroughly explain the mystery of things. Iraqi, however, was a poet; he was able to express the thought of Ibn Arabi in exquisitely succinct gems of precision. He used the simple language of love to capture the essential truth of the complementarity of *Haqq* and *Khalq*, which Ibn Arabi had so elaborately articulated; and turned the intellectual abstractions of Ibn Arabi into immediately perceived fruits-in-the-hand. Where Ibn Arabi had hovered like a bee over the blossom of Truth, examining its fragrance, Iraqi settled in the flower's heart, and drank its nectar.

Destiny, it seems, had brought Iraqi to Konya, where he was to catch his "Glimpses" of the one Reality; but he was not to remain there for long. He had found favor with one of the local rulers, the Amir, Parwanah, who built for him a retreat in the town of Tokat, and so Iraqi lived and taught there for some years. But when Parwanah was suspected by the Mongol Emperor, Abaka, of consorting with his enemies, the Amir was executed, and Iraqi fled Tokat in fear for his life.

Arriving in Cairo, Iraqi met with the Sultan there, who became very favorably impressed with him and made him the chief Shaikh of Cairo, conferring on him exceptional honors. And when, after some time, he travelled to Damascus, he was treated in a similarly reverential manner there. But he was now old, and after about a year in Damascus, he became quite ill, and sent for his son, Kabir-uddin, who had remained in Multan. With his son at his side, he died at the age of seventy-eight, in the year 1289.

Here are a few selected verses and passages from his celebrated *Lama'at*:

> Beloved, I sought You here and there,
> Asked for news of You from all I met.
> Then I saw You through myself,
> And found we were identical.
> Now I blush to think I ever searched
> For signs of You. [1]
>
> By day I praised You, but never knew it;
> By night I slept with You without realizing it,

Fancying myself to be myself;
But no, I was You and never knew it. [2]

"O You who are so unbearably beautiful,
Whose beloved are You?" I asked.
"My own," He replied;
"For I am one and one alone --
Love, lover, beloved, mirror, beauty, eye!" [3]

I sought solitude with my loved one,
Yet find there is no one here but myself.
And if there were a "someone else,"
then, truly, I should not have attained her. [4]

When I clutched at His skirt,
I found His hand in my sleeve. [5]

I am the one I love;
He whom I love is I.
Two, yet residing in a single body. [6]

If I have become the Beloved,
Who is the lover?
Beloved, Love and lover -- three in one;
There is no place for union here,
So, what is this talk of "separation?" [7]

What He takes,
He takes with His own hand from Himself;
What He gives,
He gives from Himself to Himself. [8]

Hunter, prey, bait, and trap;
Candle, candlestick, flame, and moth;
Beloved, lover, soul, and soul's desire;
Inebriation, drinker, wine, and cup --
All is He! [9]

Is it You or I -- this reality in the eye?
Beware, beware of the word, "two." [10]

"I" and "You" have made of man a duality;
Without these words,
You are I and I am You. [11]

He speaks;
He listens.
"You" and "I" are but a pretense. [12]

When shall You and I divorce ourselves
So that "You" and "I" are gone,
And only God remains? [13]

If You are everything,
Then, who are all these people?
And if I am nothing,
What's all this noise about?
You are the Totality;
Everything is You. Agreed!
Then, all that is "other-than-You" --
What is it?
Oh, indeed I know, nothing exists but You!
But, tell me, whence all this confusion? [14]

He Himself speaks of Truth;
He Himself listens.
He Himself shows Himself;
He Himself sees. [15]

The world but seems to be,
Yet it is only a blending of light and shade.
Discern the meaning of this dream;
Discriminate between time and Eternity.
All is nothing, nothing.
All is He, all is He. [16]

Listen, riffraff: Do you want to be ALL?
Then go, go and become nothing. [17]

You are nothing when you wed the One;
But, when you truly become nothing,
You are everything. [18]

Regard yourself as a cloud drifting before your Sun;
Detach yourself from the senses,
And behold your intimacy with the Sun. [19]

If you lose yourself on this path,
Then you will know for sure:
He is you, and you are He. [20]

RUMI

Jalaluddin Rumi (1207-1273) was born in the city of Balkh, in Persia. His father took his family and fled Balkh in 1219, when the Mongol hordes of Genghis Khan threatened the city. Jalaluddin's father, Baha'uddin, was a theologian and mystic, and it was he who molded the sensibilities of the young Rumi. It is said that, while the family was yet wandering through Persia, Baha'uddin took his son to meet the famous poet, Attar (d. 1230), who gave his blessings to Jalaluddin.

After long journeying, the family reached Anatolia, then under the rule of the Seljukid Turks, where they were relatively free of the Mongol threat. For a while, the family lived in Laranda (modern Karaman), where Jalaluddin was married and had a son at the age of nineteen. The father was called to a post in Konya in 1228, and took Jalaluddin along, his mother having passed away a few years earlier. Baha'uddin died a few years after they had settled in Konya, and Jalaluddin assumed his father's position as religious teacher to a small community of devotees there.

Jalaluddin studied the mystical writings of the earlier Sufi poets, like Sana'i (d. ca. 1131) and Attar, to whom he was later to acknowledge his debt, saying "Sana'i was the spirit, and Attar his two eyes; we have come after Sana'i and Attar." He was also taught and influenced by a friend and disciple of his father, Burhanuddin Mahaqqiq. But Rumi's unique soul, vision, and talent were his own. His latent mysticism and poetic exuberance were watered into full bloom by his meeting with a love-intoxicated dervish by the name of Shamsuddin [of] Tabriz.

In 1244, Jalaluddin met Shams Tabriz in the streets of Konya, and was drawn by him to the fervent life of mystical love. His relation to Tabriz was like that of a loving disciple to his Guru or Pir. Jalaluddin transferred all his ardent devotion to Shams, as only a spiritual lover can do, seeing him as the Divine manifest in his life for the sake of providing him with companionship with God. However, Rumi's sons and other family members were so jealous and outraged by the hold that Shams had on Jalaluddin's affections that they murdered Shams and threw his body in a well. At least, so the story goes. Rumi filled the void in his life by writing a book of poems of love and longing, called *Divan-i Shams Tabriz*, sometimes addressing them to Shams, and sometimes identifying with him.

His verses are full of the imagery of love, but it is the love of the soul for God. Rumi is the epitome of the mystical lover; but he also knew the "union" with his Beloved, and speaks with rare beauty of this mysterious "marriage" of the soul and God. In his great masterpiece, the *Mathnawi*, which consists of twenty-six thousand verses in the Persian language, he garbs his painful love-longing in colorful tales whose characters range from animals to legendary folk-heroes. In a rhapsody of ecstatic poetry, he tells the secrets of the mystic's heart in a thousand imaginative ways. Rumi was a natural poet; his thoughts poured out in a most amazingly varied and exuberant flood of imagery and poetic melody. For sheer effusiveness and breathtaking profundity, there has never been another like him.

The city of Konya was a gathering place for mystics, artists and intellectuals from all over the Muslim world; and Rumi lived there, famous in his own day as a spiritual Master and teacher, drawing Sufis from all over, who travelled to Konya just to meet him. After his death in 1273, Rumi quickly became recognized throughout Islam as the *Maulana*, "the Master"; and his *Mathnawi* has since been hailed as "the Persian Quran." Today the Order of the Whirling Dervishes, who trace their lineage to him, sing and dance to his songs; and the very name of "Rumi" brings tears of love to the eyes of all true lovers of God throughout the world.

Here are just a few selections from his voluminous writings:

> When I speak of adepts, He is the Master; when I peer into my
>   heart, He is the Beloved.
> When I look for peace, He is the Pacifier; when I enter the
> battlefield, He is my Sword.
> When I come to the celebration, He is the wine and the sweet-
> meats;
> When I enter the rose-garden, He is the Beauty.
> When I descend into the mine, He is the Diamond and the
> Ruby;
> When I dive into the ocean, He is the Pearl.
> When I wander in the desert, He is the Flower growing there;
>   when I ascend into the heavens, He is the Star.
> When I climb the mountain, He is the Summit; when I burn
> in sorrow, He is the Flame.
> When I ready myself for warfare, He is my Commander and
> my General;
> When I rejoice at feast-time, He is the cup-Bearer, the

Musician, and the Cup.
When I write to my Beloved, He is the Ink, the ink-Well and
the Paper.
When I awaken, He is my awakeness;
When I sleep, He is my Dream.
When I search for words to my songs, He gives rhymes to
my memory;   .
Whatever image you may paint in the mind, He is the
Painter, and He is the Brush.
If you seek a "greater," He is Greater than greater;
Leave off language and books; let Him be your Book.
Be silent, for on every side is His Light;
And even though you pass beyond all boundaries, He, the
              Judge, is there. [1]

Whatever I say in exposition and explanation of love,
When I come to love I am ashamed of that explanation.
The speech of the tongue may elucidate,
But speechless love is yet more clear.
The pen hastily writes, but when it comes to love, it shatters
in two;
When the intellect tries to explain love, it becomes helplessly
stuck, like an ass in the mud.
It is love alone that can give proper expression to love:
The proof of the Sun is the Sun itself; if you seek proof, then
do not avert your face from Him.
Those loves which are for appearance only are not love -- they
are a disgrace!
Such shows of love must be abandoned;
In its place, real love must grow. All that is other than the
true "I" must be slain. [2]

I complain of the Soul of the soul, but in truth I am not
complaining; I am only relating.
My heart is saying, "I am tormented by Him," and I am all the
              while laughing at its poor pretense.
Be just with me, O Glory of righteousness; O Thou who art
the Throne and I the threshold of Thy door!
Where, in truth, are the threshold and the Throne? In that
              place where the Beloved is, where are "we" and "I"?
O Thou Soul who art free of "we" and "I," O Thou who art
the subtle Essence of the souls of men and women,
When a man or woman unites with Thee, Thou art that One;
when their individuality is obliterated, Thou alone art.
Thou didst contrive this "I" and this "we" only so that Thou

mightest play the game of worship with Thyself,
So that all "I's" and "Thou's" should become one Soul,
immersed at last in the one Beloved. [3]

It happened that we made a journey without "we";
There our heart blossomed without "we."
That Full-Moon which was hiding from us
Put Its Face to our face without "we."
Without dying in grief for the Beloved,
We were reborn in His grief, without "we."
We are always intoxicated without wine;
We are always happy without "we."
Don't remember us as "we";
We are our own remembrance, without "we."
We are happy together, proclaiming
"Oh, we shall always be without "we."
All doors were closed to us;
And then the path of Truth
Opened without "we."
... We have passed beyond right and wrong,
Beyond both prayer and the sins of existence, without "we." [4]

... The universe was not there; only I was.
Adam wasn't there; only I was.
That light of unity was "I"; I am the Everlasting, and I am
          the prophet Elias.
The universe gets its light from me;
Adam took his form from me;
I am the All-Wise, the Knower, the Judge of all judges. [5]

Here, listen to my boast: every moment
I say that I am the water, and not the jar [containing it].
I am not the ocean [of phenomenal existence], neither am I
          not the ocean.
I am the leaf of every breeze-filled tree;
I am the wetness of the water in the stream.
Don't laugh like children! You do not understand my state.
Read a chapter from me, unfold a secret from her [the creative
Force]:
I am drunk of that wine forbidden by the lawgivers;
I am drunk of the wine of oneness; I am free of color and
          smell.
I am oblivious to this place; my mind is elsewhere;
I don't know vinegar from sugar; I don't know a vat from a

jar [i.e., he sees only God everywhere]. [6]

If there is any lover in the world, O Muslim, it is I.
If there is any believer, infidel, or Christian hermit, it is I.
The wine, the cup-bearer, the musician, the instrument and
     the music,
The beloved, the candle, the liquor and the inebriation, it is I.
The seventy-two religious sects in the world
Do not really exist; I swear by God every religious sect -- it
is I.
Earth, air, water and fire: do you know what they are?
Earth, air, water and fire -- and the soul as well; it is I.
Truth and falsehood, good and evil, pleasure and suffering,
beginning and end,
Knowledge, learning, asceticism, devotion and faith -- it is I.
Be assured that the fire of hell and its flames,
Paradise, Eden and the angels of heaven -- it is I.
Heaven and earth and all they hold: angels, demons, and men --
     it is I. [7]

JNANESHVAR

During the whole of the 13th century, while the Mongol armies were raiding Muslim lands, the Muslim armies were invading all of northern India. Since the 10th century, the conquering Islamic armies, and refugees from Turkey, Persia, Arabia and Egypt had poured into the Punjab, India's northwestern gateway, via bordering Afghanistan. It was the Turkish ruler, Sabuktigin, who, making his capital at Ghazni in Afghanistan, led the first holy Muslim campaigns against India beginning around the year 986 C.E. He was succeeded by his son, Mahmud, "the idol-breaker," who completely destroyed the sacred cities of Mathura, Kangra, and Somnath, murdering millions of Hindus, raping and enslaving the women and children, and denuding the Hindu temples of their long-hoarded wealth.

In 1182, Muhammed Ghori conquered all of Sind and the Punjab; one by one, the great cities fell: Ajmir, Delhi, Benares. In 1199, the Buddhist stronghold of Bihar was taken, and most of the 6,000 Buddhist monks were slaughtered, annihilating the last vestige of Buddhism in India. The few remaining survivors fled to Tibet, where the Buddha's teachings found a welcome home. Soon after 1200, the whole of northern India except for Rajputana, Malwa, and part of Gujerat, was under Muslim rule. Delhi became the capital of the Muslim Sultanate, and the Hindu population was reduced to virtual slavery.

This Muhammedan conquest of India continued for more than five centuries; Will Durant, in his *Story Of Civilization*, calls it "probably the bloodiest story in history." And it was justified by the basic conception of the Muslim state -- that all non-Muslims are its enemies and are to be slain. The holy *Quran,* the word of the Prophet, states emphatically that "God is one," implying universality; yet it also says, *la ila il allah,* "There is no God but Allah." And it enjoins the faithful to "Kill those who join other deities to Allah, wherever you find them. But if they shall convert ... then let them go their way." And again, "Say to the infidel, if they desist from their unbelief, what is past is forgiven them. But if they return to it, ... then fight against them to the end, until the only religion left is Allah's." Thus, the martial rulers found, in the command of their Prophet, Muhammed, the justification for a conquest spurred, in reality, by a lust for wealth and new lands.

In 1271, the year of Jnaneshvar's birth, all of northern India was under the foreign rulership of Balban, the Sultan of Delhi. His rule extended from the northern borders southward to the Vindhya mountain range, which separates the Gangetic plain of the north from the fertile Deccan of the south. Because of the tremendous obstacle they presented, these mountains prevented for quite a long time the further encroachment of Muslim rule into southern India where Jnaneshvar was born. Jnaneshvar and his family lived in the Deccan, along the banks of the Godavari river, in a town called Appegaon. They felt safe under the protection of the Hindu Raja, Ramadev, who ruled from his fortress-city of Devgiri, only a few days journey away. However, toward the end of Jnaneshvar's life-time, in 1296, a Muslim army, led by a young, ambitious warrior named Ala'uddin Khalji, was to cross the Vindhya mountains, conquer Devgiri, and threaten the region where Jnaneshvar made his home. Such were the conditions under which Jnaneshvar and his family lived.

Jnaneshvar (1271-1296), whose name (pronounced *Gyan'-esh-war*) means "the Lord (*ishvar*) of knowledge (*jnan*)," and who also called himself "Jnandev," was one of four children born to Vitthal and Rakhumabai. Vitthal, shortly after his marriage, had left

Rakhu and journeyed to Benares to become a monk at the Ashram of a well-known Swami called Ramananda. But when Ramananda happened to pass, during a tour, through the town of Alandi where Rakhu was living with her parents, he learned that his Benares disciple, Vitthal, had left his young wife there without providing her with children, as tradition required. So, on his return to Benares, Ramananda sent Vitthal back to his wife with instructions to become a householder once more, and to foster some noble children. Three boys -- Nivritti, Jnaneshvar, and Sopan, and one girl -- Muktabai, were born thereafter.

Nivritti was the eldest, being one year older than Jnaneshvar; and when Nivritti was about eight years old, he and his father travelled through the jungles to the city of Nasik. On their return, they met with a tiger on the path. Startled and frightened, father and son ran off in different directions. The boy, Nivritti, found refuge in a cave, which happened to be the home of a famous and revered yogi, by the name of Gahininath. During his short stay in the cave, Nivritti was initiated into the secrets of yoga by Gahininath, and received the blessings of this powerful Master. Later, after Nivritti had returned home, he initiated his younger brother, Jnaneshvar, and assumed the role of Guru to him. Thereafter, Nivritti and Jnaneshvar would go each day into the jungles to study the scriptures of Vedanta, to meditate, and to practice their devotions.

Their father, Vitthal, however, was at this time undergoing great difficulties; he had surrendered his brahmin caste when he became a monk (*sannyasin*), and now that he was again a householder, he had forfeited his *sannyasin* status as well. By Hindu caste laws, he was now an outcaste, an untouchable. He could not get work, no one would associate with him or his family, and there seemed nowhere to turn for justice. He felt it would be better to remove this stigma from his family by forfeiting his own life; and so one day Vitthal drowned himself in the river. Several years later, Rakhu also died, leaving the children, barely in their teens, orphaned, casteless, and required to fend for themselves.

Jnaneshvar, his brothers and sister, were yogis all; they found a home with an old Swami called Satchidananda on the grounds of an *ashram* in Nevasa, near Nasik, and lived there for several years in freedom, practicing their yoga and devotion. It was here, in 1290, that Jnaneshvar wrote his famous masterpiece, *Bhavartha Dipika,* later to be known more commonly as *Jnaneshvari.* It is a commentary, written in Marathi, on the *Bhagavad Gita*; but it is more than a mere commentary. It is a work of profound wisdom and great poetic beauty which has become deservedly famous all over the world as a guide to the spiritual life. Remarkably, it was written by Jnaneshvar when he was but nineteen years old. Two years later, he wrote a philosophical work, independent of scripture, which he called, *Amrit-anubhav*, "The Nectar Of Mystical Experience."

Jnaneshvar had realized the supreme Self, through his meditations, at a very early age. And the maturity of his learning and amazing literary ability were surpassed only by the maturity of his wisdom. In his writings, he expressed the highest knowledge possible to man in all its aspects and ramifications. Yet his style and language were such that he was able to appeal as much to the common man as to the learned. He was a revolutionary, a pioneer, in the expression of such profound mystical truths in the Marathi language; for, heretofore, all such literature was framed in the classical Sanskrit, and Marathi, the language of the common people, had been regarded as unfit for the transmission of sacred truths.

Jnaneshvar was not only an accomplished yogi and poet; he was also very well learned in the scriptural traditions of Shaivism, Vaishnavism, Yoga and Advaita Vedanta. His aim was to explain what he had realized in his meditation in terms which would be acceptable to all. Though he was a master of expression, Jnandev found words ultimately unsuitable to the conveyance of the truth of Reality. Nonetheless, he spoke of the Truth he had known simply for the sake of enjoyment. Once he declared, "There is no bondage, and no liberation; there is nothing to accomplish. There is only the joy of expounding."

Jnaneshvar, who had "seen" the Reality, knew precisely what the world is and what God is. But he knew also that, no matter what he said about it, another could take the opposite position, and be equally right. For, if he said the world and God are one, another could easily show that the Unchanging is not the same as the changing, the Eternal not the same as the temporal. And if he said the world and God are two, another could easily show that there are not two Realities; that the world is no more different from its Source than the Sun's radiating light is different from the Sun. He realized that whatever position he might take, he could not rightly tell the unspeakable Truth that he had known. If he were to say, "It is One," he would be branded a pantheist; if he were to say, "It is two," he would be called a Dualist.

Only those who, like himself, had "seen" It, could comprehend the fact that the One is both divided and undivided; that the world is an "unreal" mirage and that it is none other than the Real Itself.

Nonetheless, like all true mystics, Jnaneshvar could not help but speak of what he had known. He acknowledged the apparent duality of Purusha-Prakrti, Shiva-Shakti; but, he said, it is like "gold on gold, water on water, or sugar on sugar"; they are ultimately not-two. In his *Jnaneshvari* , he was obliged to retain the terms utilized in the *Bhagavad Gita,* and to differentiate Purusha from Prakrti; but in his *Amritanubhav,* he calls these two, Shiva and Shakti, and compares them to two lovers whose duality ceases to exist when they unite as lover and beloved. As a piece of metaphorical imagery imbued with metaphysical meaning, it is unique and unparalleled. Here is Jnaneshvar's portrait of Shiva and Shakti as inseparable lovers, from the opening portion of *Amritanubhav:*

The Union Of Shiva And Shakti

> I offer obeisance to the God and Goddess,
> The limitless primal parents of the universe.

1.   The lover, out of boundless love,
        Has become the Beloved.
        Both are made of the same substance
        And share the same food.

2.   Out of love for each other, they merge;
        And again they separate for the pleasure of being two.

3.   They are not entirely the same --
        Nor are they not the same.
        It is impossible to say exactly what they are.

4.   Their one great desire is to enjoy themselves;
        Yet they never allow their unity to be disturbed
        Even as a joke.

5.   They are so averse to separation
        That even their child, the universe,
        Cannot disturb their union.

6.   Though they perceive the universe
        Of inanimate and animate creation
        Emanating from themselves,

They do not recognize a third.

7.   They sit together on the same ground,
        Wearing the same garment of light.
        From time past remembrance they have lived thus,
        United in bliss.

8.   Difference itself merged in their sweet union
        When, seeing their intimacy,
        It could find no duality to enjoy.

9.   Because of God, the Goddess exists,
        And, without Her, He is not.
        They exist only because of each other.

10.   How sweet is their union!
        The whole world is too small to contain them,
        Yet they live happily together in the smallest particle.

11.   They regard each other as their own Self,
        And neither creates so much as a blade
        Of grass without the other.

12.   These two are the only ones
        Who dwell in this home called the universe.
        When the Master of the house sleeps,
        The Mistress stays awake,
        And performs the functions of both.

13.   When He awakes, the whole house disappears,
        And nothing is left.

14.   They became two for the purpose of diversity;
        And both are seeking each other
        For the purpose of becoming one.

15.   Each is an object to the other;
        And both are subjects to each other.
        Only when together do they enjoy happiness.

16.   It is Shiva alone who lives in all forms;
        He is both the male and the female.
        It is because of the union of these two
        That the whole universe exists.

17.   Two lutes: one note.
        Two flowers: one fragrance.

Two lamps: one light.

18.   Two lips: one word.
        Two eyes: one sight.
        These two: one universe.

19.   Though manifesting duality,
        These two -- the eternal couple --
        Are eating from the same dish.

20.   The Shakti, endowed with chastity and fidelity,
        Cannot live without Her Lord;
        And, without Her,
        The Doer-of-all cannot be.

21.   Since He appears because of Her,
        And She exists because of Her Lord,
        The two cannot be distinguished at all.

22.   Sugar and its sweetness
        Cannot be told apart,
        Nor can camphor and its fragrance.

23.   If we have the flames,
        We also have the fire.
        If we catch hold of Shakti,
        We have Shiva as well.

24.   The Sun appears to shine because of its rays,
        But the rays themselves are produced by the Sun.
        In fact, that glorious Sun and its shining
        Are the same.

25.   To have a reflection, one must have an object.
        If we see a reflection, then we infer that
        An object exists.
        Likewise, the supreme Reality which is one
        Appears to be two.

26.   Through Her,
        The absolute Void became the primal Person (*Purusha*);
        And She derived Her existence from Her Lord.

27.   Shiva formed His beloved Himself;
        And without Her presence,
        No Person exists.

28.   Because of Her form,
        God is seen in the world.
        Yet it was He
        Who created Her form of Himself.

29.   When He embraces Her,
        It is His own bliss that Shiva enjoys.
        He is the Enjoyer of everything,
        But there is no enjoyment without Her.

30.   She is His form,
        But Her beauty comes from Him.
        By their intermingling,
        They are together enjoying this feast.

31.   Shiva and Shakti are the same,
        Like air and its motion,
        Or gold and its lustre.

32.   Fragrance cannot be separated from musk,
        Nor heat from fire;
        Neither can Shakti be separated from Shiva.

33.   If night and day were to approach the Sun,
        Both would disappear.
        In the same way, the duality of Shiva and Shakti
        Vanishes, when their essential unity is seen. [1]

Later, in the same work, Jnandev elaborates on the unity of the
Self. Like Shankara before him, he had seen that the one Self is all
that is; and while he acknowledges the apparent distinction between
Shiva and Shakti, he allows no duality to mar his vision:

        Whatever form appears, appears because of Him.
        There is nothing else here but the Self. It is the gold itself
        which shines in the form of a necklace or a coin; they are
        made of nothing but gold. In the current of the river or in
        the waves of the sea, there is nothing but water. Similarly,
        in the universe, there is nothing which exists or is brought
        into existence other than the Self. Though it may be smelled,
        or touched, or seen, there is nothing else in camphor but
        camphor. Likewise, no matter how He experiences Himself,
        the Self is all that is. Whether appearing as the seen, or
        perceiving as the seer, nothing else exists besides the Self. [2]

In 1293, shortly after these works were written, Jnaneshvar,

Nivritti, Sopan, and Muktabai travelled to the holy city of Pandharpur. It was here that the famous statue of Krishna, called Vithoba, or
Vitthala, resided in a magnificent temple. Jnaneshvar and his siblings
revered this particular representation (*murti*) of Krishna as though it
were identical with the Lord Himself, and it became a focus for their
devotion. It was there at Pandharpur that Jnaneshvar wrote his most
beautiful hymns of devotion. Muktabai, his sister, was also a singer
and poet; her devotional songs, along with Jnaneshvar's, are sung in
Pandharpur and throughout Maharashtra to this day.

        Jnandev and his family quickly became well-known and
revered in the city of Pandharpur; they sang in the temples, and
Jnaneshvar read his *Jnaneshvari* aloud to appreciative crowds.
Pandharpur was, in those days, as it is today, a magnet for many yogis
and holy men; and many belonged to the little group of devotees
surrounding Jnaneshvar. One of the most famous of his Pandharpur
companions was the mystic-poet, Namadev (1271-1350), whose
devotional songs (*abhangas*) also form a glorious part of Pandharpur's sacred heritage. Others in this holy company included Choka-
dev, Sena, Narahari, and Vishobha Kechar, and the two women
devotees, Janabai and Kanhupatra.

        One day, during his stay in this city, Jnaneshvar received a
letter from a famous and powerful yogi, named Changadev, who lived
with his many disciples just outside the city. When he opened the
letter, however, Jnaneshvar found that there were no words on the
parchment; it was blank. Jnandev, much the junior of Changadev,
decided to answer this letter all the same; he guessed that though
Changadev wished to make his acquaintance, his pride prevented him
from expressing any overtures to one so much his junior. Jnaneshvar
was not intimidated by words, however, and sent his own letter in
answer to Changadev. It was this letter which led to the fruitful
meeting of these two men, but the letter is deservedly famous for
another reason; it contains the very essence of Jnaneshvar's understanding and vision, in a compressed but concise form. It is valuable
also for the glimpse it gives us into the enlightened awareness of a
remarkable saint. Here is a brief selection from that letter to
Changadev:

            Salutations to the Lord of all, who is concealed with-
        in the visible universe. It is He who causes this universe to
        appear, and it is He who causes it to vanish as well. When He
        is revealed, the universe disappears; when He is concealed, the

universe shines forth. Yet He doesn't hide Himself, nor does
He reveal Himself; He is always present before us at every
moment. No matter how diverse and varied the universe appears, He remains unmoved, unchanged. And this is just as
one would expect, since He is always one, without a second.

... It's that one pure Consciousness who becomes
everything -- from the gods above to the earth below. Objects
may be regarded as high or low, but the ocean of Consciousness, ever-pure, is all that ever is. Though the shadows on the
wall are ever changing, the wall itself remains steady and unmoved. Likewise, the forms of the universe take shape from
Consicousness -- the eternal, primordial One.

Sugar is only sugar, even though it may be made into
many forms. Likewise, the ocean of Consciousness is always
the same, though it becomes all the forms of the universe.
Various articles of clothing are made from the same cotton
cloth; likewise, the varied forms of the universe are creatively
fashioned of the one Consciousness, which remains forever
pure.

... It cannot be spoken of or spoken to; by no means
may It be comprehended by the intellect. It is always existing
full and whole; and so It shall always be. The pupil of an eye
cannot see itself; of course it is the instrument of vision -- but
it doesn't have such an ability as that. In the same way, even
the Self-realized yogi is helpless to see the Seer. Knowledge
cannot know Itself; the Perceiver cannot perceive Itself. Where
Knowledge is perfect and full, ignorance cannot exist at all.
How can even the desire to know Itself arise in absolute
Knowledge? Therefore, one should address It through silence,
by being nothing, if one would be free, all-knowing, all-
pervading; for in that "nothing" all power exists. [3]

After their meeting, Changadev invited Jnaneshvar and his
family along on a pilgrimage to Benares. They accepted, and set out
on a year-long trek through the war-torn and danger-filled northern
regions of Muslim occupied territories. This was in 1294-95. By the
time he returned to Pandharpur, Jnaneshvar had witnessed at first-
hand the state of his beloved land under the seige of the Muslim
rulers. Temples had been razed, cities looted, and the stench of
rotting bodies was everywhere.

It was in the Spring of 1296 that the Muslim warrior, Alla'-
uddin Khalji, crossed the Vindhya mountains and conquered the
unsuspecting Raja Ramadev at Devgiri, only a few days ride from
Pandharpur. And it was only months thereafter that Jnaneshvar, at the
age of twenty-five, decided to give up his life. Despite the protests of

his friends and family, Jnandev apparently felt that he had completed his earthly mission, and was resolved to end his life. Taking his companions with him, he travelled to Alandi, his mother's ancestral home, and there, by his instructions, his friends prepared a small rectangular crypt of brick and mortar. For seven days and nights, they chanted the name of God, and prayed. Then the crypt was lined with flowers, and a deerskin was placed on the floor. At the auspicious hour, Jnaneshvar seated himself on the deerskin with his *Jnaneshvari* by his side, and the crypt was sealed behind him.

Jnaneshvar had lived a mere span of twenty-five years. At an age when most men have scarcely begun their life's work, Jnandev, a poor, casteless, orphan, had ended his -- but not before having built an everlasting monument to his memory in the written masterpieces he left behind. In so few years, he had established a legacy that was to revitalize his country, his culture, his language, and to make a place for himself as an enduring presence in the hearts of his countrymen for all time.

Within a month after Jnaneshvar's self-immolation, his brothers and sister had also taken their own lives. Sopan, the youngest, gave up his life at Saswad, a few miles west of Alandi; Muktabai vanished somewhere along the banks of the Tapti river; and Nivritti ended his life at Triambakeshvar in the region of Nasik. All were barely in their twenties.

THE MEDIEVAL CHRISTIANS

In the schools of Western countries, we are still taught that Medieval philosophy was "Christian philosophy"; but of course that was true only for a very small portion of the world -- a portion that was entirely closed to all but its own small world of ideas. In Medieval Europe, the knowledge of the Upanishads, the teachings of the Taoists, of the Buddha and Shankara, -- in fact, the entire spiritual and philosophical heritage of the East, did not exist. All of Europe lived within the airtight shell of Christianity; all thought was cast in that single mold, and was approved or disapproved by the holy Roman Church.

For those born in Christian Europe, the only cultural and philosophical framework available was Christianity; just as the thinking of one born in a Muslim or Hindu culture was molded entirely by the learned bias of those traditions. It is only now, in the 20th century, when the entire world of thought is available to us, in a world made smaller by the widespread dissemination of learning, that we are able to view the wider perspective, and distinguish the universal mystical experience from the various sectarian ideologies extraneous to it.

The Christian world of the 13th century, like the Muslim and Hindu worlds of that time, experienced a great flowering of mysticism, and gave birth to some of the greatest mystics Christianity has known. The Italian ascetic hermit, Francis of Assisi (1182-1224) was a product of that century, as was Dominic of Spain (1170-1221), and Bonaventure of France (1221-1274). Contemporary with Bonaventure was the pride and joy of Christian theology, Thomas Aquinus (1225-1274). Thomas Aquinus, however, was not a mystic; that is, not until the last year of his life.

Thomas spent much of his life writing large, heavy volumes of speculative theology, in one of which he put forth the considered opinion that "man reaches the peak of his knowledge of God when he realizes that he does not know Him." Yet, in his *Summa Theologia*, he gave lip-service to the Dionysian doctrine that

> Final and perfect happiness can consist in nothing else than
> the vision of the Divine Essence. ... For perfect happiness
> the intellect needs to reach the very Essence of the First Cause.
> And thus it will have its perfection through union with God ...
> in which alone man's happiness consists, as stated above. [1]

But this brief statement of Thomas' lacks the conviction of experience; he seems to have mentioned it only as an article of doctrine, in keeping with the accepted declarations of the genuine mystics of the past.

It was only at the end of his busy lifetime of listening to lectures, discussing doctrines, writing volume on volume of argumentation, and teaching his reasonings to hundreds of inquisitive students, that one day (December 6, 1273), spent and weary, Thomas sat quietly in church after celebrating one of the Church's Feast-days, and in the utter quiet of his mind, was enlightened with the knowledge of who he was eternally. From that day onward he never took up his pen again; saying, "Compared with what has been revealed to me, all my writings are as mere straw!"

Would to God that all philosophers, scholars and theologians would take a lesson from the embarrassment of poor Thomas, and put off the urge to write their great works until *after* they have become illumined. Think what a great service all these learned doctors would perform for all posterity if only they had the patience, courage and good sense to wait until they had realized God directly before setting out in writing their learned opinions, and had attained some true God-given wisdom prior to the decision to share it with the world.

Alas, such wisdom is rare; and, where it exists, is little valued in the world. Nonetheless, a few genuinely enlightened men did exist in the Medieval Christian world; one such man was the good doctor, Meister Eckhart.

MEISTER ECKHART

While Thomas Aquinus was still teaching in Paris, Johannes Eckhart (1260-1328) was born in the village of Hochheim in Germany, and entered the Dominican monastery at Erfurt, near his village, at around fifteen years of age. There he learned Latin, logic, and rhetoric. In those days, a novice served a one-year novitiate, followed by two years of studying the Divine Office and the Constitutions of the Order; then there were five years of philosophy and finally three years of theology. For Eckhart, that three years of theology was divided between the Bible and *The Sentences* of Peter Lombard. At the end of this course, the best of the students were sent to the Studium Generale for more advanced study of scripture and theology. Eckhart, among the top students, was sent to the Studium Generale at Cologne, founded in 1248 by the famous theologian and teacher of Thomas Aquinas, Albert Magnus, who died there in 1280. Eckhart arrived there only a few years later.

In 1298, Eckhart was made Prior at Erfurt and Vicar General of Thuringia. He was then sent to Paris where he earned the title, "Master in Sacred Theology," and was thereafter referred to as "Meister" Eckhart. After leaving the Paris university in 1302, he was made Provincial of Saxony in 1303; and in 1307 he was nominated Vicar-General of Bohemia. He presided over a vast province reaching from the Netherlands in the north to Prague, and governed fifty monasteries and nine convents. Again, he was sent to Paris to occupy the chair of Theology at the university in 1311, where he had to face the disciples of Duns Scotus, who had been a popular teacher there from 1305 to 1308. Later, he taught at Strasbourg and at Cologne.

Meister Eckhart had attained great position in the Church and had acquired great learning; but he was also a man of great devotion. One night, while intently praying to his invisible Lord, his mind, suddenly made clear and bright through his one-pointed attention, became perfectly still; and in that stillness, the truth of his own and all being became perfectly clear and evident to his mind's eye. He realized, in this still, luminous clarity, that his own mind, which moments ago searched the darkness for its God, was, in fact, itself the one Reality. It had created, by its sense of "I" and "Thou," a duality where none in fact existed. And as the light of his mind grew more steady, he became more and more aware of his true nature as the one eternal Consciousness whose light fills the universe and who is the true identity of all living beings.

In this experience of unity which Christians call "the vision of God," there is no longer a veiling sense of duality; for when the " I " discovers that the "Thou" it sought is itself, then all duality vanishes, as a dream vanishes when a man awakes from sleep. When that pure and eternal "I" is known, It is the one who knows; there is no other. When It is known, It is known as the true Self which has always been the Self, despite all previous misconceptions one might have had as to one's identity. Then it is realized that this one Self is the only conscious "I" of all beings, and that it is this one Self also who is projecting all this world of forms.

Truly, there is no one here but that one Self. When He awakens us, then we realize this. First, He calls us, by causing us to become aware of His presence within us; then we are drawn to seek Him in prayer and contemplation. Like a flame within, He draws us to Himself, our Self, by an inwardly inspired love and desire. When we are purely and singly focused on Him, when the mind is stilled and clear, we awake to who we have always been, and know our eternal Identity. Meister Eckhart, speaking of this experience, said:

> As the soul becomes more pure and bare and poor,
> and possesses less of created things, and is emptied of all
> things that are not God, it receives God more purely, and is
> more completely in Him; and it truly becomes one with God,
> and it looks into God and God into it, face to face as it were;
> two images transformed into one. [1]
> ... Some simple people think that they will see God
> as if He were standing there and they here. It is not so. God

and I, we are one. [2]
    ... I am converted into Him in such a way that He
makes me one Being with Himself -- not a *similar* being.
By the living God, it is true that there is no distinction! [3]
    ... The eye by which I see God is the same as the
eye by which God sees me. My eye and God's eye are one
and the same -- one in seeing, one in knowing, and one in
loving. [4]

Eckhart, like the ancient Upanishadic *rishis*, like the Buddha
and Jesus and all other true mystics, had seen the ineluctable Truth of
all existence, had become enlightened. But how was he to speak of it?
It was so high above the understanding of ordinary men and women
that they would surely become frightened and confused on hearing of
it, and even the wisest would surely misinterpret it! Yet, how was one
to conceal the truth, and, while knowing, pretend to be ignorant?
Indeed, this truth was so exciting, so wonderful, so liberating, that,
even if no one in the world understood it, it had to be told, had to be
shouted, if not from the housetops, at least from the pulpit.
    But the difficulties facing Eckhart were two-fold; he had not
only the natural obstacle presented by the inability of language to
describe the indescribable; but there was also the stone-wall of
Christian doctrine that he had sworn to defend, and which, now, if he
were to speak faithfully of the truth, he should have to demolish. To
be sure, the Truth he had known and of which he was eager to speak
was the same Truth which Jesus had seen and of which he had spoken.
But the real purport of Jesus' teachings regarding his identity with
"the Father" had been construed over the centuries as a doctrine
relating to him alone and not applicable to all men; and so, ironically,
when Meister Eckhart began reiterating the message of Jesus regarding the identity of the human soul and God, his message was received
with horror, and regarded by all orthodox Christians as heretical and
blasphemous.
    In one of his Sunday Sermons to the simple peasants of his
congregation, Meister Eckhart took up the elucidation of those two
aspects of the one Being which enlightened sages in other lands had
long spoken of as Brahman and Maya, Purusha and Prakrti, or Shiva
and Shakti. Eckhart, like all others who have "seen" the Truth,
recognized that the divine Consciousness at once transcends and
pervades the universe. It is both the absolute, transcendent Godhead
and the projecting Power, the Creator. Yet there is no *actual* division

between these two aspects; for it is that same one Consciousness that appears as all existence.

But who can tell of this knowledge: Words are but a mockery of it. That one eternal Consciousness is beyond time, beyond the universe of phenomena; yet from It, like a thought or projected image, the world shines, like a magic-show. This world-image is projected and withdrawn in a recurrent cycle, and while it is distinguishable from the eternal Consciousness Itself, still, it is not different from the eternal Consciousness -- as a thought is not different from the consciousness from which it emanates.

Meister Eckhart, in his Sermon, made the distinction between these two aspects of the One by using the two terms, "Godhead" (*Gottheit*) and"God" (*Gott*), to represent these two aspects respectively. By "Godhead," he meant, of course, that transcendent, absolute, Silence which is forever unchanging, unmoving; and by "God" he meant the Creator, that aspect of the Divine which, like an effusive mind, continually projects the phenomenal universe. Says Eckhart:

> God and the Godhead are as different from each other
> as heaven and earth... Creatures speak of God -- but why do
> they not mention the Godhead? Because there is only unity
> in the Godhead and there is nothing to talk about. God acts.
> The Godhead does not. ... The difference between God and
> the Godhead is the difference between action and non-action. [5]

The eternal "Godhead" is man's true Being, the conscious Self from which the creative-aspect, "God," shines forth. "My real being," says Eckhart, "is above God, if we take 'God' to be the beginning of all created things. ... I [the eternal Godhead] am unborn, and in my unborn aspect I can never die. In my unborn aspect, I have been eternally, and am now, and shall eternally remain." [6] That unborn aspect, the Godhead, is experienced when, in contemplation, one enters into that Silence which exists as the Source and Ground of the mind's creative effusion.

Eckhart, having broken through into that Silence, spoke of his own experience of the unborn Self:

> In that breaking-through, when I come to be free of
> my own will and of God's will and of all His works and of
> God Himself, then I am above all created things, and I am
> neither God nor creature, but I am what I was and what I shall

remain, now and eternally. [7]
   ... When I stood in my first cause, I then had no
'God,' and then I was my own cause. I wanted nothing, I
longed for nothing, for I was empty Being and the only truth
in which I rejoiced was in the knowledge of my Self. Then it
was my Self I wanted and nothing else.. What I wanted I was,
and what I was I wanted and so I stood empty of God and every
thing. [8]

It is worth repeating that this description of a unitive Reality,
consisting of an eternal and unchanging aspect and a creative aspect
which manifests itself as the phenomenal world, is not the mere
product of a speculative theology; for Eckhart, as for all who have
"seen" it, it is a directly perceived fact. To those who have "seen"
the Truth, such descriptions as Eckhart offers of It seem perfectly
simple and obvious; yet to those who have not, it seems all a muddle.
When Eckhart spoke of these matters to the simple peasants in his
Sunday Sermon, he closed by saying to the congregation, "Whoever
does not understand what I have said, let him not burden his heart with
it; for as long as a man is not equal to this truth, he will not understand
these words, for this is a truth beyond speculation that has come
immediately from the heart of God." [9]
   To those who could not understand what he had to say
regarding the "Godhead," Eckhart did not preach the need for
learning or the study of theology; rather, he taught his congregation
to love God with a one-pointed devotion and to seek Him alone, in
whom all true knowledge and consolation is to be found:

         In God, there is no sorrow or suffering or affliction.
      If you want to be free of all affliction and suffering, hold fast
      to God, and turn wholly to Him, and to no one else. Indeed,
      all your suffering comes from this: that you do not turn
      toward God and no one else. [10]
         ... When nothing but God can console you, then,
      truly, God does console you, and with Him and in Him all
      that is joy consoles you. [11]
         ... Cleave to God, and He will endow you with all
      goodness. Seek God, and you will find God and every good
      thing as well. [12]

Meister Eckhart knew well that, no matter how ignorant the
people were of their own divine Self, if they could fully turn their
minds to God in one-pointed devotion, God Himself would reveal His

existence within them, and make them know their oneness with Him. Then all their questions would be answered without the need of books or learning. Meanwhile, however, his words were too high, too difficult, for the people to comprehend, and many complained that they understood nothing of the good Prior's Sermons.

The knowledge of the eternal Self is undoubtedly a marvellous and inestimably precious blessing; yet in a world of men unillumined by that knowledge, it may easily appear to be a curse. Just as a perfectly sane man forced to live in an asylum filled with the insane would be regarded by his fellows as abnormally mad, and would suffer to a degree unknown to the others, so it is often with the man enlightened by God's grace who must live among the unenlightened. No doubt he has the means within himself to endure the inability of others to understand him, yet still his predicament is a uniquely difficult and trying one. Meister Eckhart found himself in just such a predicament; to remain silent and acquiesce to falsehood he could not do, and to speak meant certain calumny and censure. As he spoke of his knowledge of the unitive Self in his Sermons and writings, he found his words increasingly misconstrued and increasingly suspect by the ecclesiastical authorities. In a short time, he was charged by those authorities with preaching doctrines false and heretical to the Church.

The Archbishop of Cologne, Heinrich von Virneberg, was not at all sympathetic to Eckhart's mystical views, and arranged for him to be officially charged with heresy. The Inquisitorial investigator, as it turned out, was a Dominican like Eckhart, and, perhaps because of this affiliation, found no basis for carrying charges against him. But the Archbishop was determined to protect the "true" faith, and sent two investigators from his own Order, the Franciscans, who found him guilty as charged. In 1327, Meister Eckhart was summoned to Cologne to answer to the Papal Court, and there he humbly offered answers to all the charges made against him.

In 1310, in Paris, a woman by the name of Margarette Porette had been burned at the stake by these "guardians of the faith" for publishing similar "heretical" thoughts; and Eckhart was well aware of the possibility that he too might suffer a like fate. He answered his accusers with lengthy explanations, defending his utterances with quotations from scriptural and traditional authorities, but in the end he was found guilty. On March 27, 1329, a Papal Bull was issued, declaring:

> We are indeed sad to report that in these days someone
> by the name of Eckhart from Germany, a doctor of sacred the-
> ology (as is said) and a professor of the Order of Preachers,
> wished to know more than he should, and not in accordance
> with sobriety and the measure of faith, because he turned his
> ear from the truth and followed fables. The man was led astray
> by that Father of Lies who so often turns himself into an
> angel of light in order to replace the light of truth with a dark
> and gloomy cloud of the senses, and he sowed thorns and
> obstacles contrary to the very clear truth of faith in the field
> of the Church and worked to produce harmful thistles and
> poisonous thornbushes ... [13]

However, no sentence was publicly announced against Meister
Eckhart, for, according to this same Papal Bull, he had escaped
punishment by dying just prior to the issuence of this document.
Where and how he died is unknown. He had lived nearly seventy
years, and had told to the best of his ability what had been revealed to
him. And to this day his words, though "thornbushes" to the
Church, continue to live as a monument to truth, and a source of
courage and strength to all who would pursue it.

Following is a lengthy segment from one of Eckhart's most
exhortory treatises, which reveals a side of Eckhart that is little known
or appreciated. It is, of course, the common message of the mystics,
in which all wise men and true lovers of God will recognize the voice
of a brother and true son of God:

> Let our intention be purely and only for God, and
> then truly He must perform all our works, and no person, no
> crowds of persons, and no places can hinder Him in all His
> works. In the same way, no one can hinder this man, for he
> intends and seeks and takes delight in nothing but God, for
> God has become one with the man in all his intention. And
> so, just as no multiplicity can disturb God, nothing can dis-
> turb or fragment this man, for he is one in that One where all
> multiplicity is one and is one multiplicity.
>   A man should accept God in all things, and should
> accustom himself to having God present always in his dispos-
> ition and his intention and his love. Take heed how you can
> have God as the object of your thoughts whether you are in
> church or in your cell. Preserve and carry with you that same
> disposition when you are in crowds and in uproar and dissimil-
> itude. And, as I have said before, when one speaks of simili-
> tude, one does not mean that we should pay a similar attention

to all works or all places or all people. That would be quite wrong, because praying is better than spinning, and the church is a better place than the street. But you ought in all your works to have a similar disposition and a similar confidence and a similar love for your God and a similar seriousness. Believe me, if you were constant in this way, no one could come between you and the God who is present to you.

But a man in whom God is truly absent, and who must grasp God in this thing or in that from outside, and who seeks God in dissimilar ways, be it in works or people or places, such a man does not [truly] possess God. And it may happen that some things hinder such a man, for he does not possess God, and he does not seek Him alone, nor does he love and intend Him alone; and therefore it is not only bad company that hinders him. Good company can also hinder him -- not just the street, but the church too, not only evil words and deeds, but good words and deeds as well, for the hindrance is in him, because in him God has not become all things. Were that so, everything would be right and good for him, in every place and among all people, because he has God, and no one can take God away from him or hinder him in his work.

On what does this true possession of God depend, so that we may truly have Him? This true possession of God depends on ... an inward directing of the reason and intention toward God, not on a constant contemplation in an unchanging manner, for it would be impossible to nature to preserve such an intention, and very laborious, and not the best thing either. A man ought not to have a God who is just a product of his thought, nor should he be satisfied with that, because if the thought vanished, God too would vanish. But one ought to have a God who is present, a God who is far above the notions of men and of all created things. That God does not vanish, if a man does not wilfully turn away from Him.

The man who has God essentially present to him grasps God divinely, and to him God shines in all things; for everything tastes to him of God, and God forms Himself for the man out of all things. God always shines out in him; in him there is a detachment and a turning away, and a forming of his God whom he loves and who is present to him. It is like a man [who is] consumed with a real and burning thirst, [but] who may well not drink and may turn his mind to other things. But whatever he may do, in whatever company he may be, whatever he may be intending or thinking of or working at, still the idea of drinking does not leave him, so long as he is thirsty. The more his thirst grows, the more the idea of drinking grows and intrudes [on him] and possesses him and will not leave him.

Or if a man loves something ardently and with all his
heart, so that nothing else has savor for him or touches his
heart but that, and that and nothing but that is his whole
object: truly, wherever he is, whomever he is with, whatever
he may undertake, whatever he does, what he so loves never
passes from his mind, and he finds the image of what he loves
in everything, and it is the more present to him the more his
love grows and grows. He does not seek rest, because no unrest hinders him.

Such a man finds far greater merit with God because
he grasps everything as divine and as greater than things-in-
themselves are. Truly, to this belong zeal and love and a
clear apprehension of his own inwardness, and a lively, true,
prudent and real knowledge of what his disposition is concerned with amid things and persons. A man cannot learn
this by running away, by shunning things and shutting himself up in an external solitude; but he must practice a solitude
of the spirit, wherever or with whomever he is. He must
learn to break through things and to grasp his God in them
and to form Him in himself powerfully in an essential
manner. This is like someone who wants to learn to write.
If he is to acquire the art, he must certainly practice it hard
and long, however disagreeable and difficult this may be for
him and however impossible it may seem. If he will practice it industriously and assiduously, he learns it and masters
the art.

... So a man must be pervaded with the divine
presence, and be shaped through and through with the form of
the God he loves, and be present in Him, so that God's
presence may shine out to him without any effort. What is
more, in all things let him acquire nakedness [detachment],
and let him always remain free of things. But at the beginning
there must be attentiveness and a careful formation within
himself, like a schoolboy setting himself to learn. [14]

Here, in yet another treatise, Eckhart amplifies on the necessity of remaining in touch with one's own Divinity and the Divinity in
all things, even while engaged in activities in the world. It is the
message of the *Bhagavad Gita*, of the Zen Buddhists, and of all who
have known that God is at all times present, and that the awareness of
that fact is the surest and sweetest source of peace and happiness in
this world:

... Certainly, one work differs from another; but whoever undertakes all his works in the same frame of mind, then,

truly, all that man's works are the same. Indeed, for the man
for whom God shines forth as directly in worldly things as He
does in divine things and to whom God would be so present,
for such a man things would be well. Not indeed that the
man himself would be doing worldly things, dissimilar to
God; rather, whatever external matters he chanced to see and
hear, he would refer it all back to God. Only he to whom God
is present in everything and who employs his reason in the
highest degree and has enjoyment in it knows anything of true
peace and has a real kingdom of heaven.

    For if things are to go well with a man, one of two
things must always happen to him. Either he must find and
learn to possess God in works, or he must abandon all works.
But since a man cannot in this life be without works, which
are proper to humans and are of so many kinds, therefore he
must learn to possess his God in all things and to remain un-
impeded, whatever he may be doing, wherever he may be. And
therefore if a man who is beginning must do something with
other people, he ought first to make a powerful petition to
God for His help, and put Him immovably in his heart, and
unite all his intentions, thoughts, will and power to God, so
that nothing else than God can take shape in that man. [15]

And so we see that, despite the censure of his Church, Meister
Eckhart's teachings are utterly faultless; are, indeed, identical with the
perfect teachings of the wisest of sages and the goodliest of saints.
How often, it seems, how almost invariably, the men of the world come
to despise and deprecate the seers of God, whose only aim is truth and
love. And it is, more often than not, the representatives of one or
another organized religion who most violently hate and persecute
these finest of men. These persecutors stand as a reminder to this day
of the evil inherent in man's ignorance of his own Divinity, just as
men like Meister Eckhart remind us of the goodness inherent in
man's knowledge of God, his own divine Self.

THOMAS Á KEMPIS

      Following the death of Meister Eckhart, many of those il-
lumined by the knowledge of the Self took a lesson from Eckhart's
condemnation, and were careful to avoid offending the "guardians of
the faith"; but there were a few who, inspired by Eckhart's words and
his example, found the courage to speak of their own experience of
the unitive Self. Among these, was one of Eckhart's faithful disciples,
John Tauler (1300-1361), who, like Eckhart, was a member of the
Dominican Order. "The masters of Paris," he wrote, "read big
books and turn over the leaves; that is fine, but these [like Eckhart]
read the living book wherein all things live."   The Blessed Henry
Suso (1296-1381) was another of Eckhart's disciples and defenders;
and another, the Blessed Jan Ruysbroeck (1293-1381), was a Flemish
citizen who, inspired to lead the contemplative life, formed a monastic
community at Groenendael, under the rule of the Canons Regular of
Saint Augustine.
      One of Ruysbroeck's confreres at Groenendael was a man by
the name of Gerhart Groot (1340-1384), who later formed another
contemplative community at Deventer, called "The Brethren of The
Common Life." He, like Ruysbroeck, Suso and Tauler, had become
entirely disenchanted with the theological hair-splitting of the
Scholastics and wished to return the emphasis of the Christian faith to
the holy life of devotion, and away from the preoccupation with
philosophical and theological formulations which had been the trend
since Thomas Aquinas flourished at Paris. His little band of men and
women at Deventer was but one of many who formed the growing
popular movement of return to simplicity of life centered around
interior devotion, which movement came to be known as "The New
Devotion" (*devotio moderne*). There, to Deventer, in 1376, came a
young man named Thomas Haemerlein from Kempen on the Rhine,
who was to become one of the most beloved and influential saints of
all time, known to the world as Thomas á Kempis.
      Thomas á Kempis (1380-1471) entered the Brothers of The
Common Life at the age of sixteen, was educated in that community,
and at the age of twenty-two became a monk of the Augustinian
Canons at the monastery of Mount Saint Agnes in Zwolle, near
Utrecht. There he lived, totally obscured to the world, for seventy
years, until his death on July 26, 1471. His daily work for many years

was the artful copying of manuscripts, and his daily intent was the continual awareness of God's presence. In the days he worked, and in the nights he prayed and wrote. He was eventually made Director of novitiates, and in this capacity guided the novices to spiritual life through the snares and pitfalls along the path to blessedness and joy in God.

In his solitary nights, Thomas wrote down his interior meditations, prayers, and counsels, and these pure outflowings of God's activity in him were eventually collected in the form of a small book for the spiritual benefit of those novices in his charge. In a very short time after his death, however, this little book became frequently copied and widely circulated, not only among ecclesiastics, but among the lay populace as well; and was immediately received throughout Christiandom as a supremely holy book of spiritual guidance. As the earliest Latin manuscripts of this book were untitled, for purposes of identification it was circulated under the title, *Musica Ecclesiastica,* or "Music of The Church"; but later copiers, forming a title for it from the first few words of the opening chapter, called it, *De Imitatio Christi,* or "Of The Imitation Of Christ." It is by that title that it is known to us today.

Because the book was unsigned, and its author was indifferent to fame, there is no way to be absolutely certain that *The Imitation Of Christ* was in fact the work of Thomas á Kempis; but until proven otherwise, he is considered by most scholars to be its author. Thomas wrote a few other works as well, including a biography of Gerhart Groot, the founder of The Brethren of The Common Life, but this one little book of spiritual counsels, known as *The Imitation Of Christ,* remains the primary work for which he is justly remembered and revered. It is one of a very few universally beloved classics, as much honored by non-Christians as by Christians, and held by many to be one of the most holy and perfect guides to the devotional life ever created. To Christians, it is a testimony to the Christian faith, but to contemplatives of every land and every religious affiliation, it is a universally beloved classic of devotion to God. It is the treasured heritage of men and women of all religious persuasions who savor and delight in the sweet words of all true enlightened saints and lovers of God.

Thomas, it seems, knew little of other cultures or other religious traditions, and probably knew nothing of other scriptures besides his own Bible; and so he regarded the practice of God-awareness to be a singularly Christian pursuit, inextricably bound up with Christian belief and dogma. Nonetheless, his psychological perception and his inspired intuition of truth was faultless; his pursuit of God, though colored by his own sectarian loyalties, is a perfectly universal one, applicable to all God-seekers of all times and all religious traditions. His timeless counsels on the path to God are as meaningful today as ever. Though cultures, religious doctrines, and philosophical trends may change according to the changing opinions of men, the way to God-consciousness never changes; it is the eternal legacy of all peoples of every time and persuasion.

The Imitation Of Christ may therefore be thought of as a universal handbook of spiritual contemplation. It is fashioned in three "Books" (four, if you count the spurious Book on "Communion" usually added by doctrinaire Churchmen), each of which may be regarded as representative of a progressively more interior state than the one before: In the First, the stage is set in preparing the aspirant for contemplation by freeing his mind from all exterior concerns; in the Second, the aspirant is turned to the interior examination of his own soul; and the Third leads the purified aspirant on his inward journey, by the way of love, to the threshold of God.

Typical of Thomas' advice to the spiritual aspirant are these brief excerpts:

> All that is in this world is vanity, but to love God
> and to serve only Him.

> He who seeks any other thing in religion than God
> and the health of his own soul, shall find nothing there but
> trouble and sorrow; ...

> Why have many saints been so perfectly contemplat-
> ive? Because they always studied to mortify themselves from
> worldly desires, that they might freely, with all the power of
> their heart, tend to our Lord.

> If you forsake to be comforted by worldly things, you
> may behold more perfectly the things of eternity, and you shall
> then sing continually lauds and praisings to God with great joy
> and inward gladness of heart.

But Thomas' counsels have often been criticized by ordinary (worldly) men for their apparent negation of the world; for he repeatedly calls for the "despising of the world," the need for humility and solitude, and the restraint of the outgoing senses. Yet Thomas' counsels may not truly be judged according to the purposes of ordinary men, but only according to whether or not they are appropriate to their own avowed purpose: the preparation of the soul for the fulfillment of its desire for union with God. Judged on this basis, Thomas' book of counsels has been proven time and time again by countless practicing contemplatives to be a most perfectly appropriate and trustworthy guide. It has been the special solace of renunciants and scholars, popes and laity, statesmen and kings, for over five centuries. To countless devout souls, it has proven itself to be an inestimable treasure, a marvellous and magical source of inspiration and joy.

The Imitation Of Christ reveals to us the mystic in the throes of love-longing. Thomas' pain is so nakedly apparent that his state seems to the ordinary person an unenviable, even, at times, a pathetic, one. In fact, the state of the mystic in the throes of love *is* pathetic; his ecstatic love, his ardent yearning, his intense awareness of his own mental impairments, reveal the terrible ordeal of one drawn by grace to the "vision" of God. Here, for example, in his despair over the lack of the sense of God's presence, Thomas cries out in pain and anguish:

> O Lord, the light and brightness of everlasting glory,
> the joy and comfort of all Thy children walking and laboring
> as pilgrims in the wilderness of this world! My heart cries to
> Thee by still desires without voice, and my silence speaks
> unto Thee and says thus: "How long tarrieth my Lord God
> to come? Truly, I trust that He will shortly come to me, His
> poorest servant, and comfort me and make me joyous and glad
> in Him, and deliver me from all anguish and sorrow. Come,
> Lord, come, for without Thee I have no glad day nor hour!
> Thou art all my joy and gladness, and without Thee my soul
> is barren and void. I am a wretch, and as though imprisoned
> and bound with fetters, till Thou, through the light of Thy
> gracious presence, consent to visit me and to refresh me, to
> bring me again to liberty of spirit, and to show Thy favorable
> and lovely countenance unto me...

To the normal observer, this distraught state of longing for God, evidenced by Thomas, runs counter to the peace and contentment so often claimed for the knowledge of God's eternal presence. But it is the token of a very special state of grace, granted only to

those few whom God would draw to the clear vision of Himself. It is,
admittedly, a state of discontent, of peacelessness, of extreme anguish;
yet such yearning is accompanied by the awareness that it is
precipitated by God Himself, and is the gift of His most intimate
grace. Though it stabs like a wound to the heart, it is a delicious
wound, born gladly in the hope of attainment to God. With this hope,
Thomas prays:

> Grant me, Lord, special grace to rest in Thee above
> all creatures, above all health and fairness, above all glory and
> honor, above all dignity and power, above all wisdom and
> policy, above all riches and crafts, above all gladness of body
> and of soul, above all fame and praising, above all sweetness
> and consolation, above all hope and promise, above all merit
> and desire, above all gifts and rewards that Thou mayst give or
> send besides Thyself, and above all joy and mirth that man's
> heart or mind may feel. And also above all angels and all the
> company of heavenly spirits, above all things that are not
> Thyself.
> For Thou, Lord God, art most good, most high, most
> mighty, most sufficient and most full of goodness; most
> sweet, most comfortable, most fair, most loving, most noble,
> and most glorious above all things; in whom all goodness and
> perfection is, has been, and ever shall be. And therefore what-
> soever Thou givest me besides Thyself, it is little and insuf-
> ficient to me; for my heart may not rest nor fully be pacified
> so that it ascend above all gifts and above all manner of things
> that are created, unless in Thee.
> O my Lord, most loving spouse, most pure lover and
> governor of every creature! Who shall give me wings of per-
> fect liberty that I may fly high and rest in Thee! O when shall
> I gather myself together in Thee so perfectly that I shall not,
> for Thy love, feel myself, but Thee alone, above myself and
> above all bodily things, and that Thou shalt visit me in such
> a way as Thou dost visit Thy faithful lovers? ...

Thomas' quest for the "vision" of God is the quest of all
purified souls; his is the universal voice of all who long for vision, the
archetypical, God-inspired voice of yearning which cries within the
heart of every soul for the pure Being of its own depths, the Godhood
which is always its true and eternal Self. Such yearning for God is the
clear anunciation of the soul's ascent to God, and is attainable only by
the inner working of God's grace. Such a state of yearning cannot be
understood by men in whom this grace is absent; to them, it appears to

be a false and mistaken attitude, one-sided and neglectful of the ever-existent fact of Unity. But it is a Divinely-inspired state; though it is a state of yearning and distress, it is the state of the soul drawn by God to God, just prior to its realization, or "union."   Such a soul cares nothing for the "fact"; it longs to be truly dissolved in His Unity. Ordinary men see only the distress, and fear such a state; they condemn it and regard it as a state of delusion. But it is only by such impoverishment of the soul, such death-throes of the ego, that one may ascend from man to God, from obscure darkness to the perfect light of Truth.

Here, as a final selection from *The Imitation Of Christ*, is one of Thomas' most exuberant and inspiring paeans in praise of God and of the divine Love which draws the soul to Him:

Of The Marvellous Effect Of The Love Of God

O my Lord God, most faithful lover, when Thou comest into my heart, all that is within me doth joy! Thou art my glory and the joy of my heart, my hope and my whole refuge in all my troubles. But inasmuch as I am yet feeble in love and imperfect in virtue, therefore I have need to have more comfort and more help from Thee. Consent, therefore, often-times to visit me and to instruct me with Thy holy teachings. Deliver me from all evil passions and heal my sick heart from all earthly pleasure, that I may be inwardly healed and purged from all inordinate affections and vices, and be made ready and able to love Thee, strong to suffer for Thee, and stable to persevere in Thee.

Love is a great and goodly thing, and alone makes heavy burdens light, and bears in the same balance things pleasing and displeasing. It bears a heavy burden and feels it not, and makes bitter things to be savory and sweet. The noble love of God perfectly printed in man's soul makes a man to do great things and stirs him always to desire perfection and to grow more and more in grace and goodness.

Love will always have his mind upward to God and will not be occupied with things of the world. Love will also be free from all worldly affections, that the inward sight of the soul may not be darkened or lost, and that his affection to heavenly things may not be diminished by an inordinate win-ning or losing of worldly things. Nothing, therefore, is sweet-er than love, nothing higher, nothing stronger, nothing larger, nothing more joyful, nothing fuller, and nothing better in heaven nor in earth; for love descends from God and may not rest finally in anything lower than God. Such a lover flies high, he runs swiftly, he is merry in God, he is free in soul, he gives all for All and has All in all; for he rests in one high Goodness above all things, of whom all goodness flows and proceeds. He beholds not only the gift, but the Giver, above all gifts.

Love knows no measure but is fervent without measure. It feels no burden; it regards no labor; it desires more than it may attain; it complains of no impossibility, for it thinks all things that may be done for his Beloved possible and lawful unto him. Love therefore does many great things and brings them to fruition, wherein he who is no lover faints and fails.

Love wakes much and sleeps little, and sleeping, sleeps not. It faints and is not weary, is restrained of liberty and is in great freedom. It sees causes of fear and fears not; but as a burning ember or a spark of fire, flames always upward by fervor of love unto God, and through the special help of grace is delivered from all perils and dangers.

He who is thus a spiritual lover knows well what his voice means which says: "Thou, Lord God, art my whole love and my desire! Thou art all mine and I all Thine! Spread my heart into Thy love that I may know how sweet it is to serve Thee, and to be as though I were entirely melted into Thy love." O I am immersed in love and go far above myself for the great fervor that I feel of Thy unspeakable goodness! I shall sing to Thee the song of love; and my soul shall never be weary to praise Thee with the joyful song of love that I shall sing to Thee. I shall love Thee more than myself, and not myself but for Thee. And I shall love all others in Thee and for Thee, as the law of love commands which is given by Thee.

Love is swift, pure, meek, joyous and glad, strong, patient, faithful, wise, forbearing, manly, and never seeking himself nor his own will; for whensoever a man seeks himself, he falls from love. Love is circumspect, meek, righteous, not weak, not frivolous nor heeding vain things; sober, chaste, stable, quiet and well restrained in his outward senses. Love is ... devout and thankful to God; trusting and always hoping in Him, and that even when he has but little devotion or little savor in him, for without some sorrow or pain no man may live in love. [1]

Thomas is the supreme *bhakta* of Medieval Christianity; like Narada, he revels in the love which floods his heart for God, which causes sweet tears to flow in nocturnal solitudes, and ushers in that rare intimacy with God which sends thrills of joy throughout the body and soul. The path of devotion, so perfectly epitomized in Thomas' writings, is not only a means, but is its own end as well; it is identical to beatitude, the greatest joy attainable in this life. Ultimately, it leads the soul to experience itself as the sole Divinity, beyond the division of soul and God. The separative ego so negates and consumes itself in the loving regard of God, that it no longer exists at all, and, suddenly, the previous duality of "I" and "Thou" vanishes in the clear aware-ness of Unity.

So long as the separative ego exists, the loving relationship of soul to God exists; but when the one supreme Self is realized, the relationship of soul to God is no more, and all talk of "two" is seen from that vantage point to be false, delusional. Then only the One is, without a second. But let no one imagine, who has not yet reached that "Goal," that the devotional path to God is therefore invalid, unnecessary, or dispensible. For it is one thing to admire the mountain peak of Unity from afar, and quite another to reach the summit of that mountain by the steep and arduous path of love.

≈≈≈

V. Mystics Of
The Modern Era

NICHOLAS OF CUSA

If Thomas á Kempis was the epitome of the Christian *bhakta* in the 15th century, Nicholas of Cusa (1401-1464) was that century's representative *jnani*. But these two were not so far apart in thought as they might at first appear; in fact, one may find stated in Thomas á Kempis' writings the same perennial philosophy found in Nicholas' and vice versa. Thomas á Kempis, however, was very much a figure of the Middle Ages, while Nicholas, though outlived by Thomas, is generally regarded as a transitionary figure, with one foot in the Middle Ages and one in the Renaissance era. This is due primarily to the scope of Nicholas' interests, which led him into scientific, social, and political concerns as well as strictly mystical ones.

He was born Nicholas Krebs at Cues (Cusa) on the Moselle river in the Rhineland to a well-to-do barge captain, in 1401. Like Thomas á Kempis, twenty years before him, Nicholas went as a young boy to the Brethren of The Common Life at Deventer to receive his early education. At the age of sixteen, he entered the University of Heidelberg, and then transferred to the University of Padua, where he studied Canon law, the sciences, mathematics, and Greek. He received his degree at the age of twenty-two, and thereafter decided to enter the priesthood. Nicholas studied theology at Cologne, as did Eckhart, and in 1426 became secretary to the Cardinal legate, Giordano Orsini, becoming ordained as a priest in 1430.

It would seem that around this time Nicholas collected and read a great number of classic philosophical and mystical works, including those of Plato, Eriugena, Dionysius the Areopagite, and especially Meister Eckhart. Sometime around his twenty-eighth year, he must have experienced "the vision of God" of which he was later to write so lucidly. But, in the years that followed, Nicholas became caught up in the politics of the Church and the ongoing disputes between the Church and the state, thus beginning the career of reform and reconciliation which lasted throughout his life.

Nicholas was, in his early years, a proponent of the conciliar theory of Church government (i.e., rule by council rather than by the Papacy), and was present at the Council of Basel (1431-1433); and in 1433 he presented to the Council his defense of the conciliar theory (*De concordantia catholica*) against the Papal authority. But, as the disputes dragged on, it became evident to Nicholas that the rule of a council, while sound as a theory, was impracticable, as it provided no means to end controversies, but rather tended to foster a continuous discord. Therefore, in 1435, he shifted his allegiance to the rule of the Papacy; and, in 1437, he was sent by Pope Eugenius to Constantinople to attend the Ecumenical Council at Ferrara, in the hope of mending the schism between the Greek and Roman Churches, though little came of it. Following this, in 1440, during a respite from his political labors, Nicholas wrote his best-known philosophical work, *De docta ignorantia*, "On Learned Ignorance."

The following years were years of bitter struggle within the Church, when, for a time, there were two Popes, one at Basel and one at Rome, and feelings ran high on both sides of the division. Nicholas was sent to Germany at one point to campaign for the acceptance of Eugenius as the recognized Pope, and served as an able champion. But the schism ended in 1447 with Eugenius' death, and a new Pope, Nicholas V, took the reins of sole authority. The new Pope rewarded Nicholas of Cusa for his loyalty to the Roman Papacy by making him Cardinal of San Pietro in Vincoli in 1448, and, in 1450, he was made Bishop of Brixen as well. In this office he travelled extensively throughout Germany, working for reforms in the Church, and correcting the laxity and immorality then existing in many lowland monasteries.

One of the monasteries Nicholas visited during this time was the Benedictine Abbey of Tegernsee. Nicholas had been warmly received in 1452 by the devout monks there, and in answer to their request for guidance in mystical theology, Nicholas wrote and sent to them his little book, *De visio Dei*, "On The Vision Of God," in 1453. This was also the year that he wrote his dialogue concerning the universal tolerance of all religions, *De pace fidei*, in which he asserted that "all religion[s] and the worship of God, in all men endowed with the spirit, are fundamentally one and the same, despite the diversity of their rites."

In 1459, Nicholas was recalled to Rome by his old friend, Aeneas Sylvius Piccolomini, who was now Pope Pius II, and he served there as a curial counselor, giving most of his time to his studies and writings until his death in 1464.

Nicholas was a prolific writer on the theme of mystical vision; in 1450 he had written his beautiful dialogue, *De sapienta,* "On Wisdom," and in his later years, *De possest* (1460), *De non aliud* (1462), and *De venatione sapientia* (1463), an autobiographical recounting of his search for wisdom. His primary and over-riding interest was in explaining mystical theology in accordance with his own mystical experience, but he was also aware of the great need to combine with the devotional life a love and respect for scientific knowledge in order to forge a unified and rational comprehension of reality, extending from God to all creation.

He had a natural bent toward mathematics, and used many similies and analogies from that discipline to illustrate his meaning in many of his theological works. In addition, he wrote a number of purely mathematic and scientific treatises advocating a more experimental approach to knowledge of the natural world. Among these are *Raparatio calendari* (1436), his treatment of the reform of the calendar; *De quadratura circuli* (1452), and *De staticis experimentis* (1453). In addition to his remarkable knowledge of mathematics, geometry and physical science, he was also well versed in Latin, Greek, Hebrew and Arabic. No wonder, with all his vast learning and indefatigable energy, he is sometimes regarded as the prototype of Renaissance man.

Yet, today, all of Nicholas' work seems to have been for naught. He is utterly neglected and forgotten, and few have even heard of his name. And when he is spoken of in the histories of philosophy, he is usually misrepresented to a pitiful degree. One looks with amazement and consternation at the many modern books on philosophy by authors who somehow or other are unable to comprehend the clearly unambiguous words of the great mystics of the past. Nicholas of Cusa is described, for example, in accordance with their own limited views, as a humanist, scientist, reformer, logician, philosopher, Churchman or theologian, without the slightest mention of the fact that all of what he had to say was based on his "vision of God," as he, himself, so often pointed out. What a great pity it is that so many have told the story of mystical vision so often, and so few have understood. But the mystic comes to expect this; as Nicholas, echoing the words of Lao Tze quoted elsewhere, said: "These secret things ought not to be revealed to everyone, because when they are made known they appear to many as absurdities." [1]

He knew well the futility of words to explain what can only be known through experience; and yet he spoke all the same. For what else is one to do, unless he abandon humanity altogether and play the fool? Nicholas was not of this type; he was a man of position, an active leader within the Church, and a courageous and outspoken teacher. How greatly he labored, as have so many great seers of antiquity, and how stubbornly the rationalists of the world have continued to refute him, as they have refuted his predecessors! How little the world of today has learned from all these labors. Yet, in each generation, the story of the vision of Truth is retold, even by those who recognize the futility of such telling.

Now, let us look at his works: Thomas á Kempis had felt it irrelevant to speak of the experience of unity; instead, he concentrated upon exhorting his charges to make those preparations which would enable them to experience it for themselves. Nicholas, on the other hand, had but little to say about the path, and felt a necessity to underscore the truths learned in that experience. There is not a mystic who ever lived who did not declare emphatically and often that one cannot possibly know God through the rational intellect, yet Nicholas of Cusa made this fact the object of an entire book, and brought the point home in a forceful and definitive manner to minds which, theretofore, had been unwilling to hear the message. Because so many of his time were involved in the futile exercise of dialectics, he felt called upon to make clear that no amount of reasoning, no amount of intellectual effort, could reveal That which was beyond the reach of words and intellectual conceptions. This he did in a book entitled, *On Learned Ignorance*.

In this book, he pointed out to the dialecticians that all their metaphysical and theological learning was, in fact, nothing more than ignorance; and that, when they reached that understanding which allowed them to acknowledge that all their learning had only brought them, and could only bring them, to know that they did not know, then they will have reached that state of "learned ignorance" wherefrom they could truly begin to embark on their spiritual journey to true knowledge. "Reason," said Nicholas,

> strives for knowledge and yet this natural striving is not adequate to the knowledge of the Essence of God, but only to the knowledge that God ... is beyond all conception and knowledge. [2]
>
> ... That wisdom (which all men by their very nature desire to know and consequently seek after with such great affection of mind) is known in no other way than that it is higher than all knowledge and utterly unknowable and unspeakable in all language. It is unintelligible to all understanding, immeasurable by all measure, improportionable by every proportion, incomparable by all comparison, infigurable

by all figuration, unformable by all formation, ... unimagin-
able by all imagination, ... inapprehensible in all apprehension
and unaffirmable in all affirmation, undeniable in all negation,
indoubtable in all doubt, inopinionable in all opinion; and
because in all speech it is inexpressable, there can be no limit
to the means of expressing it, being incognitable in all
cognition... [3]

But this declaration of the inability of the rational intellect to
know God is not the end but the beginning of Nicholas' message, as it
is of all mystics from the authors of the Upanishads forward. "The
Reality," says Nicholas,

which is the truth of all beings, is unattainable in its purity;
all philosophers have sought it, none has found it, as it is; and
the more profoundly learned in this ignorance, the more we
shall approach Truth itself. [4]
    Those who think that wisdom is nothing other than
that which is comprehensible by the understanding, that happiness is nothing else than what they can attain, are quite far
from the true eternal and infinite wisdom. [5]
    ... The highest wisdom consists in this, to know ...
how That which is unattainable [by the intellect] may be
reached or attained in a manner beyond [intellectual] attainment. [6]

Much of *On Learned Ignorance* and *The Vision Of God* as
well is devoted to proving by rational argument that God is quite
beyond rational comprehension. Nicholas does this by showing that
God is infinite, and therefore beyond all finite predications; and that
God is the "coincidence of opposites" (*coincidentia oppositorum*)
and is therefore beyond all thought or expression which, by its very
nature, is based on either a positive or negative assertion. Nicholas
arrived at this understanding, however, not through logic or
ratiocination, but through direct experience of God.

This "coincidence of opposites" is the very nature of the
mystical experience. As one enters into the awareness of unity, one
directly perceives that all dualities are produced by the separative
mind (or ego). As that veil of false ego is dissolved, the duality of
"I" and "Thou" disappears; the fluctuating mind is stilled, and
enters into a Stillness beyond the opposites of motion and stillness.
As this occurs, one realizes that all that stood as a barrier to this Unity,
is constructed of polarities. For example, the activity of love neces-

sitates its opposite, hatred; the recognition of beauty necessitates the recognition of ugliness; the love of knowledge begets a hatred for ignorance; our love of the true necessitates the arising of repulsion for what is false; even our love of and desire for God's vision necessitates the despising of all that obscures it. Thus we invent good and evil, likes and dislikes; we see movement and rest, and all the other pairs of opposites which go to make up our perception of our separate reality.

But, in the Unity-awareness, which is the absolute Ground of all existence, these opposites do not exist. As Nicholas says:

> Because He is Himself the absolute Ground, in which all contrariety (*alteritas*) is unity, and all diversity is identity, that which we understand as diversity cannot exist in God. [7]
> ... Just as contrariety in unity is without contrariety because it is unity, even so, in infinity, contradiction is without contradiction, because it is infinity. Infinity is simplicity itself; *contradiction cannot exist without a contrary.* [8]
> ... O Lord, my God, ... I see Thee to be Infinity Itself, wherefore nothing is alien to Thee, nothing differing from Thee, nothing opposed to Thee. For the Infinite allows no otherness from Itself, since, being Infinity, nothing exists outside It: absolute Infinity includes and contains all things. [9]

In that Infinity, or Unity, the world-appearance is experienced as a cyclic evolution and involution, or "explication" and "complication," as Nicholas puts it. Yet this primary dual motion of explication and contraction, this recurring projection and withdrawal of the world-appearance, is reconciled or resolved in the primal Unity, which is beyond all such opposites. It is unchanging, as It contains both explication and contraction. The alternating explication and contraction goes on -- as a man's breath goes on; but the One in whom this occurs remains the same Unity -- as a man remains the same whether breathing out or breathing in. That Unity is a "One," not set over against a second, but a "One" which encompasses all duality within Itself. This is the simple Truth known by all who have risen to that unitive Awareness which is the coincidence of all opposites.

Nicholas, having experienced that Unity-awareness, wherein all dualities cease to be, sees this coincidence of opposites as a sort of threshold, or wall, separating mortal awareness from God-awareness; he calls it "the wall of Paradise":

> I have learnt that the place wherein Thou art found
> unveiled is girt round with the coincidence of contradictories,
> and this is the wall of Paradise wherein Thou dost abide.
> ... Thus 'tis beyond the coincidence of contradictories
> that Thou mayest be seen, and nowhere this side thereof. [10]
> ... O God almighty, Thou dwellest within the wall of
> Paradise, and this wall is that coincidence where later is one
> with earlier, where the end is one with the beginning, where
> Alpha and Omega are one. [11]

All these polarities cease to be in the mystical "vision." There is no longer an "I" and a "Thou," no longer a universe and a God, no longer a separation between motion and rest, order and chaos, sound and silence. That One is utter Unity, and It is oneself, one's only real, eternal, Self. And the whole charade of polar opposites in comparison to that eternally undivided Self is but a misty phantasy, as little affecting that Self as a flimsy daydream. In that experience of Unity, a man realizes that *That* is always and eternally his only Identity, despite the film of separate ego and separate thought which closes back in upon him, like moss on the water, obscuring that pure Awareness. For he has seen in that Awareness that this One is the only one anywhere; that that one Consciousness, which is who he is eternally, is the source and manifestation of all that is.

Naturally, the separative mind, which exists and functions only as a producer of opposites, can scarcely be expected to fathom That which is beyond all opposites. Thought is made of opposites, and therefore connot be expected to conceive of That which produces it. It is only when the mind, having become stilled and concentrated, rises to the awareness of its own Ground and Source that this "coincidence of opposites" occurs. One may practice this concentration through the means of meditation or prayer, but one does not always succeed; it occurs, in fact, but rarely. To anyone practicing this concentrated transcendence of the ego-mind, it quickly becomes evident that it cannot be done simply by one's own efforts. There must be a "coincidence" as well of love and grace, which comes in its own time. It is "set," as it were, in the universal Will, and arises in its own due time during the ordered unfolding of the universe.

We can only become aware of that grace as it increases in us. A strong resolve arises in us to know God; our love for Him increases within us beyond what we have experienced before, and we sense a nearness, a proximity which we long to close. It draws us like a magnet, increasing within us Its own desire, until at last in a moment of yearning prayer, the veil is drawn aside, the wall of contraries is passed, and the Unity dawns within. This uncommon drawing-power experienced within is known as "grace." Everyone who has ever entered that Unity-awareness has acknowledged its agency, and his own impotency without it. Nicholas, too, acknowledges it:

> The vision of God is not seen in this world ...
> until He will make Himself visible beyond all obscurity. [12]

> ... None can attain unto Thee, ... none can possess
> himself of Thee, except Thou givest Thyself to him. [13]
> ... In beholding me Thou givest Thyself to be seen
> of me, Thou who art the hidden God. None can see Thee save
> insofar as Thou grantest a sight of Thyself, nor is that sight
> anything else than Thy seeing him that seeth Thee. [14]

When grace begins to be active within, the understanding becomes quickened and illumined, and the heart becomes filled with a tender love and yearning for God. The mind cannot bear to think of anything but God, and it turns away from all mental apparitions to focus singly on its Lord. For, as Nicholas says,

> He who seeks after wisdom with intellectual motion
> is already inwardly touched by the foretaste of the sweetness
> and its reception into the body renders the body almost incorp-
> oreal. The weight of no sensible thing can hold him down
> until he unites himself to the attracting wisdom, and this
> causes the soul to forsake the senses and to appear mad in that
> it no longer concerns itself with anything other than this
> wisdom. For such a person it is sweetness to leave this world
> and this life in order the more readily to be carried into the
> wisdom of immortality. [15]

Such is the universal experience of all who have known that grace.

Of his own mystical experience, Nicholas is typically silent in most of his written works; but, in *The Vision Of God* , written for the monks of Tegernsee, he does reveal something of his own vision. Here, he speaks of how the "Face of God" may be seen beyond the veil of all appearances and all faces:

> Thou hast at times appeared unto me, Lord, not as
> one to be seen of any creature, but as the hidden, infinite,
> God. [16]

... In all faces is seen the Face of faces, veiled, and
obscured, although it is not seen unveiled until a man enters,
beyond all faces, into a certain secret and mystic silence where
there is no knowledge or concept of a face. This mist, cloud,
darkness or ignorance into which he that seeks Thy face enters
when he goes beyond all knowledge or concept, is a state
beneath which Thy face cannot be seen except veiled; but that
darkness reveals Thy face to be there, beyond all veils. [17]
... Thou dost ravish me above myself that I may fore-
see the glorious place whereunto Thou callest me. ... Thou
grantest me to behold the treasury of riches, of life, of joy, of
beauty. ... Thou keepest nothing secret. [18]
... I behold Thee, O Lord my God, in a kind of
mental trance, ... [19]
... Thus, while I am borne to loftiest heights, I behold Thee as Infinity... [20]
... And when I behold Thee as absolute Infinity, to
whom is befitting neither the name of creating Creator nor of
creatable Creator -- then indeed I begin to behold Thee unveiled, and to enter into the garden of delights! [21]
...[In that vision] nothing is seen other than Thyself,
[for Thou] art Thyself the object of Thyself (for Thou seest,
and art That which is seen, and art the sight as well) ... [22]

It is there, in that mystical experience of infinite Unity that
one beholds the wondrous and paradoxical nature of an unchangeable and immutable One which appears as the changeable and
mutable world of multiplicity. In wonder at this ineffable paradox,
Nicholas exclaims:

O God, ... [Thou dost] seem subject to mutability,
since Thou dost never desert Thy creatures, which are subject
to mutability; ... but, because Thou art the absolute Good,
Thou art not changeable, and dost not follow what is mutable.
O the unplumbed depths of Thee, my God, who art not separate from Thy creatures, and art nonetheless beyond them! [23]

Like all others who have experienced God, and faced this
conceptual paradox, Nicholas finds it necessary, in order to explain
the nature of an unchangeable and constant Unity which appears as a
changeable and inconstant world-manifestation, to conceptually divide
the one Reality into categorically separate persona. He frames his
conception in terms identical to those used by the early Christians,
Gnostics and Hermeticists. God, he says, in His absolute and invari-
able Unity, is "the Father"; in His mysterious creative Power of

world-manifestation, He is "the Son," or "the Word"; and in His perceptible manifestation as the multiple forms of the world, He is "the Holy Spirit." Nicholas is always quick to remind us that these three are always one, and are divided conceptually only in order to make clear the various modes, or aspects, of the One.

As "the Father," God is the absolute Unity, Infinity, Eternity. The creative Power of God Nicholas explains as that potency within the Father "wherewith all things are produced from non-being to being." If God, the unchanging Unity, be called "the Father," then, says Nicholas, His Power of manifestation is "the Son":

> He is God the Father whom we might also call
> "One" or "Unity," because He necessitates being out of what
> did not exist (through His omnipotence) ... This [omni-
> potent Power of His] is the Word, the Wisdom, the Son of
> the Father; and we may regard Him as co-equal to the One or
> Unity. [24]

And the Power or Energy which is manifested by the Word, or Son, and which forms all things, is "the Holy Spirit." It is the Word that is itself manifest as the world, but to differentiate the cause, or Creator, from the effect, or the created, he uses these two terms. Thus, these three -- Father, Son, and Holy Spirit -- are but names for God, His Power of Manifestation, and the world-appearance which is the product of that Power. They are one in essence, but three when categorized according to their different characteristics. Says Nicholas:

> Thus the Essence is triune, and yet there are not three
> essences therein, since It is most simple. The plurality of
> these three is both plurality and unity, and their unity is both
> unity and plurality. [25]

Nicholas always stresses the essential unity of these three aspects of Reality, rather than their apparent plurality. For his purpose is to show that the world is nothing but the Word, and the Word is nothing but God; and that, therefore, the world is nothing but God. "What is the world," asks Nicholas, "but the manifestation of the invisible God?" [26]

This threefold categorization of Reality is, of course a formulation common to all mystics of all traditions. In the Vedantic terminology, for example, these three are *Brahman, Maya,* and *Jagat*; in the Shaivite terminology, *Shiva, Shakti,* and *samsara*; for the

Buddhists, *Dharmakaya, Purvapranidhanabala,* and *samsara*; and so
on. Nicholas' vision is, in all respects, common to all who, through
inner vision, have seen the Truth of existence and attempted to explain
it in a way comprehensible to the intellect. But this is not a mere
theological formula to be learned and mouthed by school-children. It
is to be experienced in that inner vision wherein God as man awakens
to his divine Ground and eternal Identity through a loving regard, as
that of a son to his father, or an ardent lover to her beloved.

Man is at once the Essence and the appearance; both God and
His Thought-image. When he rises in awareness beyond the appearances of the Thought-image, he knows his eternal Identity -- as a man,
waking from a dream, realizes he is not just the dream-image within a
dream, but the dreamer; or as an image in a mirror might behold him
who is the source, or original, of the image. "When anyone looks
into this mirror of Eternity," says Nicholas,

> what he sees is not the figure, but the Truth, whereof the
> beholder himself is a figure. Wherefore, in Thee, my God,
> the figure is [really] the Truth, and the Exemplar of all things
> that exist. [27]
> ... I am a living shadow and Thou the Truth... Where-
> fore, my God, Thou art alike shadow and Truth; Thou art alike
> the image and the Exemplar of myself and all men. [28]
> ... Hence, in Thee, who art Love, the lover is not one
> thing and the loved another, and the bond between them a
> third, but they are one and the same -- Thou, Thyself, my God.
> Since, then, in Thee the loved is one with the lover, and being
> loved [is one] with loving, this bond of coincidence is an
> essential bond. For there is nothing in Thee that is not Thy
> very Essence. [29]
> ... I see, Lord, through Thine infinite mercy, that
> Thou art Infinity encompassing all things. Nothing exists
> outside Thee, and all things in Thee are not other than Thee. [30]

In his little book, *De sapientia,* "On Wisdom," which is a
dialogue between a teacher and his student, Nicholas expresses most
beautifully the difference between that knowledge attainable through
intellectual learning, and that direct knowledge of God which is
"wisdom"; and he exhorts his readers to pass beyond a mere intellectual understanding to that wisdom attainable only in the vision of
God, through love and grace:

> Wisdom shining in all things invites us, with a cert-

ain foretaste of its effects, to be borne to it with a wonderful desire. For life itself is an intellectual Spirit, having in itself a certain innate foretaste through which it searches with great desire for the very Font of its own life. Without that foretaste, it could neither seek after It nor know when it had acquired It. It is due to this that it is moved toward It as its proper life. Every spirit finds it sweet to ascend continually to the very Principle of life, even though this appears inaccessible. For a persistent and continued ascent to [the Principle and Source of] life is the constituent element of increased happiness. [31]

... Just as any knowledge of the taste of something we have never actually tasted is quite empty until we do taste it, so the taste of this wisdom cannot be acquired by hearsay but by one's actually touching it with his internal sense, and then he will bear witness not of what he has heard but what he has experientially tasted in himself. To know of the many descriptions of love which the saints have left us without knowing the taste of love is nothing other than a certain emptiness. Thus it is that it is not enough for him who seeks after eternal wisdom to merely read about these things, but it is absolutely necessary that once he discovers where it is by his understanding he make it his very own. [32]

... Wisdom is not to be found in the art of oratory, or in great books, but in a withdrawal from these sensible things and in a turning to the most simple and infinite forms. You will learn how to receive it into a temple purged from all vice, and by fervent love to cling to it until you may taste it and see how sweet That is which is all sweetness. Once this has been tasted, all things which you now consider as important will appear as vile, and you will be so humbled that no arrogance or other vice will remain in you. Once having tasted this wisdom, you will inseparably adhere to it with a chaste and pure heart. You will choose rather to forsake this world and all else that is not of this wisdom, and living with unspeakable happiness you will die. After death you will rest eternally in that fond embrace which the eternally blessed wisdom of God Himself vouchsafed to grant both to you and to me. [33]

... You now have what is granted to contemplate eternal wisdom, that you may behold all things in a most simple rectitude, most truly, precisely, unconfused and perfectly, even though enigmatically. For the vision of God is not seen in this world without mystery until He will make Himself visible without darkness. And this is the facility of the difficulties of wisdom which, in proportion to your fervor and devotion, may God grant each day an increased clarity both to you and to me until He lifts us up into the glorious fruition of the Truth, where we shall remain eternally. [34]

Nicholas of Cusa was, undoubtedly, the dominant enunciator of mystical theology and wisdom in his time; but many other, more discordant, voices were soon to be heard much more loudly. The revolt against the decadence and corruption of the Roman Catholic Church which had begun in the 14th century with John Wycliffe (1320-1384) and John Huss (1373-1415), gained great popular momentum in the following century through the efforts of such men as Martin Luther (1483-1546), Zwingli (1484-1531), Calvin (1509-1564), and John Knox (1514-1572). And while there is no place in the story of mysticism for an account of the squabbles of men devoted to pursuits other than the direct realization of God, it is necessary to note that the climate of dissention prevailing during the early 16th century tended to obscure if not preclude the appearance during that time of any noteworthy mystics within the Christian community. It is not until the late 16th century that we meet again with a Christian mystic of immense stature: the universally beloved saint, Juan de la Cruz.

JUAN DE LA CRUZ

The 16th century Spaniard, Juan de la Cruz (1542-1591), known to English-speaking people as John of the Cross, spoke with such simple clarity and poetic beauty on the path of devotion, and with such psychological subtlety on the mental stages leading to "union," that all others who have spoken of these matters seem, in comparison to him, like babbling and stammering infants. Had he lived and written in our own day, still the lucidity of his spiritual vision would be a matter for wonder; the fact that he lived and wrote in the 16th century, in an age of great narrow-mindedness and religious oppression, is nothing short of miraculous.

By the time of Juan de la Cruz, the "Protestant Reformation" had stirred up a great rebelliousness against the Catholic Church within the northern European countries, but had scarcely touched Spain. The Spaniards, having recently escaped the tyranny of Islam and re-established the supremecy of Christianity and the Catholic Church, were occupied with weeding out the remains of Muslim and Jewish influences. Nevertheless, the ecclesiastical authorities of Spain were very much aware of the "Protestant" mood of the times, and were doubly suspicious of anything smacking of revolt. In a reactionary spirit of "Counter Reformation," they became even more authoritarian, more intolerant of dissension, and more given to brute force in dealing with opposition.

During the reign of Queen Isabella, from the years 1483 to 1493, the infamous Inquisitor-general, Tomas de Torquemada, tortured and murdered hundreds of thousands of "heretics" for the love of Christ. This tyrannical authoritarianism was justified on the grounds that every man's soul was in mortal danger from the wiles of the devil, and that the representatives of the Church were divinely appointed to effect every soul's salvation from the snares of that wily villain -- even if it meant exorcizing them by torture or burning.

The Christian metaphysic, or theology, of the time, in order to account for the compulsively negative tendencies in the soul (which, under the theory of reincarnation, may be explained as tendencies inherited from previous births), posited an evil being, called "the devil," who has access to the mental realm, and delights there in tempting men and women to act against their better judgement. Borrowing from ancient Jewish mythology, this theology held that the devil, in ancient times, succeeded in thus tempting the very first man and woman; whereupon God, in apparent anger, ejected them from their paradisical garden and cursed all mankind to inherit the consequences of their "original sin." However, He later sent Jesus as a mediator and savior, as a means of rescinding this curse. All those who believed in Jesus' divinity and who embraced the Christian faith as directed by the Church were to be exonerated, or saved, while all others were condemned to everlasting hell-fire.

In the 16th century, this primitive and childish myth was taken as unquestioned fact, and formed an integral part of the belief-system of practicing Christians. Indeed, all matters of faith, conduct, and even prayer, were regarded as settled and incontrovertible; and those who deviated from, or appeared to deviate from, the standards prescribed by ecclesiastical authority were suspect, and subject to prosecution by the Inquisitorial branch of the Church. Spain was, for one reason or another, particularly militant and merciless in its treatment of such deviants; nonetheless, there were a number of courageous dissenters who made known their views.

In those times, there were some daring souls who taught a method of mental recollection of God, or Truth, similar to that of the early Gnostics. They advocated a kind of mental quietude and recollection which, today, we would call "meditation"; it involved a simple emptying of the mind in perfect quietude and peace, rather than the deliberate mental engagement in petitionary pleas or visual conceptualizations of Christ. Such a method was taught by a Father Francisco de Osuna in a book published in 1537. He maintained that in such a meditation, one could experience the rising of a divine energy within the body, like the sap rising in a tree-trunk, which led to the transporting of the mind to a union with God. He had, of course, no contact with the Indian Tantric works which describe such an interior process, but had experienced it first-hand for himself.

Within a short time, the Church placed Osuna's book on the Index of prohibited books, and began a campaign of persecution against all such Illuminists, or *Alumbrados*, as they were called. One of the tenets of the *Alumbrados* was that religious ceremonies and verbalized prayers were merely preliminary, and token, practices which were unnecessary to the more spiritually advanced. Naturally, the Church could not tolerate a religious movement over which they did not preside, and over which they had no control; and many such "rebels" were imprisoned or burned at the stake in the effort to wipe out this "insidious heresy." It was in such a dangerous climate of suspicion and anti-mysticism that Juan de la Cruz was born and lived.

He was born Juan de Yepes y Alvarez on June 24, 1542, at Fontiveros, a small village about twenty-four miles northwest of Avila in the district of Old Castille. His father, Gonzalo de Ypes, had been brought up by his uncles at Toledo, his parents having died in his early childhood. The uncles, rich silk merchants, gave Gonzalo a place in their business; but when he fell in love with and married a poor silk weaver, named Catalina Alvarez, his uncles cut him off from the business and their inheritance. Gonzalo settled then with his wife at Fontiveros, until, shortly after Juan's birth, he died, leaving his widow and three sons in great poverty.

Juan endured much privation, even in his childhood; the family had little to eat other than barley bread and lentils, and little clothes or warmth during the cold winters. One of his brothers took ill, and died; and when Juan was six years old, his mother moved with the boys to the neighboring town of Arevalo, and later, in 1551, to Medina del Campo. Because of her dire poverty, Catalina could not afford to care for Juan, and he was therefore boarded at a Church orphanage, where he was well cared for, and taught to read and write.

During this time, Juan was sent out to learn a trade, but after apprenticing to a carpenter, wood sculptor, and printer, it became evident that Juan was not suited to a manual trade.

As a teenager, Juan worked for some time in a charitable hospital as an orderly, tending to the needs of patients in advanced stages of syphilis, while at the same time he attended classes at a Jesuit school, where he studied Latin grammar, history and literature. Juan was an excellent student, and his gentleness and dilligence made him a favorite with the nuns and priests with whom he worked and studied. The priest in charge of the hospital so valued Juan that he offered to assist him through his priesthood if Juan would consent to continue afterward as chaplain to the hospital. But Juan had another calling; at the age of twenty-one, he begged admittance to the Carmelite Order of Santa Ana, and was accepted as a monk in that contemplative Order. A year later, he made his profession, taking the name of Fray Juan de San Matias. But, since he required yet more education to be ordained as a priest, he was sent to the university of Salamanca for a year, where he studied scholastic philosophy and theology; and finally, in 1567, at the age of twenty-five, he was ordained.

It was just at this time that Juan met the nun, Mother Teresa de Jesus, who was then a woman past fifty years of age, and who was later to be recognized as a saint, and known to the world as Teresa of Avila. Mother Teresa had founded, some years before, at Avila, a reformed Order of Carmelite nuns, called the Discalced (barefoot) Carmelites, which was more strictly ascetic and more given to a life of contemplation than the parent Order. She had been searching for a few monks to serve as confessors and guides to her nuns in a second convent to be established at Medina; and, learning of Fray Juan through another priest, Antonio de Heredia, she met with him, and convinced him to join the new, more primitive, Order. This Juan did gladly, for he had been dissatisfied with the laxity of his own Rule, and was eagerly searching for a means to enter into a life more given to solitude and the way of prayer.

The Carmelites traced their ancestry to a group of anchorites who dwelt on Mount Carmel in Palestine in ancient times, and who adopted in the 12th century the strict Rule of Saint Albert, the Latin Patriarch of Jerusalem, which placed special emphasis on poverty, strict enclosure, fasting and prayer. By the mid-thirteenth century, this Rule was relaxed, and again made even more mild in the mid-fifteenth century by order of Pope Eugenius IV. In 1562, Teresa of

Avila founded the Discalced Carmelites, calling for a return to the primitive Rule, a return to the original ideals of the strictly contemplative life. In response to the gereral laxity of the times, many nuns joined Teresa, and her reform movement had quickly expanded and flourished.

The strict tenets of Teresa's new Order were solely directed toward the reformation of the heart, in order that it might receive the grace of divine love, and toward the focusing of the heart's intent on the pursuit of the holy union of the soul with the Divine. Thus, they called for very little of outward works or preaching, but focused entirely on a life of interior recollection and prayer, and a singular devotion to God alone, to the exclusion of all else. In the written Rule for the Reformed Carmelites, it was asserted that:

> Our desire is that they (the members of the Order)
> should be like mirrors, like shining lamps, glowing torches,
> brilliant stars, enlightening and guiding the wanderers in this
> dark world; ... raised above themselves by raptures both in-
> effable and indescribable, ... their senses transformed and more
> exalted than they gererally are in this dark life: their eyes filled
> with tears and their heart with a sweet dew productive of
> abundant fruit. [1]

After another year of theological studies at Salamanca, Juan joined Mother Teresa at Medina, and began his new life, which was to fulfill all the expectations and hopes expressed in the above Rule. In taking this new life, Juan took a new name as well; he was now Fray Juan de la Cruz, Brother John of the Cross. He and Fray Antonio moved into their new priory at the convent, which was nothing more than a broken-down farmhouse, in a place called Duruelo, not far from Fontiveros, Juan's birthplace. Here, along with the few nuns who joined them, they waked, fasted, prayed, and lived under great hardship and penance. This little band of anchorites received much notice from the surrounding communities, and after eighteen months, their population had so outgrown their small quarters that they were abandoned for a larger building in the neighboring village of Mancera.

Juan was then sent as confessor to the nuns at Teresa's original convent in Avila. There, he remained for five years, which were years of great spiritual development for him. Juan was a very small man -- under five feet; but his interior strength and dedication to God were immense. All who came in contact with him were startled by the intensity of his devotion, and the supernatural aura that seemed to surround him. He could speak only of God, and was incessantly carried into an ecstatic trance at the very thought or mention of God. The light and beauty that shone out from him greatly inspired the nuns in his charge; and all, including Mother Teresa, whose confessor he was, were greatly profited by contact with him.

The success and expansion of the Reformed Order was not, however, without its troubles. There were some who, by their zealous penances and unhealthy observances, raised a note of hysteria among the postulants; and, moreover, the spreading fame of the ascetic Order called forth much resentment and opposition from the conservative elements of the Church. Especially fierce was the opposition of the Friars of the Calced, or unreformed, Carmelite Order, who felt that they were being devalued, or even replaced, by the new Order. In retaliation, they petitioned the Carmelite Vicar-general in Italy, and succeeded in producing an order for the dissolution of the Discalced Carmelites. This, however, Mother Teresa was able to block by some political maneuvering of her own, and the tension between the two factions increased.

At this point, Fray Juan and some of his brother monks were kidnapped by the Calced Brothers and were imprisoned for a few days, until being released by an order from the Papal nuncio, Ormaneto, who favored the Discalced monks. However, when Ormaneto died suddenly, the Discalced brothers and nuns were left friendless. In the place of Ormaneto, a new nuncio (Papal representative) was appointed who had no liking for Teresa's new Order; and he ordered the Discalced priests to resign their offices and turn over their charges to the Calced Order. They refused to do this, and, led by Fray Juan and his companion, refused as well to elect as Prioress anyone other than Mother Teresa. This, of course, incensed the Carmelite Vicar-general, and through his emissary, Tostado, he ordered the rebel monks and nuns excommunicated, and a new Prioress sent to replace Teresa.

As a further blow, and to punish the instigators of this rebellion, the general's emissary sent a band of armed men to arrest and carry off Fray Juan and his companion to a Calced priory. There, Juan was flogged mercilessly, and then taken blindfolded to the city of Toledo -- that infamous bastion of the Inquisition. There, a trial was held, presided over by Tostado, in which Juan was charged with disobedience to his superior. Juan respectfully told them that he was under orders from the Papal legacy to retain his office, and that, in any event, he was under obligation to his holy vows to follow the primitive Rule of the Discalced Friars.

Juan was thereupon found guilty of rebellion and contumacy, and condemned to an unspecified term of imprisonment. He was thrown into a closet six feet by ten feet which had served as a privy to an adjoining guest-chamber. This was in December of 1557. His home for the next nine months was this small stone privy-closet, lit only by a small hole at the top. He was given a board covered by a rug to lie on, and was fed on scraps of dry bread and an occasional sardine.

He was given no bath or change of clothes during this entire time, so he became covered by lice and sores. During the winter months, he endured freezing cold, and in the summer months the stifling heat. On Fridays, which were Feast days, he was taken to the refectory where the Friars sat at their table, and made to kneel in the center of the room, taking a bit of dry bread and water like a dog. At this time, the Prior would admonish and taunt Juan with reproaches, after which all the monks would in turn strike him vigorously across his bared shoulders with a cane. Juan bore all this without a word.

It was during this nine months in his tiny cell that Juan wrote down, on scraps of paper given to him by a sympathetic jailer, the verses which were to comprise his most famous and exquisite poetry on the "dark night" of the soul, and its union with its Lord. It was there, in this most wretched physical state, that his mind, freed from all but God, his only solace, experienced that illumination which he calls the "divine marriage" of the soul and God. Much later, when he was asked by a nun if any consolations had been given him during his imprisonment, he replied, "My daughter, one single grace of those that God gave me there could not be paid for by many years of prison."

By August, the heat in his stone dungeon was suffocating, and he felt that he must get away from there or die soon. At this time, he had a dream in which the blessed Virgin appeared to him, and told him that he would soon escape and be free. On this inspiration, he began to look for an opportunity to escape. One day, his jailer, concerned to grant his prisoner a little air, left the door to his cell ajar during the afternoon while the other monks were resting; and Juan crept out of his cell for the first time into the adjoining chamber to peer out the window, and examine his surroundings. His room was in a high castle-like monastery abutting a cliff that jutted up just over the Tagus river. The forward part of the monastery gave into a walled courtyard adjacent to the city walls of Toledo. If he cut up his rug into strips, he thought, he could drop down onto the battlements and make his way to the courtyard, and from there into the city.

Having made his plan, he worked each day that his door was left open, on loosening the screws that held the padlock in place, so that when the time came he could easily force open the door. The time came on August 14. At around two o'clock in the morning, when the two Friars who were staying in the adjoining guest-chamber were asleep, he pushed open his door, and, taking with him his strips of cloth, made his way through the room and out the window, landing on a pile of rocks, only to find himself in a walled courtyard from which there seemed no escape. Finally, however, despite the darkness, he located a low point in the wall and managed to climb over it. After hiding in the city till daybreak, Juan made his way to a Carmelite convent where he was sheltered by sympathetic nuns, and then whisked away to safety the following night.

According to one nun who saw him not long after this, Juan looked "like a dead man, with nothing but skin on his bones, so drained and exhausted he could hardly speak!" But, in time, he recovered, and it was arranged that he be sent as temporary Prior of a hermitage far away on the Andalusian border, where he would be safe from his enemies. Here, amid the quiet splendors of the Spanish countryside, Juan lived very happily for some time in the company of the gentle hermits who dwelt in this remote place. Through the recommendation of Mother Teresa, he also became the confessor to the nuns of a nearby convent. And it was at this time as well that he began to write the commentaries to the few poems which he had written or begun during his imprisonment.

In 1581, the Pope authorized the Discalced Carmelites to form a separate province from that of the Calced brothers and sisters, and they were finally free to develop in their own way. Juan was now Rector of the Carmelite college which he founded at the university of Baeza; and, in 1582, he was sent to Granada as Prior of a new convent. There he remained for three years, teaching, counseling, and giving much time to the completion of his written commentaries on his earlier poems. In 1588, he was made Prior at Segovia, and became an elected officer in the governing body of the Order. From this time on, he became more and more embroiled in the agonizing political machinations going on around him, and more and more frustrated at his impotence to arrest the increasing degeneracy of the Order.

Mother Teresa, on whose contemplative ideals the new Order had been founded, was now dead, and there were many new voices in the Carmelite hierarchy calling for the expansion of the Order, foreign missions, and greater participation in the role of teaching and preaching -- quite opposite to the interior life to which Juan de la Cruz was committed. But Juan was no match for the calculating political expertise of his adversaries in the Order, and the ambitious administrators had their way. The contemplative movement begun by a few brave and solitary souls had snowballed into a large, diversified organization, less interested in sanctity than in its own expansion.

The politically ambitious Vicar-general of the Order, Doria, realizing that Juan was an obstacle to his own complete control of the Order, began contriving to discredit him, so as to put him out of the way. Thus, in the following elections of the Chapter, Juan was overruled by those currying favor with the Vicar-general, and was deprived not only of his office but of his Priory as well, and was sent to a remote and lonely hermitage-farm at La Penuela. Meanwhile, his detractors made every effort to collect evidence of some misdeed on his part as a pretext for stripping him of his habit. In addition, the Inquisitorial branch of the Church was simultaneously engaged in a thorough examination of his teachings on the grounds of suspicion that he was practicing the *Alumbrado*, or Illuminist, heresy.

However, his detrators were never to have their way. Juan contracted a fever from an inflammation on his right foot shortly after arriving at La Penuela, and very soon thereafter tumors began appearing all over his body. The Prior of Ubeda, in whose infirmary Juan sought treatment, had long held a grudge against him and made Juan's last days as bitterly uncomfortable and harsh as possible. And on the 14th of December, 1591, Juan died.

It is said that the sweet fragrance emitting from his body was such that people came from all around to touch it, or to steal a piece of cloth or bandage which had been on his person. And even nine months later, when Juan's body was disinterred for reburial, still it had not decayed, and still it gave forth a sweet aroma. In their eagerness to have a relic of the saint, various factions claimed his fingers, toes, and eventually all his limbs, leaving only a head and torso to be enshrined at Segovia. Indeed, it was because of the evidence of holiness in his life and in his death, and the popular outcry for his beatification, that Juan's enemies were prevented from destroying his written works and erasing his name from the pages of history.

Today, Juan's small collection of mystical verse is recognized by conoisseurs of literature as the jewel in the crown of Spanish poetry; yet Juan was not primarily, or deliberately, a poet. His few verses were not contrived as literature, but spilled out of his heart as an attempt to give expression to his inexpressible experiences of interior grace, and the meeting, or union, with his beloved God. On their own, they are very beautiful in their simple and economical style; but the fullness of their meaning, in all its rich complexity, was necessarily so obscure, owing to their brevity and symbolism, that Juan felt impelled to write lengthy and elaborate commentaries explaining them verse by verse. It is by these poems and their illuminating commentaries that we know of the depths and heights to which Fray Juan attained; and it is by them that we are possessed of an unparalleled guide for the soul on its journey to union with God.

Juan's prose works, each corresponding to one of his short poems, are *The Ascent of Mount Carmel, The Dark Night* (which was intended as part of *The Ascent*), *The Spiritual Canticle*, and *The Living Flame Of Love.* The path he expounds in these works is not, in the least way, different from that shown by the devotional saints of all religious traditions; his distinction lies, rather, in the keen clarity of his perception of the progressive psychological stages along the way, and the amazingly lucid and convincing way in which he describes these stations. Anyone who has travelled the path of divine love -- whether Hindu, Jew, Buddhist or Sufi -- must stand in awe, and thrill with delight, before these written works of Fray Juan de la Cruz; for no more true and perfect description of the mystical path of devotion could ever be imagined.

One who is searching for worldly pleasure, success, or applause, will not find the path to these among his pages. The goal of the mystic is Truth, God, the Highest -- in short, the ultimate perfection and beatitude. For the lover, all this is summed as "union with the Beloved." To be united with God is to be dis-united with the separative ego; to see the one Self is to become blind to the desires and appetites of the individual self. The knowledge, pleasure, and enjoyment of God is obtained internally and not externally; and therefore the knowledge, pleasure and enjoyment of the phenomenal world is not included in it. Just as one who looks eastward cannot see the west, and one who looks westward cannot see the east, likewise,

those who look to the Eternal, the Absolute, do so only by looking
away from the transient, the phenomenal; and those who look to the
transient, phenomenal world necessarily look away from the Eternal.
Make no mistake: though these two are undoubtedly complementary
aspects of the same one Reality, they are, to the vision, mutually
exclusive. Juan expresses this fact in this way:

> The high things of God are foolishness and madness
> to man... Hence the wise men of God and the wise men of
> the world are foolish in the eyes of each other, for to the one
> group, the wisdom and knowledge of God is imperceivable,
> and to the other, the knowledge of the world is imperceivable.
> Wherefore the knowledge of the world is ignorance to the
> knowledge of God, and the knowledge of God is ignorance to
> the knowledge of the world. [2]

The wisdom of God lies in a direction opposite to the wisdom
of the world, but to the normally active and outgoing mind, such a
180° turn-around is as difficult as holding back a raging river or a
dozen wild horses.   To Juan, this total denial of the outgoing
tendencies of the mind and will is like a "dark night" for the soul.
And in his poem, called *The Dark Night,* he tells of the journey of the
soul to union with God in allegorical terms, describing a midnight
rendezvous of a lover with her beloved. In his commentary on this
poem, he explains that he describes this journey as taking place on a
dark night because, in setting out on this journey, the soul must be
emptied of all appetite or desire for what belongs to the phenomenal
world; and this, to the soul, is like darkness. Secondly, the path itself
is dark, as it may not be negotiated by the light of the reasoning
intellect, but in the darkness of faith alone. Thirdly, says Juan, God,
Himself, the Objective and End of the journey, is profound darkness
to the mind and senses accustomed to the light of the world.
      The necessity of a one-pointed focus of the soul toward God,
and therefore a renunciation of all other objectives, is declared by all
the saints who have ever reached that Goal to be absolutely essential to
success. Meister Eckhart and Thomas á Kempis seemed never to tire
of repeating this truth; and Juan de la Cruz devotes almost the whole
of his book, *The Ascent Of Mount Carmel,* to making clear that one
who wishes to know God must be ready to renounce all other desires
and goals:

Now a man may be striving for a perfect union in this life through grace with That to which through glory he will be united in the next. But, manifestly, the perfect union in this life through grace and love demands that he live in darkness to all the objects of sight, hearing, imagination, and everything comprehensible to the heart, that is, to the soul.

A man, then, is decidedly hindered from the attainment of this high state of union with God when he is attached to any understanding, feeling, imagining, opinion, desire, or way of his own, or to any other of his works or affairs, and knows not how to detach and denude himself of these impediments. His goal transcends all of this, even the loftiest object that can be known or experienced. Consequently, he must pass beyond everything to unknowing. [3]

To deprive oneself of the gratification of the appetites in all things is like living in darkness and in a void. ... Hence, we call this nakedness a night for the soul. For we are not discussing the mere lack of things; this lack will not divest the soul, if it [still] craves for all these objects. We are dealing with the denudation of the soul's appetites and gratifications; this is what leaves it free and empty of all things, even though it possesses them. Since the things of the world cannot enter the soul, they are not in themselves an encumbrance or harm to it; rather, it is the will and appetite dwelling within it that causes the damage. [4]

... To reach satisfaction in all, desire its possession in nothing. To come to possess all, desire the possession of nothing. To arrive at being all, desire to be nothing. To come to the knowledge of all, desire the knowledge of nothing. To come to the pleasure you have not, you must go by a way of no pleasure. To come to the knowledge you have not, you must go by a way of unknowing. To come to the possession you have not, you must go by a way of poverty. To come to be what you are not, you must go by a way of non-existence.[5]

... The road and ascent to God, then, necessarily demands a habitual effort to renounce and mortify the appetites; the sooner this mortification is achieved, the sooner the soul reaches the top. But until the appetites are eliminated, a person will not arrive, no matter how much virtue he practices. For he will fail to acquire perfect virtue, which lies in keeping the soul empty, naked, and purified of every appetite.[6]

... Until slumber comes to the appetites through the mortification of sensuality, and until this very sensuality is stilled in such a way that the appetites do not war against the spirit, the soul will not walk out to genuine freedom, to the enjoyment of union with its Beloved. [7]

In addition to the renunciation of the appetites, there is yet another, complementary, ingredient in the successful attainment of union with God; and that is grace. Grace is, of course, ever-present, and is the hand that upholds an aspirant every step of the way; but the grace of divine love, the grace of extreme longing for God, is a very special and highly significant grace. The desire for God, says Juan, "is the preparation for union with Him. ... If a person is seeking God, his Beloved is seeking him much more. And if a soul directs to God its loving desires, God sends forth His fragrance by which He draws it and makes it run after Him." [8] And yet this love is an afflictive and joyless love, until it is consummated; for, though it enters sweetly, it brings the soul near to death before its work is done:

> The very fire of love which afterwards is united with the soul, glorifying it, is that which previously assails it by purging it, just as the fire that penetrates a log of wood is the same that first makes an assault upon it, wounding it with its flame, drying it out, and stripping it of its unsightly qualities until it is so disposed that it can be penetrated and transformed into the fire.
>
> Spiritual writers call this activity the purgative way. In it a person suffers great deprivation and feels heavy afflictions in his spirit, which ordinarily overflow into the senses, for this flame is extremely oppressive.
>
> In this preparatory purgation, the flame is not bright for a person, but dark. If it does shed some light, the only reason is that the soul may see its miseries and defects. It is not gentle, but afflictive. Even though it sometimes imparts the warmth of love, it does so with torment and pain. And it is not delightful, but dry. Although sometimes out of His goodness, God accords some delight in order to strengthen and encourage it, the soul suffers for this before and afterwards with another trial. Neither is the flame refreshing and peaceful, but it is consuming and contentious, making a person faint and suffer with self-knowledge. Thus, it is not glorious for the soul, but rather makes it feel wretched and distressed in the spiritual light of self-knowledge which it bestows.
>
> At this stage a person suffers from sharp trials in his intellect, severe dryness and distress in his will, and from the burdensome knowledge of his own miseries in his memory, for his spiritual eye gives him a very clear picture of himself. In the substance of his soul he suffers abandonment, supreme poverty, dryness, cold, and sometimes heat. He finds relief in nothing, nor is there a thought that consoles him, nor can he even raise his heart to God, so oppressed is he by this flame.

... A person's sufferings at this time cannot be exaggerated;
they are but little less than the sufferings of purgatory. [9]

Yet, as the soul draws nearer to God, through this infused flame of love, its suffering grows even more intense as it longs solely for the consummation of that love, in the perfect meeting with the Beloved. Brought, by grace, to utter humility and nothingness, it is prepared to make that final ascent:

> The soul, through love, is brought to nothing, and
> knows nothing save love ... accompanied by a kind of im-
> mense torment and yearning to see God. So extreme is this
> torment that Love seems to be unbearably rigorous with the
> soul, not because He has wounded her ... but because He left
> her thus, suffering with love, and did not slay her for the sake
> of seeing and being united with Him in the life of perfect
> love. [10]

Only when the soul is brought to this state of yearning is it truly able, by its proximate intimacy, to ask in heart-felt earnest:

> Reveal Your presence,
> And may the vision of Your beauty be my death;
> For the sickness of love
> Is not cured
> Except by Your very presence and image!

> The soul, desiring to be possessed by this immense
> God, for love of Whom she feels that her heart is robbed and
> wounded, unable to endure her sickness any longer, deliberately
> asks Him ... to show her His beauty, His divine essence, and
> to kill her with this revelation, and thereby free her from the
> flesh since she cannot see and enjoy Him as she wants. She
> makes this request by displaying before Him the sickness and
> yearning of her heart, in which she perseveres suffering for
> love of Him, unable to find a cure in anything less than this
> glorious vision of His divine essence. [11]

Juan speaks of this state of the soul from his own experience, and it is the experience of all who have attained the vision of God through the path of divine love. It is because of their universality that his writings endure as a supremely valuable encouragement and guide to all seekers of Truth. When Juan speaks of his experience of "union," however, it is clear that he is under certain restraints, owing to the position of the Church on such matters. He had attained the highest enlightenment, and the most sublime heights of spiritual vision, yet he remained very cautious in the written expression of this highest of realizations.   Had he spoken more distinctly about his experience of "union,"   he would surely have been charged with heresy.

In order to speak at all of the experience of the unity of God and the soul, and yet at the same time uphold the ultimate Dualism between the soul and God, which was (and is) a basic tenet of his Church, he said that, in the spiritual union, the soul "feels" like it is one with God; the soul "feels" that everything in the world is God. And on many occasions, he found it most prudent to say, simply, that, "what God communicates to the soul in this intimate union is totally beyond words."

Juan would never have thought of declaring that the soul, in its experience of union, realizes its essential unity with God. He knew very well that to do so would have sealed not only his own fate but the fate of his writings as well. Even so -- cautious and guarded as he was in his choice of words -- Juan was not able to elude the suspicion of the Inquisitors, nor the subtle influence of their looming presence. Several of his major prose works are presented to us today, minus their final chapters; either Juan deliberately broke off his writing prior to commenting on the final verses of his poems, which deal with the experience of "union," or his writings on this theme were regarded as so dangerous by his censors that they were destroyed after his death. Whichever is the case, it is clear that the powerful hand of "the defenders of the faith" played a role in molding the written express- ion of Juan's experience of God. Here is what Juan *does* say (with the editorial help of his censors) about his experience of oneness with God:

> What God communicates to the soul in this intimate union is totally beyond words. One can say nothing about it just as one can say nothing about God Himself that resembles Him. For in the transformation of the soul in God, it is God who communicates Himself with admirable glory. In this transformation, the two become one, as we would say of the window united with the ray of sunlight, or of the coal with the fire, or of the starlight with the light of the Sun. [12]
> ... The soul thereby becomes divine, becomes God, through participation, insofar as is possible in this life.
> ... The union wrought between the two natures, and the com- munication of the divine to the human in this state is such that even though neither changes their being, both appear to

be God. [13]

Juan was a supremely great spiritual Master, a devotional saint
of the highest order. His experiences, many previously uncharted in
Christian doctrines, would be more recognizable in the context of the
scriptures of the Tantric yogis. In *The Spiritual Canticle*, for example,
he speaks, in couched terms, of the awakening of the inner fire (the
Kundalini-Shakti), its purifying course through the subtle nerves, the
piercing of the lotuses, or chakras, and the attendant opening of these
psychic centers, revealing super-natural "virtues" in the soul.   He
speaks of the hearing of the inner music, and the tasting of the inner
nectar, familiar to yogis who have managed to awaken their higher
spiritual centers. And he speaks of the permanent "liberation" which
is experienced by one who is habitually experiencing "union"   with
God:

> Having been made one with God, the soul is some-
> how God through participation. Although it is not God as
> perfectly as it will be in the next life, it is like the shadow of
> God. Being the shadow of God through this substantial trans-
> formation, it performs in this measure in God and through God
> what He, through Himself, does in it. For the will of the two
> is one will, and thus God's operation and the soul's is one. [14]
> ... When there is union of love, the image of the
> Beloved is so sketched in the will and drawn so vividly, that it
> is true to say that the Beloved lives in the lover and the lover
> in the Beloved. Love produces such likeness in this transform-
> ation of lovers that one can say each is the other and both are
> one. The reason is, that in the union and transformation of
> love, each gives possession of self to the other, and each
> leaves and exchanges self for the other. Thus each one lives
> in the other and is the other, and both are one in the transform-
> ation of love. [15]
> ... Thus, no one ... can disturb the soul that is liber-
> ated and purged of all things and united with God. She enjoys
> now in this state a habitual sweetness and tranquility which
> is never lost or lacking to her. [16]

The testimony of Juan de la Cruz's attainment is not only in
his writings but in his life. He was truly a man transformed, by love,
in God; and all who came in contact with him were awed by the
glorious light of his presence. He was the epitome of the *jivan-mukta,*
the *bodhisattva,* the *faqr,* and the *parabhakta*. Here, in his pure and
simple style, he sings of that Love which was his sole quest, his

precious attainment, and his ultimate Identity:

> In the inner wine cellar
> I drank of my Beloved; and, when I went abroad
> Through all this valley,
> I no longer knew anything,
> And lost the herd which I was following.
>
> There He gave me His breast;
> There He taught me a sweet and living knowledge;
> And I gave myself to Him,
> Keeping nothing back.
> There I promised to be His bride.
>
> Now I occupy my soul
> And all my energy in His service;
> I no longer tend the herd,
> Nor have I any other work
> Now that my every act is love. [17]

> ... What more do you want, O soul! And what else
> do you search for outside, when within yourself you possess
> your riches, delights, satisfactions, fullness, and kingdom --
> your Beloved whom you desire and seek? Be joyful and glad-
> dened in your interior recollection with Him, for you have
> Him so close to you. Desire Him there, adore Him there. Do
> not go in pursuit of Him outside yourself. You will only
> become distracted and wearied thereby, and you shall not find
> Him, nor enjoy Him more securely, nor sooner, nor more
> intimately than by seeking Him within you. [18]

KABIR

As we turn once again to India, several truly great represent-atives of the mystical tradition stand out during the period of the 15th and 16th centuries. One of these is the universally celebrated poet-saint, Kabir.

Of the life of Kabir (1440-1510), very little is known, despite the abundance of legends surrounding him. He is said to have been born in Benares, India, to a Muslim family, but they may have been low-caste Hindus who had recently converted to Islam in name only, as was the case of many in those times of Muslim oppression. His father was named Niru, and his mother, Nimá. Of his childhood and youth we know nothing. It is apparent, however, from the evidence of his later life, that he must have gained some education and experience of both Hindu and Muslim religious teachings. He speaks lovingly, in his poetry, of his Guru; but who that Guru was is not known. The legend which tells of his having received spiritual initiation from the famous Hindu Guru, Ramananda, is dubious; since Ramananda preceded Kabir by perhaps a century.

Also, his marital status is unclear; some biographies, written long after his lifetime, claim that Kabir was married, and that he had two children -- a boy, Kamal, and a girl, Kamali. Others say he was a *brahmacharya*, a celibate, who never married. Some say his family-trade was that of weavers, and that Kabir also practiced this trade. But, in fact, the only suggestion of this is Kabir's reference to himself in one of his songs as "the weaver of Kashi," which may have been only a reference to his caste.

Kabir, it seems, lived at least part of his life in Benares, a city teeming with people of both Hindu and Muslim faiths. Benares, known to the Hindus as Varanasi, or Kashi, was, to orthodox brahmins, a holy city of grand temples and bathing ghats even before the coming of the Buddha in the 5th century B.C.E. For many centuries thereafter, it was honored by Buddhists as the place of the Buddha's first Sermon, and many stupas and monasteries were located there. Later, when the Muslim conquerors came to India, the city was captured by them and renamed Benares. It became the home of many ornate mosques, and a place of pilgrimage to the faithful of Islam. Thus, over the centuries, Benares has been a holy gathering place for the worshipful of the Hindu, Buddhist, and Muslim traditions.

In the late 15th and early 16th centuries, during the lifetime of Kabir, Benares was still under Muslim domination, but, by this time, the community of Islam had reconciled itself to co-existing peacefully alongside the large Hindu population; and thus the city was, as it is today, a great melting-pot of diverse cultures and religious sects. Hindus carried on their worship and their ritual bathings, while nearby the mullahs called the faithful of Islam to prayer from the mosque-tops. Privilege still fell to the Muslims, however; and to avoid the *jiziya* tax imposed on the Hindu subjects, and perhaps to escape the stigma of a low caste as well, many families officially converted to Islam, while retaining much of their Hindu customs and cultural heritage.

In those days, as now, both the Hindu and Muslim popula-tions consisted almost entirely of orthodox religionists for whom religion meant the practice of those traditional observations and ritu-als associated with their own sectarian heritage. Most of those pandits and mullahs with whom Kabir came in contact, it seems, were of this type. Kabir, who had plumbed the depths of mystical vision, who had known the one Self, no doubt felt as though he were in a world of madmen, and that he was totally surrounded by stupidity and religious bigotry on every side. Thus, if Kabir seems a bit strident, a bit too critical of the popular mentality and the prevailing exclusivism of both the Hindu and the Muslim religious leaders, we must remember his time and his circumstances.

In an age and in a place where all men believed their own exclusive rituals and practices to be the be-all and end-all of religious accomplishment, and fought bitterly with one another over such trivialities, Kabir felt impelled to speak, in order to urge the peoples of both faiths to go beyond mere outward practices, and onward to the full transformation of the mind, toward the ultimate goal of oneness with the one all-pervading Being. What separated Hindu from Muslim, he explained, was merely the differences in their traditional names and rituals; the goal was one and the same for all men, what-ever means they adopted to achieve it.

From the vantage point of that absolute Unity, the sectarian practices of either faction could justifiably be regarded as absurd. The Hindu's bowing to a stone idol, or the telling of beads, if the purpose of mental one-pointedness on God was forgotten, was truly useless and absurd; as was the Muslim's practice of pilgrimage and ritual prayer. Kabir had no intention of entering into dispute with such people, nor of disparaging the genuine efforts of anyone. He merely wished to point out to both Hindu and Muslim that the aim of both their earnest endeavors was the awareness of the one Truth, the same one and only Reality. For this, he said, it is best to obtain the guidance of one who has already attained that awareness -- a Guru, or a Pir, who could guide them correctly to the attainment of God.

As he, himself, was such a knowing Guru, he offered this advice to all who cared to follow it: 'Keep the mind rooted in Truth by the steadfast remembrance of God; keep His name continually in your mind by repeating it with every breath. The mind will thereby become colored with God-awareness; and all will be seen as it truly is: as God.' For Kabir, the name of God was *Rama* or *Hari*; but he acknowledged that other names were equally suitable, so long as it brought to mind the one Lord, the common Truth of all being. 'In this way, ' said Kabir, 'the mind will be prepared for the vision of God. For, when the mind becomes so colored with the name of God that it sees, in the daylight hours, nothing but God manifest in every form, and, in the hours of darkness, remains fastened to God in His secret inner recesses, it will become entirely merged in God, and know itself as that infinite and eternal One.'

Kabir has often been accused of being critical to both Muslims and Hindus, but his criticism is really aimed toward all those partisans of orthodoxy of every religious persuasion who hold their small sectarian views and practices to be the only correct ones, and somehow more divinely sanctioned than any others. To Kabir, this was only politics. He had clearly experienced the one Reality which Muslims call by the name of Karim, and Hindus call Ram; and he knew that there was only one Truth, and one alone. Furthermore, he could say with all certainty that the knowledge of the Truth was to be obtained, not through this or that ritual observance, but through an inner reformation of the heart, and a one-pointed devotion to God within oneself.

Strictly speaking, Kabir was neither Muslim nor Hindu -- if we consider those designations to signify a person who follows the externals of this or that religious tradition. Kabir was a Self-realized sage; he had passed beyond all sectarian notions, beyond all names and forms, and rested in the supreme knowledge of the one, nameless, Reality. Sometimes, however, in order to get across the point that the God of the Muslims and the God of the Hindus was one, he spoke of

his Lord as "Ram-Allah." And, not surprisingly, both the pandits
and the mullahs were offended and incensed by this attempt of his to
associate the one with the other. Having no understanding beyond
their own learned traditions, each faction felt that their basic beliefs
were being trampled and blasphemed. To brahmins, he was a *mleccha*
(outcaste), and to devout Muslims, he was a *kafr* (infidel).

Kabir was thereupon called to answer for his teachings by
some angered mullahs, and was brought before Sikander Lodi, the
Sultan, at Jaunpur. The learned representatives of orthodoxy wanted
to make an example of him, but the Sultan, apparently swayed by
reason, refused to prosecute him. Instead, Kabir was told to leave the
city of Benares, and take his philosophy elsewhere. Thereafter, Kabir
wandered for some time around the area of Jaunpur, and in Manikpur
and Jhusi as well.

The dates of Kabir's birth and death vary; some say he lived
from 1398 to 1448; others say it was 1440 to 1510. Most accounts
agree, however, that, after much wandering, teaching, and gathering of
disciples, he died in the city of Maghar, in the district of Gorakpur. It
is really not necessary to know all the details of the life and death of a
saint, of course; the lives of those who have attained the Eternal take
place beyond their external circumstances, and they, themselves, attach
little importance to time or place. Kabir's testament of Truth is
identical to that of all others like him, and his voice is indistinguishable from those of all other true lovers and knowers of God.

It is ironic that today Kabir is regarded as a great Guru of the
Hindus, and a great Pir of the Muslims. Legend has it that when he
died, his Hindu followers wished to cremate his body, while the
Muslim followers wished to bury him, according to their separate
customs. While thus arguing, one mourner lifted the shroud covering
Kabir's body, and behold! the body had disappeared; and in its place
were two bouquets of flowers, one for the Hindus and one for the
Muslims.

Today, Kabir is known and honored throughout the world for
his many intensely provocative songs. Not one of them, however, was
written down by Kabir; they were transmitted orally for nearly a
century before being written down by his followers for the enjoyment
and enlightenment of succeeding generations. Several independent
collections of these songs exist; one, called the *Bijak*, is the sacred
book of the Kabir Panth, the sect of Kabir's present-day followers.
Another collection is included in the holy book of the Sikhs, called

the *Adi Guru Granth*; and yet another group of songs, of questionable authenticity, was compiled by the Dadu Panthis, the followers of the 16th century saint, Dadu, and is called the *Kabir Granthavali*.

Why did Kabir sing so many songs? Why did Jnaneshvar? Or Dattatreya? Or Milarepa? Not solely, as some might think, for the purpose of saving the world. No; the world is already saved. It is always securely in the hands of God. No; they sang because the Truth requires to be sung. It is the nature of God to express Himself as this world; and it is the nature of those who have known their identity with God to sing of Him and His presence. Their singing and the effect of their singing, they leave in the hands of God. For such men, what Jnaneshvar said is perfectly true: "There is no bondage or liberation; there is nothing to accomplish. There is only the joy of expounding."

Following, is a brief selection of Kabir's sayings and songs taken from the sources mentioned above:

> You and I are of one blood; one life exists in us
> both. From one mother the world is born; what then is this
> sense of separateness? We have all come from the same
> country; we all drink from the same fountain; yet the ignorant
> divide us into innumerable sects. [1]

Does [the Muslim's God] Khuda, live only in the mosque?
Is [the Hindu's God] Ram, only in idols and holy grounds?
Have you searched and found Him there?
You imagine that Hari [Vishnu] is in the East, and Allah is in
    the West;
But search for Him only in the heart -- that is where Ram and
Karim both live.
Which, then, is false, the Quran or the Vedas? False is the
man who does not see the Truth.
It is One; It is the same One in all. How can you imagine
that It is two?
Says Kabir: O Lord, every man and every woman are Your
own forms;
I am the simple child of Allah-Ram; He is my Guru, my Pir.[2]

Brother, where did your two gods come from? Ram, Allah;
Keshav, Karim; Hari, Hazrat -- so many names!
There may be many golden ornaments, but there is one gold;
it has no two-ness in it.
Merely for the sake of exposition, we make of the One, two.

Mahadev, Muhammed; Brahma, Adam; Hindu, Turk; all the
same earth.
Vedas, Quran; mullahs, brahmins; many names, but the pots
are all made of the same clay.
Kabir says: both sides are engaged in disputing; neither
attains to Ram.
One slaughters goats, one slaughters cows; they squander
their lives in argument. [3]

The river and its waves are the same; where is the difference
between the wave and the water?
When it rises it is water; when it falls it is water. Tell me,
where is there any distinction?
... So many bodies, so many opinions! But my Beloved,
though invisible, is in all these bodies.
There is no life at all without the Beloved; the Self lives as
            each and every one.
What, then, O friend, are you searching for like a fool?
The object of your quest is within you, as the oil is in the
sesame seed.
As the pupil is in the eye, so is the Lord in the body;
The deluded do not know Him, and search for Him without. [4]

The lock of error shuts the gate; open it with the key of Love.
By opening the door, you shall wake the Beloved.
Kabir says: O brother, do not pass by such good fortune as
this! [5]

Are you ready to cut off your head and place your foot on it?
If so, come; Love awaits you!
Love is not grown in a garden, nor sold in the marketplace;
Whether you are a king or a servant, the price is your head,
and nothing less.
Yes, the cost of the elixer of love is your head!
Do you hesitate? O miser, It is cheap at that price! [6]

Love based on a desire for gain is worthless.
God is desireless; how could one with desire attain the
Desireless?
When I was conscious of individual existence, the love of
the Master filled my heart;
When the love of the Master filled my heart, my sense of
selfhood was dissolved.
O Kabir, this path is too narrow for two to travel. [7]

O brothers, the love of God is sweet! It is conferred by the

Master, and grows sweeter every day.
Wherever I go, I offer obeissance to the Lord; whatever I do
is an act of worship to Him.
In sleep, I reverence Him; I bow my head to no other. Whatever I utter is His name.
Whatever I hear reminds me of Him; whatever I eat or drink
is to His honor.
To me, society and solitude are one; for all feelings of duality
have left me.
I have no need to practice austerity, for I see Him smiling
everywhere as the supreme Beauty in every form.
Whether sitting, walking, or performing actions, my heart
remains pure, for my mind remains fixed on God.
Says Kabir: I have experienced the divine state, beyond both
joy and suffering; and I am absorbed in That.
O brothers, the love of God is sweet! [8]

This swan has taken its flight to the great lake beyond the
mountains; it no longer needs to search for the ponds
or pools.
Your Lord lives within you; what do you search for outside?
Kabir says: Listen, O brother, the Lord who has ravished my
eyes, has united Himself with me. [9]

Rama has possessed me; Hari has enchanted me! All my
doubts have flown like migratory birds in winter.
When I was mad with pride, the Beloved did not speak to me;
But when I put on the robe of humility, the Master opened
my inner eye,
Dyeing every pore of my body in the color of love.
Drinking the elixer from the cup of my emptied heart, I
slept on His bed in divine ecstasy.
The devotee meets Hari as gold meets a gold-solvent; the
pure heart melts into its Lord. [10]

O scholars, you are mistaken; there's no creator or creation
there [in the experience of Unity].
There's no radiant form, no time, no word, no flesh, or faith;
no cause or effect, or even a thought of the Vedas.
There's no Hari or Brahma, no Shiva or Shakti, no pilgrim-
ages or rituals;
There is no mother, no father, no Guru; think! Is it two
or is It One?
Kabir says: If you understand this, you are the teacher and
I am the disciple. [11]

There, what form or shape is there to describe? What second, what "other," is there to see?
In the beginning, there is no Aum, or Veda. Who can trace His birth?
There, no sky exists, no moon or Sun; no father's seed, no air, fire, water, or earth.
Who can name Him, or know His will? Who can say from whence He comes?
Remembering the Void, the simple One, a light burst forth [within me]; I offer myself to that Existence who is non-existence. [12]

Whatever he does, the wise man retains the awareness that he is the Self; the ignorant, even though they practice virtue, remain in bondage.
In the middle of the inner sky, there is a flame shining; It is not the doer, nor does It speak.
If I say, "He is One," it is a lie; if I say, "He is two," I am guilty of slander.
Kabir knows Him as He is, but cannot express Him.
The devotee who can stay in that place where the Invisible
             and the manifest are one,
Like a lamp in the doorway, illumines both what is within and what is without.
As a piece of cloth is not different from the threads which comprise it,
So Brahman is not different from the world, and the world is not different from Brahman.
O Kabir, there is no difference between the world, the Creator, and Brahman; Brahman is in all and all is in Brahman.
The fire is one, whether it burns in a lamp or a torch; so Brahman is all, and in Him exist all souls, God, and the world.
Unity is the essence of the teachings of all the saints;
Laugh at Kabir if you do not become perfect by living in accord with this truth! [13]

NANAK

The same social conditions which spawned a Kabir gave birth, around the same time, to a number of similarly inclined, albeit lesser gifted, sages throughout India. One such figure was the Hindu sage, Nanak, whose teachings are virtually indistinguishable from Kabir's. While he offered nothing outstandingly original, his songs reveal him to be a devout and sincere mystic; and his place in history as the first Guru of the Sikhs earns for him a place in our story.

Prior to the 19th century, when the biographers and hagiographers of India began to glean from the West a sense of the need for accuracy, forthrightness, and objectivity in dealing with historical data, nearly all saintly biographies from that land suffered from the overzealousness of their devout, but too imaginative, authors. They are frequently so embellished with fanciful stories of supernatural occurrances, and imaginary conversations and events, that it is usually very difficult to separate out the few facts from the abundance of fictions. The extant biographies of Nanak are no exception to this rule. They were written by Sikh partisans of the 16th century who, possessing the bare bones of the facts about the life of their hero, felt the need to enhance their story with elaborate invention in the interest of exalting Nanak to a position of assured reverence. Once we strip off the flabby flesh of improbable phantasy, the bare bones of the story of Nanak seem to be the following:

Nanak (1469-1539) was born in early May of 1469 to a Khatri farmer named Kalu in the small jungle village of Talwandi, which is now called Nanakana, and is located on the banks of the Ravi river, about fifty-five miles northwest of Lahore in the Punjab (now a territory of Pakistan). As a child, Nanak attended school, and tended cows for his father. It seems that he did not care much for the rural life, however, and proved of little use to his father. As he seemed unfit or unwilling to adopt the life of a farmer and herdsman, he went to live at Sultanpur, with a brother-in-law, named Jairam, who held a post there as a petty government officer. Nanak, through his brother-in-law, also obtained a post with the government, as a stewart, or storekeeper, in the Commissariat. Shortly thereafter, at the age of eighteen, he became married.

Nanak's was not a happy marriage; it seems his wife was something of a nag, and often accused him of improvidence. The fact was, however, that Nanak, in his position of storekeeper at the government Commissariat, was able to generously supply some needy families with extra food and occasional monetary help; and because of his charitable generosity, he was unable to provide luxuries for his own family. Despite his apparently growing disinterest in his wife, however, Nanak fathered two sons; Sri-chand, when he was thirty-two years of age, and Lakshmi-das, four years later. By this time, he had worked at the Commissariat for sixteen years.

It was during this time at Sultanpur, while working at the Commissariat, that Nanak began to awake to the spiritual life, and took to joining with a Muslim friend, named Mardana, in singing devotional songs and attending religious lectures. It was around this time also that Nanak apparently came near to drowning in a canal where he regularly bathed; and this near-death experience generated in him a profound spiritual awareness of the eternal Self. Thereafter, he proclaimed to his friends and family that he had been taken up to God, and had known Him directly. He was utterly transformed by the experience, and inspired to teach others of the all-pervasive God whom he had known. Thereupon, he quit his job, and, renouncing worldly life, set out as a religious mendicant, taking his Muslim friend, Mardana, with him.

It is reported that once, during his wanderings, he was taken prisoner for a time by the armed troops of the then Sultan, Babar. It was still a time of Muslim conquest, and everywhere throughout the Punjab, and in other parts of India as well, cities were being burned and pillaged, Hindu temples razed, and many citizens murdered or enslaved. Nanak sings in his poetry of the times and the terrible plight of the people suffering under the Muslim yoke; and especially of those of the households of the Hindu nobility, the once-wealthy and proud, the princes and princesses, who were now slaves of their captors:

> The tresses that adorned these lovely heads,
> And were parted with vermillion,
> Have been shorn with cruel shears;
> Dust has been thrown on their shaven heads.
> They lived in ease in palaces,
> Now they must beg by the roadside,
> Having no place for their shelter.
> Glory unto Thee, O Lord of Glory!
> Who can understand Thy ways, O God?

Surely Thy ways and dispensations are strange!

When these whose heads are shorn were married,
Fair indeed seemed their bridegrooms beside them.
They were brought home in palanquins carved of ivory.
Pitchers of water were waved over their heads
In ceremonial welcome.
Ornate and glittering fans waved above them.

At the first entry into their new homes,
Each bride was offered a gift of a thousand rupees;
Another thousand they received when each took her post in
her new home;
Coconut shreddings and raisins were among the delicious
          delicacies served to them at their tables.
These beauties once lent charm to the couches on which
they reclined;
Now they are dragged away, with ropes 'round their necks,
Their necklaces snapped and their pearls scattered.

Their beauty and wealth were once their greatest assets;
Now their beauty and wealth are their greatest liabilities.
Barbarous soldiers have taken them as prisoners and disgraced
them.
God casts down, God exalts, whomsoever He will.

If these people had taken heed to the future,
Need they have been reduced to such a plight?
Pursuing worldly love and sensual pleasure,
The princes of Hindustan have lost their heads.
Desecration and desolation follow in the footsteps of the
great Moghal, Babar.
None, none in Hindustan can eat his supper in peace.

... Few, some very few,
From this havoc return home,
And others enquire of them
About their lost dear ones.
Many are lost forever,
And weeping and anguish are the lot of those who survive.
Ah, Nanak, how completely helpless mere men are!
It is God's will that is done, for ever and ever. [1]

In nearly every song of Nanak's, we may find this same
declaration of the dependence of man upon the will of God. Men
who have not experienced the one all-pervasive Reality directly find
this view difficult to comprehend or to accept; for it seems to them to

negate the independence of man's will, and to foster an attitude of
fatalism and a lack of initiative. But those who, like Nanak, have seen
the Truth, know, with a certainty beyond all doubt, that He is the only
one who exists anywhere, and that all is done in perfect accordance
with his will; that, in fact, He is doing everything. Says Nanak:

> By His will all is created;
> Through His will, all life pulsates.
> Under His will, death has dominion
> Over all creation and all life.
> By His will also the blessed abide in His eternal Truth.
> All-pervasive, omnipotent, is His will;
> Such, O Nanak, is the helplessness of man. [2]

This unwavering surety that nothing occurs that is not done by
the One, is the mark of the true mystic. To the claim that this view is
detrimental to initiative, the mystic asks, "Since He is doing everything, why should initiative be excluded from His creation? Does He
manifest in every way except only initiative?" the man who takes
God's will as his own, does not cease to will; he wills, but it is God who
wills through him. And he who has seen the Truth recognizes that he
cannot will other than what God wills; he is so one with God, that to
will against God's will would be to will against himself -- and there is
no will in him for that. When we assert our freedom of will, it is
God's freedom in us that we assert, for he is our soul, our Self. We
are aware of our freedom to will, but we cannot will against what that
supreme Intelligence within us shows us is our true good. Thus, while
we are ultimately free as God to will as we see fit, as individual selves,
we are bound by the will of that greater Self who is God. As Nanak
tells us:

> Man in himself has no independent power
> Either to live or to die, to swim or to drown.
> All things are as the Creator ordains;
> Birth and death are both by His will.
> His will is supremely sovereign, in the beginning and
>   in the end. [3]

Similarly, as Nanak so often proclaims, no man approaches
God or sees Him except by His will. No one reaches God through the
various "methods" of meditation, or the "techniques" of yoga; no
effort to reach him through solitary contemplation or ascetic practi-
ices, unless it is His will, will bear any fruit. We are given to know

within ourselves when we are called to Him, and when we are not; when we are to serve with our actions, and when we must go within. For all things occur in His time, and not in our own; by His inspiration within us, and not by our own; according to His wishes, and not our own. All things move together of one accord; assent is given throughout the universe to every falling grain; and every soul moves through life, from one state of being and awareness to another, as He ordains; and each grows, and draws nearer to His vision as He ordains as well. "By God's grace alone," says Nanak, "is God to be grasped. All else is false, all else is vanity."

He who has known God has known also this one certainty: that it was God's grace that led him to it, and framed him in readiness for it, and prepared his heart and mind for it; and it was God alone who lifted him to that embrace. Says Nanak:

> He whom Thou makest to know Thee, he knows Thee.
> And his mouth shall forever be full of Thy praises. [4]
> ...Liberation and bondage depends upon Thy will; there is
> no one to gainsay it.
> Should a fool wish to, suffering will teach him wisdom. [5]

During his sojourns, Nanak is reported to have travelled as far eastward as the city of Benares. It is possible that during this visit he came in contact with the songs of Kabir; perhaps even with Kabir himself. But eventually, after an unspecified length of time, Nanak returned from his wanderings to his home in Talwandi, there remaining only a short time with his wife and children. Then, once again, he set out on his wandering career. This time, instead of entering the southern lands as before, where warfare was still going on, he headed northward into Kashmir. In his travels, he met with many yogis and ascetics of various sects: Siddhas, Naths, Shaktas, bhaktas, and Avadhuts. By travelling so widely, he gained first-hand knowledge of the various religious traditions and views prevalent throughout the land.

When he had returned from his northward journey, Nanak headed westward, apparently through Afghanistan and Persia, to reach the pilgrimage-place of the Muslims, at Mecca, in Arabia. It was there, so the story goes, that, while lying down for the night, he inadvertently pointed his feet in the direction of the Ka'abah, the enshrined stone regarded by faithful Muslims as "the receptacle of God." And when a devout Muslim, observing this, angrily reproached him for pointing his feet "toward God," Nanak replied, ironically, "O Kazi, please turn my feet in the direction where God is not."

After his long wanderings, extending over a vast area, Nanak returned to his family, and took them to the village of Kartarpur, on the Ravi river, where he had been given some rich farmland. There, in his later years, he settled down as a wheat farmer. A commune of devotees gathered there, and Nanak generously shared with all who came both his grain and the wisdom he had acquired.

Nanak belonged to that great, unnameable, tradition of those who have realized the universal Self, and are therefore quite beyond any mere formalized religious dogmas; nonetheless, Nanak's teachings in no way diverged from those of the Upanishadic tradition into which he was born. Like Kabir, he knew both Hinduism and Islam in their orthodox formulations, but, having realized the one Goal of both traditions, he was able to advise the votaries of each religion to go beyond the mere outward observances which divided sect from sect; and to seek to know their one common Lord directly, within their own hearts. His teachings were, therefore, in no way different from those of all the Self-realized saints who had lived before him, going back to the earliest times.

It was only much later, long after Nanak's death, that his discples, and particularly those to whom the mantle of succession had been passed, established a separate and independent sect, which eventually grew to be the large militant religious organization called the *Sikhs* ("Disciples"); and which, when often persecuted in its long and bitter history, set itself in armed opposition to both Muslim and Hindu authorities. And while Nanak has always been honored as the *Adi Guru* ("Original Guru") and the mystical authority of the Sikhs, he cannot be accounted responsible for the militant organization which succeeded him, any more than Jesus can be held responsible for the Crusades or the Inquisition. He was a saint, a true knower of God, and what he taught was the perennial teaching of all those who have known the indivisible unity of all existence.

Nanak ended his days in peace at Kartarpur, surrounded by his friends, family, and a small band of devotees. And it is interesting to note that the early biographers of Nanak tell a story of his corpse's miraculous disappearance which is very similar to the one told of Kabir. In the version concerning Nanak, the Muslim and Hindu devotees had come to pay respects to Nanak on his deathbed, and they argued among themselves over whether his corpse was to be cremated or buried. Nanak, overhearing them, said, "If the bouquet of flowers brought by the Hindus remains fresh at my death, they may cremate my body; if the bouquet of the Muslims remains fresh, they may bury it." And, after Nanak died, sure enough, when someone removed the shroud, Nanak's body was gone, but there remained two bouquets, both of which were still fresh. It is a story which makes one think of the tale of the disappearance of the corpse of Jesus as well, and gives rise to wonder at the exaggerated claims and misguided zeal of disciples at every time and place.

During his many years of travelling, Nanak had written down many of his musings and inspirational songs of God; and, after his death, these were passed on to his successors. It was Guru Arjan, the head of the sect from 1581 to 1606, who compiled these songs of Nanak's, and combining them with the songs of Kabir, Namadev, and other earlier saints, formed the holy book of the Sikhs, the *Adi Guru Granth*. Here are just a few of the many songs of Nanak's included in that book:

> It is not through thought that He is to be comprehended,
> Though we strive to grasp Him a hundred thousand times;
> Nor by outer silence and long deep meditation
> Can the inner silence be reached;
> Nor is man's hunger for God appeasable
> By piling up world-loads of wealth.
> All the innumerable devices of worldly wisdom
> Leave a man disappointed; not one avails.
> How then shall we know the Truth?
> How shall we rend the veils of untruth asunder?
> Abide by His will, and make your own His will, O Nanak;
> write this in your heart. [6]

> Those who believe in power,
> Sing of His power;
> Others chant of His gifts
> As messages and manifestations from Him.
> Some sing of His greatness,
> And His gracious acts;
> Some sing of His wisdom
> Difficult to understand.
> Some sing of Him as the fashioner of the body,
> Who destroys what He has fashioned;
> Others praise Him for taking away life
> And restoring it anew.

Some proclaim His Existence
To be far, desperately far, from us;
Others sing of Him
As present everywhere,
Meeting us face to face.

To sing truly of the transcendent Lord
Would exhaust all vocabulaties, all human powers of
expression;
Yet millions have sung of Him in innumerable strains.
His gifts to us flow in such plenitude
That man wearies of receiving what God bestows.
Age on unending age, man lives on His bounty;
Carefree, O Nanak, the glorious Lord smiles. [7]

Were my span of life to extend to a million years,
And if I could live upon the air alone,
Never assailed by sleep, in a deep dark cave
Where neither the light of the Sun nor the light of the moon
Could pierce down to distract me,
Even so, my God, I could not know Thy worth,
Nor say how great is Thy name.

Were I to hover like a bird,
Soaring through innumerable skies,
And vanish beyond the range of mortal vision,
Self-sustained, without need for food or drink,
Even so, my God, I could not know thy worth,
Nor say how great is Thy name.

Were I to study unmeasured loads of books,
And become the master-scholar of their lore,
And if I had a pen to write with the speed of the wind,
A pen filled with inexhaustible ink.,
Even so, my God, I could not know Thy worth,
Nor say how great is Thy name. [8]

Lord, Thou mighty River, all-knowing, all-seeing,
I am like a little fish in Thy great waters;
How shall I sound Thy depths?
How shall I reach Thy shores?
Wherever I go, I see Thee only,
Yet, snatched out of Thy waters, I die of separation.
I know not the fisher,
I see not the net,
But, flapping in my agony, I call upon Thee for help.

O Lord, who pervadeth all things,
In my folly, I thought Thou wert far;
But no deed I do can ever be out of Thy sight.
Thou art all-knowing, and all things Thou seest;
I am not worthy to serve Thee,
Nor do I glory in Thy name.

Thy gifts are my portion;
There is no other door
To which I may go.
This, then, is the humble prayer
Of Thy servant, Nanak:
Accept my mind and my body
As devoted unto Thee.

The Lord is near, the Lord is distant,
And the Lord is between these two as well;
He watcheth His creation,
And hears His creation, for He is all.
Nanak, whatever the Lord wills,
That comes to pass. [9]

I have lost my nights in sleep,
I have lost my days in pursuit of sensual pleasures.
Oh, how cheaply we sell this precious human life!

Fool, you have forgotten God;
You will have to repent hereafter.
Even on the morrow, utter shall be your despair.
On earth man sets no bounds
To his heaping up of wealth,
But does not desire the Lord, the truly boundless.
Truly, they lose the Lord, who gain this world.

If wishes were wealth, beggars would be millionaires;
But it is not by wishes, but by deeds
That the ultimate Goal is reached.
Nanak, the Creator watcheth over His creation;
His is the final Judgement:
The how and why of it, no man knows. [10]

This is the greatest sickness of the soul:
To forget even for a second, the Beloved.
There is no comfort hereafter
For him whose heart is empty of God.

Through the grace of the Guru,
The tired soul has refreshment;
The praise of God banishes worldly desire.
Day and night, O anxious heart of mine,
Say and repeat: "Praise be to God."
But that man is rare indeed
Who never forgets the name of God.

When the light of the soul blends with the universal Light,
And the human mind commingles
With the Mind of all things,
Then our petty being,
With its violence, doubt and sorrow, disappears.
Through the grace of the Guru,
Such spiritual union takes place.
They are blessed in whose hearts the Lord resides.

Let that man be in love with the body,
And make the body his spouse,
Who wishes to live the life of the senses.
Do not love that which does not endure:
The Spouse of the righteous is the Lord;
On His couch, they enjoy His love. [11]

Let my tongue become a hundred thousand tongues,
Let the hundred thousand be multiplied twenty-fold,
And with each tongue, many hundred thousands of times,
I wold repeat the holy name of the Lord.
Thus, let the soul, step by step,
Mount the stairs to the Bridegroom,
And become one with Him. [12]

DADU

In India, during the 16th century, there lived many great illumined saints. We have already mentioned Kabir and Nanak; there was also Chaitanya (1485-1533), the love-intoxicated *bhakta* of Bengal; Vallabha (1479-1531), the great mystic-philosopher and *acharya*; and Eknath (1548-1609), the gentle Maharashtran mystic and poet. But there was one who is especially worthy of inclusion in our story for the simple clarity of his vision and the universality of his message: his name was Dadu. Like Kabir and Nanak, he stood quite alone between the quarrelling factions of Hinduism and Islam, and proclaimed the unity of all men in God and the universality of the message of all who have known Him. "Ask of those who have attained God," he said; "all speak the same word. All the saints are of one mind; it is only those in the midst of the way who follow diverse paths. All the enlightened have left one message; ... It is only those in the midst of their journey who hold diverse opinions." [1]

Dadu (1544-1603), whose name is an affectionate diminutive of the common Muslim name, Allahdad, was born at Ahmedabad, on the banks of the Saraswati river, to a Muslim merchant named Lodi Ram and his wife, Basri. From his early youth, he was gifted with a curious intellect and a love of learning. It is said that, at the age of eleven, he received the blessing of a wandering holy man, and from that time began to take interest in the knowledge of God.

At the age of eighteen, he left his home to live the religious life of prayer and meditation. He wandered from city to city between the regions of Gujerat and Rajputana as a mendicant, until, sometime around the age of twenty-five, he took up his abode in the town of Sambhar, on the shores of the Salt Lake, in the Moghul province of Ajmer. There, he came into contact with a number of spiritual teachers, and came under the tutelege of one called Shaikh Buddhan; but he was to claim no lineage from any tradition save the one common tradition of all mystics, and no teacher save the one interior Teacher common to all.

It was at Sambhar that Dadu became married, and fathered four children; two sons and two daughters. As a householder, he practiced the trade of a cotton-carder; yet the holiness and authority of his discourses among his friends quickly earned for him a reputation as a holy man, and he began to attract a following of devoted disciples. Like Kabir, whom he greatly admired, Dadu knew both the Muslim and Hindu mystical traditions, and preferred not to be associated exclusively with either. He had experienced the One to whom both Muslims and Hindus aspire, and attempted, by his teachings, to reconcile them in understanding of their common pursuit. He had known God directly, and had seen, therefore, how foolish are those who squabble over their petty ideas of God, and their various modes of external worship and behavior:

> One says "Swami," one says "Shaikh"; neither grasps the
> mystery of this world.
> One speaks of "Rama" and the other of "Allah," but they
> have not known either Rama or Allah!
> ... Says Dadu: I am neither a Hindu or a Muslim. I follow
> none of the Six Systems [of philosophy]; I worship
> the Merciful.
> Dadu belongs to neither faction: he is the slave of Allah-
> Rama. He who is without form or limitation, He
> alone is my Guru. [2]

Naturally, such words as these were offensive to the orthodox Muslim legalists; and soon Dadu became a controversial figure in Sambhar, and found he had as many enemies as friends. A Muslim official, by the name of Buland Khan, assaulted Dadu, beat him, and had him jailed for his self-proclaimed infidelity to the doctrines of Islam. Shortly thereafter, Dadu decided to leave Sambhar. At the age of thirty-five, he moved to Amber, and was well-received there by the local Hindu ruler, Raja Bhagwan Das, and was supplied by him with a comfortable retreat on the shores of Lake Maota.

Bhagwan Das, while a Hindu, was brother to one of the wives of the Muslim emperor, Akbar; and was a commander of the royal armies. While at the emperor's court one day, he had occasion to mention to the emperor the presence in his kingdom of Dadu; and Akbar, who was always eager to meet with the saintly of all religious persuasions, remarked that he would like to meet him. Soon thereafter, a meeting was arranged between Dadu and Akbar at the emperor's palace at Sikri. To appreciate this historical meeting, it is necessary to know something about Akbar.

Padashah Akbar (d. 1605) was a descendent of the great conqueror, Babur (d. 1530). Babur, in whose veins flowed the blood of the Turkish ruler, Timur (the Tamerlane of English literature) and Genghis Khan, the Mongol, was succeeded by his son, Humayun, who was twenty-three when he ascended the throne as emperor of Hindustan. Humayun's son, Akbar, then came into power in 1556, at the age of thirteen, after his father fell from his library staircase and died as a result. Thereafter, Akbar proved himself a superior Commander-in-chief of the armies, and an indefatigable ruler of an ever-widening empire.

Akbar was an ambitious and ruthless warrior, and a crafty administrator, who accomplished the conquest and consolidation of nearly all of India under his rule; but he was also a man of unusual curiosity and tolerance concerning all religious traditions -- a trait highly uncharacteristic of Muslim rulers of India up to that time. It is said that he had been influenced from his early youth by the teachings of the Sufis, and that he, himself, sought "to attain the ineffable bliss of direct contact with the Divine reality."

In his eagerness to know as much as possible about the religious traditions of the various factions existing in his Empire, he met frequently with representatives of Sufism, Hinduism, Jainism, Zoroastrianism and Christianity. His interest was no doubt partly spiritual, partly intellectual, and partly political. In the naive hope of establishing a religious synthesis in which all religious ideals would be reconciled in one universal religion to be adopted throughout India, he built a universal "House of Worship," and proclaimed his new religion, with himself as its titular and infallible head.

While this "new religion" was not to last beyond his own rule, it must be conceded that it had widespread beneficial effects throughout India, in establishing, at least, a temporary truce between the various warring religious factions. Though his attempt to form a universal religion, founded on Imperial decree rather than on direct spiritual experience, was naive and doomed to failure, it had the value of fostering a time of peace and tolerance between the Muslim and Hindu populations. It was, thus, under such tolerant and generous conditions, that Dadu was welcomed to the palace of Akbar in the Spring of 1584.

According to the account preserved by Dadu's followers, when Dadu arrived at the palace, he was first met by the emperor's representatives whose custom it was to interview those with whom Akbar was to meet. These representatives were Shaikh Abu-l Fazl and Raja Birbal. Abu-l Fazl, one of Akbar's closest and most trusted advisors on religious matters, was himself a true Sufi. He greeted Dadu with these words: "We esteem you highly, O saintly Dadu, and desire to know more of your teaching. What God do you worship, and what is the manner of your worship?"

"The God we worship," said Dadu,"is the Creator of all things. Our teaching is to hold Him in constant remembrance. Our mode of worship is to subdue the senses, and sing the praise of Rama. To be sure, God is other than His name; He can neither be uttered or comprehended. But men, for their own purposes, have given Him various names. Beholding in Him some attribute, they have given Him the name of that attribute. He deals graciously, and they call Him *Dayal*, the Gracious; as Protector of His creatures, He is styled *Gopal,* the Cowherd; as dwelling within the heart, He is known as *Rama*; as showing mercy, He is *Rahim,* the Compassionate; as He who is beyond man's reach, He is called *Allah*; as unseen, He is known as *The Invisible*; as fashioner of all things, He is *Creator;* as transcending all limitation, He is the *Absolute*; as drawing men's hearts to Himself, He is *Mohan*, the Charmer; as pervading the universe, He is the *Omnipresent*. He accepts the homage of His true worshippers, and they witness His presence in the world." [3]

Abu-l Fazl and Birbal were delighted with Dadu's conversation, and immediately made arrangements for him to see the emperor, Akbar. When, at last, Dadu was ushered into the royal presence, Akbar, after greeting him courteously, asked about his religious views, and Dadu explained to him the inner state of constant recollection of God. "But how," Akbar asked, "is this inner state to be attained?" And Dadu replied, quoting a Persian verse:

The soul, filled with passionate yearning, stands expectant
at the door of vision;
The surrendered heart dwells every moment in the Divine
Presence, watchful, alert. [4]

"First," said Dadu, "a man must cease from the indulgence of the body, which binds him to the world. He must abandon all hope in the three worlds, and the Changeless One will surely reveal Himself." They continued to talk of spiritual matters in this manner for some time, and, at the close of their interview, Akbar invited Dadu to return another time; but Dadu declined the invitation. Nonetheless, before Dadu returned to Amber, Akbar sent for him to bid farewell, and Dadu went as bidden. "Tell me," said Akbar, in this, their last meeting, "how one so enmeshed in the world's affairs as I am may find God. I am ready to love Him with every power of my being, and to school my heart in truth, if thus I may learn His secret."

"Well spoken!" said Dadu; "Well spoken, indeed! That is the sum of all I have to say. May God keep you ever in this frame of mind."

Akbar bowed his head. "Swami," he said, "you have given and I have received."

With this, Dadu returned the emperor's bow, and bestowed the blessing hitherto withheld: "I pray the indwelling God to keep you continually in His protection and favor." [5]

That evening, everyone gathered together to sing religious hymns, and to honor Dadu before his departure. And in the morning Dadu returned to Amber, where he was congratulated by Bhagwan Das on the splendid impression he had made on the emperor.

This little scenario of Dadu with the emperor Akbar is interesting as a look into the court-life of the time, but even more so as a portrait of Dadu, who appears as natural and sincere in the emperor's presence as on the dusty roads with his disciples. We see these same qualities in the many songs and utterances of Dadu which were collected after his death. Dadu had set down in written form, at different times throughout his life, his thoughts, convictions, and experiences of God. Extending over a long period of time, they vary from prayers to spiritual directives, from yearning for God to proclamations of His unity. In all of these songs and utterances, one senses a real man, blunt and ordinary at times, but always totally honest with himself, and utterly impatient with phoniness and pretense.

Dadu's songs remind us a good deal of those of Kabir or Nanak, but they have a quality of roughness and independence which is wholly his own. He was openly critical of all that smacked of "the business of religion," and most especially of those who paraded as Gurus and accumulated disciples for their own agrandizement, wealth and power. "The disciple is the cow," said Dadu; "and the Guru is the milker of the cow. Great care does he take of his cow, and well he might, when he makes his living by him!"

Dadu, himself, was a true Guru, in the best sense of the word. He had attained the Highest, yet he never seemed to posture or lose sight of his own humble station before God. Some of his songs of yearning for the vision of God, for example, remind us of the tenderest of the Hebrew Psalms, or the writings of the Christian saint, Juan de la Cruz:

Ah me! oft do I feel such pangs of separation from my
      Beloved that I am like to die unless I see Him.
Maiden, hearken to the tale of my agony; I am restless without
      my Beloved.
In my yearning desire for the Beloved I break into song day and
      night; I pour out my woes like the nightingale.
Ah me! Who will bring me to my Beloved? Who will show
me His path and console my heart?
Dadu says: O Lord, let me see Thy face, even for a moment,
and be blessed. [6]

He sits close at hand; he hears everything, yet He doesn't
answer me.
Dadu casts himself on Thee; take away this life of mine.
Everyone I see is happy; no one is in distress.
Yet sore distressed is thy servant Dadu, because I see Thee
not face to face.
No one in all the world is in such deep distress as I; I weep
floods of tears in my longing to meet the Beloved.
I find Him not, neither can I find peace without Him. Tell
me, how can I continue to live?
He who wounded me is the only one who can heal me.
Sighing for the vision, this lonely one lives apart; enduring
the pangs of separation, Dadu awaits Thy coming,
O Hari!
He who ardently yearns for the meeting, like a fish taken out
of water,
He alone beholds Thy vision; he is joined to Thy Spirit.
This lonely one, separated from Rama, does not find Him;
Dadu writhes like a fish, till Thou hast mercy
upon him. [7]

Dadu continued to live in Amber for many years, teaching his
disciples and writing his songs of love to his Lord. But, as at Sambhar,
there were many of the orthodoxy, Hindu and Muslim alike, who
resented his words, which they interpreted as critical of their beliefs.
And so, after fourteen years in Amber, Dadu was forced to leave that
city, and for nearly ten years thereafter, he moved from town to town
and city to city with his close disciples, welcomed everywhere he went
by both peasantry and royalty; until, at the city of Nairana, in the year
1603, in the company of his many beloved disciples and his two sons,
he passed away.

The many songs and utterances (Bani) which Dadu left
behind comprise today the holy-book of the Dadu-panthis. Here are

just a few:

> Be done with self and worship Hari; cast off worldly desire
> in mind and body.
> Cherish goodwill towards every living creature; this, says
> Dadu, is the sum of religion.
> He is the true saint who bears enmity to none;
> There is but one Spirit, and he has no enemy.
> I have made diligent quest: truly, there is no second.
> In every man is the one Spirit, whether he be Hindu or
> Muslim.
> Both brethren have alike hands and feet, both have ears;
> Both brethren have eyes, be they Hindus or Muslims.
> When you look in the mirror of ignorance, there appears to
> be two;
> When error is dispelled and ignorance vanishes, there is no
> "other."
> To whom then will you bear enmity, when there is no other?
> He from whose Being all sprang, the same One dwells in all.
> In every man is the one Spirit; hold Him therefore in reverent
> respect.
> Recognize that Spirit in yourself and others; it is the manifest-
> ation of the Lord.
> Why give pain to any when the indwelling Rama is in every
> man?
> O revered Self, give peace and contentment; For there is none
> but Thee in all the three worlds.
> When the soul perceives the Self, then are all souls brethren;
> Give your heart to Him who is the Creator of all.
> When a dog wanders into a palace of mirrors, it sees its own
> reflection everywhere, and begins barking.
> See how the One has likewise become many, and angrily
> seeks to destroy itself.
> All souls are brother-souls, the offspring of one Womb;
> Consider this truth! Who, then, is the other, O foolish man?
> All came in one likeness; it was the Lord who sent them;
> They have all taken different names, and thus become
> separate.
> Worship the divine Self, and bear hatred toward none;
> In this worship you will find peace, in hatred only sorrow. [8]

> Teach me, O Hari, to reverence Thy pure Name, that my
> heart may be glad in Thy worship.
> Make my heart to overflow with love, devotion, yearning,
> O Hari!
> Make me gentle in speech and humble of bearing, rejoicing in

Thy presence, O Rama!
Fill me with spiritual longing, detachment from the world, and
           a loving heart.
May I steadfastly cherish the desire to remain ever-devoted to
Thy feet.
Grant me quiet contentment and self-control, and keep my
heart firmly directed toward Thee.
O Ever-Present, awaken me to the sense of Thy constant
presence.
O Mohan, grant me knowledge, and the power of meditation,
that my mind may continually turn to Thee.
O Lord of the humble, grant that the Light of lights may
illumine Dadu's heart. [9]

While the mind is unstable, there can be no union;
When the mind becomes stable, He will be found with ease.
How can the mind remain firm without some resting place?
It merely keeps wandering here and there.
It will become stable only when you settle it on the remem-
brance of God.
Where you hold fast to His Name with a steadfast mind --
there, says Dadu, is Rama.
Delight in the remembrance of Hari; then will the mind
become steadfast.
When it has tasted the fellowship of love, it will not move
away a single step.
When it is fixed on the One within, it finds no joy in other
attractions;
Fixed firmly there, it does not wander anywhere else.
Like a gull, perched on a boat's mast in mid-ocean, the mind,
After it has grown weary of flying here and there, has found its
           resting-place.
Then only does my soul find peace and happiness, when my
mind has become stable,
Steadfastly fixed on Rama. If only one could learn this
secret!
The pure mind is stable; its joy is in the name of Rama.
In this way, you too shall find the vision of Him who is
supreme and perfect Bliss. [10]

Wonderful is the Name; it holds the truth of the three
worlds.
Considering this, O heart, repeat it night and day.
Wonderful is the Name; let the heart never forget Hari.
Let His image dwell in the heart; cherish it with every breath.

When you cherish Him with every breath, one day He will
come to meet you.
... Abandon all other means of approach, and devote yourself
to the Name of Rama. [11]

... The Creator has many and diverse names:
Choose the name that comes to mind; thus do all the saints
practice remembrance.
The Lord who endowed us with soul and body -- worship
Him in your heart;
Worship Him by that name which best suits the moment. [12]

Many great scholars there are, and brave imparters of
wisdom;
Religious garbs are endless. But rarely is one found who is
wholly devoted to God's service.
... If you can understand I will speak: There is one
                    ineffable Truth;
Be done with the leaves and branches, and go for the root.
What does mere garb signify?
Devising all manner of costumes, men array themselves
[as devotees];
Yet how few take the way of self-effacement and the
worship of Hari!
All the world are actors; rare is the real sadhu.
... There is but one Spirit; the Lord is in all.
Therefore, let your union be with the Lord, not with a
sect or mode of dress.
Rosaries and sect-marks are of no avail; what have I
to do with them?
Within me is One who is mine; day and night I take His
Name.
All look to the outward appearance, and do not perceive
what is within;
The outward is what is shown to the world, but Rama
reveals Himself within.
Hari, the all-knowing Lord, accepts only what is of the heart;
To Rama, the truth is dear, despite a thousand pretenses.
Hari receives, not the word spoken by the lips, but the
intent of the heart.
... True love is the most wondrous of signs; the soul who
aches for the vision of God is the true sadhu. [13]

Without a torturing thirst, how should one drink the bliss
          of communion with the Lord?
O God, give me an aching desire to behold the vision of Thee!
Desire [for God] does not arise without the pain of separation;
How could love exist without this pain?
Without love all is false, try however hard you may.
The pain of separation is not born of words; desire [for God]
is not born of words.
Love cannot be found through words. Let no one put his
faith in them. [14]

Where Rama is, there I am not; where I am, there Rama
is not.
This mansion is of delicate construction; there is no place
for two.
While self remains, so long will there be a second;
When this selfhood is blotted out, then there is no other.
When I am not, there is but One; when I obtrude, then two.
When the veil of "I" is taken away, then does the One become
as It was. [15]

Have done with pride and arrogance, conceit, envy, self-
assertion;
Practice humility, and obedience; worship the Creator.
When a man has abandoned false pride, arrogance, and vain-
glory,
When he has become humble and meek, then does he find
true bliss.
Prince and beggar alike must die; not one survives.
Him you should call "living" who has died and yet lives.
My enemy "I" is dead; now none can smite me down.
'Tis I who have slain myself; thus, being dead, I live.
We have slain our enemy, we have died; but he is not
          forgotten;
The thorn remains to vex us. Consider and lay this truth
to heart:
You will only find the Beloved when you are as the living
dead;
Only by losing yourself can you find Him who knows all.
When you regard yourself as nothing, then you will find
the Beloved.
Recognize, therefore, by quiet reflection, from whence this
thought of self arises.
Becoming as the living dead, enter onto the path;
First bow down your head, then may you venture to plant

your foot [on this path].
Know that the path of discipleship is exceedingly hard;
The living dead walk it, with the Name of Rama as their
guide.
So difficult is the path, no living man may tread it;
He only can walk it, O foolish man, who has died and lives.
Only he who is dead can tread the path that leads to God;
He finds the Beloved, and leaps the fearsome gulf.
He that is alive shall die; and only by dying inwardly shall
he meet with the Lord.
Forsaking His fellowship, who could endure when trouble
comes?
O when will this dominion of self pass away? When will the
heart forget every "other"?
When will it be made wholly pure? When will it find its
true home?
When I am not, then there is One; when I intrude, then two.
When the curtain of "I" and "Thou" is drawn aside, then do I
become as I was [in the Beginning]. [16]

My enemy "I" is now dead; now none can slay me.
'Tis I who have slain myself; I have died, and yet live.
While the thought of self remains, so long are there two.
When this selfhood is destroyed, then there is no second.
Then only will you find the Beloved, when "I" and "mine" are
wholly lost.
When "I" and "mine" are no more, then shall you find the
                    pure vision.
"I" and "mine" are a load upon the head; you die with the
weight of it.
By the grace of the Master, remove it and lay it down.
In front of [the true] I, stands the [false] I; for this reason,
He remains hidden.
When this selfhood passes away, the Beloved is revealed.
Hide yourself where no one can see you;
See and show forth only the Beloved. Then you shall find
                    eternal happiness.
If there is no inward thought of self, but the mouth still
utters the words, "I" and "Thou,"
Let no one make this a matter of reproach; for it is in this
way that they ["I" and "Thou"] hold communion
with one another.
When others see that devotee who, having abandoned self,
is wholly devoted to Rama,
Then they too are led toward the Lord. [17]

Omniscient God, it is by Thy grace alone that I have been
blessed with vision of Thee.
Thou knowest all; what can I say?
All-knowing God, I can conceal nothing from Thee.
I have nothing that deserves Thy grace.
No one can reach Thee by his own efforts; Thou showest
        Thyself by Thine own grace.
How could I approach Thy presence? By what means could
        I gain Thy favor?
And by what powers of mind or body could I attain to Thee?
It hath pleased Thee in Thy mercy to take me under Thy wing.
Thou alone art the Beginning and the End; Thou art the
Creator of the three worlds.
Dadu says: I am nothing and can do nothing.
Truly, even a fool may reach Thee by Thy grace. [18]

Many have spoken and passed on, but the mystery remains
        unsolved.
We too speak, but what more can we say?
What do I know, what can I speak, concerning that almighty
        One?
What knowledge have I of His manner of being? It utterly
        passes my comprehension.
How many have spoken and passed on; even the wisest have
spent their powers in vain.
... There, neither silence nor speech exists; no "I" nor "Thou,"
no self or other, neither one nor two.
If I say "One," there are two; if I say "two," there is but One.
The Magician who devised this play -- go and enquire of Him.
How He fashioned the many from the One, let the Master
        Himself make plain. [19]

SEVENTEENTH AND EIGHTEENTH CENTURY MYSTICS

One looks in vain to the 17th and 18th centuries for a mystic of truly universal proportions. Christendom spawned its Jacob Boehme (1575-1624) and George Fox (1624-1691), its Thomas Traherne (1636-1674) and William Law (1689-1761); but they seem small and narrow in their views and attainments when compared to the spiritual giants of the past whose utterances transcend all narrow confines of sectarian dogma. The Hindu religious tradition boasts of its Tulasidas (1532-1623), Tukaram (1598-1650), and Ramadasa (1608-1681); but they seem only to echo the Jnaneshvars and Namadevs who came before them, without the special genius of their predecessors. They were great devotees, and enlightened men, to be sure, but the lustre of their jewel appears to shine but dimly through the excrudescence of tradition binding them to their limited place in history. Like their Christian counterparts, they seem bogged in the stagnant waters of their own tradition's long-established customs and vocabularies.

There were no giants produced during those centuries by Islam, Judaism, or Buddhism either. It seems to have been a period of calcification and provincialism in every religious tradition. The genius of the times was focused in another direction, having caught the faint glimmer of a dawning new age of freedom -- religious, intellectual, and political. The great minds of those centuries, the Bacons, Galileos, and Newtons, were exploring the cosmos to discover its secrets in the endeavor to certify by the light of reason what before had been relegated to the misty domain of revelation. The declarations of those who claimed revelation or tradition as their authority too often conflicted with reason, and it became clear that a new test-standard for truth was required: observation and empirical proof. Thus a new age of science was born. The focus of the world's attention had shifted from the metaphysical to the physical, from the abstract to the concrete, from the Spirit to the form, and from faith in the doctrines of established religions to a faith in the new god, Reason.

Rationalists, such as Descartes, Spinoza, Leibnitz, and Kant, dominated the attention of Western philosophers; while political theorists like Hobbes, Locke and Hume held the ear of the activists, the reformers. In Europe and elsewhere, religion appeared to have failed in providing a solution to man's most passionate aspirations due to its inherent subjectivity and the unreliability of diverse claims of revelation. Religious ideals had proven to be too readily perverted and abused; but the newly deified Reason seemed to open the way to a new dawn, a New Age, wherein a universally reliable and testable world-view would be revealed. It was an unrealizable dream, of course, but it was the dream which captured the imagination of all the world, and seemed to hold out a new hope for a grand practicable solution for all the ills that flesh is heir to.

The mystical ideal of a life given to the simple regard of God had become so entirely obscured and camouflaged by dogma -- the dogma of Judaism, Christianity, Hinduism, Islam, Buddhism, those bulwarks of separatism and concretized tradition -- that the demolition crew of Reason's advocates were required to batter down its walls, crumble its bricks, and boldly destroy it utterly, in order to break free of its mentally confining bastions. Freedom -- spiritual, intellectual, and political -- became the new religion; and, intoxicated with fervor for a new liberation from the confines of tradition, the religious, intellectual and political leaders of men called loudly the battle-cry of Revolution. And with the advent of new means of printing and distributing ideas, the battle-cry was heard 'round the world.

If there were great seers of God during those times, they remain unknown to us. Even had they existed, and had they made themselves known, their voices would not have been heard above the din and outcry of men so intoxicated with the opiate of unbridled freedom. The 17th and 18th centuries which ushered in the Age of Reason, political freedom, and industrialization, were glorious centuries of ideation and action, but they were "the Dark Ages" of mystical vision. For such vision is possible only to those who are capable of transcending the foment of ideation and action, finding in the uncluttered stillness of the mind the Source of all ideation and action.

These centuries hummed with the busiest and most dramatic of outcries, conflicts, and victories, and paved the way for the proud materialistic society of today. But no Upanishadic rishi, no Socrates, no Buddha, no Jesus or Shankara, was heard even to whisper beneath the tumult. It was not until the 19th century that the voice of a supremely great and universal visionary was to be heard. Like the other sublime souls who've so rarely appeared, this man lived, obscured to all but a few, in his own small place on the earth; but, like those immortal, God-like manifestations of the past, his life and message was to send out shock-waves 'round the world to awaken, delight and enrapture the slumbering souls of men everywhere. His name was Ramakrishna.

RAMAKRISHNA

Gadadhar Chattopadhyaya, later to be known as Sri Rama-krishna, was born to Khudiram and Chandra Devi on February 18, 1836, in the small Indian village of Kamarpukur, in Bengal. When Gadadhar was born, his father was already in his sixties; he had two brothers, one of whom was more than thirty years older than himself, and two sisters, one twenty-six years older than he, and one three years younger. Khudiram, a tenant farmer of the brahmin caste, died when the boy was only seven.

It was at this age that young Gadadhar began to take a strong interest in religion; he loved to listen to the stories from the *Puranas*, and to spend his time with the wandering *sannyasins* who passed through Kamarpukur on their way to the nearby holy city of Puri. Gadadhar was a gay and precocious child, but even at the age of seven, his mind seemed to be lifted up into some abstract realm of consciousness, beyond the child's world of play and games. One summer day, as he was walking along a narrow path dividing the rice-paddies, munching from a basket of puffed rice, he gazed overhead at the dark clouds gathering in the sky, and just then a flock of snow-white cranes flew by against that blackening sky. Gadadhar became so overwhelmed by the contrasting beauty of this scene that he fell unconscious to the ground, and was later found by some villagers in that condition, his puffed rice scattered about him on the ground. Later, recalling that moment as an adult, he said that he had felt such emotion that his heart seemed about to burst, and he became swallowed up in ecstasy.

At the age of nine, Gadadhar was invested with the sacred thread, as all brahmin boys are, and he began at that time to take an interest in meditation at the small shrine to the family deity, Raghuvir, an aspect of Vishnu. It was at this time also that he had the opportunity to play the part of Shiva in a village play, put on to celebrate the holiday of Shivaratri. When he was dressed in the accoutrements of Shiva, Gadadhar became so completely identified with his part that his mind grew withdrawn and distant, and he was scarcely aware of his surroundings. Once on stage, he seemed to the audience the very image of Shiva; tears flowed from his eyes and he stood lost in deep contemplation, with a radiance on his face that struck everyone as strangely authentic in one so young.

Gadhadhar was a very artistic and creative child; he loved to make mud-sculptures of the various gods, and to paint pictures representing scenes from the Puranas. And after his initiation into the art of drama, he organized his young friends into a troupe to perform plays in the village mango orchard. There they would put on scenes from the epics, like the *Ramayana* and the *Mahabharata*. Gadadhar loved to act out scenes from the life of Krishna, especially those from the *rasalila*, the story of the exquisite love-play between Krishna and the cowherd girls and boys. He was equally convincing in the role of Krishna or of Radha; he could play the female roles with great skill, imitating the coquettish walk and movements of the women he had seen in the village.

When Gadadhar was around thirteen, his elder brother, Ramkumar, who was now forty-four, and the head of the family, went to Calcutta to earn money for the family. There, he opened a school of Sanskrit, while also serving as priest to a number of families -- a function reserved only for those of the brahmin caste. After a few years, Ramkumar sent for Gadadhar to join him as a helper. Gadadhar, now sixteen, travelled to Calcutta and learned from his brother how to recite the Sanskrit *slokas* of the priest's office, and to assist in the decorating and worshipping of the deity images. Ramkumar hoped to teach his younger brother all the branches of priestly learning, such as the *Shastras* containing caste-laws, astrology, and so forth, which would enable him to earn a living; but Gadadhar seemed to have little interest in such things. He delighted so much in worship, the singing of devotional songs, and quiet meditation, that his brother often became impatient with his lack of a practical sense.

In 1855, a new temple was built on twenty acres of ground just outside of Calcutta, at Dakshineswar, on the east bank of the Ganges; and Ramkumar was hired to serve as its priest. It was a large complex, containing a beautiful garden, courtyard, bathing terrace, and a number of separate temples, dedicated to the various aspects of God. The main temple was devoted to the Mother, the divine creative Power of the universe, called *Kali*; and several minor temples were devoted to Shiva and Vishnu. It was a very wealthy woman of the *sudra* (the lowest) caste, named Rani Rasmani, who financed and oversaw this huge enterprise, and who had selected Ramkumar for the position of priest of the main, Kali, temple.

Gadadhar was at first reluctant to enter the service of this woman of low caste, but the beauty of the place, and the kind regard shown him by the Rani and her son-in-law, Mathur, overcame his initial reluctance, and he accepted the position of assistant priest in the temple of Kali. It proved an idyllic home for Gadadhar, one in which he would remain for the remainder of his life. Here, in the company of his brother, and a nephew, his boyhood friend, Hriday, who shortly joined him, he spent his days decorating and worshipping the deity image of Kali in the lavish temple. In his free time, he meditated in the nearby woods, or bathed in the Ganges, or spoke with his friends in his comfortable little room attached to the temple.

Gadadhar was very happy in his new life; he became totally absorbed in the worship of the divine Mother, whether in his official duties or in his free moments of meditation; and both the Rani and her son-in-law, Mathur, who served as temple manager, became very fond of this beaming youth who brought with him such heart-felt devotion and spiritual joy into the temple. It was around this time that he began to be called "Ramakrishna," a name combining two of the names for God, and it is by that name that he is known to the world today. But this was but the beginning of Ramakrishna's spiritual life. In the following years, as his devotional fervor increased, he was to pass through many stages of intense longing, dark despair, and to ascend to the heights of mysical vision, realizing in himself the absolute Truth of all existence.

In 1856, Ramakrishna's brother, Ramkumar, died; and Ramakrishna was persuaded to accept the position of head priest in the Kali temple. This coincided with a period of great longing which arose in Ramakrishna for some inner experience of the divine Mother, some inner proof of Her existencce; and he began to spend his nights alone in the nearby forests, in an abandoned cremation grounds, where he would meditate on the all-pervasive God as the divine Mother, Kali. Like an infant child deprived of its mother, he would weep and cry out, "O Mother, where are you? Can't you show yourself to me!" And when, in the mornings, he would appear, bleary-eyed and as if drunken, even his nephew and close comrade,

Hriday, would wonder if he was not becoming deranged from thinking so much on Kali.

Soon his restless longing became so intense, and his Mother's absense so bitter to him, that Ramakrishna felt that he would prefer to die rather than suffer so. What happened then, he tells in his own words:

> I felt as if my heart were being squeezed like a wet towel. I was overpowered with a great restlessness and a fear that it might not be my lot to realize Her in this life. I could not bear the separation from Her any longer. Life seemed to be not worth living. Suddenly my glance fell on the sword that was kept in the Mother's temple. I determined to put an end to my life. When I jumped up like a madman and seized it, suddenly the blessed Mother revealed Herself. The buildings with their different parts, the temple, and everything else vanished from my sight, leaving no trace whatsoever, and in their stead I saw a limitless, infinite, effulgent Ocean of Consciousness. As far as the eye could see, the shining billows were madly rushing at me from all sides with a terrific noise, to swallow me up! I was panting for breath. I was caught in the rush and collapsed, unconscious. What was happening in the outside world I did not know; but within me there was a steady flow of undiluted bliss, altogether new, and I felt the presence of the Divine Mother. [1]

Yet this was but the first of Ramakrishna's many intimate encounters with the Divine; he had experienced the truth of the scriptures, and was satisfied that all this world of forms was only the manifold expression of the one all-pervasive Creatrix -- the divine Prakrti, the Logos, the creative Power of God. But this experience merely whetted his appetite for spiritual knowledge, and he became even more one-pointedly fixed on his Mother, Kali, as the one and only object of his perception -- whether open-eyed in the world of forms or deep in meditation on his beloved Kali within. Now, his official devotions in the temple became the familiar loving play of a child with its mother, and he would talk to her image and tuck her on the chin, and behave in such an unorthodox manner that the temple officials began to wonder seriously about his sanity.

Once, when Ramakrishna fed the rice intended as the ritual offering to Kali to the temple cat, an official who had seen this act complained to Mathur, the manager. But nothing came of this, as Ramakrishna, himself, explains:

>The Divine Mother revealed to me in the Kali temple
>that it was She who had become everything. She showed me
>that everything was full of Consciousness. The image was
>Consciousness, the altar was Consciousness, the water-vessels
>were Consciousness, the door-sill was Consciousness, the
>marble floor was Consciousness -- all was Consciousness. I
>found everything inside the room soaked, as it were, in Bliss,
>the Bliss of God. I saw a wicked man in front of the Kali
>temple; but in him also I saw the power of the Divine Mother
>vibrating. That was why I fed a cat with the food that was to
>be offered to the Divine Mother. I clearly perceived that all
>this was the Divine Mother -- even the cat. The manager of
>the temple garden wrote to Mathur Babu, saying that I was
>feeding the cat with the offering intended for the Divine
>Mother. But Mathur Babu had insight into the state of my
>mind. He wrote back to the manager: "Let him do whatever
>he likes. You must not say anything to him." [2]

The statue (*murti*) of Kali, the Divine Mother, which stood in
the shrine of the main temple was made of black basalt, and decorated
from head to foot in golden ornaments and rich silk brocades. She
stood upright on the prostrate body of Shiva, a garland of skulls
draped 'round Her neck, and a string of severed arms around her
waist. In one of Her four hands She held a severed human head; in
another, a blood-stained sword; another hand offered gifts of wealth,
and the fourth was held palm-outward in a gesture signifying "Have
no fear." Some early artist conceived Her thus, deriving Her attributes from the descriptions of the seers and philosophers who spoke of
the creative Energy of the universe whose foundation is the
unchanging and unmoving Absolute (*Shiva*); and who, while giving
life and pleasures with one hand, takes them away with the other. She
is the impartial Mother Nature, whose bloody sport all this world is;
whose parade of time (*kali*) brings all things to birth, fruition, and
ultimately to death.

To Ramakrishna, this artist's representation of the abstract
Principle of creation was no mere statue. He focused all his heart and
mind on Her, imbuing Her with life and personality. To him, She was
his Mother; and so intense was his devotion that he often visualized
Her in his meditations, or caught glimpses of Her youthful form
strolling about in the garden during his waking hours. But this
"divine madness" was soon to take a new turn.

Suddenly, Ramakrishna began to worship God as Rama, the

God-incarnation of the epic literature; and he began to identify himself with Rama's monkey-servant, Hanuman. It was no doubt the same predilection which enabled him to identify easily with various persona as an amateur actor, which now enabled him to identify so completely with Hanuman. He began hopping about like a monkey, and ate only fruits and roots. At times, he strolled about naked and carefree, causing embarassment to everyone. Once, when his patroness, Rani Rasmani, was in the temple during the singing of devotional songs, Ramakrishna turned suddenly, and slapped her across the face. Everyone present was greatly alarmed, but the Rani admitted that her mind had wandered, and she had been thinking of an impending court case, and defended Ramakrishna's action as justified. But many of Ramakrishna's associates were by now quite concerned for his sanity. His mother in Kamarpukur heard of his state, and requested the temple officials to send him back to his village for a "change of air."

Ramakrishna was now twenty-three; his mother was sure that what he really needed to get his feet back on the ground was a wife. And so, with Ramakrishna's approval, a wife was found for him, in a neighboring village: a girl just five years old, by the name of Saradamani. Such a youthful marriage was considered in India a betrothal to be consummated in true marriage when the child reached puberty. But the marriage was never, in fact, consummated; after a year and a half in Kamarpukur, Ramakrishna returned to Dakshineswar and his beloved Kali. Immediately, his divine "madness" resurfaced. He spent nearly all his time in meditation and prayer, giving scarcely any time to sleep. With the death of the Rani, in 1861, Mathur, her son-in-law, became the sole executor of the temple, and as he was reverently devoted to Ramakrishna, he looked after every need of the divinely intoxicated priest.

Around this time, a woman came to Dakshineswar who was to have a great influence on Ramakrishna. She was known only as "the Brahmani." She was a wandering *sannyasini* (renunciant) in her fifties, and a learned practitioner of the Tantric path. Recognizing in Ramakrishna the signs of an advanced devotee, she took him under her charge, teaching him the philosophy and practice of the Tantric sadhana. She became convinced that he was not only a saintly and extremely pure devotee, but was a rare and extraordinary being, similar to the legendary God-incarnations such as Rama and Krishna. She openly declared to everyone that Ramakrishna was an *Avatar*, an incarnation of God Himself. To corroborate her claim, the Brahmani invited two learned pandits to the temple, and, with Ramakrishna sitting among them, she described to them his condition. Soon, the pandits also were convinced, and everyone agreed that Ramakrishna was, indeed, a special incarnation of God. Upon hearing this, Ramakrishna declared, "Just imagine! Well, I'm glad to learn its's not a disease, after all."

Through the tutelege of the Brahmani, Ramakrishna learned of the scriptures which supported and gave explanations of the experiences he was having: the burning sensation, the intense longing, the great joy of devotion he felt, and his experiences of the all-pervasive Reality -- all were documented and explained to him as manifestations of divine grace which had been experienced by saints and seers throughout India's long spiritual history. Moreover, he learned of the Tantric conception of the interior Shakti known as Kundalini, and became even more aware of the process of spiritual development going on within him. He could trace the movement of living energy rising from the base of his spine, through his body, and upward, into the cranial region. When he sang his love-songs to God, and when he prayed and meditated in the nearby grove, he felt these changes in his body, corresponding to the changes in his consciousness. When that energy reached the crown of his head, he would lose all sense of the world around him, and become lost in an infinite sea of Bliss.

The Brahmani also taught him the various *bhavas*, or attitudes, through which a man may worship and attain union with his Beloved. For a time, Ramakrishna practiced the *bhava* of motherly love toward Rama, identifyting with the mythological mother of Rama, and enjoying the tender relationship to God of a mother to its child. At another time, he took the *bhava* of Radha, the female consort of Krishna in the Puranas; and in this attitude, he enjoyed the love of a maiden for her Lover. Ramakrishna, the young man, like Ramakrishna, the child, had a seemingly infinite capacity for play-acting and total identification with whatever identity he chose to assume. And due to this proclivity he was able to experiment wholeheartedly with nearly every kind of mental attitude, and, through each, reach an exalted state of devotion, which might have been the lifelong attainment of a lesser-gifted person.

Toward the end of 1864, when Ramakrishna was 28, a new character entered the Dakshineswar scene. His name was Totapuri.

He was, like the Brahmani, a wandering renunciant; and, like the Brahmani, he was to become a mentor to Ramakrishna, and a great influence in his life. Whereas the Brahmani was a learned practitioner of the Tantric path, and most suited to Ramakrishna's inherent tendencies; Totapuri was an austere Vedantist, whose philosophy left no room for devotional fervor; he was a strict *Advaitist*, or Nondualist, in the manner of Shankara.

While the experience of Unity is the same for all, the attitude of the devotee and that of the Non-dualist, or the *bhakta* and the *jnani*, are necessarily quite different. Ramakrishna, up to this time, had followed his natural bent toward the devotional attitude; as a *bhakta*, he approached his God in a relational manner, rising thereby to the awareness of his oneness with God by the path of love. But here was something new; Totapuri was sternly and ascetically Nondualistic; that is to say, he did not acknowledge the validity of the relational path; for him, the soul (*jiva*) and the Self (*Atman*) were ever one. Totapuri had spent many years meditating on the Absolute, and had attained the direct realization of absolute Unity in his meditation; and he held unswervingly to the truth of what he had known in that experience. For him, all these practices of various devotional *bhavas* were mere imagination, irrelevant and contradictory to the ultimate truth of Unity. The gods and goddesses which Ramakrishna had been worshipping for so long were, to him, mere phantasies of a delude mind.

When Totapuri, the ascetic yogi, met Ramakrishna while passing through the Dakshineswar temple on his visit to the Ganges, he recognized in Ramakrishna a ripeness for the Vedantic teachings of Non-duality, and he asked Ramakrishna if he would like to be initiated by him. Ramakrishna, after asking permission from his "Mother," Kali, responded that he would. Totapuri first initiated Ramakrishna into monkhood (*sannyasa*), during which he was asked to renounce everything that tied him to the world -- caste, sex, society, everything. Then Totapuri began teaching Ramakrishna, the *sannyasin*, of the great truths of Vedanta: "Brahman," he said,

> is the only Reality, ever pure, ever illumined, ever free,
> beyond the limits of time, space, and causation. Though
> apparently divided by names and forms through the inscrut-
> able power of Maya, that Enchantress who makes the
> impossible possible, Brahman is really One and undivided.
> When a seeker merges in the beatitude of samadhi, he does

not perceive time and space or name and form, the offspring of
maya. Whatever is within the domain of maya is unreal.
Give it up. Destroy the prisonhouse of name and form and
rush out of it with the strength of a lion. Dive deep in search
of the Self and realize It through samadhi. You will find the
world of name and form vanishing into void, and the puny
ego dissolving in Brahman-Consciousness. You will realize
your identity with Brahman, Existence-Knowledge-Bliss
Absolute. [3]

Then, asking Ramakrishna to meditate, concentrating on the
space between the eyebrows, Totapuri told him to withdraw his mind
from all thoughts, imaginations, and worldly objects. Of this effort to
meditate in this manner, Ramakrishna later said:

> In spite of all my attempts, I could not altogether
> cross the realm of name and form and bring my mind to the
> unconditioned state. I had no difficulty in taking the mind
> from all the objects of the world. But the radiant and too
> familiar figure of the Blissful Mother, the Embodiment of
> the essence of Pure Consciousness, appeared before me as a
> living reality. Her bewitching smile prevented me from
> passing into the Great Beyond. Again and again I tried, but
> She stood in my way every time. In despair I said to Nangta
> (*Ed. note*: "Nangta" refers to Totapuri): "It is hopeless. I
> cannot raise my mind to the un-conditioned state and come face
> to face with Atman." He grew excited and sharply said:
> "What? You can't do it? But you have to!" He cast his eyes
> around. Finding a piece of glass, he took it up and stuck it
> between my eyebrows. "Concentrate the mind on this point!"
> he thundered. Then with stern determination I again sat to
> meditate. As soon as the gracious form of the Divine Mother
> appeared before me, I used my discrimination as a sword and
> with it clove Her in two. The last barrier fell. My spirit at
> once soared beyond the relative plane and I lost myself in
> samadhi. [4]

Ramakrishna remained in a deep trance of samadhi for three
days; and it was only by the strenuous efforts of Totapuri that his
mind was gradually brought down again to the relative plane. Totapuri was amazed and flabbergasted; "Is it possible," he exclaimed,
"that this man has attained in one day what it took me forty years to
attain! It is nothing short of a miracle!"

Ramakrishna had seen the Reality from both sides of the coin;
he knew the One in both Its aspects, the absolute Consciousness, and

Its relative manifestation. Whether he called It "Mother" or "Brahman," It was the same One. As he was later to explain:

> Kali is none other than He whom you call Brahman.
> Kali is the primal Shakti. When It is inactive, we call It
> Brahman. But when It has the function of creating, preserving
> or destroying, we call That Shakti or Kali. He whom you call
> Brahman, She whom I call Kali, are no more different from
> each other than fire and its power of burning. [5]

> ... When I think of the Supreme Being as inactive --
> neither creating nor preserving nor destroying --, I call Him
> Brahman or Purusha, the Impersonal God. When I think of
> Him as active-- creating, preserving, destroying--, I call Him
> Shakti or Maya or Prakriti, the Personal God. But the
> distinction between them does not mean a difference. The
> Personal and the Impersonal are the same thing, like milk and
> its whiteness, the diamond and its lustre, the snake and its
> wriggling motion. It is impossible to conceive of the one
> without the other. The Divine Mother and Brahman are one. [6]

Ramakrishna enjoyed the company of Totapuri for nearly a year, after which the sturdy Avadhut continued on his wandering career. Ramakrishna is said thereafter to have entered once again into deep samadhi for a period of nearly six months, during which time his body was kept alive by a kindly monk who, recognizing his state, managed to push into his mouth a few morsels of food daily.

Shortly after this time, Ramakrishna, in his eagerness to corroborate for himself the essential unity of all religious paths, became a practitioner of each of the major religions in turn. Finding a Muslim Pir, he learned to follow the customs of Islam, and, praying to Allah, realized the goal of that religion. Later, he began to listen to readings of the Bible, and became utterly devoted to Jesus, experiencing divine ecstasy at the very thought of the Christ. One day, while walking in his favorite grove, meditating on Jesus, he saw coming toward him a man with large beautiful eyes, and serene countenance and fair skin, and he realized that it was Jesus. As they embraced, the form of Jesus merged into his own. He also recognized the divinity of the Buddha, and the Tirthankaras of Jainism, and the Gurus of the Sikh tradition. "I have practiced," he said,

> all religions -- Hinduism, Islam, Christianity -- and I have also
> followed the paths of the different Hindu sects. I have found
> that it is the same God toward whom all are directing their

steps, though along different paths. You must try all beliefs
and traverse all the different ways once. Wherever I look, I
see men quarreling in the name of religion -- Hindus, Moham-
medans, Brahmos, Vaishnavas, and the rest. But they never
reflect that He who is called Krishna is also called Shiva, and
bears the name of Shakti, Jesus, and Allah, as well --
the same Rama with a thousand names. ... Let each man
follow his own path. If he sincerely and ardently wishes to
know God, peace be unto him! He will surely reach Him. [7]

In 1867, Ramakrishna paid a visit to his home in Kamarpu-
kar, and met again, for the first time since his marriage, with his wife,
Sarada. She was now fourteen, and eagerly receptive of her
husband's spiritual wisdom. She was an unusually pure and devout
child, and she recognized the extraordinary holiness of her husband.
She gladly entered his service as a disciple and servant. In January of
1868, Ramakrishna set out with Mathur and a party of one-hundred
and twenty-five devotees to travel on pilgrimage to some of the holy
places of India which had been held in reverence in song and legend
for centuries. He journeyed by foot and by boat to Benares,
Allahabad, Vrindavan and Mathura, and back to Calcutta, meeting
with many saintly devotees during his travels. In 1870, he took
another trip -- this time to Nadia, the birthplace of Chaitanya, the 16th
century love-intoxicated saint of Bengal.

Thereafter, Ramakrishna settled down at Dakshineswar, with
Sarada joining him. He had long ago renounced worldly attachments
in order to remain solely conscious of the ever-present reality of God;
he was a monk, and his relationship with his wife was one of a Guru
and disciple. Shortly after she joined him, he placed her on an altar
and worshipped her as the Divine Mother, Kali; and ever afterward he
looked upon her as the very embodiment of the Divine. One day,
while massaging his feet, Sarada asked her husband, "What do you
think of me?" And Ramakrishna answered:

> The Mother who is worshipped in the temple is the
> mother who has given birth to my body and is now living in
> the *nahabat* (*Ed. Note*: a small building on the temple grounds
> into which his mother had moved); and it is She again who is
> stroking my feet at this moment. Indeed, I always look on
> you as the personification of the blissful Mother, Kali. [8]

As for the experience of Sarada during this time, she relates:

I have no words to describe my wonderful exaltation
of spirit as I watched him in his different moods. Under the
influence of divine emotion he would sometimes talk on
abstruse subjects, sometimes laugh, sometimes weep, and
sometimes become perfectly motionless in   samadhi. This
would continue throughout the night. There was such an
extraordinary divine presence in him that now and then I would
shake with fear, and wonder how the night would pass.
Months went by in this way. Then one day he discovered that
I had to keep awake the whole night lest, during my   sleep, he
should go into samadhi -- for it might happen at any moment;
and so he asked me to sleep in the *nahabat.* [9]

In the years that followed, Ramakrishna, the "mad   priest of
Dakshineswar," became increasingly recognized as Ramakrishna,
"the Master." He had not studied philosophy from books, but he
had experienced in himself the direct knowledge of Reality over
which philosophers merely theorize. Those who came to him with
their questions regarding spiritual life received their answers, not from
the book-knowledge of a pandit, but from one who lived day and
night in intimate contact with the living reality of God. Many
distinguished scholars, doctors, and accomplished yogis came to
Dakshineswar to sit at his feet and listen to the words of one who
spoke of the reality of God from his own, most intimate, experience.

The 19th century had seen a great decline in religious faith
throughout India. Under the British rule begun in 1757, the young
men and women, educated in the Western manner, with Western ideals
of material progress, had become disillusioned with the ancient ideals
of Indian religious culture. They had rejected the mystical ideas and
the ancient scriptures of their Indian heritage, and looked upon these
as superstitious mumbo-jumbo from a retarded past. They adopted
Western clothes, Western customs, and strived to absorb themselves
into the efficient British civilization which had overspread their own
ancient, seemingly outdated, culture. But Ramakrishna, this slightly-
built, stammering priest living on the out-skirts of the city was to serve
as a great transformative force, recalling the people of India, as
Shankara, Jnaneshvar, and Chaitanya had done before him, to the rich
spiritual heritage which was their most precious and most significant
birthright.

Ramakrishna represented, as no other of his time could do, the
living synthesis and culmination of all the long Indian tradition of
spiritual attainment and knowledge which had accumulated over the

centuries. He bridged the chasm between Dualism and Non-dualism, between the Impersonal and the Personal God, between *bhakti* and *jnan*, through his own realization and revelation of their essential unity. During the last ten years of his life, many learned and famous people from all walks of life came to see him. Many became his devoted disciples, visiting him weekly or daily. Among these were Keshab Chandra Sen, the leader of the religious reform organization called the Brahmo Samaj, Pundit Shashadhar, and Bankim Chatterji, the famous novelist and dramatist, and many more.

As his many devotees came to sit in his small room in the temple-grounds, Ramakrishna would often sing to them the devotional songs of the mystic-poet, Ramprasad, and other Bengali saints. And as he sang, he would be lifted up into ecstasy, and merge into the Absolute. Then he would stop his singing, and sit lost in a rapturous silence, a lustrous radiance shining forth from his face. All who saw him thus were moved and dumbstruck by the ease with which he rose from the lower state of consciousness to the Highest. Almost daily, he entered into deep samadhi, completely unaware of the world around him; and then, coming down again, as it were, to the appearance of God as the world of forms, he would merrily speak to his listeners of his Divine Mother, and her inseparable identity with Brahman, the Absolute.

But those to whom Ramakrishna was most drawn were the young men, as yet untainted by fixed opinions, and unsaddled by worldly responsibilities. Many such young men began coming to see him, and remained to become transformed by his lilting voice, his guileless wisdom, and his gentle touch. These were to become his future monks and teachers who would take his message to every part of the world. No doubt the most famous, and perhaps the most gifted of these young men was Narendra Datta, a nineteen-year old university student who would later become known in the West as well as throughout India as Swami Vivekananda (1863-1905).

When Narendra first came to see Ramakrishna, he was a member of the Brahmo Samaj, a liberal religious organization which preached universal toleration and the reform of certain Hindu practices such as caste discrimination and suttee. He was one of those youths, typical of the time, who was enthralled with European values, and who had little if any sympathy for what he regarded as the backward "superstitions" of his country's past. But when he met Ramakrishna, he got a great shock. He had come with a group from the Brahmo Samaj, and Ramakrishna had immediately asked him to sing a few devotional songs. After he did so, the Master took him by the hand and led him to a verandah. Here they were alone; and the Master said to him, "Ah, you have come very late. Why have you been so unkind as to make me wait all these days? My ears are tired of hearing the futile words of worldly men. Oh, how I have longed to pour my spirit into the heart of someone fitted to receive my message."

But Narendra was a proud and independent youth, and a bit of a snob. He was certain that this man who had addressed him so familiarly on their first meeting was undoubtedly mad and completely egotistical. After they had rejoined the others, Narendra asked him, "Sir, have you seen God?" And Ramakrishna replied, "Yes, I have seen God. I have seen Him more tangibly than I see you. I have talked to Him more intimately than I am talking to you." Continuing, the Master said, "But, my child, who wants to see God? People shed jugs of tears for money, wife, and children. But if they would weep for God for only one day they would surely see Him."

Narendra was baffled. He had never heard anyone say that they had seen God. And this man spoke with such certainty and such assurance about such matters that it seemed almost commonplace to him. Narendra was hooked; and thereafter, he returned again and again. And each time he did, he found his resistance melting a little more each time. All his plans, all his ambitions, seemed to be overturned; and now all he could think of was God -- and this strangely lovable man who seemed to be the very personification of all that was holy and Godlike.

When, on a subsequent visit to Dakshinesvar, Naren received the touch of Ramakrishna's hand, he felt suddenly overwhelmed with emotion, and felt that the room and the whole outer world was melting away. "What are you doing to me!" he cried out; "Don't you know I have my father and mother at home!" And when Ramakrishna, with a laugh, removed his hand, Narendra regained his sense of the concreteness of the world. In the years that followed, Narendra became a regular visitor to Dakshineswar, and learned the wisdom of God at the feet of this amazing man whom he now regarded as his Master. After the death of Ramakrishna in 1886, he would be the one to take this wisdom across the ocean to America, and to share his Master's vision with the New World.

In April of 1885, Ramakrishna came down with an inflammation of the throat, and a doctor was called in. He was advised not to speak so much and to avoid singing and over-exertion. Naturally, Ramakrishna found it impossible to follow this advice, and the problem with his sore throat became increasingly worse, till at last it began to bleed. The doctor announced that the Master had cancer of the throat. In September, Ramakrishna was moved to Syampukur, where his disciples could remain with him and attend his needs day and night. As he could not eat anything but liquids due to the pain, his body became increasingly emaciated. Yet through it all, the Master remained in an exalted state of mind, radiant as usual in the flush of his superconscious joy.

In December, he was moved to a more comfortable garden-house at Cossipore, and for eight months more the Master continued to dwindle in strength. Sarada, Narendra, and many other young men stayed with him and nursed him day and night. It was during these months that a great bond of brotherhood was forged between these future monks, and it was during this time that Ramakrishna revealed to each of them the course they were to follow after his death. Shortly before his end, he said to them as they gathered around his bed, "Do you know what I see? I see that God alone has become everything. Men and animals are only frameworks covered with skin, and it is He who is moving through their heads and limbs. I see that it is God Himself who has become the block, the executioner, and the victim for the sacrifice."

On Sunday morning, August 15, 1886, Ramakrishna lifted his head, and cried out, "Kali! Kali! Kali! " and lay back again. At 11:30 A.M. he was gone.

Ramakrishna was born a simple child in an obscure little village in the countryside of India, but today his words and his vision live on in the hearts of millions. Perhaps no one else in modern times has so profoundly effected the mind of modern man as this humble, delicate, soul, so far removed from the bustling, busy world of contemporary civilization. His laughing eyes, his playful smile haunt us and will continue to haunt us from every corner of our minds. He lived as the incontrovertible proof of the possibility of a life filled with purity, love, and the ever-present vision of God -- a proof from which we can never hide. And wherever men speak of the highest, whenever men recount the wisest, however men envisualize the greatest, the name of Ramakrishna will be heard, and the sound of his voice will echo in our hearts.

Today, a mere one-hundred years have passed since his death, and already the story of his life and immensity of his vision is known throughout the world. This is due in great part to one of Rama-krishna's frequent visitors, a young school teacher, named Mahendra-nath Gupta, known simply as "M," who kept a record of the conversations of the Master which he personally witnessed. He had a fortunate gift for remembering these conversations almost verbatim, which he then recorded in a book, called *The Gospel Of Ramakrishna*. It is this book which provides for us an intimate portrait of the great saint of Dakshineswar. The following collection of the utterances of Ramakrishna are taken from it:

On The Unity Of All Religions

Some people indulge in quarrels, saying, "One cannot attain anything unless one worships our Krishna," or "Nothing can be gained without the worship of Kali, our Divine Mother," or "One cannot be saved without accepting the Christian religion." This is pure dogmatism. The dogmatist says, "My religion alone is true, and the religions of others are false." This is a bad attitude. God can be reached by different paths." [10]

You may say that there are many errors and super-stitions in other religions. I should reply: Suppose there are. Every religion has errors. Everyone thinks that his watch alone gives the correct time. It is enough to have yearning for God. It is enough to love Him and feel attracted to Him. Don't you know that God is the inner Guide? He sees the longing of our heart and the yearning of our soul. Suppose a man has several sons. The older boys address him distinctly as "Baba" or "Papa," but the babies can at best call him "Ba" or "Pa." Now will the father be angry with those who address him in this indistinct way? The father knows that they too are calling him, only they cannot pronounce his name well. All children are the same to the father. Likewise, the devotees call on God alone, though by different names. They call on one Person only. God is one, but His names are many. [11]

The inferior devotee says, "God exists, but He is

very far off, up there in heaven." The mediocre devotee says, "God exists in all beings as life and consciousness." The superior devotee says, "It is God Himself who has become everything; whatever I see is only a form of God. It is He alone who has become maya, the universe, and all living beings. Nothing exists but God." [12]

Further, some say that God has form and is not formless. Thus they start quarrelling. ... One can speak rightly of God only after one has seen Him. He who has seen God knows really and truly that God has form and that He is formless as well. He has many other aspects that cannot be described.

Once some blind men chanced to come near an animal that someone told them was an elephant. They were asked what the elephant was like. The blind men began to feel its body. One of them said the elephant was like a pillar; he had touched only its leg. Another said it was like a winnowing-fan; he had touched only its ear. In this way, the others, having touched its tail or its belly, gave their different versions of the elephant. Just so, a man who has seen only one aspect of God limits God to that alone. It is his conviction that God cannot be anything else. [13]

On The Identity Of Brahman And Shakti

He is indeed a real man who has harmonized everything. Most people are one-sided. But I find that all opinions
point to the One. All views -- the Shakta, the Vaishnava, the
Vedanta -- have that One for their center. He who is formless
is, again, endowed with form. It is He who appears in different forms. The attributeless Brahman is my Father. God with
attributes is my Mother. Whom shall I blame? Whom shall I
praise? The two sides of the scale are equally heavy. [14]

Nothing exists except the One. That One is the
supreme Brahman. So long as He keeps the "I" in us, He
reveals to us that it is He who, as the Primal Energy, creates,
preserves, and destroys the universe.
That which is Brahman is also the Primal Energy.
Once a king asked a yogi to impart knowledge to him in one
word. The yogi said, "All right, you will get Knowledge in
one word." After a while a magician came to the king. The
king saw the magician moving two of his fingers rapidly and
heard him exclaim, "Behold, O king! Behold!" The king
looked at him amazed, when, after a few minutes, he saw the
two fingers becoming one. ... The implication of the story is
that Brahman and the Primal Energy at first appear to be two.
But after attaining the knowledge of Brahman, one does not see
the two. Then there is no differentiation; it is One, without a
second, Advaita -- non-duality. [15]

Brahman is Shakti; Shakti is Brahman. They are not
two. These are only two aspects, male and female, of the
same Reality -- Existence-Knowledge-Bliss Absolute. [16]

Brahman and Shakti are identical, like fire and its
power to burn. When we talk of fire we automatically
mean also its power to burn. Again, the fire's power to burn
implies the fire itself. If you accept the one, you must accept
the other. [17]

The phenomenal world belongs to that very Reality
to which the Absolute belongs; again, the Absolute belongs
to that very Reality to which the phenomenal world belongs.
He who is realized as God has also become the universe and
its living beings. One who knows the Truth knows that
it is He alone who has become father and mother, child and

neighbor, man and animal, good and bad, holy and unholy, and so forth. [18]

On The Illusory Ego

Under the spell of God's maya, man forgets his true nature. He forgets that he is heir to the infinite glories of his Father. [19]

Maya is nothing but the egotism of the embodied soul. This egotism has covered everything like a veil. All troubles come to an end when the ego dies. If by the grace of God a man but once realizes that he is not the doer, then he at once becomes a *jivanmukta* [a liberated being]. Though living in the body, he is liberated. He has nothing else to fear. [20]

"I" and "mine" -- that is ignorance. By discriminating, you will realize that what you call "I" is really nothing but *Atman* [the Self]. Reason it out. Are you the body or the flesh or something else? At the end , you will know that you are none of these. You are free from attributes. Then you will realize that you have never been the doer of any action, that you have been free from virtue and faults alike, that you are beyond righteousness and unrighteousness. [21]

The jnani -- the Vedantist, for instance -- always reasons, applying the process of "Not this, notthis." Through this discrimination he realizes, by his inner perception, that the ego and the universe are both illusory, like a dream. Then the jnani realizes Brahman in his own consciousness.
... In that state a man no longer finds the existence of his ego. And who is there left to seek it? Who can describe how he feels in that state -- in his own Pure Consciousness -- about the real nature of Brahman? Once a salt doll went to measure the depth of the ocean. No sooner was it in the water than it melted. Now who was to tell the depth? ... Then the "I," which may be likened to the salt doll, melts in the Ocean of Existence-Knowledge-Bliss Absolute, and becomes one with It. Not the slightest trace of distinction is left. [22]

The Vedantist says, "I am He." Brahman is real and the world illusory. Even the "I" is illusory. Only the Supreme Brahman exists." [23]

Even after attaining samadhi, some retain the "servant ego," or the "devotee ego." The bhakta keeps this "I-consciousness." He says, "O God, Thou art the Master and I am Thy servant; Thou art the Lord and I am Thy devotee." He feels that way even after the realization of God. His "I" is not completely effaced. Again, by constantly practicing this kind of "I-consciousness," one ultimately attains God...

One can attain the Knowledge of Brahman too by following the path of bhakti. God is all-powerful. He may give His devotee *Brahmajnana* [the knowledge of Brahman] also if He so wills. But the devotee generally doesn't seek the Knowledge of the Absolute. He would rather have the consciousness that God is the Master and he the servant, or that God is the Divine Mother and he the child. [24]

On Grace And Surrender To God

One cannot see God without purity of heart. Through attachment to "woman and gold" the mind has become stained -- covered with dirt, as it were. A magnet cannot attract a needle if the needle is covered with mud. Wash away the mud and the magnet will draw it. Likewise, the dirt of the mind can be washed away with the tears of our eyes. This stain is removed if one sheds tears of repentence and says, "O God, I shall never again do such a thing." Thereupon God, who is like the magnet, draws to Himself the mind, which is like the needle. Then the devotee goes into samadhi and obtains the vision of God.

You may try thousands of times, but nothing can be achieved without God's grace. One cannot see God without His grace. Is it an easy thing to receive the grace of God? One must altogether renounce egotism; one cannot see God as long as one feels "I am the doer." ... God doesn't easily appear in the heart of a man who feels himself to be his own master. But God can be seen the moment His grace descends. He is the Sun of Knowledge. One single ray of His has illumined the world with the light of knowledge. This is how we are able to see one another and acquire varied knowledge. One can see God only if He turns His light toward His own Face. [25]

A man does not have to suffer any more if God, in His grace, removes his doubts and reveals Himself to him. But this grace descends upon him only after he has prayed to God with intense yearning of heart and practiced spiritual discipline. The mother feels compassion for her child when she sees him running about breathlessly. She has been hiding herself; now she appears before the child.

...It is His will that we should run about a little. Then it is great fun. God has created the world in play, as it were. This is called Mahamaya, the Great Illusion. Therefore one must take refuge in the Divine Mother, the Cosmic Power Itself. It is She who has bound us with the shackles of illusion. The realization of God is possible only when those shackles are severed. [26]

On The Path Of Devotion

The path of knowledge leads to Truth, as does the path that combines knowledge [*jnan*] and love [*bhakti*]. The path of love too leads to this goal. The way of love is as true as the way of knowledge. All paths ultimately lead to the same Truth. But as long as God keeps the feeling of ego in us, it is easier to follow the path of love. [27]

Do you know how a lover of God feels? His attitude is: "O God, Thou art the Master, and I am Thy servant. Thou art the Mother, and I am Thy child." Or again: "Thou art my Father and Mother. Thou art the Whole, and I am a part." He doesn't like to say, "I am Brahman." [28]

The man in whom longing for God manifests its glories is not far from attaining Him. What are the glories of that longing? They are discrimination, dispassion, compassion for living beings, serving holy men, loving their company, chanting the name and glories of God, telling only the truth, and the like. When you see these signs of longing in an aspirant, you can rightly say that for him the vision of God is not far to seek. [29]

You will feel restless for God when your heart becomes pure and your mind free from attachment to the things of the world. Then alone will your prayer reach God. A telegraph wire cannot carry messages if it has a break or some other defect.

I used to cry for God all alone, with a longing heart. I used to weep, "O God, where art Thou?" Weeping thus, I would lose all consciousness of the world. My mind would merge in the *Mahavayu* [the infinite sky of Consciousness].

How can one attain yoga? By completely renouncing attachment to worldly things. The mind must be pure and without blemish, like the telegraph wire that has no defect. One must not cherish any desire whatever. The devotion of a man who has desire is selfish. But desireless devotion is love for its own sake. You may love me or not, but I love you; this is love for its own sake.

The thing is that one must love God. Through intense love one attains the vision of Him. The attraction of the husband for the chaste wife, the attraction of the child for its mother, the attraction of worldly possessions for the worldly man -- when a man can blend these three into one, and direct it all to God, then he gets the vision of God. [30]

The sum and substance of the whole matter is that a man must love God, must be restless for Him. It doesn't matter whether you believe in God with form or God without form. You may or may not believe that God incarnates Himself as man. But you will realize Him if you have that yearning. Then He himself will let you know what He is like. If you must be mad, why should you be mad for the things of the world? If you must be mad, be mad for God alone. [31]

TWENTIETH CENTURY MYSTICS

At the turn of the century, two independent American scholars, Richard M. Bucke and William James, published their investigations into the mystical experience. Bucke's *Cosmic Consciousness* (1901), and James' *Varieties Of Religious Experience* (1902), included numerous personal accounts of such experiences, and documented their occasional occurrence in the lives of, otherwise, ordinary people. Their scholarly efforts met with a great deal of interest -- but from the relatively small community of religious scholars and students only; and, while both books continue to be reprinted and read by students of mysticism, the over-all effect on the Western religious culture has been negligible.

Within the Western Judeo-Christian tradition, as in all religious traditions, the number of genuine mystics has always been few, and the unitive aspect of mystical experience has always been frowned upon by the official Church; but, since the Protestant Reformation of the 17th and 18th centuries, the mystical element in Christianity has become almost non-existent. The theocentric devotion of Medieval Catholicism has given way to anthropocentric Protestantism and secular humanism; and the emphasis of Christianity, in much of the Western world, has become focused almost exclusively on social and humanitarian goals.

There were, of course, a few exceptional individuals, like Evelyn Underhill (1875-1941) and Thomas Merton (1915-1968), who sought to return the focus of Christianity to theocentric devotion and interior contemplation; but their influence was slight, and did little to stem the degenerative trend of mainstream Christianity. This trend was most evident in 20th century America, where the Christian ethic had been most effectively adapted to the materialistic view of Western society. It is not surprising, therefore, that the renewed call to theocentric devotion and mystical realization was to come from outside the Western Christian tradition, from the mystical saints and sages of the East.

When Ramakrishna's disciple, Swami Vivekananda (1863-1902), came to America in 1893 to attend the Chicago World's Parliament of Religions, he attracted a great deal of attention, and his subsequent lectures in America on the universal goal of Self-realization stirred the hearts and minds of many. Only a few years later,

Swami Rama Tirtha (1873-1906), another illumined sage of India, came to the West, and similarly inspired those who came to hear him. The Sufi, Pir Hazrat Inayat Khan (1888-1950) came in 1910. Another enlightened pilgrim to America was the enchanting Parama-hansa Yogananda (1893-1952), who came in 1920 and remained to found his Self-Realization Fellowship in California, helping to spread the teachings of Yoga in America.

But in those early decades of the 20th century "Yoga" was still widely regarded as synonymous with chicanery, and Swamis were caricatured in the popular press as snake-charmers and charlatans. The Western world had completely lost sight of the great mystical tradition of antiquity, and was scarcely prepared to offer a warm welcome to the mystical teachings of the East.

In those early decades of this century little was known in the Christian West of the mystical philosophies of foreign lands, and few were willing to even listen to their representatives. The great Depression and the two great wars turned the full attention of the Western world to political and practical affairs rather than to spiritual or philosophical ones, to the means for bodily survival rather than the liberation of the soul. Still, there were a few, even during those awful war years, who advanced the call to mystical knowledge. And there were a few also who gave witness to the truth of God in their very lives, such as the martyred saints, Mohandas K. Gandhi (1870-1948), and Father Maximilian Kolbe (1894-1941). It is such as these who prove the Divinity inherent in man, and who serve as the examples and guides for all who would manifest God's love in this world.

Many valuable studies and translations of mystical works were also published around this time. Swami Nikhilananda published the first English translation of *The Gospel Of Ramakrishna* in 1942; Aldous Huxley published his *The Perennial Philosophy* in 1944, and many popular translations of Vedantic texts, such as the *Upanishads,* the *Bhagavad Gita, Srimad Bhagavatam Purana* and the *Viveka-chudamani* were made by Swami Prabhavananda of the Hollywood Vedanta Society during those years.

It was not until the 1950's, however, that the new availability of inexpensive paperback volumes served to familiarize an increasing segment of the public with the past mystics of every religious tradition. The works of D.T. Suzuki, R.H. Blyth, Christmas Humph-ries, Philip Kapleau and other Buddhist scholars created a great deal of interest in Zen Buddhism; and the publication of ancient Sufi works translated by A.J. Arberry and R.A. Nicholson brought about an increased familiarity with that tradition as well. By the 1960's, a largescale Renaissance of mysticism had surfaced in the West. During that decade, hundreds of scholarly works and translations of mystical literature were published in Europe and America, and thousands of eager young minds were awakened to the life of devotion and meditation on the Self.

Many recent and contemporary saints, such as Ramana Maharshi (1879-1950), Swami Shivananda (1887-19630, Sri Auro-bindo (1872-1950), Sai Baba of Shirdi (d. 1918), and Meher Baba (1894-1969), were introduced to the Western world through the printed page; and in the 1970's the lives of other Eastern sages became known in the West: great Siddhas like Nityananda Baba (d. 1961), Neem Karoli Baba (d. 1973), the alluring Ananda Mayee Ma (1896-1982), and the ubiquitous Sathya Sai Baba (b. 1926).

It was in the '70's that many "Gurus" from the East, quick to capitalize on this "new wave" of consciousness and the growing enthusiasm for Self-realization, began to appear both in Europe and America. During those years, the West was host to Maharishi Mahesh Yogi, Eknath Easwaren, Swami Satchidananda, Swami Muktananda, Amrit Desai, Sant Kirpal Singh, Thich Nhat Hanh, Sri Chinmoy, and many others. A number of large communities and organizations sprang up during that time, each centered around one or another of these "Masters" from the East, and young men and women from every walk of life gathered in droves around these Gurus in search of the high-road to enlightenment. It was a time not unlike that of the establishment of the Gnostic and Christian communities in the 1st and 2nd centuries or the establishment of various religious communities in Medieval Europe.

However, such periods of widespread mystical fervor among the populace are invariably brief; and what begins as a popular devotional movement usually calcifies within a short period of time into an institutionalized program of ritual and proselytization; and the fervent attention to God soon descends to an attention to the administrative and financial demands of a complex religious organ-ization. By the 1980's, this inevitable transformation had become nearly complete, and the "meditation revolution" had all but run its course. The popular mood of mystical elation evidenced in the 60's and 70's had dwindled; and the reactionary suspicion of things "spiritual," fanned by a number of scandals associated with some of the better known "Gurus," served to put an end to the great spiritual movement begun in the 60's.

But there were many irreversible advances made during those decades in our understanding of the subtleties of consciousness and the method of its evolutionary play. Much light has been shed on the working of the mysterious *Kundalini-Shakti* by those luminaries in whom this evolutionary energy had evolved and become demonstrably manifest. Pioneers such as Swami Muktananda (1906-1982), Gopi Krishna (1903-1984), and Hiroshi Motoyama (b. 1925), by their courageous explorations into uncharted regions of spiritual transformation, have provided us a glimpse into the subtleties of our own psycho-physical reality, and made clear the path for the evolution of mankind.

No doubt it is much too early to count the saints and sages produced during this century, or to assess their influence; that judgement must be left to some future generation. Still, it is clear that our 20th century has given birth to a worldwide recognition among the learned that the philosophy of mysticism is a universal and perennial one, and not merely the quaint conceit of a few misguided zealots, nor the property of any one of the many diverse sectarian religions.

We have seen in this century an unparalleled availability of knowledge concerning the literature of past and foreign cultures, and along with this, the widespread dissemination of mystical literature from every land and every time. And, while this literature remains primarily in the hands of the learned few, it has greatly altered, by its influence, the religious and philosophical climate of the world. No longer is it possible for the votaries of any one religious sect to lay claim to an exclusive franchise on the Truth or the special dispensation of God; for the accumulation of the products of scholarship, and the means to produce and distribute literature throughout the world has made the world a much smaller place and brought the greatest written works of the mystics of all traditions within the reach of nearly everyone.

It is necessary to say, however, that, despite this increased familiarity with the tenets of the perennial philosophy of mysticism, there has not necessarily been a corresponding increase during this century in the number of genuine mystics. Indeed, it would seem that the disparity between the knowledge of the mystics and that of the overwhelming majority of humanity is as great as it was in the past, and there appears no reason to doubt that it shall remain so for a very long time.

The genuine followers of the perennial philosophy shall remain few, not because it requires great understanding, but because the following of that philosophy requires so great a moral courage and unflagging determination. The philosophy of mysticism, unlike some others, is not dependent upon intellect for confirmation, but upon experiment. It remains incomprehensible to all but those who are willing to carry out the experiment with their very lives.

When we look closely at the lives of the great mystics the world has known, can we imagine that it is only coincidental that the lives they led are so similar? Can we imagine that the genius of a Buddha, a Jesus, Plotinus, Shankara, or Nityananda is in the least way separable from the moral courage their lives displayed? They bartered everything that men hold dear in order to know the Truth directly. They dared to see God, not counting the cost; so drawn to the love of Truth, the love of God, that they willingly released all other interests to focus one-pointedly on That alone.

The modern mystic would do well to note the condition and circumstances of the lives of the mystics contained in this book, for such conditions are not likely to be, for him or her, any different. Not one of the aforementioned mystics, insofar as I can tell, ever earned a penney from his written works, nor escaped the calumny and ridicule of the ignorant majority. Indeed, nearly all were censured, if not hounded, by even the so-called "learned" community, and lived, for the most part, rejected or ignored by their intellectual peers. Some, of course, were persecuted and put to death; many were ostracized, and none lived without the most severe trials of penury and social isolation. It was then, and no doubt long shall be, the price to be exacted for a life lived for Truth and the attainment of transcendent knowledge.

≈≈

APPENDIX [1]

It should be abundantly evident from the foregoing study that throughout the ages men and women have come face to face with God, the absolute Source and Ground of all existence; and that it is this very experience which constitutes the one common thread that binds together in unity all the great religious and philosophical traditions which have existed since time began, and all that shall exist in the future. Each of the great mystics included in this book spoke in his own language, his own restricted terminology, and the consequence is that today many regard each of these efforts to reveal the nature of reality as disparate and unrelated "philosophies" or "religions." But the experience of the one Reality is the same for all, of course; and in all the declarations of the many prophets, saints, and messiahs, we can hear the attempt to convey a common knowledge based on that common vision.

We have seen, also, that each of the mystics who have attempted to describe the reality experienced in this vision have described it, in a similar way, as an indivisible Unity containing two, *apparently distinct*, aspects: an eternally unchanging and constant aspect, and an aspect that appears changing and inconstant. To those who have never experienced that Unity, such declarations about It must appear illogical and self-contradictory. But, say the mystics, however paradoxical it may seem to the rational intellect, that is simply and truly the nature of the one reality.

In order to explain that reality which is both the eternal God and the world of forms, a reality which appears to possess two such incompatible aspects while remaining one reality, it became apparent very early on, historically, that it was necessary to introduce two terms, each to designate one aspect of this dual-faceted Being, yet which would in no way represent two separate and distinct entities, but one -- a One with two faces. In every language, therefore, and in every religious and philosophical tradition, we find these two, designated as Male and Female, and called by countless different names. Here, listed according to their source, are just a few of these many sets of terms:

Source	The One	Its Creative Power
Vedas	Prajapati	Prthivi
Judaism	Jahveh	Chokmah
Upanishads	Brahman	Maya
Samkhya	Purusha	Prakrti
Taoism	Tao	Teh
Buddhism	Nirvana	Samsara
Heraclitus	Zeus	Logos
Philo	Theos	Logos
Christianity	Father	Son (Logos)
Gnosticism	Mind	Thought
Plotinus	The One	Nous
Shaivism	Shiva	Shakti
Chan/Zen Buddhists	Hsin/Kokoro	Nien/Nen
Kabbalists	En Sof	Sefirot
Sufis	Haqq	Khalq
Eckhart	Gottheit	Gott
Ramakrishna	Brahman	Kali

The history of both religion and philosophy has all too often told the story of the struggles of the proponents of one set of these terms to establish supremacy over the proponents of another set of terms. But since each set of terms is synonymous with the others, let us, for the moment at least, in the interest of avoiding the confusion of multiple terminologies, agree to select one of these sets of terms for our present use. Let us use the terms, "Shiva" and "Shakti," with the understanding that we might just as readily use any others of the combinations of terms listed above.

As the mystics tell us, the universe is a manifestation of an insubstantial, creative Energy. This Energy, or Shakti, has no independent existence of its own, but is simply a "projection" of pure Consciousness, or Shiva; and is similar to the thought-energy projected in the form of a dream-image by an individual mind. Thus, Shiva and Shakti -- the transcendent Absolute and the Energy which manifests as the phenomenal world -- are simply polar aspects of the same one and only Being. These two are not even a hair's breadth apart; they are but two different perspectives on the same reality. And the duality created by conceptually dividing Shiva from Shakti is only an apparent and artificial one, as they constitute an indivisible unity.

This complementarity of Shiva and Shakti may be illustrated by an analogy with the ocean and its waves: Consider an infinite ocean; if we regard its "water-ness," the ocean is one constant whole. But if we regard its "wave-ness," that same ocean is a multiplicity of incessantly changing forms. The ocean is the one reality that is manifesting as all the waves; and, though the waves form and dissolve, form and dissolve, the ocean as a whole remains the same, continually unchanged and unaffected. This is exactly what the mystic experiences in his awakening to the universal Self; he appears to be but one of the many manifestations of reality, but he is, in fact, the one Reality Itself, forever unchanging, eternal.

Shankara, the great expounder of the philosophy of unity, called this apparent duality between the many and the One, a "superimposition":

> Like ripples on the water, the worlds arise from,
> exist in, and dissolve into, the supreme Lord, who is the
> material cause and support of everything.
>   The manifested world of plurality is superimposed
> upon the eternal, all-pervading Lord whose nature is Existence-
> Consciousness, just as bangles and bracelets are superimposed
> on gold. [2]

Another way of explaining the "superimposition" of the phenomenal world on God is by analogy with the ordinary experience of the superimposition of a thought or mental image upon one's own consciousness. Notice how a thought is superimposed upon the background of pure mental awareness: the projected thought has a definite reality of its own, albeit a temporary one; and yet it does not mar or alter in any way that background consciousness. The thought-form or image and the background consciousness exist simultaneously, with a definite distinction between them; however, the thought is formed not only *on* consciousness, but *of* consciousness -- just as a wave is formed not only on, but of, the ocean.

All the mystics concur that it is in a way very similar to this that the phenomenal world of forms is projected upon the supreme Consciousness. The world and God are separate and distinct, but the world has no independent existence; it is formed not only on, but of, God. In the mystic's vision, one's own body is recognized for what it really is: a form whose substance is the universal substance; and one's consciousness is recognized for what it really is: the only Consciousness that is. And then one knows that he has no other, nor ever had any other, identity but the One who alone is.

Still, while the ocean is the only reality underlying the waves, the waves *do* exist. No one would deny it. It is equally undeniable that, while that pure Consciousness (Shiva) is the only reality underlying all forms of life, individual beings *do* exist. Clearly, we live simultaneously in two frameworks of reality: that of the divisible world of multiple phenomena, and that of the eternal Self, the unbroken Whole. All the great issues and arguments of science, philosophy and theology are solved in one stroke by the understanding of the dual-sidedness of reality. From the standpoint of my Shakti-identity, my life in the universal drama is fixed and determined; from the standpoint of my Shiva-identity, as the eternal Self, I am ever free, and remain unaffected by the changes taking place within the manifested world. When I identify with my Shakti-form, I am Shiva's servant; I worship Him as my Lord. When I identify with Shiva, my eternal Self, there are not two, but only one; and I am He.

This complementarity of identities necessitates two entirely different mental attitudes, or states of awareness: when we focus on the Self, we become aware, "I am the one infinite Existence-Consciousness-Bliss"; but when we take the attitude of love toward God, we become aware, "I am Thy creature and Thy servant, O Lord." And it is the paradoxical fact that both attitudes are correct and valid which accounts for the confused oscillation many dedicated truth-seekers feel between the attitude of Self-knowledge (*jnan*) and devotion to God (*bhakti*).

To say, "I am He," as did al-Hallaj, or Shankara, is offensive to the bhakta, for it denies the separate existence and fallibility of the individual soul; and to say, "I am the servant of God," does not satisfy the jnani, for it asserts a duality where none in fact exists. I am convinced that, if we are to speak truly and to live realistically, it is necessary to embrace *both* attitudes, and to relinquish the logic which begs for an either/or approach to identity. The greatest contemplatives who ever lived, having pondered this quandary, have come to the same conclusion, and have taken a position which defies categorization into one classification or another. For example, the Blessed Jan Ruysbroeck, a 14th century disciple of Meister Eckhart, wrote:

Though I have said before that we are one with God,
... yet now I will say that we must eternally remain other than
God, and distinct from Him. ... And we must understand and
feel *both* within us, if all is to be right with us. [3]

And in the folowing song of Kabir, we can hear the perfect
blending of the devotion of the bhakta and the unitive knowledge of
the jnani:

> Whatever I utter is His Name;
> Whatever I hear reminds me of Him.
> Whatever I eat or drink is to His honor.
> To me, society and solitude are one,
> For all feelings of duality have left me.
> I have no need to practice austerity,
> For I see Him smiling everywhere
> As the supreme Beauty in every form.
> Whether sitting, walking, or performing actions,
> My heart remains pure, for my mind remains fixed on God. [4]

Just as Shiva and Shakti cannot be separated one from the
other, neither can the jnani and the bhakta be separated; though
mutually exclusive, they co-exist as complements in everyone. As our
knowledge grows, we must learn to adapt our vision of the world to
accept and embrace such apparently contradictory views. We must
learn to feel comfortable with the notion that a quantity of energy is
both a wave and a particle; that our lives are determined, and that we
are free; that our identity is both the Whole and the part. We are the
universal Self, we are God; and we are also the individualized "soul"
which consists of the mind and its own private impressions. We are
the Ocean; but we are also the wave.

We are Shiva, but we are also Shakti. We are perfect, but we
are also imperfect. We are the eternal Reality, but we are also the
ephemeral image It projects on Its own screen. We are indeed the
Dreamer, but we are also the dream. We are entitled to say, "I am
Shiva!" but so long as the Shakti-mind exists, it must sing the song of
love and devotion to its Lord. While we live and move in this
phantasmagoria, we are His creatures, and are utterly dependent upon
His grace. Therefore, if we truly understand our own double-faceted
reality, we must learn to sing two songs: one, the song of our own
immortal Self; and the other, the song of love for God. Neither,
without the other, is complete.

If we are to learn anything from this protracted examination
of the dual-sidedness of our own nature, it is that, if we can but peer
beyond the appearance of multiplicity, we can become aware of the
unity of all things, the unity and ever-presence of God, the supreme

Self. With such a refined vision, we will then be able to see that not only are we the Self, but everything around us is also the Self. The subject is the Self; the object is the Self. Truly, no matter who or what I see or speak to, it is really only my own Self. If we could really grasp the truth of this, what a revolution would occur in our thinking and behavior!

Just as waves on the ocean are only water, just as golden ornaments are only gold, so all the various forms in the universe are only forms of our own Self. Becoming aware of this, we would begin to revel in that joy which had been missing in our lives before. We would begin to drink the nectar of the unending love for which we had been thirsting before. And we would begin to take delight in just being and living and acting in the world in a way we had been unable to before.

The knowledge once gained from an experience of "enlightenment" is a means of escape from any real ensnarement in anxiety or fear from that time on. It is a supramental *knowing* which asserts itself whenever needed, and provides a surety which can never be shaken. The perceptual division of subject from object does not cease; the world goes on, even for the enlightened. It is just that he *knows* in his heart, with an indomitable certainty, that he and the universe are one.

Just as a chess-player retains the awareness that the warfare between his opponent and himself is merely a temporary game of role-playing, and that at the end of the game both the red and the black pieces will be thrown into the same box; in the same way, one who has clearly experienced the undivided Reality retains the knowledge of the ultimate unity, and sees the play of subjects and objects as the ongoing pretense, or play, of the one Self. Listen to what Jnaneshvar has to say on this theme:

> There is nothing else here but the Self. Whether
> appearing as the seen or perceiving as the seer, nothing else
> exists besides the Self. ... Just as water plays with itself by
> assuming the forms of waves, the Self, the ultimate Reality,
> plays happily with Himself. Though there are multitudes of
> visible objects, and wave upon wave of mental images, still
> they are not different from their witness. You may break a
> lump of raw sugar into a million pieces, still there is nothing
> but sugar. Likewise, the unity of the Self is not lost, even
> though He fills the whole universe. He is seeing only His
> own Self -- like one who discovers various countries in his

imagination, and goes wandering through them all with
great enjoyment. [5]

But how are we to attain this unitive state of awareness? Until
we are lifted into the "experience of unity" by the grace of God,
duality must continue to exist for us. When that experience is about
to happen to a person, that person's mind becomes irresistably withdrawn from worldly concerns, and becomes centered instead upon
one all-consuming love, a singular sort of love, for the very source of
love within. And in the process of consummating this love, solitude is
procured, giving the mind the opportunity to become detached from
the pull of distracting thoughts and sense-impressions; and the mind is
then focused with great intensity upon its aim. Consciousness, like an
unflickering flame in a windless room, becomes pure and clear. And
then suddenly it knows who it has always been.

It is God's grace which manifests in us as that divine love that
draws us so compellingly toward the experience of unity. This love is
not the ordinary kind of love between a subject and an object,
however; for in this case the subject and the object, and the love itself
are one. Nor is this love the result of a conclusion based on a rational
premise; it is an inner experience. It is something quite real --
breathtakingly and intoxicatingly real. It stirs from within, and
centers on itself within. It is not a rationally thought-out construction
based on philosophical principles, but a sweetness that is itself the
object of devotion. It is this Love that bhaktas love. It has no location
but the human heart, yet its source is the universal Being. It is His
gracious gift, and only those who have expeienced it know what it is.
It is of this love that Ramakrishna sang:

How are you trying, O my mind, to know the nature of God?
You are groping like a madman locked in a dark room.
He is grasped through ecstatic love;
How can you fathom Him without it?
When that love awakes, the Lord, like a magnet, draws to Him
    the soul. [6]

Such longing for God always precedes the experience of enlightenment, because it is the natural expression, the unfailing indicat-
or, of a shift in consciousness toward the transcendent Unity. All of
the outer events as well as the inner ones will conspire to bring one's
life to that point where enlightenment is experienced. When it is time
for it to come, it will produce itself, and it will announce its coming by

a great wave of love that steers the heart irresistably to the source of that love, and eventually reveals itself unaided from within.

Consider the great Shankara's final message to the disciple in his *Vivekachudamani* :

> Gurus and scriptures can stimulate spiritual aware-
> ness, but one crosses the ocean of ignorance only by direct
> illumination, *through the grace of God.* [7]

No one has ever realized God except those to whom He has revealed Himself. On this point all Self-realized beings are unanimously agreed. As one commentator says in the *Malini Vijaya Vartika* : "The learned men of all times always hold that the descent of grace does not have any cause or condition, but depends entirely on the free will of the Lord." If it were dependent upon conditions, it would not be absolute and independent grace. According to yet another Tantric scripture, the *Tantraloka*, "Divine grace leads the individual to the path of spiritual realization. It is the only cause of Self-realization and is independent of human effort."

The experience of Self-realization occurs when the mind is concentrated to a fine laser-point and focused in contemplation of God; but this happens only by the power of the universal Self, of God Himself. This is not a denial of the efficacy of self-effort, but merely an assertion that every effort or desire to remember Him, every intensification of concentration on Him, is instigated by Himself, for He is our own inner Self, the inner Controller. It is He who inspires, enacts, and consummates all our efforts.

Among the Christian mystics, we find complete agreement on this issue. Saint Bernard of Clairvaux, for example, says: "You would not seek Him at all, O soul, nor love Him at all, if you had not been first sought and first loved." Meister Eckhart also acknowledges this truth, saying: "It is He that prays in us and not we ourselves." And the Blessed Jan Ruysbroeck concurs:

> Contemplation places us in a purity and radiance
> which is far above our understanding, ... and no one can
> attain to it by knowledge, by subtlety, or by any exercise
> whatsoever; but he whom God chooses to unite to Himself,
> he and no other can contemplate God. [8]

We find the same agreement among the Sufi mystics, the Hindus and the Buddhists. It is always so -- always. And though the

attempt is often made by charlatans to translate the description of the
mental state of the mysitc at the time of his experience of unity into a
sort of "method" or "scientific technique" for the attainment of
God, no one has ever claimed that such a technique has actually
produced the advertised result. For, by themselves,the practices of
shallow breathing, fixed stares, and cessation of thought, will never
produce the experience of unity. This experience comes only by the
will of God. Nanak, the great Guru of the Sikh tradition, stated the
matter plainly when he said, "Liberation from bondage depends upon
Thy will; there is no one to gainsay it. Should a fool wish to,
suffering will teach him wisdom." [9]

When He draws the mind to Himself, the mind becomes still
automatically. It is not necessary to attempt to still the mind by
austere practices or artificial methods. The body becomes still, and
the mind becomes still, when the heart is yearning sincerely for Him
alone. Everything happens very naturally by His grace: One begins
to begrudge the mind any thought save the thought directed to God;
and, with the aim of centering the mind continually on Him, one
begins to sing His name in the inner recesses of the mind. It doesn't
matter what name is used; Christians call Him "Father"; Muslims call
Him "Allah," or "Karim"; Jews call Him "Adonai"; and Hindus
call Him "Hari" or "Ram." Love responds to whatever name is
called with love. To one who loves, His name is nectar; it is like a cold
drink of water to a thirsty man. It is no discipline, nor is it an
austerity. It is the refreshment of life. It is the sweetness of peace, and
the delight of delights.

Since there is really nothing else but that infinite Being wherever one may look, that awareness dawns, as one begins to sing the
name of God within the heart; and the bliss of recognizing one's own
Self both without and within begins to well up. The more one sings
His name, the more one revels in that bliss, and the more clearly one
perceives His continual presence. Inherent in that perception is all
mercy, all right judgement, all tenderness, all loving-kindness. It is the
natural devotion by which a man's heart is transformed, and by which
he becomes fit for the vision of God.

Therefore, say the mystics, we must forge our link with God,
and He will lead us to Himself. He will draw us to love Him, for He
Himself is that Love that awakens in us as love for God. He will draw
us to seek Him in prayer and in silent longing, for He is our own
heart. Follow, and you will reach Him. Draw near to Him in the

silence of the night and He will reveal Himself to you as your very deepest Self, your eternal Identity. Keep on loving Him, keep on trusting in Him to guide you, and keep on praying to Him. When He puts into your heart the desire to know Him, He will lift aside the veil and reveal that, all along, it was Him who prayed, who sought, who sorrowed, as you; and that, all along, it was you who forever lives beyond all sorrow, as God -- forever blissful, forever free.

≈≈

About The Author

Swami Abhayananda was born Stan Trout in Indianapolis, Indiana on August 14, 1938. After service in the Navy, he settled in northern California, where he pursued his studies in philosophy and literature. In June of 1966, he became acquainted with the philosophy of mysticism, and experienced a strong desire to realize God. Abandoning all other pursuits, he retired to a solitary life in a secluded cabin in the mountain forests near Santa Cruz, California; and, on November 18, of that same year, became enlightened by the grace of God.

He spent four more years in his isolated cabin, and subsequently met Swami Muktananda who visited Santa Cruz in 1970. Shortly thereafter, he joined Muktananda in India, as his disciple, and later lived and worked in Muktananda's Oakland, California ashram. In May of 1978, he returned to India and was initiated by his master into the ancient Order of *sannyas*, and given the monastic name, "Swami Abhayananda," which, in Sanskrit, means "the bliss of fearlessness."

Abhayananda was then assigned to teach the knowledge of the Self in New York, then in Philadelphia, Chicago, and Oklahoma City. In 1981, he left Muktananda's organization, and went into retreat once again, this time for seven years, in upstate New York. It was during this time that all of Abhayananda's books were written, and Atma Books was founded to publish them.

At present, Swami Abhayananda is residing in the Olympia area of western Washington state, where he continues to teach, write, and publish his works on the knowledge of the Self.

NOTES

Introduction

1. *Svetasvatara Upanishad*, 3
2. *Mundaka Upanishad*, 3:1
3. *Svetasvatara Upanishad*, 1
4. *Saddharma bundarika*, 15:21; Radhakrishnan, S., 1962, p. 600.
5. New Testament, *Book of John*:10:30

Pre-History Of Mysticism

1. Langdon, S., 1909; p. 13
2. Brihadaranyaka Upanishad: 1:4:1-5
3. Edwin, Irwin, 1956; pp. 353-357
4. Gimbutas, M., 1982,

Vedic Hymnists

1. *Rig Veda*, x.82
2. *Rig Veda*, v.84
3. *Tandya Maha Brahmana*, xx.14.2
4. *Rig Veda*, i.164.46
5. *Ibid.*, x.114
6. *Ibid.*, x.129.1
7. *Ibid.*, x.129.2-7
8. *Ibid.*, x.90.1-5; Prabhavananda, S., 1963; p. 32.

Early Egyptians

1. Budge, W., 1959; pp. 40-41
2. Campbell, J., 1962; pp. 86-88
3. Budge, W., 1959; pp. 37-40 (quoting Brusch, Dr. H., 1929; pp. 96-99)

The Jews

1. Hestrin, 1991; pp. 50-58
2. Old Testament, *Proverbs*: 8:22-30
3. *Ibid.*, *Ecclesiasticus*: 1;1-6
4. *Ibid.*, *Ecclesiasticus*: 24
5. *Ibid.*, *Second Isaiah*:: 45:4-7
6. *Ibid.*, *Psalms*: 24
7. *Ibid.*, *Psalms*: 11
8. *Ibid.*, *Psalms*: 42
9. *Ibid.*, *Psalms*: 13
10. *Ibid.*, *Psalms*: 139

The Upanishadic Seers

1. Valmiki, *Ramayana*
2. *Katha* Upanishad, IV; based on Mascaro, Juan, 1965
3. *Kena* Upanishad, II; *Ibid.*
4. *Kaushitaki* Upanishad, III.8; *Ibid.*
5. *Mundaka* Upanishad, III.1; *Ibi6*.

Isha Upanishad, I.7; *Ibid.*
7. *Brihadaranyaka* Upanishad, IV.4.25; *Ibid.*
8. *Katha* Upanishad, IV; *Ibid.*
9. *Svetasvatara* Upanishad, II.1; *Ibid.*
10. *Taittiriya* Upanishad, I.5; *Ibid.*
11. *Ibid.*, II.6; *Ibid.*
12. *Katha* Upanishad, II; *Ibid.*
13. *Ibid.*, VI; *Ibid.*
14. *Ibid.*, II; *Ibid.*
15. *Svetasvatara* Upanishad, III; *Ibid.*
16. *Kena* Upanishad, II; *Ibid.*
17. *Maitri* Upanishad, VI.24; *Ibid.*
18. *Ibid.*, VI.19-23; *Ibid.*

Kapila

1. Old Testament, *I John*: 2:15-16
2. *Brihadaranyaka* Upanishad, I.6
3. *Isha* Upanishad, I.1
4. *Svetasvatara* Upanishad, VI
5. *Ibid.*, IV
6. *Ibid.*, VI
7. *Samkhypravacana*-bhasya,

Bhagavad Gita

1. *Bhagavad Gita*, 1:47; based on Mascaro, Juan, 1962
2. *Ibid.*, 2:18
3. *Ibid.*, 2;53
4. *Ibid.*, 3:27-28
5. *Ibid.*, 4:11
6. *Ibid.*, 5:20-21
7. *Ibid.*, 5:24
8. *Ibid.*, 6:18-21
9. *Ibid.*, 6:23-27
10. *Ibid.*, 7:9-11
11. *Ibid.*, 7:12-14
12. *Ibid.*, 7:25
13. *Ibid.*, 7:18-19
14. *Ibid.*, 8:18
15. *Ibid.*, 8:20
16. *Ibid.*, 8:21-22
17. *Ibid.*, 9:7-15
18. *Ibid.*, 10:8-10
19. *Ibid.*, 9:34
20. *Ibid.*, 11:12-13
21. *Ibid.*, 11:54-55
22. *Ibid.*, 13:20-23
23. *Ibid.*, 13:26
24. *Ibid.*, 13:27-34
25. *Ibid.*, 14:4
26. *Ibid.*, 15:16-17
27. *Ibid.*, 15:18-20
28. *Ibid.*, 13:16
29. *Ibid.*, 18:7-8
30. *Ibid.*, 18:46-48
31. *Ibid.*, 3:35

33. *Ibid.*, 2:47
34. *Ibid.*, 2:55
35. *Ibid.*, 3:17-19
36. *Ibid.*, 3:30

Taoist Sages

1. Legge, J., 1962; pp. 37-38, Intro.
2. Lao Tze, *Tao Teh Ching*, 25
3. *Ibid.*, 1
4. *Ibid.*, 1
5. *Chuang Tze*, 22
6. *Tao Teh ching*, 4
7. *Ibid.*, 52
8. *Ibid.*, 6
9. *Ibid.*, 16
10. *Ibid.*, 21
11. *Ibid.*, 21
12. *Ibid.*, 37
13. *Ibid.*, 51
14. *Ibid.*, 14
15. *Ibid.*, 26
16. *Ibid.*, 28
17. *Ibid.*, 38
18. *Ibid.*, 50
19. *Ibid.*, 70
20. *Ibid.*, 16
21. *Chuang Tze*, Ch. 11
22. *Ibid.*, Ch. 22
23. *Tao Teh ching*, 2
24. *Chuang Tze*, Ch. 12
25. *Ibid.*, Ch. 5
26. *Tao Teh Ching*, 16
27. *Chuang Tze*, Ch. 13
28. *Ibid.*, Ch. 4
29. *Tao Teh Ching*, 56
30. *Ibid.*, 19
31. *Ibid.*, 1
32. *Ibid.*, 14
33. *Ibid.*, 2
34. *Chuang Tze*, Ch. 6
35. *Ibid.*, Ch. 8
36. *Ibid.*, Ch. 23
37. *Ibid.*, Ch. 6

The Buddha

1. *Dhammapada*, Ch. 11, Babbitt, I., 1965;
2. *Sutra On Cause And Effect In The Past And Present*, Suzuki, D.T., 1961; p. 49f.
3. *Ibid.*, p. 121
4. Chuang Tze,
5. Suzuki, D.T., *op. cit.*
6. *Buddha's Sermon at Benares*, Stryck, L., 1968; pp. 52-53
7. *Ibid.*
8. *Ibid.*
9. *Ibid.*
10. *Ibid.*
11. *Ibid.*
12. *Ibid.*
13. *Ibid.*
14. *Dhammapada*, op. cit.

15. *Tao Teh Ching*, 33
16. Ashvagosha, Stryck, *op. cit.*, p. 285
18. Padma-Shambhava; Stryck, *op. cit.*, p. 315

The Pre-Socratic Greeks

1. Hippolytus, *Refutation Of All Heresies*, VI.18
2. Hicks, 1966, Vol. II; p. 411
3. *Ibid.*, p. 419
4. *Ibid.*, p. 419
5. *Ibid.*, p. 423
6. Adapted from fragments of Heraclitus found in Freeman, K., 1962; pp. 24-34. Fragment nbr. 1
7. *Ibid.*, nbr. 2
8. *Ibid.*, 17
9. *Ibid.*, 28
10. *Ibid.*, 72
11. *Ibid.*, 104
12. *Ibid.*, 108
13. *Ibid.*, 113
14. *Ibid.*, 41
15. *Ibid.*, 78
16. *Ibid.*, 124
17. *Ibid.*, 114
18. *Ibid.*, 47
19. *Ibid.*, 101a
20. *Ibid.*, 107
21. *Ibid.*, 45
22. *Ibid.*, 101
23. *Ibid.*, 54
24. *Ibid.*, 116
25. *Ibid.*, 115
26. *Ibid.*, 88
27. *Ibid.*, 29
28. *Ibid.*, 13
29. *Ibid.*, 9
30. *Ibid.*, 18
31. *Ibid.*, 26
32. *Ibid.*, 49
33. *Ibid.*, 50
34. *Ibid.*, 30
35. *Ibid.*, 16
36. *Ibid.*, 34a
37. *Ibid.*, 102
38. *Ibid.*, 80
39. *Ibid.*, 23
40. *Ibid.*, 10
41. *Ibid.*, 60
42. *Ibid.*, 103
43. *Ibid.*, 8
44. *Ibid.*, 51
45. *Ibid.*, 125
46. *Ibid.*, 85
47. *Ibid.*, 43
48. *Ibid.*, 131
49. *Ibid.*, 112
50. *Ibid.*, 119
51. Xenophanes, *Ibid.*; pp. 20-23

Socrates

1.   Xenophon; Benjamin, A., 1965; p. 8
2.   Plato, *Republic*, Bk. VII.517; adapted from Hamilton, E., 1969
3.   Plato, *Apology*, 28A,B.; trans. by Hugh Tredennick, from Hamilton, *op. cit.*, p. 14
4.   Plato, *Apology*, 29C-30C; *Ibid.*, pp. 15-16
5.   Plato, *Apology*, 41D-42A; *Ibid.*, pp 25-26
6.   Plato, *Phaedo*, 117D-118; *Ibid.*, pp. 97-98
7.   Xenophon, *Memorablia*, 4:8:11; Benjamin, *op. cit.*, pp. 140-141
8.   Plato, *Laws*, 903B-C; Jowett, *op. cit.*
9.   Plato, *Timaeus*, 90-90C; *Ibid.*
10. Plato, *Republic*, 490A-B; *Ibid.*
11. Plato, *Rebublic*, 611B-C; *Ibid.*
12. Plato, *Republic*, 532B; *Ibid.*
13. Plato, *Phaedrus*, 247C-E; *Ibid.*
14. Plato, *Timaeus*, 28C; *Ibid.*
15. Plato, *Phaedrus*, 249C; *Ibid.*
16. Plato, *Laws*, 716C; *Ibid.*
17. Plato, *Symposium*, 212A; *Ibid.*

Philo Judaeus

1.   Old Testament, *Exodus*: 4:22
2.   Philo, *De confusione linguarum*, 136-137; Winston, 1981; p. 90
3.   Philo, *Legum Allegoriorum*, 2:86; *Ibid.*, p. 93
4.   Philo, *De fuga et inventione*, 50-52, *Ibid.*, p. 93
5.   Philo, *Quod a Deo somm.* 19; *de posteritate Caini,* 63; *De vita Mosis,* II. 134
6.   Philo, *That The Worst Is Wont To Attack The Better; Ibid.*, p. 90
7.   Philo, *De posteritate Caini,* 18.63; *Ibid.*
8.   Philo, *Quod Deus sit immutabilis,* 30.144; *Ibid.*
9.   Philo, *De posteritate Caini,* 14-16; *Ibid.*
10. Philo, *Allegorical Interpretations,* III.9
11. Philo, *On Dreams,* I.60
12. Philo, *On Drunkenness,* 145f., 152
13. Philo, *Who Is The Heir?* 69f.
14. Philo, *De mutatione nominum,* 12.82
15. Philo, *De migratione Abrahae*, 31.169
16. Philo, *De specialibus legibus,* I.16
17. Philo, *Legatio ad Gaium,* I.4-5
18. New Testament, *Book of John*: 1:2

The Early Christians And Gnostics

1.   New Testament, *John*: 1:1
2.   Ibid., *John*: 1:2
3.   Athenasius, *Contra Arianos*, I.24-25; Bettenson, 1956; p. 382
4.   *Ibid.*, pp. 389-390
5.   Athenagorus; Wilson, 1959; pp. 385-386
6.   Tertullian, *Adversus Praxaen*, 26; Bettenson, 1956; p. 179
7.   Ireneus, *Adversus Haereses*, III.18.1; *Ibid.*, p. 113
8.   Athenasius, *De Incarnatione,* 17; *Ibid.*, p. 397
9.   Athenasius, *Contra Arianos,* III.31; *Ibid.*, p. 398
10. *The Nicene Creed*
11. Jonas, 1958; pp. 89-90
12. *Ibid.*
13. Pseudo-Apuleius, Asclepius, 41; *Ibid.*, pp. 267-268
14. *Pistis Sophia*, ch. 32; *Ibid.*, p. 68
15. Simon Magus, *Apophasis Megale* ("The Great Exposition"), quoted by Hippolytus of Rome, *Refutatio Omnium Heresium*, VI.8; adapted from Roberts & Donaldson, 1892, Vol. VI, pp. 208-210
16. Creed of the Valentinians, according to Ireneus, *Adversus Haereses,* 1.21.4
17. Hippolytus, *Refutatio Omnium Heresium* VI.29.5ff. Roberts & Donaldson, *op. cit.*
18. Plotinus, *Enneads*, II.1-2; Turnbull, 1934; p. 63
19. *Ibid.*, pp. 65-66
20. *Poimander, Corpus Hermeticum,* 1.11; based on translation by Yates, F., 1964; p. 23
21. *Asclepius, Corpus Hermeticum,* II; *Ibid.*, pp. 42-43
22. *Poimander, Corpus Hermeticum,* 1.11; *Ibid.*, pp. 31-32
23. *Poimander, Corpus Hermeticum,* 1.12; *Ibid.*, pp. 33-34

Plotinus

1.   Plutarch, *De Iside et Osiride*, 67
2.   Maximus of Tyre, *Diss.*, XI.9-10
3.   Plotinus,*Ennead s*, III:7:1; Mackenna, 1956
4.   Porphyry, *Life Of Plotinus*, Turnbull, 1936; p. 6
5.   *Ibid.*, p. 4
6.   *Ibid.*, p. 5
7.   Plotinus, *Enneads*, 45:3:11; *Ibid.*, p. 106
8.   *Enneads*, 10:5:6; *Ibid.*, p. 158
9.   *Enneads*, 27:4:2-5; *Ibid.*, p. 118
10. *Enneads*, 22:6:4; *Ibid.*, p. 184
11. *Enneads*, 22:6:4; *Ibid.*, p. 184
12. *Enneads*, 5:5:2; *Ibid.*, p. 180
13. *Enneads*, 1:8; *Ibid.*, p. 48
14. *Enneads*, 26:3:5; *Ibid.*, p. 100
15. *Enneads*, 33:9; *Ibid.*, p. 68
16. *Ibid.*, 30:3:8; pp. 113-114
17. *Ibid.*, 44:5:15-16; pp. 162-163
18. *Ibid.*, 49:5:13; p. 162
19. *Ibid.*, 26:3:4; p. 101
20. *Ibid.*, 47:1; p. 76
21. *Ibid.*, 30:3:10; p. 116
22. *Ibid.*, 38:6:35; p. 204

23. *Ibid.*, 9:6:10; p. 221
24. *Ibid.*, 9:6:11; p. 222
25. *Ibid.*, 1:9; p. 49
26. *Ibid.*, 15:3:2; p. 89
27. *Ibid.*, 46:12-13; p. 36
28. *Ibid.*, 46:16; p. 37
29. *Ibid.*, 36:10; pp. 40-41
30. *Ibid.*, 1:6; p. 47
31. *Ibid.*, 32:5:8; p. 165
32. *Ibid.*, 38:6:34; p. 203
33. *Ibid.*, 49:5:17; p. 163
34. *Ibid.*, 47:3:3; p. 83
35. *Ibid.*, 38:6:22-23; p. 199

Dionysius

1. *Mystical Theology*, I.; Editors of The Shrine Of Wisdom, 1965; p. 10
2. *Letter To Dorotheus, a Minister*; Hathaway, 1969; p. 134
3. *Mystical Theology*, II.; *op. cit.*, p.1 2
4. *Ibid.*, III; p. 14
5. *Ibid.*, V; p. 16
6. *Ibid.*, I; p. 10
7. *Ibid.*, I; p. 10
8. *Ibid.*, II; p. 12
9. *Ibid.*, I; p. 11
10. *Ibid.*, V; p. 16
11. *Ibid.*, IV; p. 15
12. *Letter To Titus, The Bishop*; Hathaway, *op. cit.*; p. 157
13. *Celestial Hierarchies*, I; Editors of The Shrine Of Wisdom, *op. cit.*, p. 21
14. *The Divine Names*, IV.14; Rolt, 1920; 15. *The Divine Names*, IV.23; *Ibid.*
16. *Ibid.*, IV.24
17. *Ibid.*, IV.34
18. *Ibid.*, IV.35

Narada

1. *Bhagavad Gita*, 9:29
2. Narada, *Bhakti Sutras*, 3-5
3. *Ibid.*, 51-61
4. *Ibid.*, 7-9
5. *Ibid.*, 19
6. *Ibid.*, 67-73
7. *Ibid.*, 28-33
8. *Ibid.*, 34-38
9. *Ibid.*, 62-66
10. *Ibid.*, 74-81
11. *Ibid.*, 84

Patanjali

1. *Katha* Upanishad, 6
2. *Bhagavad Gita*, 6:10-28
3. Patanjali, *Yoga Sutras*, 2
4. *Ibid.*, 3-4
5. *Ibid.*, 20-26

The Tantra

1. *Vishnu Purana*, I.8
2. *Spanda karika*
3. *Paramartha-sara*
4. *Linga Purana*
5. *Hatha Yoga Pradipika*
6. *Kularnava Tantra*, 5.111-112
7. *Malini Vijaya Vartika*
8. *Kularnava Tantra*, 12.25
9. Vasugupta, *Shiva Sutras*, 2.6
10. *Paramananda Tantra*
11. *Jnanarnava Tantra*, 24.41
12. Shankara, *Sundaryalahari*
13. Kshemaraj, *Pratyabijnahridayam*
14. *Vijnanabhairava*
15. *Tripurarahasya*
16. *Kularnava Tantra*, 9.42
17. *Ishvarapratyabijna Vimarshini*
18. *Ishvarapratyabijna*, 11-12
19. *Spandakarika*, 3:3
20. Kshemaraj, *Pratyabijnahridayam*

Shankara

1. Shankara, *Vivekachudamani;* Prabhavananda, 1947; p. 59
2. *Ibid.*, p. 62
3. Shankara, *Atma Bodha*: 26-27
4. Shankara, *Vivekachudamani; op. cit.*, p. 76
5. Shankara, *Commentaries on The Vedanta Sutras;* Thibaut, 1962, Vol. II, p. 173
6. *Ibid.*, 1:1:5; Vol. I, p. 51
7. *Ibid.*, 3:2:37; Vol. II, p. 174
8. *Ibid.*, 2:3:42Vol. II, p. 61
9. *Ibid.*, 1:3:12; Vol. I, p. 171
10. *Ibid.*, 2:3:41; Vol. II, p. 59
11. *Ibid.*, 1:1:11; Vol. I, p. 61
12. *Ibid.*, 2:1:16; Vol. I, p. 330
13. Shankara, *Vivekachudamani; op. cit.*, p. 71
14. Shankara, *Atma Bodha*: 48
15. Shankara, *Vivekachudamani; op. cit.*, p. 51
16. Shankara, *Atma Bodha:* 38
17. Shankara, *Vivekachudamani; op. cit.*
18. *Ibid.*; p. 69
19. *Ibid.*, p. 97
20. *Ibid.*, p. 106
21. *Ibid.*, p. 131

Dattatreya

1. Reprinted from Abhayananda, S., *Dattatreya: The Song Of The Avadhut*, Olympia, Wash., Atma Books, 1992

Milarepa
1. Evans-Wentz, 1971; p. 234
2. *Ibid.*, p. 245
3. *Ibid.*, pp. 245-247
4. *Ibid.*, pp. 259, 261, 262, 270, 271, 27

The Ch'an And Zen Buddhists

1. Stryck & Ikemoto, 1965;
2. Suzuki, 1970; pp. 23-24
3. Chung-yuan, 1975; pp. 72-73
4. *Ibid.*, p. 71
5. *Ibid.*, p. 60
6. Suzuki, 1960; p. 111
7. Chung-yuan, 1975
8. Suzuki, 1961; p. 336
9. Suzuki, 1960; pp. 76-82
10. Suzuki, 1960; pp. 89-103
11. Suzuki, 1961; p. 319
12. Chung-yuan, *op. cit;* p. 141
13. Suzuki, 1960; p. 127

Al-Hallaj

1. Nicholson, 1963; p. 151
2. Schimmel, 1975; pp. 62-64
3. Anonymous
4. Schimmel, *op. cit.*; p. 77

Jewish Mysticism

1. Ibn Gabirol, *Fons Vitae*, V.30
2. *Ibid.*, I
3. *Ibid.*, I
4. *Ibid.*, III.204
5. Ibn Gabirol, *The Royal Crown*; Zangwill, 1923, 1974; pp. 82-88
6. *Ibid.*
7. *Ibid.*; p. 16
8. *Ibid.*; pp. 3-5
9. Zohar, Sholem, 1949; p. 27
10. Zohar, Seltzer, 1980; p. 433

Ibn Arabi

1. Schimmel, 1975; p. 261
2. Affifi, 1939; p. 21
3. *Ibid.*; p. 11
4. *Ibid.*; p. 11
5. *Ibid.*; pp. 10-11
6. *Ibid.*; p. 21
7. Austin, 1980; p. 125
8. Landau, 1959; pp. 83-84
9. *Ibid.*; p. 83
10. Ibn Arabi, *Meccan Revelations*, I
11. Austin, *op. cit.*; p. 92
12. *Ibid.*; p. 98
13. *Ibid.*; p. 137
14. *Ibid.*; p. 108
15. *Ibid.*; p. 136
16. *Ibid.*; pp. 126-127

17. *Ibid.*; p. 88
18. *Ibid.*; p. 126
19. *Ibid.*; p. 153
20. *Ibid.*; p. 153
21. Landau, *op. cit.;* p. 79

Iraqi

1. Chittock & Wilson, 1982; p. 120
2. *Ibid.*; p. 124
3. *Ibid.*; p. 111
4. *Ibid.*; p. 95
5. *Ibid.*; p. 117
6. *Ibid.*; p. 125
7. *Ibid.*; p. 76
8. *Ibid.*; p. 96
9. *Ibid.*; p. 110
10. *Ibid.*; p. 77
11. *Ibid.*; p. 103
12. *Ibid.*; p. 80
13. *Ibid.*; p. 127
14. *Ibid.*; p. 99
15. *Ibid.*; p. 80
16. *Ibid.*; p. 119
17. *Ibid.*; p. 10
18. *Ibid.*; p. 112
19. *Ibid.*; p. 123
20. *Ibid.*; p. 120

Rumi

1. *Divan-i Shams*; Nicholson, 1898
2. *Mathnawi;* Winfield, 1898
3. *Ibid.*
4. *Divan-i Shams; op. cit.*
5. *Ibid.*
6. *Ibid.*
7. *Mathnawi; op. cit.*

Jnaneshvar

1. *Amritanubhav*, Abhayananda, 1989; pp. 114-118
2. *Ibid.*; pp. 193-194
3. *Changadev Pasashti, Ibid.*; pp. 237-241

Medieval Christians

1. *Summa Theologia*, II.1.8

Meister Eckhart

1. Treatise A.2, Colledge & McGinn, 1982; p. 222
2. Sermon 6, *Ibid.*; p. 188
3. *Sermon 18*, Blackney, 1941; p. 181
4. Sermon 23, *Ibid.*; p. 206
5. Sermon 27, *Ibid.*; pp. 225-226
6. Sermon 52, Colledge & McGinn, 1982; pp. 202-203

7.   Sermon 52, *Ibid.*; p. 203
8.   Sermon 52, *Ibid.*; p. 200
9.   Sermon 52, *Ibid.*; p. 203
10. Treatise A.1, *Ibid.*; p. 211
11. Treatise A.2, *Ibid.*; pp. 220-221
12. Treatise C.5, *Ibid.*; p. 251
13. Papal Bull, *Ibid.*; p. 77
14. Treatise C.6, *Ibid.*; pp. 252-254
15. Treatise C.7, *Ibid.*; p. 255

Thomas á Kempis

1.   Abhayananda, 1992; pp. 102-105

Nicholas of Cusa

1.   *De sapientia*; Dolan, 1962; p. 105
2.   *De venatione sapientiae,* Ch. xii; Beck, 1969; p. 64
3.   *De sapientia*, I, Dolan, *op. cit.*; pp. 105-106
4.   *De docta ignorantia,* I.3; Heron, 1954;
5.   *De sapientia;* Dolan, *op. cit.;* p. 108
6.   *Ibid.*; p. 105
7.   *De visio Dei,* II; Salter, 1960; pp. 12-13
8.   *Ibid.*, XIII; p. 61
9.   *Ibid.*; p. 62
10. *Ibid.*, IX; p. 44
11. *Ibid.*, X; p. 49
12. *De sapientia*, I; Dolan, *op. cit.*; p. 127
13. *De visio Dei,* III; Salter, *op. cit.*; p. 31
14. *Ibid.*, V; pp. 19-20
15. *De sapientia*, I; Dolan, *op. cit.;* p. 110
16. *De visio Dei,* XII; Salter, *op. cit.*; p. 54
17. *Ibid.*, VI; p. 26
18. *Ibid.*, XXV; p. 29
19. *Ibid.*, XVI; p. 78
20. *Ibid.*, XIII; p. 59
21. *Ibid.*, XII; p. 57
22. *Ibid.*, XII; p. 56
23. *Ibid.*, XV; p. 74
24. *De sapientia*, I; Dolan, *op. cit.;* p. 113
25. *De visio Dei,* XVII; *op. cit.*; p. 82
26. *De possest,* II.2; Dolan, *op. cit.*
27. *De visio Dei,* XV; *op. cit.*; p. 72
28. *Ibid.*, XV; p. 73
29. *Ibid.*, XVII; pp. 81-82
30. *Ibid.*, XIV; p. 66
31. *De sapientia*, I; Dolan, *op. cit.*; p. 107
32. *Ibid.*, pp. 111-112
33. *Ibid.*; pp. 115-116
34. *Ibid.*; p. 127

Juan de la Cruz

1.   Brenan, 1973; p. 12
2.   *Spiritual Canticle*, Stanza 26:13 Kavanaugh & Rodriguez, 1973; p. 514
3.   *The Ascent Of Mount Carmel,* II.4.4; *Ibid.*; pp. 113-114
4.   *Ibid.*, I:3-4; pp. 76-77

5.   *Ibid.*, I:13:11; pp. 103-104
6.   *Ibid.*, I:5:6; p. 83
7.   *Ibid.*, I:15:2; p. 106
8.   *The Living Flame Of Love*, III:26-28, *Ibid.*; p. 620
9.   *Ibid.*, I:19-21; pp. 586-587
10. *Spiritual Canticle*, I:18, *Ibid.*; pp. 422-423
11. *Ibid.*, I:11:2; pp. 448-449
12. *Ibid.*, 26:4; p. 512
13. *Ibid.*, 22:3-4; p. 497
14. *The Living Flame Of Love*, III:78, *Ibid.*; p. 641
15. *Spiritual Canticle*, 12:7, *Ibid.*; p. 455
16. *Ibid.*, 24:5; p. 503
17. *Ibid.*, 26-28; pp. 511, 518-520
18. *Ibid.*, I:8; p. 419

Kabir

1.   Bijak
2.   Bijak, Sabda 97
3.   Bijak, Sabda 30
4.   Bijak, Shastri, 1941; pp. 52-53, 41
5.   Bijak, *Ibid.*; p. 41
6.   Bijak, *Ibid.*; p. 48
7.   Bijak, *Ibid.*; p. 38
8.   Bijak, *Ibid.*; p. 49
9.   Bijak, *Ibid.*; p. 46
10. Bijak, *Ibid.*; p. 37
11. Bijak, Sabda 43
12. Bijak, Ramaini 6
13. Bijak, Shastri, *op. cit.*; pp. 42-43

Nanak

1.   Rag Asa, Singh et all, 1960; pp. 87-88
2.   Sri Rag, *Ibid.*; p. 71
3.   *Ibid.*; p. 83
4.   *Ibid.*; p. 57
5.   *Ibid.*; p. 42
6.   *Ibid.*; p. 29
7.   *Ibid.*; p. 30
8.   Sri Rag, *Ibid.*; p. 66
9.   Sri Rag, *Ibid.*; p. 69
10. Rag Gauri Bairagan, *Ibid.*; pp. 84-85
11. Sri Rag, *Ibid.*; p. 67
12. *Ibid.*; p. 47

Dadu

1.   Bani 190, 191; Orr, 1947; pp. 93-94
2.   *Ibid.*; p. 62
3.   *Ibid.*; pp. 32-33
4.   *Ibid.*; p. 33
5.   *Ibid.*; p. 33-34
6.   Psalm 7, Pad 151; *Ibid.*; p. 66
7.   *Ibid.*; pp. 174-175
8.   *Ibid.*; pp. 191-192
9.   Psalm 181, *Ibid.*; p. 124
10. *Ibid.*; pp. 170-171
11. *Ibid.*; p. 141
12. *Ibid.*; p. 140

13.   *Ibid.*; p. 103
14.   *Ibid.*; p. 168
15.   Parcha, *Ibid.*; p. 66
16.   Jiwat Mritak, *Ibid.*; pp. 105-106
17.   *Ibid.*; pp. 162-163
18.   *Ibid.*; p. 142
19.   Hairan, *Ibid.*; p. 101

Ramakrishna

1.   Nikhilananda, 1942; pp. 13-14
2.   *Ibid.*; pp. 15-16
3.   *Ibid.*; p. 28
4.   *Ibid.*; p. 29
5.   Rolland, 1952; p. 156
6.   Nikhilananda, *op. cit., p. 32*
7.   *Ibid.;* p. 35
8.   *Ibid.*; p. 38
9.   *Ibid.*; p. 38
10.   *Ibid.*; p. 191
11.   *Ibid.*; p. 112
12.   *Ibid.*; p. 265
13.   *Ibid.*; p. 191
14.   *Ibid.*; p. 490
15.   *Ibid.*; p. 242
16.   *Ibid.*; p. 271
17.   *Ibid.*; p. 108
18.   *Ibid.*; p. 328
19.   *Ibid.*; p. 218
20.   *Ibid.*; pp. 168-169
21.   *Ibid.*; p. 208
22.   *Ibid.*; p. 148
23.   *Ibid.*; p. 181
24.   *Ibid.*; p. 171
25.   *Ibid.*; pp. 173-174
26.   *Ibid.*; p. 116
27.   *Ibid.*; p. 104
28.   *Ibid.*; p. 134
29.   *Ibid.*; pp. 202-203
30.   *Ibid.*; p. 375
31.   *Ibid.*; p. 449

Appendix

1.   Reprinted from Abhayananda, S.,
      The Supreme Self, Fallsburg, N.Y.,
      Atma Books, 1984
2.   Shankara, *Atma Bodha*, 8-9
3.   Jan Ruysbroeck, *The Sparkling Stone*, X
4.   Kabir; Shastri, 1941; p. 49
5.   Jnaneshvar, *Amritanubhav;* VII;
      Abhayananda, 1989;
6.   Nikhilananda, 1941; p. 607
7   Shankara, *Vivekachudamani;* Prabhava-
      nanda, 1947; p. 131
8   Jan Ruysbroeck, *The Sparkling Stone*, IV
9.   Nanak; Singh *et all,* 1960; p. 42

BIBLIOGRAPHY

Introduction

1. Campbell, Joseph, *The Masks Of God*, Vol. I: *Primitive Mythology*, N.Y., Viking Press, 1959; Vol. II: *Oriental Mythology*, 1962
2. Van Over, Raymond (ed.), *Sun Songs: Myths From Around The World*, N.Y., New American Library Mentor Books, 1980
3. Watts, Alan, *The Two Hands Of God: Myths Of Polarity*, N.Y., Macmillan Collier Books, 1969

Pre-History Of Mysticism

1. Campbell, Joseph, *Historical Atlas Of World Mythology, Vol. I, Part I: Mythologies Of The Primitive Hunters And Gatherers*, N.Y., Harper & Row, 1988
2. Gimbutas, Marija, *The Goddesses And Gods Of Old Europe: Myths And Cult Images*, Berkeley, University of California Press, 1982
3. Langdon, Stephen, *Sumerian And Babylonian Psalms*, Paris, Librairie Paul Geuthner, 1909
4. Edwin, Irwin (ed.), *The Works Of Plato: The Jowett Translation*, N.Y., Modern Library, 1956
5. Marshack, Alexander, *Roots Of Civilization*, New York; McGraw-Hill, 1972

Vedic Hymnists

1. de Barry, William T. (ed.), *Sources Of Indian Tradition*, N.Y., Columbia Univ. Press, 1958
2. Muller, Fredrich Max, *The Vedas*, Calcutta, Susil Gupta Ltd., 1956
3. Prabhavananda, Swami, *The Spiritual Heritage Of India*, Holllywood, Vedanta Press, 1963

The Early Egyptians

1. Budge, Sir Wallis, *Egyptian Religion*, N.Y., University Books, 1959
2. Brusch, H., *Religion Un Mythologie*, 1929
3. Campbell, Joseph, *Masks Of God: Oriental Mythology*, N.Y., Viking Press, 1962

The Jews

1. Dimont, Max I., *Jews, God, And History*, N.Y., Penguin Books, 1962
2. Hestrin, Ruth, *"Understanding Asherah--Exploring Semitic Iconography*, Biblical Archaeology Review, Sept./Oct., 1991 (Vol. XCII, No. 5), Washington D.C.
3. Ginzberg, Louis, *The Legends Of The Jews*, N.Y., Simon & Schuster, 1961
4. Potok, Chaim, *Wanderings: History Of The Jews*, N.Y., Alfred A. Knopf, 1978

Upanishadic Seers

1. Mascaro, Juan, *The Upanishads*, Middlesex, Penguin Books, 1965
2. Nikhilananda, Swami, *The Upanishads* (Four Vols.), N.Y., Harper & Bros., 1956
3. Radhakrishnan, S., *Indian Philosophy* (Vol. I), Longon, Geo. Allen & Unwin, 1962

Kapila

1. Keith, A.B., *The Samkhya System: A History Of Samkhya Philosophy*, London, Oxford Univ. Press, undated
2. Johnston, E.H., *Early Samkhya*, Delhi, Motilal Banarsidas, 1974

Bhagavad Gita

1. Mascaro, Juan, *The Bhagavad Gita*, Middlesex, Penguin Books, 1962
2. Nikhilananda, Swami, *The Bhagavad Gita*, N.Y., 1964
3. Tapasyananda, Swami, *Srimad Bhagavad Gita*, Mylapore, Sri Ramakrishna Math, 1984

Taoist Sages

1. Legge, James, *The Texts Of Taoism*, N.Y., Dover Books, 1962
2. Waley, Arthur, *The Way And Its Power*, London, 1933
3. Yutang, Lin, *The Wisdom Of Lao Tze*, N.Y., Modern Library, 1948

The Buddha

1.   Babbitt, Irving (tr.), *The Dhammapada,*
     N.Y., New Directions, 1965
2.   de Barry, Theodore (ed.), *The Buddhist*
     Tradition In India, China And Japan,
     N.Y., Modern Library, 1969
3.   Ling, Trevor, *The Buddha,* N.Y., Chas.
     Scribner's Sons, 1973
4.   Stryck, Lucien (ed.), *The World Of The*
     Buddha, Garden City, N.Y., Doubleday,
     1968
5.   Suzuki, D.T., *Essays In Zen Buddhism,*
     1st Series, N.Y., Grove Press, 1961

The Pre-Socratic Greeks

1.   Freeman, Dathleen, *Ancilla To The*
     Pre-Socratic Philosophers, Cambridge,
     Harvard University Press, 1962
2.   Guthrie, W.K.C., *A History Of Greek*
     Philosophy (2 Vols.), Cambridge, Cam-
     bridge Univ. Press, 1962
3.   Hicks, R.D. (trans.), *Diogenes Laertius:*
     Lives Of The Philosophers, Cambridge,
     Harvard University Press, 1966

Socrates

1.   Benjamin, Anna S. (trans.), *Recollections*
     Of Socrates by Xenophon, Indianapolis,
     Bobbs-Merrill Co., 1965
2.   Hamilton, Edith & Cairns, H. (trans.),
     Plato: The Collected Dialogues, Prince-
     ton, Princeton Univ. Press,(Bolingen
     Series), 1969
3.   Jowett, Benjamin, *Dialogues Of Plato,*

4.   Levin, Richard, *The Question Of*
     Socrates, N.Y., Harcourt Brace & World
     Co., 1961

Philo Judaeus

1.   Winston, David (trans.), Philo Of Alex-
     andria -- The Contemplative Life, Gi-
     ants, And Selections, Ramsey, N.J.,
     Paulist Press, 1981
2.   Wolfson, Harry A., *Philo: Foundations*
     Of Religious Philosophy In Judaism,
     Christianity And Islam (2 Vols.),
     Cambridge, Harvard Univ. Press, 1947

Jesus of Nazareth

1.   Durant, Will, *Ceasar And Christ,* N.Y.,
     Simon & Schuster, 1944
2.   May, Herbert G. & Metzger, Bruce M.
     (eds.), *The New Oxford Annotated Bible*

With The Apocrypha, N.Y., Oxford University Press, 1977

The Early Christians And Gnostics

1.   Amidon, Philip R. (trans.), *The Pan-*
     arion of St. Epiphanius, Bishop of Sal-
     amis-Selected Passages, N.Y., Oxford
     University Press, 1990
2.   Barnstone, Willis (ed.), *The Other Bible,*
     San Francisco, Harper Collins, 1984

3.   Bettenson, Henry (ed.), *The Early*
     Church Fathers, London, Oxford Univ.
     Press, 1956
4.   Grant, R.M., *Gnosticism And Early*
     Christianity, N.Y., Harper & Row, 1956

5.   Jonas, Hans, *The Gnostic Religion,*
     Boston, Beacon Press, 1958
6.   Magill, Frank N. & McGreal, I.P. (eds.),
     Masterpieces Of Christian Literature,
     N.Y., Harper & Row, 1963
7.   McGiffert, Arthur C., *A History Of*
     Christian thought, Vol. I: Early And
     Eastern; Vol. II: The West From
     Tertullian To Erasmus, N.Y., Charles
     Scribner's Sons, 1933
8.   Pagels, Elaine, *The Gnostic Gospels,*
     N.Y., Random House, 1979
9.   Randolph, Kurt, *Gnosis* (trans. by R.M.
     Wilson), N.Y., Harper & Row, 1983
10. Roberts, Rev. A. & Donaldson, J. (eds.),
     The Ante-Nicene Christian Library,
     Edinburgh, T. & T. Clark, 1892
11. Wilson,   (trans.), *The Ante-Nicene*
     Fathers, Vol. II: Justin Martyr And
     Athenagorus,
12. Wolfson, Harry A., *The Philosophy Of*
     The Church Fathers, Cambridge,
     Harvard University Press, 1970
13. Yates, Frances A., *Giordano Bruno And*
     The Hermetic Tradition, Chicago, Chic-
     ago University Press, 1964

Plotinus

1.   MacKenna, Stephen (trans.), *Plotinus:*
     The Enneads, London, Faber & Faber,
     1956
2.   Turnbull, Grace H. (ed.), *The Essence*
     Of Plotinus, N.Y., Oxford University
     Press, 1934

Dionysius

1.   Editors Of The Shrine Of Wisdom
     (trans.), *Mystical Theology And The*

Celestial Hierarchy, Fintry Brook, England, Shrine Of Wisdom, 1965

2. Hathaway, Ronald F. (trans.), *Hierarchy And the Definition Of Order In The Letters of Pseudo-Dionysius,* The Hague, Martinus Nijhoff, 1969

3. Rolt, C.E. (trans.), *Dionysius the Areopagite on The Divine Names and The Mystical Theology,* London, Society for Promoting Christian Knowledge, 1920

Narada

1. Prabhavananda, Swami (trans.), *Narada's Way Of Divine Love,* Hollywood, Vedanta Press, 1959

Patanjali

1. Prabhavananda, Swami, *How To Know God: The Yoga Aphorisms Of Patanjali,* Hollywood, Vedanta Press, 1953

The Tantra

1. Beane, Wendell C., *Myth, Cult And Symbols In Shakta Hinduism,* Laiden, Netherlands, E.J. Brill, 1977

2. Kumar, Pushpendra, *Shakti Cult In Ancient India,* Varanasi, Bhartiya Publishing Hse., 1974

3. Pandit, M.P., *Gems From The Tantras* (1st & 2nd Series), Madras, Ganesh & Co., 1970

4. Singh, Lalan P., *Tantra: Its Mystic And Scientific Basis,* Delhi, Concept Publishing Co., 1976

5. Sinha, Indra, *The Great Book Of Tantra,* Rochester, Vermont, Destiny Books, 1993

Shankara

1. Chinmayananda, Swami, *Shankara, The Missionary,* Bombay, Central Chinmaya Mission Trust, 1978

2. Mayeda, Sengaku (trans.) *A Thousand Teachings: The Upadeshasahasri of Shankara,* Tokyo, University of Tokyo Press, 1979

3. Nikhilananda, Swami, *Atmabodha,* Madras, Sri Ramakrishna Math

4. Prabhavananda, Swami (trans.), *The Crest-Jewel Of Discrimination,* Hollywood, Vedanta Press, 1947

5. Thibaut, George (trans.), *The Vedanta Sutras Of Badarayana* (2 Vols.), N.Y., Dover Publications, 1962

Dattatreya

1. Abhayananda, S.(trans.), *Dattatreya: The Song Of The Avadhut,* Olympia, Washington, Atma Books, 1992

2. Chetanananda, Swami (trans.), *Avadhut Gita Of Dattatreya,* Calcutta, Advaita Ashram, 1984

Milarepa

1. Chang, Garma C.C. (trans.), *The Hundred Thousand Songs Of Milarepa* (2 Vols.), New Hyde Park, N.Y., University Books, 1962

2. Evans-Wentz, W.Y., *Tibet's Great Yogi, Milarepa,* N.Y., Oxford Univ. Press, 1971

The Ch'an And Zen Buddhists

1. Chung-yuan, Chang, *Original Teachings Of Ch'an Buddhism,* N.Y., Pantheon Books, 1975

2. Dumoulin, Heinrich, *A History Of Zen Buddhism,* Boston, Beacon Press, 1969

3. Stryck, L. & Ikemoto, T., *Zen Poems, Prayers, Sermons, Anecdotes, Interviews,* Garden City, N.Y., Doubleday Anchor Books, 1965

4. Suzuki, D.T., *Essays In Zen Buddhism, First Series,* N.Y., Grove Press, 1961; *Second Series,* N.Y., Samuel Weiser, 1970; *Third Series,* N.Y., Samuel Weiser, 1971

5. Suzuki, D.T., *Manual Of Zen Buddhism,* N.Y, Grove Press, 1960

The Sufis

1. Arberry, A.J., *Muslim Saints And Mystics,* Chicago, University of Chicago Press, 1966

2. Arberry, A.J., *Sufism: An Account Of The Mystics Of Islam,* London, George Allen & Unwin, 1950

3. Shah, Idries, *The Way Of The Sufi,* N.Y., E.P. Dutton, 1970

Al-Hallaj

1. Nicholson, R.A., *The Mystics Of Islam,* London, Routledge & Kegan Paul, 1963

2. Schimmel, Annemarie, *Mystical Dimensions Of Islam,* Chapel Hill, Univ. of North Carolina Press, 1975

408 HISTORY OF MYSTICISM

Jewish Mysticism

1. Husik, Isaac, *A History Of Medieval Jewish Philosophy*, N.Y., Atheneum, 1974
2. Hyman, Arthur & Walsh, James a., *Philosophy In The Middle Ages,* N.Y., Harper & Row, 1967
3. Scholem, Gershom G., *Major Trends In Jewish Mysticism*, N.Y., Schocken Books, 1946
4. Scholem, Gershom G. (ed.), *Zohar: The Book Of Splendor--Basic Readings From The Kabbala*, N.Y., Schocken Books, 1949
5. Scholem, Gershom G. *Kabbala*, N.Y., Quadrangle/New York Times Book Co., 1974
6. Seltzer, Robert M., *Jewish People, Jewish Thought: The Jewish Experience In History*, N.Y., Macmillan Publishing Co., 1980
7. Zangwill, Israel (trans.), *Selected Religious Poems Of Solomon Ibn Gabirol* (Ed. by Israel Davidson), Philadelphia, Jewish Publication Society, 1923, 1974

Ibn Arabi

1. Affifi, A.E., *The Mystical Philosophy Of Muhyic Din-ibnul 'Arabi*, Cambridge, AMS Press, 1939
2. Austin, R.W.J. (trans.), *Ibn Al-Arabi: The Bezels Of Wisdom,* N.Y., Paulist Press, 1980
3. Landau, Rom, *The Philosophy Of Ibn 'Arabi*, London, George Allen & Unwin, 1959

Iraqi

1. Chittock, W.C. & Wilson, Peter L. (trans.), *Fakhruddin Iraqi: Divine Flashes*, N.Y., Paulist Press, 1982

Rumi

1. Aresteh, A. Reza, *Rumi The Persian,* Lahore, Sh. Muhammed Ashraf, 1965
2. Nicholson, R.A., *Divan-i Shams Tabriz: Selected Poems Of Jalaluddin Rumi,* Cambridge, 1898
3. Whinfield, E.H., *The Masnavi,* London, 1898

Jnaneshvar

1. Abhayananda, S. (trans.), *Jnaneshvar: The Life And Works Of The Celebrat-* ed *13th Century Indian Mystic-Poet,* Olympia, Washington, 1989
2. Pradhan, V.G. (trans.), *Jnaneshvari* (2 Vols.), London, George Allen & Unwin, 1968

The Medieval Christians

1. Jones, Rufus, *The Flowering Of Mysticism*, N.Y., Macmillan, 1939
2. Katsaros, T. & Kaplan, N., *The Western Mystical Tradition,* New Haven, College & University Press, 1968
3. Petry, Ray C. (ed.), *The Library Of Christian Classics, Vol. XIII: Late Medieval Mysticism*, Philadelphia, Westminster Press, 1957

Meister Eckhart

1. Blackney, Raymond B., *Meister Eckhart, A Modern Translation,* N.Y., Harper Torchbooks, 1941
2. Colledge, E. & McGinn, B. (trans.), *Meister Eckhart: The Essential Sermons, Commentaries, Treatises, and Defense,* Ramsey, N.J., Paulist Press, 1982
3. Evans, C. de B., *Eckhart*, London, 1924

Thomas á Kempis

1. Abhayananda, S. (ed.), *Thomas á Kempis: On The Love Of God,* Olympia, Washington, Atma Books, 1992
2. Klein, Edward J., *The Imitation Of Christ*, N.Y., Harper & Bros., 1941

Nicholas Of Cusa

1. Dolan, John P. (ed.), *Unity And Reform: Selected Writings of Nicholas de Cusa,* Notre Dame, University of Notre Dame Press, 1962
2. Beck, Lewis W., *Early German Philosophy*, Cambridge, Mass., Belknap Press of Harvard Universtiy Press, 1969
3. Heer, Friedrich, *The Intellectual History Of Europe*, (Trans. by Jonathon Steinberg), Cleveland, World Publishing Co., 1966
4. Heron, Germain (trans.), *On Learned Ignorance*, New Haven, Yale University Press, 1954
5. Salter, Emma G. (trans.), *The Vision Of God*, Frederick Ungar Publishing Co., 1960

Juan de la Cruz

1. Brenan, Gerald, *Saint John Of The Cross: His Life And Poetry*, London, Cambridge University Press, 1973
2. Kavanaugh, K. & Rodriguez, O. (trans.), *The Collected Works Of John Of the Cross*, Washington D.C., ICS Publications, 1973

Kabir

1. Shastri, H.P. (trans.), *Indian Mystic Verse*, London, Shanti Sadan, 1941
2. Tagore, Rabindranath, *One Hundred Poems Of Kabir*, London, 1915
3. Westcott, Rev. G.H., *Kabir And The Kabir Panth*, Varanasi, Shartiya Publishing House, 1907

Nanak

1. McLeod, W.H., *Guru Nanak And The Sikh Religion*, Oxford, Clarendon Press, 1968
2. Singh, Trilochan, et all (eds.), *Selections From The Sacred Writings Of The Sikhs,* London, Geo. Allen & Unwin, 1960
3. Trumpp, Dr. Ernest, *The Adi Granth,* New Delhi, Munshiram Manoharlal, 1970

Dadu

1. Orr, W.G., *A Sixteenth Century Indian Mystic*, London, Lutterworth Press, 1947
2. Tripathi, Chandrika P., *The Bani Of Dadu*, Allahabad, Belvedere Press, 1924

17th And 18th Century Mystics

1. Bronowski, J., *The Western Intellectual Tradition*, N.Y., Harper Torchbooks, 1960
2. Jones, Rufus M., *Spiritual Reformers in The 16th And 17th Centuries*, Boston, Beacon Press, 1959

Ramakrishna

1. Chetanananda, Swami (ed. & trans.), *Ramakrishna As We Saw Him,* St. Louis, Vedanta Society of St. Louis, 1990
2. Nikhilananda, Swami (trans.), *The Gospel Of Sri Ramakrishna,* N.Y., Ramakrishna-Vivekananda Center, 1942
3. Prabhavananda, Swami (ed.), *Vedanta For The Western World*, Hollywood, Vedanta Press, 1947
4. Rolland, Romain, *The Life Of Rama-*

krishna,

20th Century Mystics

1. Baba, Meher, *The Everything And The Nothing,* Berkeley, The Beguine Library, 1963
2. Bucke, Richard M. *Cosmic Consciousness*, E.P. Dutton & Co., N.Y., 1901, 1964
3. Craig, Mary, *Six Modern Martyrs,* N.Y., Crossroad Publ. Co., 1985
4. Dass, Ram, *Miracle Of Love: Stories About Neem Karoli Baba,* N.Y., E.P. Dutton, 1979
5. Hatengdi, M.U. & Chetanananda, Swami, *Nityananda: The Divine Presence*, Cambridge, Mass., Rudra Press, 1984
6. Huxley, Aldous, *The Perennial Philosophy,* World Publishing Co., N.Y., 1944
7. Mahadevan, T.M.P., *Ramana Maharshi: The Sage Of Arunachala*, London, Geo. Allen & Unwin, 1977
8. Muktananda, Swami, *Play Of Consciousness*, So. Fallsburg, N.Y., S.Y.D.A. Foundation, 1979
9. Rama Tirtha, Swami, *In Woods Of God-Realization*, Lucknow, India, Rama Tirtha Pratisthan, 1956
10. Singh, Kirpal, *The Japji,* Bowling Green, Va., Sawan Kirpal Publications, 1981
11. Suzuki, D.T., *Mysticism: Christian & Buddhist*, N.Y., Harper & Bros., 1957
12. Underhill, Evelyn, *Mysticism*, N.Y., E.P. Dutton, 1961
13. Vivekananda, Swami, *Jnana-Yoga*, N.Y. Ramakrishna-Vivekananda Ctr., 1955
14. Yogananda, Paramahansa, *Autobiography Of A Yogi,* Los Angeles, Self-Realization Fellowship, 1981
15. Yogananda, Paramahansa, *Man's Eternal Quest,* Los Angeles, Self-Realization Fellowship, 1982

ILLUSTRATIONS

I would like to offer my thanks and acknow-
ledgements to the following sources for permission to publish the photos contained in this
book:

1.   Musée de l'Homme, Paris.
2.   Achille Weider, Zurich.
3.   "Public domain. From Alexander
      Marshack.
4.   "Neolithic figurines from Romania,"
      by D. Berciu, *Antiquity*, XXXIV, No.
      136 (1960): 283-284.
5.   "Neolithic figurines from Romania,"
      by D. Berciu, Antiquity, XXXIV, No.
      136 (1960): 283-284.
6.   Deutches Archaeologisches Institut,
      Athens.
7.   Archaeological Survey of India, New
      Delhi.
8.   Marshall, Sir John (ed.), *Mohenjo-
      Daro and the Indus Civilization,* London,
      Arthur Probesthain, 1931; Vol. I, pp. 51.
9.   Mumford, John, *Ecstacy Through Tantra,*
      St.. Paul, Minn., Llewellyn Publications,
      1994; p. 14. Photo by Melissa Jade.
10.   Danielou, Alain, *Hindu Polytheism,*
      N.Y., Bollingen Foundation, 1964
      [Bollingen Series 73]; plate 1. Photo by
      Raymond Burnier. Reprinted by
      permission of Princeton University Press.
11.   Campbell, Joseph, *The Mythic Image,*
      Princeton, Princeton University Press,
      1974; p. 397. Reproduced by permission
      of Princeton University Press.
12.   Campbell, Joseph, *The Mythic Image,*
      Princeton, Princeton University Press,
      1974; p. 369. Reproduced by permission
      of Princeton University Press.

Note: Efforts have been made to identify and
request permission from those holding copy-
rights to the photos appearing in this book. If
we have failed to identify and acknowledge
any, please notify us and we shall correct the
error.

INDEX